Charting a New Course:
Natural Language Processing and Information Retrieval

THE KLUWER INTERNATIONAL SERIES
ON INFORMATION RETRIEVAL

Series Editor:
W. Bruce Croft
University of Massachusetts, Amherst

Charting a New Course:
Natural Language Processing and Information Retrieval

Essays in Honour of Karen Spärck Jones

Edited by

John I. Tait

University of Sunderland,
School of Computing and Technology,
Sunderland, United Kingdom

 Springer

A C.I.P. Catalogue record for this book is available from the Library of Congress.

ISBN-10 94-017-8167-2 Springer Dordrecht, Berlin, Heidelberg, New York
ISBN-10 1-4020-3467-9 (eBook) Springer Dordrecht, Berlin, Heidelberg, New York
ISBN-13 978-94-017-8167-1 Springer Dordrecht, Berlin, Heidelberg, New York
ISBN-13 978-1-4020-3467-1 (eBook) Springer Dordrecht, Berlin, Heidelberg, New York

---

Published by Springer,
P.O. Box 17, 3300 AA Dordrecht, The Netherlands.

Printed on acid-free paper

Table of Contents

JOHN I. TAIT

PREFACE

I first met Karen Spärck Jones in 1977 in Chelmsford, Essex, England (of all places), at a seminar to which my undergraduate teachers Richard Bornat, Patrick J. Hayes and Bruce Anderson had invited me. It was a meeting which would change and enrich my life in many ways, and for which I will always be grateful to these men to whom I owe so much.

In April 1978 I began a Ph.D. under Karen's supervision in Cambridge, cementing a relationship which continues to this day, and indeed is one of the reasons I ended up editing this volume.

I found Karen a highly stimulating supervisor and colleague, if not always easy to get along with. Indeed I believe some of our best work flowed precisely on those occasions when our discussions were, at the least, full and frank, disputatious and sometimes of extraordinary length. I can remember one occasion when Karen and I, and to an extent Bran Boguraev, spent over 6 hours arguing about an issue and in the end agreed to differ! From the areas about which we could agree there came one paper (Boguraev, Sparck Jones and Tait, 1982) from the areas about which we could not agree, Karen produced another paper (Sparck Jones, 1983), which I think stands as an excellent brief exposition on the subject (even if I still disagree with parts of its position). These two papers (I believe) were the first two computational linguistic papers from Cambridge on the subject of English compound nouns, starting a tradition of study which continues to this day, and indeed is reflected in the paper by Ann Copestake and Ted Briscoe in this volume.

Quite a number of years ago I decided that Karen's contributions to the range of fields in which she has worked was such that a volume of this sort was appropriate, and that I should try to ensure it was produced. In 2001 I began sounding out various people to see whether there was sufficient support to make the production of a book viable. I was overwhelmed with the strength and range of support for the idea. Karen has always been a controversial and outspoken figure, but my concerns that that would over shadow other opinions and feeling about her were misplaced. Initially I had not intended or expected to be the editor, but Keith van Rijsbergen, in particular, took me to one side and made it clear he thought I should take on the challenge myself.

J. I. Tait (ed.), *Charting a New Course: Natural Language Processing and Information Retrieval. Essays in Honour of Karen Spärck Jones.* vii–ix
© 2005 Springer.

This initiated what has been something of an odyssey, over what turned out to be an extraordinarily difficult period in Karen's life. First her own serious illness and then the untimely death of her husband Roger Needham cast a shade over the production of the book. Karen has bounced back from these difficulties in an exceptional and unique manner, further increasing my respect and admiration for her.

One of Karen's great gifts is a profound intellectual rigour and ability to see when claims are not fully supported by experimental evidence or reasoned argument. She has made many major contributions over a range of fields which are represented in this book.

However it is sometimes not appreciated how well rounded a person Karen is. I remember her not only our academic work together, but also her interest in jewellery, in church architecture, and in sailing. The latter is what stimulated the title of the book, prompted by David Harper. Thank you, David for getting us onto a nautical course! The final form was a joint effort from Barbara Grosz, Keith van Rijsbergen and Yorick Wilks, so thanks are due to all of them, and indeed all those who contributed to the debate, as well.

It is perhaps worth noting the somewhat unusual approach we have adopted to Karen's name. Wherever possible and sensible we have adopted the (probably more proper) form with a two-worded surname and an umlaut: *Karen Spärck Jones*. However, since it seems to continue to be the case that many automatic systems do not properly support umlauts, so in consultation with Karen we have generally used the form *Karen Sparck Jones* in references and the like in the belief that this will assist students and other scholars to find the referenced material.

The book is structured in five or six parts. Following Mark Maybury's introduction and overview of Karen's achievements, there are two chapters on early work (defined as prior to about 1975) from myself and Yorick Wilks, and Stephen Robertson. Next there are four chapters on Information Retrieval (IR) from Keith van Rijsbergen, Martin Porter, Donna Harman and Gareth Jones. This is followed by four chapters on Natural Language Processing (NLP) from Mark Maybury, Arthur Cater, Ann Copestake and Ted Briscoe, and Stephen Pulman. The third section covers one of the overarching themes of Karen's career, evaluation, and contains two contributions (one from Donna Harman and one from Robert Gaizauskas and Emma Parker) which really draw together the themes of NLP and IR from the previous sections. Finally there are two chapters from Peter Willett and Yorick Wilks which relate Karen's work to more recent broader developments, specifically chemoinformatics, and to Artifical Intelligence

This brings me to one of my clearest conclusions from editing this book. Karen has produced a body of work which has never been so relevant as it is today. Despite the fact that some of it goes back over 40 years even the very early work can be studied with profit by those working on recently emerging topic, like the semantic web and bioinformatics. Indeed recently one of my own students who works on information dioscovery within the semantic web paradigm, after dismissing most of what has been done in IR since the 1970's waved what turned out to be Karen's thesis at me saying "but this is really worth reading"!

I would also like to thank Robbert van Berckelaer of Springer (formerly Kluwer) and Bruce Croft, the series editor, for their enthusiasm and unfailing support for the project during what has turned out to be a lengthy and tortuous journey.

Finally, I'd like to thank all those who have contributed to this volume in different ways, whether it be as authors, through reviewing or by giving encouragement and advice. At the risk of omitting someone important in addition to the authors I'd like to thank Ursula Martin, Queen Mary, University of London; Steve Pollitt, View-Based Systems Ltd; John Carroll, University of Sussex; Barbara Grosz, Harvard University; Wendy Hall, University of Southampton; Candy Sidner, Mitsubishi Electric Research Laboratories (MERL); Bonnie Webber, University of Edinburgh; Bran Boguraev, IBM TJ Watson Research Center. Hiyan Alshawi, Google; Bruce Croft, University Massachusetts Amherst; David Harper, Robert Gordon University Aberdeen.

John Tait, University of Sunderland.

REFERENCES

Boguraev, B.K., K. Sparck Jones and J.I. Tait, "Compound Nouns - a Problem for Inference". Language, Reasoning and Inference, University of Edinburgh, 1982.

Sparck Jones, K. "So what about parsing compound nouns" Automatic Natural Language Parsing, K. Sparck Jones and Y. Wilks, Ellis Horwood, Chichester, 1983.

MARK T. MAYBURY

KAREN SPÄRCK JONES

Professor of Computers and Information (emeritus) and Computing

"Her energy and enthusiasm are truly legendary. Everyone who meets her is
deeply impressed by the commitment and drive which she demonstrates in
abundance. That this energy is backed by an exceptional intellect makes for a
powerful combination."

- Stephen Robertson, at the degree ceremony for
Karen Spärck Jones's honorary doctorate at City University

1. IN THE BEGINNING

From her early days, Karen exhibited signs of genuine intellectual curiosity. Her
initial education was deep and broad - she read history and philosophy. As a teacher
and researcher, Karen mastered knowledge of the past and created technology of the
future. Karen's extraordinary life as a computing pioneer is summarized in the
timeline in Figure 1. Karen became involved with information retrieval (IR), in her
own words, "for respectable intellectual reasons" but began serious IR work in the
mid sixties through a "funding accident." Working at the Cambridge Language
Research Unit (CLRU) founded by the legendary Margaret Masterman was,
according to Karen, "originally a lively discussion group interested in language and
translation, subsequently funded to do research on automatic translation."

From 1955 to 1958 the CLRU explored the value of Roget's thesaurus within the
context of machine translation and, subsequently, document retrieval. For
translation, the headwords from *Roget's Thesaurus* (325,000 words classified into
1073 headwords organized into 15 classes) were used for sense disambiguation
during transfer so that, for example when the word "spend" occurred before "day" or
"night" it was translated using its sense of "passing time" not dispersing money. For
retrieval, *Roget's* enabled word substitution so that, for example, a word like "eat"
could be matched with "food".

Karen's doctoral research explored methods to exploit thesauri for language
processing while fellow PhD student Roger Michael Needham was creating text-
based methods for constructing retrieval thesauri (Masterman, Needham and Sparck
Jones 1958). Roger Needham's 1961 Cambridge PhD was on information retrieval,
focusing in particular the application of digital computers to classification and
grouping, using clump theory to classify archeological data (Needham and Sparck

J. I. Tait (ed.), *Charting a New Course: Natural Language Processing and Information
Retrieval. Essays in Honour of Karen Spärck Jones.* xi–xxiii
© 2005 Springer.

Jones 1964). Karen married Roger in 1958, they built a house, and in 1961 bought their first boat, later sailing round the east coast in an 1872-vintage Itchen Ferry Cutter.

2. DISSERTATION RESEARCH

Karen's doctoral thesis (Sparck Jones 1964) was a cornerstone for research in the areas of synonymy and semantic classification. Karen proposed that a thesaurus could be constructed from sets of synonymous word senses derived by substitution in sentential contexts. Karen classified dictionary entries from the Oxford English Dictionary into semantic categories (headwords) found in Roget's Thesaurus to create an ideal resource for language processing. This led later to a core idea that word classes could be derived by clustering based on lexical cooccurrence. Karen's thesis was so novel and fundamental that twenty two years later it was published as a book by Edinburgh University Press (Sparck Jones 1986). Yorick Wilks and John Tait present a "Retrospective of 'Synonymy and Semantic Classification'" in Chapter One.

3. EARLY RESEARCH: A SCIENCE IS BORN

It is hard to imagine that when Karen came to the CLRU to do research on computing and language, there was not even one computer. Someone commented at the time that they were "Like children playing with invisible mice". Yorick Wilks recalls "doing parsing with Hollerith card sorting machines". Perhaps ironically CLRU staff did what has become, if now automated, a core element of modern language research methodology: corpus based processing. For example, at that time Mark Allford, who taught Russian and German, did some of the first corpus analysis in math and thermodynamics. He discovered that 1,000 terms would support reading 90% of text in mathematics whereas about 5,000 words were required for social sciences.

A rigorous scientist unsatisfied with only plausible arguments for ideas and seeking truth, using the Cranfield collection Karen began testing to see if classification would enhance recall in retrieval (i.e., return more relevant documents). Karen learned that collection frequency weighting of terms (aka inverse document frequency (IDF)) was cheap, useful, effective and applicable to many document collections. Donna Harman outlines in Chapter Five, the considerable influence of IDF on IR and NLP.

Because of the inability to predict the effectiveness of methods or explain performance, however, Karen also realized early on the many data variables and system parameters in indexing and retrieval systems demanded a finer descriptive and analytic framework. Early on detailed analytic experiments led her to suspect the argument that keyword clustering could enhance recall (Sparck Jones and Barber 1971), and she later discovered keyword clustering enhanced precision. Karen readily learned from others, exemplified by her adoption of Cornell's approach to testing across collections. Seeking to address the challenges associated with establishing collections to enable the scientific community to perform systematic comparative evaluations led Karen and colleagues to explore ideal test collections. When Keith van Rijsbergen returned from Australia to take up his Royal Society fellowship in Cambridge, Karen and Keith received a grant from the British Library to do a report on the 'need and provision of an ideal test collection'. Keith gathered the data and worked out a preliminary design and authored a report on the need and provision of an 'ideal' test collection (Sparck Jones and van Rijsbergen 1975/6). This was followed by a report on a design study for the 'ideal' information retrieval test collection (Sparck Jones and Bates 1977). Finally, there was a report on the statistical bases of relevance assessment for the 'ideal' information retrieval testcollection (Gilbert and Sparck Jones 1979). The subsequent Text Retrieval and Evaluation Conference (TREC) was heavily influenced by the design for the ideal test collection. Donna Harman outlines Karen's contributions to TREC in Chapter Eleven.

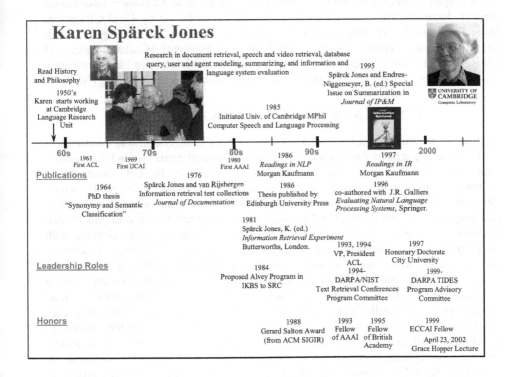

Figure 1. Karen Spärck Jones Time Line

Karen recognized the key role of experimentation and evaluation (Sparck Jones 1986) in scientific progress for many tasks such as document classification, retrieval, and translation. She embarked upon "a major series of comparative experiments" including larger scale tests both to understand indexing and retrieval but also to demonstrate generally applicable techniques. Karen reflected "I wanted to feel satisfied that the tests were valid, in being properly controlled and with performance properly measured. I believed that the standard of my own experiments, as well as those of others, needed to be raised, in particular in terms of collection size" (Sparck Jones 1988a; p. 4). Stephen Robertson elaborates on Karen's early work on IR experiments and test collection design in Chapter Two.

Experimentation on collections led to "depression" at the lack of results from classification but "exhilaration" that collection term frequency weighting was useful and reliable. Rigorous and grueling experiments (many input, indexing, and output parameters, multiple test collections and request sets, and hundreds of runs on thousands of documents) ensured validity of results. One important discovery was the value of relevance weighting (Robertson and Sparck Jones 1976; Sparck Jones 1979a, Sparck Jones and Webster 1980) even with little relevance information (Sparck Jones 1979b). Karen credits influential examples set by Cyril Cleverdon, Mike Keen and Gerry Salton and notes collaborations with her colleagues (Keith van Rijsbergen, Stephen Robertson) and research assistants (Graham Bates and Chris Webster). Discouraged by the lack of "snap, crackle and pop" in IR research, she returned to the then more dynamic area of natural language processing (NLP).

4. INTELLIGENT KNOWLEDGE BASED SYSTEMS

Amidst her scientific contributions to IR and NLP, in 1984, Karen was instrumental in the establishment of the Intelligent Knowledge Based Systems (IKBS) research area, one of four key areas in the Alvey Program funded by the UK's Science and Engineering Research Council (SERC). She proposed IKBS to the SERC which ultimately funded several hundred project teams drawn from industry, university, and polytechnics. An element of the program including creating instructional video lectures (the Alvey tapes) in areas such as logic programming, dealing with uncertainty, image understanding, machine learning, natural-language processing and of course expert systems, as well as starter kits with tools and instructional guides to help disseminate knowledge more broadly. The program also established a series of "community clubs" in a broad range of application areas including financial services (e.g., the Small Company Health Adviser), insurance, data processing (e.g., the Help Desk Adviser for data-processing installations), econometric modeling, real-time manufacturing planning, real-time quality control of processing plants, quantity surveying, transport-route planning, and water-industry construction planning. Khurshid Ahmad (University of Surrey) worked on an Alvey project at the time addressing knowledge based systems for water distribution network control and rehabilitation of sewer systems. Khurshid recounts:

> Karen advanced the cause of information retrieval, especially knowledge-based IR, consistently, persistently, and laudably, throughout her career. Her views on the power and the limitations of intelligent systems are amongst most lucid ones: this was exemplified in a feature article on her and other leading intelligent systems

academics in the London-based Observer newspaper - a magazine article in which she was dressed as hiker or climber - during the Alvey Programme period. Karen's playful sense of humor was ever present.

Although an academic, Karen's influence on the business community was also felt. Bob Moore of Microsoft Research recalls the mentorship Karen provided during 1985-1987 when he went to Cambridge to set up a research group for SRI International with an initial focus on natural-language processing. He notes:

> At that time I was not many years out of grad school, and it was to be my first management position. I had only a vague understanding of the business side of contract research, and no knowledge at all about how things worked in the UK. Fortunately for me, Karen believed that expanding the base of NLP research in Cambridge by helping SRI was a Good Thing, so she virtually took me by the hand and guided me through the ins and outs of the local funding environment, including providing many introductions within the research departments of British companies, whose support we needed to provide matching funds to receive the Alvey grant.

5. NATURAL LANGUAGE FRONT ENDS TO DB

An early desire of artificial intelligence systems was to ease the human burden of access to not only unstructured sources like free text but also to structured sources like databases. Challenge language problems such as discourse (e.g., anaphora and ellipsis), sense ambiguity, indirect and partial language, and implicit statements, among others, vexed researchers. Karen and others recognized the importance of knowledge and inference in enhancing human natural language interaction with databases (Boguraev, Copestake and Sparck Jones 1986). This included the ability to detect and correct user presuppositions or misconceptions and to make inferences from their statements or the data itself (e.g., generalizations, deductions) to improve quality and naturalness.

6. NATURAL LANGUAGE ACCESS TO UTILITIES AND HETEROGENEOUS INFORMATION-INQUIRY SYSTEM

Karen and her collaborators investigated several rich forms of natural language access in the context of utility interfaces and inquiry systems. In the utility system case, in Menunet (Brooks and Sparck Jones 1985) users could access hierarchically organized menus by simply stating a particular action (e.g., "send" or "find"). The system would automatically construct a presentation of the various linguistic forms of accessible menus based on this input thus providing direct language access to a large number of possibly interrelated office automation functions.

In the second case of inquiry systems, language access was provided to a diverse set of information sources, from structured databases to unstructured text collections. Karen's interest in this form of "question answering" included an early recognition of the need for inference (Boguraev and Sparck Jones 1983, Sparck Jones and Tait 1984, Sparck Jones 1983, Boguraev et al. 1986). In order to bridge the gap between structured and unstructured sources, an unconventional approach was the use of shallow processing of knowledge. Unlike most conventional knowledge based systems, knowledge was viewed as representing relations among word senses rather than formally representing models of the world. Thus while inference was rather limited to such operations as establishing linguistic relations, substitutions, generalizations and refinements, it was also broader and potentially derivable automatically from on-line dictionaries or even unstructured document collections.

A natural extension of early work in natural language access to databases was the ability to question and get natural language answers and explanations from both structured and unstructured sources, such as the web. Arthur Cater addresses Question Answering in Chapter Eight.

7. TEXT SUMMARIZATION

The first collection of papers related to document summarization appeared in 1995 in a special issue on Text Summarization of the *Journal of Information Processing and Management* (Sparck Jones and Endres-Niggemeyer 1995). This had roots in a 1993 Dagstuhl Seminar "Summarizing text for intelligent communication" in which Karen helped pull together an international group to focus on this important language application area.

In her characteristic style of crisply clearly characterizing the nature and scope of a problem, Karen articulated clearly the importance of distinguishing input factors (e.g., source form, subject type, unit), purpose factors (e.g., situation, audience, use), and output factors (e.g., material, format, style) with respect to summarization (Sparck Jones 1999). Early on, she forwarded important ideas such as the use of rhetorical structure and/or discourse purpose segmentation to enhance extraction of relevant units from source texts (Sparck Jones 1993).

8. MULTIMEDIA INFORMATION RETRIEVAL

Always pursuing novel directions, Karen in collaboration with others drew upon the foundations of IR and speech and language processing to move in the direction of retrieval of radio and television broadcasts. Her team was awarded a SIGIR best paper for their innovative research on the retrieval of spoken documents from multiple index sources (Jones, Foote, Sparck Jones and Young 1996) and the ACM Multimedia Conference best paper in the same year (Brown, Foote, Jones, Sparck Jones and Young 1996).

The Video Mail Retrieval Using Voice project developed robust unrestricted keyword spotting algorithms and adapted existing text-based information retrieval techniques to work effectively on voice and video data types. The Multimedia Document Retrieval (MDR) project (1997-2000) explored research into the audio indexing and retrieval of sources such as broadcast news (Johnson, Jourlin, Sparck Jones and Woodland 2001).

9. READINGS

Karen's influence has not only been by her personal scientific contributions but her service to several research communities. Through her continuous, multi-decade service as a teacher, director and conductor of research, she influenced multiple generations of IR, speech and language scientists. She has not only enabled and shaped cadres of scientists and engineers, but she has also has enhanced the quality and efficiency of the research community through the application of her significant knowledge and experience to the organization of the scientific literature. In addition to survey articles, she has collaborated to bring to life two instrumental readings: *Natural Language Processing* (Grosz, Sparck Jones and Webber 1986) and *Information Retrieval* (Sparck Jones and Willet 1997).

10. MPHIL IN COMPUTER SPEECH AND LANGUAGE PROCESSING

Not content with shaping the literature, Karen took an active and innovative role in graduate education in speech and language processing. Karen worked in the Computer Laboratory since 1968, but wherever she was she acted as a pioneer in research and an innovator in education. Collaborating with the late Prof. Frank Fallside from Engineering at Cambridge and Steven G. Pulman from the Computing Laboratory, Karen helped establish the first M. Phil. in Computer Speech and Language Processing at Cambridge in 1985 (renamed Computer Speech, Text, and Internet Technology in 2001). The interdisciplinary course was run jointly by the Engineering Department Speech Group and the Computer Laboratory Natural Language Processing Group with the assistance of the Department of Linguistics and the MRC Applied Psychology Unit. Consisting of two terms of lectures and practicals followed by a three month project and resulting thesis, the course introduced students to an interdisciplinary approach drawing students and lecturers from linguistics, psychology, computer science/artificial intelligence, engineering and mathematics. The program was distinguished by its balance of in-depth practical and theoretical grounding and strong links with industrial research laboratories.

Its course lecturers over the years (including Steve Young, Steve Pulman, Phillip Johnson-Laird, Ted Briscoe, Ann Copestake, Phil Woodland, Tony Robinson, Sarah Hawkins, Francis Nolan) and demonstrators were directly involved in leading edge research within the university and in collaboration with other European, US, and Japanese industrial and academic laboratories. Prof. Steve Young (University of Cambridge) notes that:

Over the time that Karen taught on the course there were approximately 320 graduates - many of whom are now well-known in either the speech or language field (or both) such as Michael Collins, Ted Gibson, Phil Woodland, Julian Odell, Philip Monaco, Tony Robinson, Simon King .... The course has grown in strength over the years with application rates now approaching 200 per year. To cater for the increased demand we recently increased the target number of places from 20 to 30.

In summary, Karen was instrumental in helping to establish an extraordinary educational team at Cambridge, now as a major international centre for education and research in speech and language processing.

11. ADVISOR

In addition to her active technical engagement with her research assistants in the multiple areas of endeavor noted above, Karen's mark is seen in the lives of dozens of researchers who have gone on to influence numerous scientific communities, from information retrieval, to intelligent agents, to automated summarization, to language generation. Table 1 shows Karen's Ph.D. students, whose topics span the broad areas of information retrieval, machine translation, expert systems, user modeling, and natural language processing, reflecting Karen's wide ranging interests and influence.

12. PROFESSIONAL SERVICE AND HONORS

Throughout the years Karen has served her professional community in multiple capacities including as a Member of the Foresight Programme Panel on Information Technology, the Committee on Linguistics in Documentation, the Executive Committee of the Museums Documentation Association, the Department of Philosophy Advisory Board at Carnegie Mellon University, and the Advisory Committee for the Research and Innovation Centre of the British Library.

Table 1. Karen Spärck Jones Ph D students (partial)

Doctoral Candidate	Subject	Start	Finish	UCAM TR #
Martin Porter		1967	1969	
Branimir Konstatinov Boguraev	Automatic resolution of linguistic ambiguities		1979	TR-11
Arthur William Sebright Cater	Analysis and inference for English		1982	TR-19
John Tait	Automatic summarising of English texts	1978	1983	TR-47
Hiyan Alshawi	Memory and context mechanisms for automatic text processing		1984	TR-60
David Carter	Interpreting Anaphors in Natural Language Text		1986	
Richard Barber	Expert Systems	1983	1990	
Victor Poznanski	A relevance-based utterance processing system	1985	1990	TR-246
Derek G. Bridge	Computing presuppositions in an incremental language processing system	1986	1991	TR-237
Mark T. Maybury	Planning multisentential English text using communicative acts	1986	1991	TR-239
Richard C. Hutchings	Natural language processing	1986	1991	
Malgorzata E. Stys	Discourse structure and machine translation	1992	1998	
Richard I. Tucker	Automatic summarising and the CLASP system	1993	1999	TR-484
Oi Yee (Olivia) Kwong	Word sense selection in texts: an integrated model	1996	2000	TR-504
Martin Choquette	Automatic information retrieval	1996	2001	
Donnla B. Nic Gearailt	Natural language processing	1997	2002	

In 1988, Karen was awarded the Gerard Salton Award from the ACM Special Interest Group in Information Retrieval (SIGIR) for her research achievement. Karen served as Vice President of the Association for Computational Linguistics in 1993 and then became President in 1994. She has been a member of the DARPA/NIST Text Retrieval Conferences Program Committee since 1994, and of the DARPA Translingual Information Extraction Detection and Summarization (TIDES) Program Advisory Committee since 1999. In 1993 Karen became a Fellow of the American Association of Artificial Intelligence (AAAI) "for contributions to applied natural language research;leadership of an internationally renowned natural language processing research group; and work as an educator." In 1999 she became a Fellow of European Coordinating Committee for Artificial Intelligence (ECCAI) for making significant and sustained contributions to artificial intelligence. In 1995 she was elected a Fellow of the British Academy. And in 1997 Karen Ida Boalth Spärck Jones gained admission to the degree of Doctor of Science, Honoris Causa, from City University. Then, in 2002, Karen gave the prestigious Grace Hopper Lecture which serves "the dual purpose of recognizing successful women in engineering and of inspiring students to achieve at the highest level". Characteristic of her enthusiasm and drive, the final words on the slides to her talk "Language and Information: Old Ideas, New Achievements" (Sparck Jones 2002a) regarding statistical language and information processing read "GO FOR IT!" Topping off this impressive list of accolades, on July 23rd, 2004 in Barcelona, Spain Karen Spärck Jones received the ACL's Lifetime Achievement Award.

13. KAREN THE PERSON

Those who had the honor of learning from and with Karen immediately recognize her challenging but generous approach. She demanded clarity in communication, coherence and cohesion in writing, and evidence and persuasiveness of argument. Rob Gaizauskas (University of Sheffield) recalls being terrified by his first meeting with Karen but soon understood her "intensity and genuine concern for others doing a good job", benefiting from her academic guidance in the now widespread GATE. Ralph Wesichedel (BBN) has always been impressed with Karen's "passion for excellence, desire to bring out the best in others, and her commitment to evaluation progress".

Karen possesses an uncanny capacity to use all of her senses and apply her active scientific mind to exploit the environment around her to discovery for new knowledge. For example, Jeremy Bennett (University of Bath, England) reported how Karen, a contributor to the analysis of compound nominals, discovered a school signpost visible when driving from Cambridge to Newmarket, UK containing eight nouns in a row (a record?): "The Horse Race Betting Levy Board Apprentice Training School". Ann Copestake and Ted Briscoe describe noun compounds in Chapter Nine.

Another notable characteristic of Karen is her rich use of metaphor in her principally scientific writing. For example, in her writings she warned of techniques that are simply "bombinating in the void" or of the "rush to climb on the information bandwagon." She argued for solid scientific progress as opposed to "just inventing copy for the salesman". She described how the "the library schools [will] train the professionals to guard the sacred flame of bibliographic control". And she wrote how we need to "drive useful roads through the enormous jungle we are currently just viewing on day trips from the outside".

Her well-developed sense of humor is evident throughout her writings. In the introduction to the *Readings in NLP*, for example, she notes "There is a widespread belief that AI-oriented NLP research began in the late sixties, and an equally widespread myth that the early workers in machine translation were all crooks or bozos" (p. xiii)

Throughout the years, Karen was an inspiration to her colleagues. For example, Professor Yorick Wilks (University of Sheffield), states that:

> the most remarkable thing about Karen is that, as is now clear many years later, she pioneered a whole field of statistical, data-driven semantics, but, because of the vicissitudes of the times and the [CLRU] laboratory where she worked, she could not publish or continue to work in it, so she went off and founded a very distinguished career in something completely different, only returning to her early interests many years later. I think this is unique in the history of our field.

A comment echoed both others, Candy Sidner notes her admiration for Karen throughout the years. Ed Hovy (USC/ISI) calls Karen the "éminence grise" describing her as "the voice or reason and historian of the field."

14. THE FUTURE

We are all blessed that Karen remains an active and influential language scientist and engineer. This is more poignant today with the recently published *Computer Systems: Theory, Technology and Applications: A Tribute to Roger Needham* (Herbert and Sparck Jones 2004), a collection tribute to the tragic passing of Karen's husband. If the past is any indicator, Karen will likely surprise us again. A laypersons guide to security (Sparck Jones 2002b) and journal article on privacy (Sparck Jones,2003b) are just the latest installments. Past performance suggests she will apply her formidable talents to a practical application area of language process that has some core scientific challenge. We look forward to Karen continuing to spark action in herself and others!

Mark Maybury, MITRE Corporation

ACKNOWLEDGEMENTS

I thank Keith van Rijsbergen (University of Glasgow) and Yorick Wilks (University of Sheffield) for their corrections on and contributions to earlier drafts.

REFERENCES

Alshawi, H. 1984. Memory and context mechanisms for automatic text processing. PhD thesis. UCAM-CL-TR-60

Boguraev, B. K. 1979. Automatic resolution of linguistic ambiguities. PhD thesis. UCAM-CL-TR-11

Boguraev, B. K. and Sparck Jones , K.1983. A natural language front end to databases with evaluative feedback. (1983 ICOD-2 Workshop on New Applications of Databases) In Gardarin and Gelenbe (eds.) 1984. New Applications of Databases. London: Academic Press.

Boguraev, B. K., Copestake, A. A. and Sparck Jones , K. 1986. Inference in natural language front ends for databases. In Meersman and Sernadas (eds.). Knowledge and Data (DS-2): Proceedings of IFIP WG 2.6 Working Conference. Amsterdam: North-Holland.

Bridge, D. G. 1991. Computing presuppositions in an incremental language processing system. PhD thesis. UCAM-CL-TR-237.

Brown,M.G. , Foote, J.T., Jones, G.J.F., Sparck Jones, K. and Young, S.J. Open-Vocabulary Speech Indexing for Voice and Video Mail Retrieval, Proceedings of ACM International Conference on Multimedia, Boston, U.S.A., pp307-316, November 1996 (Best Paper Award) (reprinted in Readings in Multimedia Computing and Networking, Eds. Kevin Jeffay and HongJiang Zhang, Morgan Kaufman Publishers, 2002).

Brooks, P. and Sparck Jones, K. 1985. Menunet: using index menus to enhance access to system utilities. University of Cambridge, Computing Laboratory.

Cater, A. W. S. September 1981. Analysis and inference for English, PhD thesis. UCAM-CL-TR-19.

Gilbert, H. and Spärck Jones, K.1979. Statistical bases of relevance assessment for the 'ideal' information retrieval test collection, British Library Research and Development Report 5481, Computer Laboratory, University of Cambridge.

Grosz, B., Sparck Jones , K. and Webber, B. (ed.) 1986. Readings in Natural Language Processing. Los Altos, CA: Morgan Kaufmann, CA.

Herbert, A. and Sparck Jones, K. (eds.) 2004, *Computer Systems: Theory, Technology, and Applications Series*: Monographs in Computer Science XVII.

Johnson, S. E., Jourlin, P., Sparck Jones , K. and Woodland, P. C. 2001. Information retrieval from unsegmented broadcast news audio. International Journal of Speech Technology, 4: 251-268.

Jones, G. J. F., Foote, J. T., Sparck Jones , K. and Young, S. J. 1996. Retrieving spoken documents by combining multiple index sources. SIGIR 96 Proceedings of the 19th Annual International ACM SIGIR Conference on Research and Development in Information Retrieval (SIGIR 96), 30-38. Best paper award.

Kwong, O. Y. September 2000. Word sense selection in texts: an integrated model. PhD thesis. UCAM-CL-TR-504.

Masterman, M., Needham, R. M., and Sparck Jones, K. (ed.) 1958. "The analogy between mechanical translation and library retrieval", Proceedings of the International Conference on Scientific Information. National Academy of Sciences, National Research Council, Washington, DC, Vol 2, 917-935.

Maybury, M. T. December, 1991. Planning multisentential English text using communicative acts, PhD thesis. UCAM-CL-TR-239.

Needham, R. and Sparck Jones, K. 1964. Keywords and clumps. Journal of Documentation, 20 (1): 5-15.

Poznanski, V. 1992. A relevance-based utterance processing system, February 1992. PhD thesis. UCAM-CL-TR-246.

Robertson, S.E. and Sparck Jones , K. 1976. Relevance weighting of search terms. Journal of the American Society for Information Science, 27: 129-146.

Sparck Jones, K. 1964. Synonymy and Semantic Classification. PhD thesis. University of Cambridge; with additional chapter, "Twenty years later: a review", Edinburgh: Edinburgh University Press, 1986.

Sparck Jones, K. 1979. Experiments in relevance weighting of search terms. Information Processing and Management. 15, 3, (1979), 133-144.

Sparck Jones , K. and Barber, E. O. 1971. What makes an automatic keyword classification effective? Journal of the ASIS, 22: 166-175.

Sparck Jones, K. and van Rijsbergen, C. 1975. Report on the need for and provision of an ideal information retrieval test collection. British Library Research and Development Report 5266, Computer Laboratory, University of Cambridge.

Sparck Jones, K. and van Rijsbergen, C. J. 1976. Information retrieval test collections. Journal of Documentation 32: 59-75.

Sparck Jones, K. and Bates, R. G. 1977. Research on a design study for the 'ideal' information retrieval test collection, Computer Laboratory, University of Cambridge, BL R&D report 5428.

Sparck Jones, K. 1979a. Experiments in relevance weighting of search terms. Information Processing and Management, 15: 133-144. reprinted in Key Papers in Information Science, Griffith (ed.) 1980.

Sparck Jones, K. 1979b. Search term relevance weighting given little relevance information. Journal of Documentation. 35: 30-48.

Sparck Jones, K. and Webster, C. A. 1980. Research on relevance weighting 1976-1979. Computer Laboratory, University of Cambridge. (BL R&D Report 5553).

Sparck Jones, K. (ed.) 1981. Information Retrieval Experiment, Butterworths, London. http://www.nist.gov/itl/div894/984.02/projects/irlib.

Sparck Jones, K. 1983. Shifting meaning representations. Proceedings of the Eighth International Joint Conference on Artificial Intelligence (IJCAI). 621-623.

Sparck Jones, K. and Tait, J. I. 1984. Automatic search term variants generation. Journal of Documentation. 40: 50-66. See also Spärck Jones , K. and Tait, J. I. 1983. Automatic search term variants generation for information retrieval. University of Cambridge, Computing Laboratory. BL R&D report 5793.

Sparck Jones, K. 1986. What sort of thing is an AI experiment? In Partridge and Wilks (eds.) Workshop on the Foundations of Artificial Intelligence: A Source Book. Cambridge: Cambridge University Press.

Sparck Jones, K. 1988a. A look back and a look forward. Gerard Salton Award Talk. ACM. 13-29.

Sparck Jones, K. (ed.) 1988b. User models, discourse models, and some others. Computational Linguistics, 14(3): 98-100.

Sparck Jones K. 1993. Discourse modeling for automatic summarizing. Technical Report 29D, Computer Laboratory, University of Cambridge.

Sparck Jones, K. 1994. Natural language processing: she needs something old and something new (maybe something borrowed and something blue, too). Presidential Address, Association of Computational Linguistics. http://www.cs.columbia.edu/acl, http://xxx.lanl.gov/cmp-lg/9512004.

Sparck Jones, K. 1994. Finding the information wood in the natural language trees. Video (Grace Hopper Celebration of Women in Computing), University Video Communications. Stanford, 1995..

Sparck Jones, K. and Endres-Niggemeyer, B. (eds) 1995. International Journal of Information Processing and Management: Special Issue on Text Summarization. 31(5).

Sparck Jones, K. and Galliers, J. R. 1996. Evaluating Natural Language Processing Systems, Berlin: Springer.

Sparck Jones, K., Jones, G. J. F., Foote, J. T. and Young, S. J. 1996 Experiments in spoken document retrieval. Information Processing and Management, Berlin.

Sparck Jones , K., and Willett, P. 1997. (eds.) Readings in Information Retrieval. San Francisco, CA: Morgan Kaufmann, CA.

Spärck Jones, K. 1999. Automatic summarising: factors and directions. In Mani, I. and Maybury, M. (eds.) Advances in Automatic Text Summarization, Cambridge, MA: MIT Press. (http://xxx.lanl.gov/cmp-lg/9805011). 1-12.

Sparck Jones, K., Gazdar, G. and Needham. R. (eds.). 2000. Computers, Language and Speech: Integrating formal theories and statistical data. Philosophical Transactions of the Royal Society, Series A, Volume 358, issue no. 1769, pp. 1255-1266.

Spärck Jones, K. 2001. Natural language processing: a historical review.

Spärck Jones, K. 2002a. Language and information: old ideas, new achievements. Grace Hopper Lecture, University of Pennsylvania, 23 April 2002, slides and references.

Spärck Jones, K. 2002b. Computer security – a layperson's guide, from the bottom up. Computer Laboratory Technical Report 550. University of Cambridge. http://www.cl.cam.ac.uk/TechReports/UCAM-CL-TR-table.html.

Spärck Jones, K. 2003a. Document Retrieval: Shallow Data, Deep Theories; Historical Reflections, Potential Directions. ECIR 2003: In Fabrizio Sebastiani (Ed.): Advances in Information Retrieval, 25th European Conference on IR Research, ECIR 2003, Pisa, Italy, April 14-16, 2003, Proceedings. Lecture Notes in Computer Science 2633 Springer, 1-11.

Spärck Jones, K. 2003. Privacy: What's different now? Interdisciplinary Science Reviews. 28(4): 287–292.

Tait, J. I. 1983. Automatic summarising of English texts. PhD thesis. UCAM-CL-TR-47.

Tucker, R. January 2000. Automatic summarising and the CLASP system. PhD thesis. UCAM-CL-TR-484.

YORICK A. WILKS AND JOHN I. TAIT

A RETROSPECTIVE VIEW OF SYNONYMY AND SEMANTIC CLASSIFICATION

1. INTRODUCTION

Karen Spärck Jones' Cambridge PhD thesis of 1964 has had an interesting and unusual history. Entitled Synonymy and Semantic Classification (henceforth SSC) it was reproduced only in the simple mimeo book form then used by the Cambridge Language Research Unit where she worked. It was finally published in 1986, in an Edinburgh University Press series[1] Even that late publication managed to be ahead of a great deal of later work that recapitulates aspects of it, usually from ignorance of its existence. There is no doubt that SSC was developing statistical and symbolic techniques for the use of what we now call language resources so far ahead of other work that it was almost impossible for contemporary researchers to understand the book or to relate it to their own activity. At the time SSC was being written, Olney and Revard (1968) were exploring the content of Webster's Third Dictionary quantitatively on punched cards at Systems Development Corporation (where Sparck Jones also was by chance, joining in their work during 1967) and their work met a similar lack of reception, it, too, being twenty to thirty years ahead of its time.

2. A BRIEF OVERVIEW OF SYNONYMY AND SEMANTIC CLASSIFICATION

SSC begins with a review of the implications of the use of the computer as a tool to study natural language text. It discusses the need for precision of representation (in dictionaries, grammars and thesauri) for automatic processing, but rapidly moves to a deeper discussion of meaning, focussing in particular on the claim that in the context of a coherent text (fragment) different words will be used in senses with related meanings. There is a developed example in which *canal* and *road* are cited as means of communication. Roget's thesaurus is then put forward as a means of operationalising this intuition. The approach adopted finds strong echoes in much later work by Morris and Hirst (1991) and Ellman and Tait (2000), which do not really share the same intellectual heritage.

Sparck Jones then moves on to consider the notion of semantic relations between words: her focus is on synonymy and on Lyons (1961), although a range of other

---

[1] SSC page references refer to the Edinburgh edition.

1

John I. Tait (ed.), *Charting a New Course: Natural Language Processing and Information Retrieval. Essays in Honour of Karen Spärck Jones.* 1–11
© 2005 Springer.

relations (including antonymy, hyponymy, logical implication, Lyon's incompatibility and so on) and a range of other authors are mentioned. Chapter Two ends with a proposal to test a notion of synonymy based on substitution, reducing a subtle and complex notion to an empirically testable notion, without losing sight of the limitations of the test.

Chapter Three and Four develop this notion of synonymy based on substitution by using the notion of a row or set of close synonyms (cf Wordnet synsets). The discussion is sophisticated in many ways, but suffers from the use of an obscure notion of a *ploy* (a kind of semantic interpretation), from considering the context of the use of a word only in terms of the sentence (and not more broadly), and from the attempt to move between a specific *word-use* and a *word-sign* (string of characters) without any intermediate notion of morphology (strictly graphology) or intermediate word senses. This is not to say that taking on these notions would necessarily simplify the discussion: but they sometimes make the discussion hard to follow to at least one of the current authors' eyes. The chapter moves on to a fascinating discussion of a notion of semantic distance (likeness) between words (and then between phrases) based on similarity of their occurrence patterns in thesaurus rows.

Chapter Six describes a series of Practical Experiments, using an analysis of Richards' book "English through Pictures" which reports some success in building a simple prototype system of the kind described in the previous chapters.

The thesis concludes with some manual experiments concerning the feasability of discovering the semantic relationships between words in coherent text and then argues that, taken together, these experiments support the notion that there is conceptual repetition in discourse (p 200).

A brief summary like this is inevitably unfair to the original. Some passages, even now, reveal a deep understanding of aspects of language which we have yet to fully face up to in Computational Linguistics (CL). For example, some of the discussion of metaphor in Chapter Two and Three, and the kind of conflict between specific use and overtones of a word derived from its whole range of uses (SSC, p86) shows great sophistication.

We now return to the strengths and weaknesses of SSC which we outlined at the beginning of this section. We will then pass on to highlight some aspects of this work which resonate with more recent developments in Computation Linguistics and Information Retrieval, despite the fact that it is now over forty years old.

3. STRENGTHS AND WEAKNESSES OF SSC

SSC has three great strengths. First, SSC brought together Information Retrieval (IR) methods with linguistic semantics and CL for the first time, a link that is now accepted and productive (as well as the subject of her 1999 AIJ article (Sparck Jones 1999), and thus an interest spanning her career). In saying that, we do not imply SSC is about IR, but that the underlying clustering algorithm she applied in it to thesaurus rows was the so called Theory of Clumps (1962) of Needham and Parker-Rhodes, a development in automated classification of Tanimoto's (1958) original idea for derived clusters as a basis of IR. The principal originality of SSC was to take an IR clustering algorithm and apply it to features that described not physical objects or documents but other words or features at the same level as the classifiers themselves, and to which they were bound by a defined relationship of semi-synonymy. The kinds of associative nets/clumps she derived have been rediscovered many times since by others, probably in part because her thesis was not published e.g. Schvaneveldt's Pathfinder networks (1990) which were patented for IR.

Secondly, SSC's use of Roget's Thesaurus is possibly the first use of an established machine-readable linguistic/lexical resource in CL, apart perhaps from the roughly contemporary quantitative computations with Websters' Third Dictionary by Olney and Revard at SDC mentioned above. The widespread use of linguistic resources, such as machine-readable dictionaries, as a basis for NLP did not become commonplace until the late Eighties, when among the earliest contributors were members of her own laboratory, such as Bran Boguraev (Boguraev and Briscoe, 1989).

Thirdly, SSC shows an appreciation of the need to evaluate ideas about language processing by experiments on realistic samples of language using well-defined tasks, a matter we now take for granted but, when SSC was written, Artificial Intelligence (AI) was still in the heyday of its toy systems with tiny sets of examples.

However, the principles underlying SSC as well as its implementation and evaluation, unfair as it perhaps is to raise these modern notions for work done 40 years ago, still do give rise to real problems and we set out some problems with SSC that were always evident and have not changed with time (as its virtues have in the list above).

There are serious short comings in the discussion of the experiments which are very hard to interpret: there is a lack of detail (for example algorithmic descriptions) preventing judgements being made about the scalability of the algorithms. There is also a lack of clarity about the experimental set ups: some are clearly manual, some apparently automatic, one probably semi-automatic. The general notion underlying the experiments is very clear: namely, applying the theory of clumps to features, where in SSC the features were words whose features were being-corow-members, which should have resulted in clumps of words associated by the clump algorithm. But the matrix inversions required for that computation were very large and almost certainly not tractable over a data base the size of Roget. The whole of Roget's thesaurus was put onto punch cards by Betty May, but only a sample can have been used in the experiments described in SSC. Chapter 6 note 14 clearly implies the adaption of the ideas to the practicalities of computing with then available machines.

One of the problems in interpreting SSC today is confusion between what was achieved with the then available computing engines and knowledge of software engineering, and what could have been achieved if Sparck Jones had had today's computers and software engineering and further was doing this work with the benefit of the insights on language we have gained over the intervening 40+ years.

There is also a failure to grasp the problems posed by basing the synonymy analysis on the use of words in context, presumably the meaning of this word in this sentence (for simplicity let us confine ourselves to writing) in this text at this time to this reader, as opposed to a word sense in a dictionary. Indeed, there is a slide between the two, with the definition of word-use on page 79 being concerned with "ployed" sentences versus page 122 where word-use is defined by existence in a row. The discussion in Chapter 4 seems to show Sparck Jones is aware of the problem, but she shies away from the introduction of a intermediate layer between word-use and word-sign, one that corresponds to what we all now refer to, without much sign of scepticism, as a word-sense. One might (then or even now) put forward the objection that this is introducing an artificial abstract notion into a system which is otherwise entirely dependent on directly observable phenomena in language. But might not the avoidance of this (conventional) abstraction be the reason the system has the problems it undoubtedly has, dealing with the more complex relations like hyponymy or antonymy?

These last arise from a definition of likeness (SSC p102) which seems to gloss over the previous distinction between word-use and signs. Sparck Jones is clearly aware that there are complex relations between notions of substitution, hyponymy, homonymy, and synonymy, but only the first is given an operational definition with any plausibility.

In modern terms, there may be a parameter of the machine learning algorithm in which every occurrence of every sign (to use SSC's terminology) has its own row (cf SSC p90) and a much smaller collection of rows emerge, but there is a danger of hyponyms and synonyms occurring in the same row. Antonymy, too, must be part of word meaning but the structure seems unable to take account of this.

The output from unsupervised methods is notoriously hard to interpret: given clumps of row-associated words from the program, why would they be better clumps than those provided by the Thesaurus heads themselves? No answer to this could have been expected at the time, and is barely available now: there is an awareness in Chapter 7 of the need to measure this output against some operational task, such as machine translation, though that was of course beyond the scope of SSC. The basis of the property of co-row-ness (for words) is that of substitution-preserving-some-property: Sparck Jones discusses this notion and its evident circularity yet she goes on to adopt it and then identify that with Thesaurus rows. She refers to, and is clearly aware of, Quine's critique of any such notion as circular (1953). There is a double sleight of hand here: even if substitution does provide a test of rowness, why should we accept Roget's rows as passing it, as she clearly does in order to get a data set ? One could say that SSC's rows are ambiguous between an emergent property of language use (corresponding to unsupervised learning in more modern usage, and Parker-Rhodes & Needham's clumping) and artefacts extracted from a human constructed resource: such as Roget's rows, and, later, Miller's (2000) synsets (corresponding to supervised learning perhaps).This is perhaps best illustrated by considering the question: if the practical experiments of Chapter Six had produced row systems quite unlike Roget, what would this have meant for the (implicit) hypothesis of the whole thesis ?

SSC is presented explicitly as a search for emergent semantic primitives; but how do (or could) these emerge from these computations? Yet, by using Roget she already assumes such a set (the 1000 heads of Roget): so why is that set worse (or better) than any she derives, or might derive with further computation? Perhaps what is lacking, in modern terms, is an understanding of the need for an objective function, allowing us to distinguish more and less optimal solutions the need for which is now so well understood in unsupervised machine learning.

This might seem a long list of problems. However in view of the groundbreaking nature of the work, the intellectual tradition from which it sprang, the extraordinarily limited computational environment in which it was undertaken, they are comparatively minor, and in no way detract from the major strengths.

4. A FURTHER TWENTY YEARS LATER: SPARCK JONES'S VIEW OF SSC AFTER 20 YEARS.

Sparck Jones wrote a new introduction to SSC when it was finally published, 20 years late, in the Edinburgh University IT series, run by one of the present authors. Perhaps the most striking feature of her retrospective, as compared to the original SSC, is the emphasis on semantic primitives and the explicit opening claim that "The thesis proposes a characterisation of, and a basis for deriving, semantic primitives, i.e. the general concepts under which natural language words and messages are categorized (p.1)".

This view of SSC is not one that a reader of the original thesis would necessarily come to from its text, although it makes perfect sense if we take semantic primitives to mean the topic markers that are the 1000 or so Roget heads, such as 324 SOFTNESS. However, and as noted in the previous section there are some problems with reconciling this notion of predefined primitives and truly emergent ones. In her retrospective discussion Sparck Jones widens comparisons at this point, describing such primitives as domain dependent (e.g. SHIP-as-a-type) by contrast with more general notions of semantic primitive in the work of Katz (1972), Wilks (1975) and Schank (1975), and which was criticised by Lewis (1970), Pulman (1983) and others.

These latter primitives (usually equivalent to notions such as such as human, physical object, movement etc.) she takes as being general rather than domain dependent, which suggests the two types could all be fitted together in some very semantic hierarchy with physical object near the very top and types of ship at the bottom; and this is something like what one gets in Wordnet and indeed in the hierarchy Roget himself offers at the start of his Thesaurus. That Sparck Jones sees these two types of primitive as closely related, as is shown by the original appendix to SSC on Thesauri and Synonym dictionaries , a historical excursus that covers both types of primitive and remains for some the best thing in the book.

In the structures associated with the LDOCE dictionary (Procter, 1978) and both types are given as quite separate hierarchies (of semantic and domain terms) and dictionary entries are decorated with both as features independently. Again, in much recent work on word-sense disambiguation (e.g. Yarowsky (2000), Wilks and Stevenson (1997)) both types of hierarchy have been used as separate information sources, combined ultimately by the algorithm, but where it can be seen that one type tends to disambiguate verbs and the other nouns. None of these considerations are definitive as to whether there are two levels or types of primitives or not, or whether the difference is merely one of degree and domain. Sparck Jones certainly distinguishes two roles for primitives, as do many authors, namely being definitional of sense (as in a dictionary) and being selective for particular senses (as in a disambiguation program) but that distinction has no implications for the one- or two levels of primitive issue.

5. THE VIEW OF SEMANTICS EMBODIED IN SSC

As noted above, SSC was perhaps the first attempt to capture computationally the elusive notion of linguistic relations or fields, one well established in the descriptive literature (Lyons, 1961) but with no formal or computational basis up to that point. It is notion close to some Continental notions of text structure and meaning, ones that have received wide popular discussion, and in which the meaning of any symbol depends, by a relation of contrast, on its relation to other symbols, rather than to objects in the world, as in the basic, rather simple minded, version of Anglo-Saxon philosophy.

Of course linguistic or semantic fields are a subtle and complex subject. A later review (Lyons, 1977, Chapter 8) points out some commonalities, but also contradictions and contrasts between different field theories. In the most accessible form of the theory, there is postulated some sort of meaning surface lying between the lexemes of a language and the world of language use. Particular lexemes are then related to areas of this meaning surface. Most field theorists are concerned with changes in the meaning of language over time, and this creates an odd contrast with SSC, which, like almost all computational work which followed it, takes a rather static, or at least snap shot, view of language. As we have noted, all field theorists share a focus on lexical semantics, in terms of the relations between words and other words or the whole vocabulary, which is presumably what made the approach attractive to Sparck Jones, but they also share a difficulty in formalising the notion of field in a consistent and useful way.

Much of the discussion of SSC shies away from putting forward anything which cannot be directly observed in text. In the end SSC resorts to concepts as additional, artificial, constructs lying outside observable language. One might say the work is caught between Skinner and Saussure, having on the one side the poverty of sticking to the merely observable and on the other problem of subjecting the abstract to empirical verification. In a later overview of her work in IR (Sparck Jones, 2003) she refers to a simple principle underlying everything she does as "taking words as they stand" a position already present in SSC, before Sparck Jones began her distinguished career in IR, namely a reluctance to decorate words with logical, primitive semantic, or other linguistic codings (as opposed to relations). This was something shared, in an interdisciplinary way, with linguistic field theorists and their Continental counterparts. Against this, it could be argued that, by accepting, as she did, the overarching a priori architecture of Roget, all derived from a single mind by intuition, Sparck Jones was accepting a great deal of decoration beyond the words themselves. Conversely, it can be argued, changing sides as it were, that nothing violates that principle in using a thesaurus or a dictionary because the decorations are only more words, as are the Thesaurus heads of Roget themselves.

6. OTHER RESONANCES BETWEEN SSC AND MORE MODERN WORK IN MT, NLP AND IR.

The discussion of the likeness between words and phrases in Chapter Three of SSC, referred to in section 2 above as a form of semantic distance, finds many echoes in later query expansion techniques, like pseudo-relevance feedback or local feedback (Xu and Croft, 1996). These techniques presume that terms which co-occur in documents with query terms are semantically related to query term uses. They rely on the implicit existence of an empirically derived thesaurus, or clump dictionary, on which similarity calculations of the sort described in SSC can be computed.

The introductory material to Chapter Five contains a couple of oddities which hide really quite deep insights.

First, there is discussion of the very large number of rows in which a word might be placed reflecting the very fined grained distinctions of sense which might be required for high-quality machine translation. However, oddly, there is no discussion of how one might link these to another natural language. Was Sparck Jones perhaps thinking that some form of parallel corpora would solve this problem given the automatic procedure? Or was the problems posed by the need to link the source and target languages simply missed?

Secondly, initially she proposes to distinguish every sentence position of every use of a word, but this abandoned on grounds of efficiency. However retaining this position would imply the learning not only of a synonym dictionary but also of a corresponding grammar in some sense. Further it might imply a finite model of language (in the absence of a generative component). It is hard to believe these restrictions were an oversight in view of the sophistication of the discussion elsewhere. Sparck Jones and her collaborators clearly understood such a process might imply learning or deriving a grammar stored in the thesaurus (Masterman, Needham and Sparck Jones 1958), but perhaps not its implications for the underlying model of language.

7. WHAT WAS THE SSC COMPUTATION/ALGORITHM?

It is clear that Sparck Jones in SSC made use of the Theory of Clumps, an unsupervised classification algorithm, deriving ultimately from Tanimoto and refined by Roger Needham (her husband) and Frederick Parker-Rhodes at CLRU. The Theory of Clumps (from now on TC) which she found ultimately unsatisfactory for her purposes (see the quotation above) was an algorithm that took a set of objects x classified by a set of features y and produced clumps or sets drawn from x which expressed natural subsets of x in terms of the assigned features. An aspect of TC which Sparck Jones liked and drew attention to (as did Roger Needham) was that it had a feature close of Wittgenstein's notion of family resemblances namely that subsets, so found, did not need to share any common feature at all and hence this notion was not at all part of the old Necessary and Sufficient Conditions tradition for being a thing of a certain sort.

Roger Needham's thesis was classic application of TC, outside IR that is, and he took a set of Greek pots classified by a range of features (colour, handles, decorative figures etc.) and produced plausible sets of pots based on the core notion of TC that things should be seen as alike if they tended to have the same features, or had separately the features that other things had as common features etc. It was thus an associative rather than definitional model of similarity and would have fallen under Firth's phrase about words and "knowing them by the company they keep". Things in the same clump would tend to keep the same company in terms of features.

Sparck Jones's application of TC was thus more original than taking objects and features as quite different sorts of thing: she realised that both could be words and that words as features could be used to classify words as objects Thus her classification relationship was that of appearing in the same row in Roget 's thesaurus. Elsewhere in this paper we discuss the implications of that assumption of classification as a form of synonymy but here we simply note that, in TC terms, co-row words were features of any given member word, where the co-row members were derived from the OED by seeking in entries for semi-synonyms and testing their substitutability (intuitively) within the example sentences given in the dictionary.

Given this assumption, TC could proceed, which meant first a matrix of features against objects was constructed, notionally at least, and here, since the matrix is symmetrical (both sides being in principle the whole vocabulary of Roget words) we can imagine a matrix with something of the order of 50K rows and columns. At this point forms of the TC algorithms come into play, of which the most basic is a measure of how close any two rows (derived as above) are. Sparck Jones adopts a rough and ready measure of the number of common words in two rows divided by the total number of distinct words in both i.e. their intersection divided by their union.

The main TC algorithm then runs and produces tentative clumps of objects based on the object-feature associations established in this way. These clumps should, being empirically based on associations in a corpus (the OED) yield better groups than Roget heads (considered as groupings of semi-synonyms). On p.183 she writes of assuming that we now have a better thesaurus than Roget 's, but one of the same kind, and one that might be tested against Roget in simple Machine Translation (MT) experiments.

This shows clearly that the clump output from SSC was of the same type as Roget heads themselves and, at one point, she discusses a possible recursive procedure for organizing the clumps produced by the program into a flat hierarchy more like Roget itself.

The account above must be treated with caution because of the different way experiments were handled and described then and now, and in large measure because, as we noted earlier, the 50K square matrix could not be constructed with the computers then available, nor were there as many techniques then for representing large very sparse matrices in alternative, more compressed, forms. Hence whatever experiments she did were necessarily on very small samples and she shows a sample of 500 rows and describes an experiment based on 180 rows (p.170), the maximum number her program could handle. An output clump is given as a set of rows deemed sufficiently close (p.172) and there is an extensive discussion (pp.176-181) of how this should be evaluated (by comparing it with

Roget or by doing say machine translation and getting a better result than with Roget) which shows the attention to detail in and general importance of evaluation procedures which is most striking for its time.

8. THE PRACTICAL EXPERIMENTS AND THEIR RELATION WITH MODERN EXPERIMENTAL WORK IN IR AND MT/NLP

We now take for granted the need to verify hypotheses in language processing by conducting large scale experiments. TREC and DUC (elsewhere in this volume), SENSEVAL (Edmonds and Kilgarriff, 2002), and and DARPA's MT competitions, are all modern examples of this approach. They rely on enormous volumes of data, and careful standardisation of tasks to produce their results. They provide an opportunity to compare systems, theories and approaches which was denied earlier language workers. They also could not be carried out without the computer's ability to process large volumes of language data in a verifiable and repeatable manner.

Despite the shortcomings in the experimental work and its description noted above, there is no doubt that SSC represents an early land mark on the journey that led to these modern destinations. The scale of the experiments is puny by today's standards. 533 rows were extracted from English through Pictures, and experiments were conducted on 500 rows extracted from the Oxford English Dictionary (compared to 28000 bigram collocations in the 1.2 Million documents processed for Sunderland's TREC 2002 experiments (Stokoe, Oakes and Tait, 2003)). However, given the puny computational resources available at the time, these experiments must have seemed daunting in the extreme. Particularly creditworthy is the clear understanding of the limitations of the experiments shown by the small sample size (p178) although oddly it now appears that skewedness of sense distributions in even very large samples might be a feature of real language (Krovetz and Croft, 1992; Stokoe and Tait 2003). It was of course impossible for Sparck Jones to know this in 1964.

9. CONCLUDING REMARKS

We can say that while the theory of clumps was not wholly satisfactory in itself, it has been of importance for other reasons. It was intended to be a theory of classification that explicated our intuitive idea of a set of things that are somewhat loosely related by family resemblances, which was the basis of the notion of conceptual classes of the kind that seemed appropriate to retrieval (Sparck Jones, 1971).

We have highlighted three great strengths of this work: the bringing together of automatic classification with linguistic semantics and computational linguistics; the use of a preexisting machine readable resource (Roget); and the appreciation of the need for experimental work on the largest scale feasible. These three aspects of the work make it far ahead of its time. In rereading the book we have found many insights which would have seemed profound and far sighted in the 1980's or even the 1990's.

Synonymy and Semantic Classification is not a widely read or referenced work: this is perhaps a product of it only having been properly published over twenty years after its original acceptance as a thesis. Despite the inevitable shortcomings of such early work. It can still be read with profit by any student of the relevant fields, and the material covered, and issues raised, are as central to the study of these fields as they were in 1964. The Appendix on the history of artificial languages remains of strong independent interest. The thesis was to serve as worthy foundation of a long and successful career, and it provided themes followed by Karen throughout.that period. We hope this review will stimulate wider reading of the book so it can finally achieve the recognition it deserves.

Yorick Wilks was awared a PhD from the University of Cambridge in 1968 following a period of study at Pembroke College. He was a contemporary of Karen Spärck Jones at the Cambridge Language Research Unit. He is a leading international authority on Natural Language Processing and Artificial Intelligence, and a permanent member of ICCL, the International Committee on Computational Linguistics. He was Professor of Linguistics and then Computer Science at the University of Essex, before moving to New Mexico State University. Since 1993 he has been Professor of Computer Science and Director of ILASH, the Institute of Language, Speech and Hearing, at the University of Sheffield, where he is also a member of Senate and a member of the Committee on Committee Membership.

John Tait is Professor of Intelligent Information Systems and Associate Dean of Computing And Technology at the University of Sunderland. He obtained a BA in Computing Science at the University of Essex in 1976 during the period of study for which he first met Yorick Wilks, prior to Wilks' appointment at Essex. This kindled a lifelong interest in computerized language processing, In 1983 he was awarded a Ph.D. from the University of Cambridge for a thesis entitled "Automatic Summarising of English Texts" for which he was supervised by Karen Spärck Jones. Following a varied career in industry he took up a position as Senior Lecturer at Sunderland in 1991, being promoted to Professor in 1997.

ACKNOWLEDGEMENT

One of the authors would like to thank Chris Stokoe for accumulating some data on the Sunderland TREC work for comparison with Spärck Jones's experiments.

REFERENCES

Boguraev, B. and T. Briscoe (eds) Computational Lexicography for Natural Language Processing, Longman, London, 1989.

Edmonds, P. and A. Kilgarriff Introduction to the Special Issue on evaluating word sense disambiguation systems Natural Language Engineering 8(4) 2002.

Ellman, J. and J.I. Tait, "On the Generality of Thesaurally derived Lexical Links" Proceedings of JADT 2000, the 5th International Conference on the Statistical Analysis of Textual Data eds. M. Rajman &

J.-C. Chappelier. March 2000, Swiss Federal Institute of Technology, Lausanne, Switzerland. Ecole Polytechnique de Federale Lausanne, Switzerland. Pp 147-154.

Katz, J.J. Semantic Theory, Harper and Row, New York, 1972.

Krovetz, R and W.B. Croft Lexical Ambiguity and Information Retrieval ACM Transactions on Information Systems 10(1). 1992

Lewis, David, `General Semantics, Synthese, 22, 18-67, 1970

Lyons, J. A structural Theory of Semantics and its Application to some Lexical Sub-Systems in the Vocabulary of Plato , Ph.D. Thesis, University of Cambridge, 1961. Published as Structural Semantics, No. 20 of the Publications of Philological Society, Oxford, 1963.

Lyons, J, Semantics , Cambridge University Press, Cambridge, England. 1977.

Masterman, M., R.M Needham and K. Sparck Jones The Analogy between Mechanical Translation and Library Retrieval Proceedings of the International Conference on Scientific Information. Vol 2 917-935. Washington DC. 1958

Morris, J. and G. Hirst, Lexical Cohesion Computed by Thesaural Relations as an Indicator of the Structure of Text. Computational Linguistics 17(1). 1991.

Miller, G.A., M. Chodorow, Fellbaum , P. Johnson-Laird, R. Tengi, P. Wakefield, and L. Ziskind. WordNet - a Lexical Database for English, Cognitive Science Laboratory, Princeton University., 2000

Needham, R. and F. Parker-Rhodes, A method for using computers in information classification, in Proc. IFIP62, The Hague, 1962.

Olney, J., Revard, C., and Ziff, P. Some monsters in Noah's Ark. Research memorandum, Systems Development Corp., Santa Monica, CA 1968.

Procter P.et al. The Longman Dictionary of Contemporary English. Longman, Burnt Mill, Herts.1978

Pulman, S. Word meaning and belief, Croom Helm, Beckenham, Kent, 1983.

Quine, W.V.O. From a logical point of view, Cambridge, MA, 1953.

Schank, R. Conceptual Information Processing, North Holland, Amsterdam, 1975.

Schvaneveldt, R. Pathfinder Networks, Ablex, Norwood, NJ, 1990.

Sparck Jones , K, Dictionary Circles, SP-3304, System Development Corporation, Santa Monica, CA 1967.

Sparck Jones, K. Theory of Clumps in Encyclopedia of Library and Information Sciences, (eds.) A. Kent and M. Lacour. Vol.5. New York: Marcel Dekker, 1971.

Sparck Jones, K. Information retrieval and artificial intelligence, Artificial Intelligence 114 (1999) 257-281.

Sparck Jones, K. Document Retrieval : Shallow Data, Deep Theories, Historical Reflections, Potential Directions, in (Advances in Information Retrieval ECIR 2003), (ed.) F. Sebastini, Springer, Berlin, 2003, 1-11.

Stokoe, C., M. Oakes and J. Tait Word Sense Evaluation in Information Retrieval Revisited Proceedings of the 26th ACM SIGIR Conference on Research and Development in Information Retrieval (SIGIR 2001), Toronto, July 2003. 159-166

Tanimoto, T. An elementary theory of classification and prediction, IBM Research, Yorktown Heights, 1958.

Wilks, Y. Primitives and Words, in (eds.) R. Schank and B. Nash-Webber, Theoretical Issues in Natural Language Processing, BBN Inc., Cambridge, MA, 1975.

Wilks, Y. and Stevenson, M. Sense tagging: Semantic tagging with a lexicon. In Proceedings of the SIGLEX Workshop Tagging Text with Lexical Semantics: What, why and how?, 47--51, Washington, D.C., 1997

Yarowsky, D. Hierarchical Decision Lists for Word Sense Disambiguation., Computers and the Humanities, 34(2):179-186, 2000.

Xu, J. and W.B. Croft Query Expansion using Local and Global Document Analysis Proceedings of the 19th Annual International ACM SIGIR Conference on Research and Development in Information Retrieval (SIGIR 96), H.P. Frei, D. Harman, P. Schauble and R. Wilkinson (eds), Zurich, Switzerland. 1996.

STEPHEN ROBERTSON

ON THE EARLY HISTORY OF EVALUATION IN IR

1. INTRODUCTION

Karen Spärck Jones has been involved in experimental work on information retrieval systems since the 1960s. She, along with Cyril Cleverdon, who started it all, must be regarded as a major architect of the prevailing model of how we should conduct laboratory experiments and evaluations. Unlike Cleverdon, she never built her own test corpus from scratch. While some researchers are happy to leave the construction of test corpora to others, and simply use the results, this fact made her all the more sensitive to difficult and delicate issues of methodology in all aspects of IR experimentation.

This paper attempts an overview of the developing ideas in IR experimentation and evaluation, from their early beginnings to the start of TREC at the beginning of the 1990s. It is not specifically about Karen's work, but as is right and proper, her contribution looms large.

2. EARLY DAYS: PHILOSOPHIES AND ANECDOTES

Information retrieval systems have been with us for a long time. The phrase itself was coined by Calvin Mooers in the 1950s, though the concept predates the phrase. It might also be observed that the concept predates computers, and in fact computers were not seriously used in information retrieval until the 1960s. The early history of IR involves things like card catalogues or indexes, printed indexes, and various pre-computer forms of mechanisation, including punched cards of various kinds. But the technology was only ever a means to an end, and the more serious issues concerned how information might be represented for retrieval. If there was little discussion of the idea of free-text indexing before the 1970s, this was not so much because it was technologically infeasible (although this was the case) as because few people thought it could possibly work well enough.

One dominant feeling about some of the early IR work is that there is a strong philosophical element. Some people really believed that the world could be described in terms of an hierarchical classification scheme such as UDC. Others, equally wedded to the idea of formal classification, nevertheless saw the world in terms of facets which required to be synthesised into descriptions. Still others preferred the notion of synthesis from atomic concepts.

Hand-in-hand with these basic principles went examples: anecdotes. You might illustrate why your basic principle was correct and another's was not by means of an

John I. Tait (ed.), *Charting a New Course: Natural Language Processing and Information Retrieval. Essays in Honour of Karen Spärck Jones.* 13–22

example. Textbooks on IR from that period abound in such examples. One of the classic examples, the 'venetian blind', was supposed to demonstrate why simple term co-ordination would not work: such co-ordination could not distinguish between a venetian blind and a blind Venetian[1]. Such examples are reminiscent of the role of examples in work on theoretical linguistics at around the same time. It might be said that it took linguistics rather longer than information retrieval to relegate such examples to the sidelines and adopt a statistical view of the phenomena of interest.

The idea of an experiment

In the late fifties and early sixties, some people in the field began to consider that the dominant combination of broad philosophy and anecdote was insufficient to promote the development of good information retrieval systems. There began to be a suspicion of broad philosophy as a good guide to system design (quite aside from the difficulty of choosing among the rival philosophies), and a suspicion of anecdote as providing justifications for broad philosophies. The alternative seemed to be to treat system design as an empirical science: to try to design and conduct experimental investigations of what works and what doesn't.

So then the question became, how do we do an experiment? Probably one of the reasons that Cyril Cleverdon became such a dominant influence in this period was that he was not afraid to try! For all the obvious methodological difficulties of making a valid and useful experiment in this area, Cleverdon was ready to take them on.

3. SOME EXPERIMENTS

Cleverdon had a hand in a number of experiments, large and small, in the period from the late fifties on. But his major contribution was through the two experiments conducted at the institution of which he was then the librarian: the Cranfield College of Aeronautics.

Cranfield 1

The first Cranfield experiment, which took place between 1958 and 1962 (Cleverdon, 1962), was directly aimed at the 'competing philosophies' idea. A collection of documents (research papers and reports) from the College library was indexed using four separate schemes: UDC (a traditional hierarchical library classification scheme); alphabetical subject headings; a facetted classification scheme (a system allowing the synthesis of subject labels by combining terms from different facets); and Uniterms (a system of single-word index terms, designed to be combined at search time). Each system was administered and searched by experts in that scheme.

---

[1] There was famously a Doge of Venice who was blind.

Since the experiment was intended to show how well each scheme worked in terms of retrieving appropriate documents, queries were required, together with some form of evaluation of appropriateness. Although there was already some awareness of the subtleties of relevance, there remained a notion that each query had one or more 'correct' answers, and that evaluation could be thought of as moderately objective. The Cranfield 1 methodology was designed around this idea. A small number of research papers authored by faculty members of the College were identified as 'source' documents. The author of each paper was approached and asked to specify a question representing the information need with which they started, before writing the paper. Thus the paper was taken as a (or *the*) correct response to the query.

Each system was then searched (manually, by the experts) for each query. The primary measure of system effectiveness was the proportion of source documents retrieved (which might be taken as a measure of recall). The expert proponents of each system were all somewhat shocked by the result, which indicated rather small differences between the systems. The facetted classification scheme, which arguably had the strongest theoretical basis, actually came off worst. The experts in that system then decided that the failure was due to the method used for representing their complex subject labels in an alphabetical form for searching, a method known as *chain indexing*[2]. They replaced it by a system providing more access points, and re-ran the experiment; facetted classification then moved from bottom to top position.

This result, too, was somewhat shocking. The idea that the most important component of the facetted classification scheme had nothing to do with the core analysis of the scheme, and related only to its subsequent representation, was not really compatible with the perceived overriding importance of the basic philosophy.

Methodologically, the source document method came in for a considerable amount of criticism. For one thing, it was recognised by the experimenters that a second measure (what we now call precision) was required, and indeed relevance judgements of system outputs were made for this purpose (though of course that meant that the definition of relevance used in the precision measure was different from that used in the recall measure). For another, the idea of the source document being a complete, or even good, representative of what one would want the system to retrieve was clearly problematic. These considerations made a significant impact on subsequent methodological developments.

Cranfield 2

The second Cranfield experiment took place between 1962 and 1966 (Cleverdon, Mills, & Keen, 1966). Here the emphasis was still on indexing, but no longer on

---

[2] Chain indexing was originally developed to generate in a logical and controlled way multiple index entries from a classification code or formally organised string of related terms. It relies heavily on assumptions about hierarchies, and strictly limits the number of index points generated. As a result some combinations that are implicit in the string are not given explicit entries in the index. In the experiment, this resulted in good documents being missed.

competing philosophies, rather on the details of how indexing languages are built up. Each document was indexed using free index terms (words or phrases) selected from the text of the document; the resulting terms from the whole collection were then subjected to various combinations of conflation operations (synonyms, morphological variants, generically related terms etc.) to generate the variant indexing languages to be tested. The most-quoted result was that the best performing language was one based on single words, with very little conflation (morphological variants and strict synonyms). A result which was reported somewhat less was that if they started with phrases rather than single words, the best result (only slightly less good than the best single words one) was obtained with a lot of conflation. However, the impression taken by many observers was that the use of simple natural language for indexing was as good as any more complex scheme. It was partly for this reason that much of the following work took the view that simple automatic indexing by extracting all the words (as we now take for granted) was a good place to start – the interesting questions were at the search end. It is arguable whether the Cranfield 2 results really supported such a view, but they certainly encouraged it.

Methodologically, Cranfield 2 made several advances over Cranfield 1 (though inevitably it generated just as many methodological arguments). The collection used for the experiments was much smaller, 1400 documents, than that used for Cranfield 1 – this was partly to allow relatively complete relevance judgements. The 221 queries were again generated by the source document method; however, the retrieval of source documents was not the issue, indeed they were removed from the collection. Instead, relevance judgements were made by expert judges. The pool of documents which each judge looked at was not the whole collection, but the result of a first pass over the collection by students. (This aspect generated a lot of argument.) Recall-precision graphs were used for evaluation.

The Cranfield 2 collection of 1400 documents and 221 queries, and a subset of 200 documents used for some of the experiments, became famous as *the* Cranfield test collection. This was made available to researchers outside the Cranfield team, and became the first and one of the most widely-used of the portable test collections. This aspect is further explored below.

MEDLARS

The experiment on the MEDLARS Demand Search Service (a predecessor to Medline) (Lancaster, 1969) was one of the first big experiments on an operational system. The document collection was the real Index Medicus / MEDLARS database (brief bibliographic records indexed using MeSH subject headings), and the queries were real requests put to the MEDLARS system by medical researchers and other users. No attempt at a complete recall base was made, but the documents judged for relevance (by the original requesters) included some retrieved by the MEDLARS staff from other systems, as well as those retrieved by the MEDLARS system itself[3].

---

[3] This use of other systems to find relevant documents that had been missed by the system under test represents the first attempt to deal with the issue of recall in large collections (where the scanning of

This allowed an estimate of recall as well as a measure of precision, but more importantly, it allowed a detailed failure analysis. All documents retrieved by the system but judged non-relevant, and all those found by other systems and judged relevant but not retrieved by MEDLARS, were examined in detail, to provide a taxonomy of failures. As a result of the experiment, a number of changes were made (to the MeSH scheme, to the guidelines for indexers, to the guidelines for searchers, to the training of intermediaries, etc.).

Although the failure analysis method is more honoured in principle than followed in practice, and in any case is in some ways more difficult now than it was then, it was an important development. In general, the attempt to evaluate a system in a realistic usage environment was a precursor of wider concerns (outside the laboratory framework) related to users, user-system interaction, and eventually user information seeking behaviour. In fact, one of the most interesting results of that experiment was something which was initially regarded as an aside from the main thrust of the experiment. Some of the requesters were able to visit MEDLARS intermediaries who helped them formulate their queries in MEDLARS standard form (Boolean operations on MeSH headings). Others sent in their requests by letter, and intermediaries used the letters to formulate queries. The question was: "How much does it help to have a face-to-face interview at this stage?". The answer was: "It hinders!". The training of intermediaries was modified as a result.

One consequence of the real-life situation in which the experiment took place was that no follow-up study was made – no experiment was conducted after the changes had been put into effect. Another was that the resulting set of documents, requests and relevance judgements was not really suitable for further experimentation.

Clustering and term weighting

Meanwhile, outside the world of libraries and documentalists, the fledgling science of computing was beginning to tackle interesting problems like information retrieval. (MEDLARS was a computer-based system, indeed was one of the earliest in a tradition that went on to dominate commercial information retrieval for a generation, but was strictly the product of the pragmatic world of publishing, dissemination, librarianship and documentation, rather than a result of computer science research.)[4]

---

the entire collection by the user is out of the question). It anticipates a number of later approaches, including the pooling method of TREC.

[4] In this world of Inspec and MEDLARS, Dialog and Orbit, computers became tools for information retrieval by the back door. They were first used extensively by publishers in the process of generating printed indexing and abstracts journals such as Index Medicus. Then it became apparent that all the machine-readable data that was lying around as a result might have other uses.

It is somewhat unfair to lump "documentation" in with the others in this pragmatic world – the field of documentation had a strong theoretical component and can be said to be the main intellectual forebear of the modern field of information retrieval – as witness the contributions of Robert Fairthorne in the fifties and sixties, both to ideas of mechanisation and of evaluation.

In computer science laboratories, most notably at Harvard and then Cornell in the United States and in Cambridge in Britain, people like Gerard Salton and Karen Sparck Jones were beginning to explore ideas which would eventually, though slowly, change information retrieval completely. But some of the earliest ideas to be explored look like attempts to reproduce in automated form some information-organisational mechanisms that humans made use of. Thus one of the early concerns was with clustering – automatically derived classification schemes – applied to information objects. The objects might be documents (as in the traditional library model) or words (something like the more recent documentation ideas of facetted classification and co-ordinate indexing).

The genesis of the statistical revolution – whereby statistical ideas came to the forefront of IR – was already present in this work. However, it received a considerable boost when researchers, Sparck Jones and Salton amongst them, began to realise the central importance of term weighting and document scoring functions. From the seminal *idf* paper (Sparck Jones, 1972) of the early seventies, through to the language models and other methods of the present day, statistical ideas have if not dominated, at least come to occupy an essential central role in IR.

4. METHODS: RE-USING TEST COLLECTIONS

The centrality of experimentation

In order to test their ideas and methods, those researchers who were working on IR as a computational task needed some suitable test material. It can be argued that the developing statistical view of IR fitted very well with the experimental approach to the field. It was no longer a question (as it was in the days of anecdote) of an answer to a user request being right or wrong; rather, a system might be able to say, on the basis of limited evidence, that a document is more or less likely to be more or less helpful to the user. Likelihood replaces logic; experimental observation replaces assertion.

The Cranfield experiment had created the basic ground rules for such experimentation. As different researchers took it up and refined it in the sixties and seventies and eighties, the tradition acquired a canonical status: this was the way to do experiments in information retrieval. In retrospect, we can see the refinement process and the canonical status in two distinct lights. On the one hand, it was a process of tightening the rules to ensure as far as possible the repeatability of experiments and the validity of results (good). On the other hand, it was a process of tightening the rules to create a dogma (bad). Both facets are in evidence today.

The test corpus paradigm

Such researchers seldom had the sources or resources to construct their own test corpora, but the materials which had been carefully (and expensively) put together for experiments like Cranfield looked like obvious candidates. Thus IR lead where many other computational fields struggled to follow in later years – in the provision and re-use of test corpora.

The Cranfield test collection was the first such corpus, and is still in use at the time of writing, some 38 years after the end of that experiment. Sparck Jones made extensive use of it; indeed the first book by Sparck Jones (Sparck Jones, 1971) relies entirely on Cranfield for its experimental base. She was also instrumental in making other corpora available, notably a significantly larger one developed by Vaswani at the National Physical Laboratory in the UK, known as the NPL collection. She helped to establish standards formats and descriptions for such corpora, and to disseminate them among the IR community.

In the United States, the Cranfield corpus was less well-known, but there were several others in common use. Michael Keen, one of the co-authors of Cranfield 2, went to work at Cornell with Salton, and was instrumental in constructing a MEDLARS test corpus, based on Lancaster's work but actually a small collection like Cranfield. Others were a CACM collection (material taken from the journal) and the NPL collection.

The Cranfield legacy

It is worth exploring some of the characteristics of Cranfield-style IR test methodology, taken together with the test data, which made it so attractive. For one thing, this was research that was based firmly in the requirements of users, but without the need to actually interact with users. The entire user experience was conveniently encapsulated in the test data, in particular in the queries and relevance judgements; in computational terms, it was there in the machine, along with the system to be tested. Researchers could be seen to be responding to user needs, without having to find users and set up real (difficult, expensive, time-consuming, and often ultimately inconclusive) user experiments. Furthermore, any experiment could be re-run any number of times, without requiring a new set of users each time.

This approach to IR experimentation has many limitations; one might describe them as internal and external ones. The external ones have to do mainly with that encapsulated user experience – it is clear that the user experience that is encapsulated is a very much impoverished one (limited to asking an initial text question and then judging documents). Anything richer, however, requires real users to be involved – in every experiment, not just in some initial data creation stage.

Internal limitations have to do with internal standards. Even assuming that we can encapsulate the user experience to the extent needed for a test collection, do particular test collections provide that encapsulation as well as they might? The Cranfield collection, for example, is not very large, and it covers a very specific subject area. Perhaps more importantly, it was designed for a specific experiment, and is not necessarily very well suited to the multitude of new purposes to which it is put. There were a few other collections around in the early seventies; the variety was an advantage, but each collection had its own limitations. (Sparck Jones & van Rijsbergen, 1976)

The 'ideal' test collection

By the middle 1970s, the dissatisfactions with the existing test collections were mounting. The desire for a large(r) general purpose test collection with extensive relevance judgements was apparent. Sparck Jones initiated and led (Sparck Jones & van Rijsbergen, 1975; Sparck Jones & Bates, 1977; Gilbert & Sparck Jones, 1979) a thorough investigation of the requirements for such a collection and how they might be satisfied. This putative new corpus was named the 'ideal' test collection (the quotation marks were quite deliberately inserted at an early stage of the investigation: the implication was that while one could not hope to achieve a truly ideal collection, the aim was high).

The 'ideal' collection studies were based in the U.K. and mainly involve the U.K. IR research community. A lot of effort went into them; the outcomes included an analysis of the costs and other resources required to set up such a collection. Unfortunately, the bottom line was 'too much'. It would have required the entire U.K. government budget for basic information research for a few years.

So the project was shelved. It was never quite killed off, but lay there, gathering dust, for over a decade.

The Book

When people report experiments in information retrieval, they give more or less thought to describing and discussing the methods used, or explaining the decisions taken in selecting methods; this may be of interest, but is not normally the main focus of either the work or the report, let alone of any subsequent journal- or conference-paper distillation. The knowledge, understanding and experience about experimentation in IR which developed in the sixties and seventies was actually quite hard for a newcomer to discover, buried as it was in the appendices of dense and hard to find research reports. Sparck Jones saw this as a problem, and put together a collection of papers as a book to address this issue (Sparck Jones, 1981).

It was not her way to confine her work in the creation of an edited book to selecting the authors and letting them get on with it. She acted as an editor in the strongest sense: she constructed a carefully-designed structure for the book, involving authors at this stage, and expecting and encouraging them to adapt their conceptions of their own contributions to this broader view. The result is a broad-ranging compendium and analysis of experimental methods, covering not just the Cranfield laboratory tradition, but experiments in the context of operational systems and services as well. One cannot claim that *Information Retrieval Experiment* is the best of its kind, for the simple reason that neither before nor since has any competitor ever appeared. One can, however, simply point to its excellence.

5. WHAT HAPPENED NEXT

In the decade following publication of the Book, the tradition of laboratory experiment in IR went through a somewhat fallow period. To be sure, many experiments were run, mostly with the existing test collections such as Cranfield,

CACM and NPL. But efforts in the direction of the design or construction of new collections, or the development of experimental methods, were little in evidence.

The situation changed dramatically in 1991. The Text REtrieval Conference, TREC, revived the tradition in a major way. In doing so, it drew extensively on the work done a decade and a half earlier, by Karen Spärck Jones and others, on the 'ideal' test collection. Karen herself, who had concentrated on her NLP work for some years, was drawn back into the IR field, took enthusiastic part in TREC, and wrote (among other things) a great series of 'Reflections on TREC' papers.

TREC has come so much to dominate our view of information retrieval experimentation that it must be hard for new entrants to imagine the field without it. However, the era that preceded TREC, particularly the twenty years up to and including the publication of *Information Retrieval Experiment*, were a rich period for information retrieval research, to which the present must inevitably remain indebted.

Stephen Robertson obtained his PhD at University College London, but spent most of his academic career at City University, London. In 1998 he moved to Microsoft Research in Cambridge where he leads a group concerned with Information Retrieval and Analysis. He retains a part-time professorship at City. In 1976 he was the author, with Karen Sparck Jones, of a probabilistic theory of retrieval which has been moderately influential. Further development of this model led to the BM25 scoring function, used in the Okapi experimental system. He has participated in successive rounds of the TREC Text Retrieval Conference, on a variety of tasks, as well as undertaking more user-oriented experiments. At Microsoft he is involved in the construction of a new evaluation environment, and continues to work on probabilistic models and evaluation methods.

He was given the Tony Kent Strix Award of the Institute of Information Scientists in 1998, and the Salton Award of the ACM SIGIR in 2000.

REFERENCES

Cleverdon, C. W. (1962). *Report on the testing and analysis of an investigation into the comparative efficiency of indexing systems.* Cranfield, U.K.: College of Aeronautics. (Aslib Cranfield Research Project)

Cleverdon, C. W., Mills, J., & Keen, E. M. (1966). *Factors determining the performance of indexing systems.* Cranfield, U.K.: College of Aeronautics. ((2 vols.) Aslib Cranfield Research Project)

Gilbert, H., & Sparck Jones, K. (1979). *Statistical basis of relevance assessment for the 'ideal' information retrieval test collection.* Cambridge, U.K.: Computing Laboratory, University of Cambridge.

Lancaster, F. W. (1969). MEDLARS: Report on the evaluation of its operating efficiency. *American Documentation, 20*, 119–148.

Sparck Jones, K. (1971). *Automatic keyword classification for information retrieval.* London, U.K.: Butterworths.

Sparck Jones, K. (1972). A statistical interpretation of term specificity and its application in retrieval. *Journal of Documentation, 28*, 11–21.

Sparck Jones, K. (Ed.). (1981). *Information retrieval experiment.* London, U.K.: Butterworths.

Sparck Jones, K., & Bates, R. G. (1977). *Report on a design study for the 'ideal' information retrieval test collection.* Cambridge, U.K.: Computing Laboratory, University of Cambridge.

Sparck Jones, K., & van Rijsbergen, C. J. (1975). *Report on the need for and provision of an 'ideal' information retrieval test collection.* Cambridge, U.K.: Computing Laboratory, University of Cambridge.

Sparck Jones, K., & van Rijsbergen, C. J. (1976). Information retrieval test collections. *Journal of Documentation, 32,* 59–75.

C.J. VAN RIJSBERGEN

THE EMERGENCE OF PROBABILISTIC ACCOUNTS
OF INFORMATION RETRIEVAL

'If you correlate each individual document with the properties of those patrons who would judge it relevant, you get one interpretation. If, on the other hand, you correlate each individual patron with the properties of those documents that he would judge relevant, then you get a different interpretation.'

Maron, 1983, p. 103

1. INTRODUCTION

It is almost half a century ago that the first accounts were given of the probabilistic processes and structures underlying the phenomena of information retrieval. We have now become used to talking about a 'probabilistic model' for IR, but in those early days it was far from obvious whether such a model existed. Even now it is not entirely clear what sense of model is appropriate. In science we have theories that account for the phenomena, the observable structures and processes, which may postulate processes and structures not directly accessible to observation (Van Fraassen, 1980). Models are then commonly thought of as interpretations of such theories; this is the logical view. Another view is that models are a kind of picture of the processes and structures under study. It is not easy to see how these views of theory and models fit with IR. Therefore, I shall only use the word 'model' in the conventional sense of labelling a particular model: a formally, often mathematically, defined approach to some aspect of IR.

Let us begin at the beginning. Possibly the first person to seriously propose probability theory as a basis for *indexing* was Maron in collaboration with Kuhns (Maron and Kuhns, 1960). His approach was to pose the question: 'What is the probability that a document indexed by a given description will satisfy the information need of a user who has described his need in an identical way?' (Maron, 1965). Maron and Kuhns in their 1960 paper had given an algorithm for computing this probability by interpreting the weight of an index term I, relative to a given document, as an estimate of the probability that if a user were to read the document in question and find it to satisfy his information need, then he would describe his need in terms of I. For this they used Bayes' Theorem to calculate, an inverse probability inference, the probability of relevance of a document with respect to query I in terms of the estimated likelihood of term I being assigned as an index term. This gave an answer to the question posed above. It provided the probability that if a user described his need in terms of request I, then he will find that the

John I. Tait (ed.), *Charting a New Course: Natural Language Processing and Information Retrieval. Essays in Honour of Karen Spärck Jones.* 23–38

document in question satisfies that need or is relevant. They called these latter probabilities relevance numbers and proposed that they be used to rank the documents resulting from a request. In fact Maron (1965) claimed that '...this ranking (ordering) provides an optimal strategy in going through the class of retrieval documents.' We shall refer to this as Model I. Fuhr presented a generalisation of Model I in 1986, and further refinement in Fuhr (1989).

In 1976 Robertson and Sparck Jones wrote what is now a seminal paper describing a second probabilistic model, Model II. This second approach was somewhat different from that of Maron and Kuhns, whose approach was that a probability that a document is relevant to a query is based on the probability that a user who likes the document would have used this query. In Model II, on the other hand, the aim is to calculate, by estimation, the probability that a randomly selected document that possess a subset of all the possible properties will be judged relevant by the inquiring user. This is markedly different from Model I where a putative set of users is used to estimate the likelihood mentioned above, whereas in Model II a random set of relevant documents is used to estimate the probability that any relevant document would have a property, or a combination of properties.

It is clear that this second model was not influenced very much by the Maron and Kuhns, but is was heavily influenced by the earlier work of Barkla (1969) and Miller (1971). In two earlier papers one by Robertson (1974) and Sparck Jones (1975) they both refer to the original work of Barkla and Miller. It is interesting to show how, for example, Miller's work foreshadowed Model II. Miller gave a simple derivation of what I am tempted to call Model $I\frac{1}{2}$, the reason for which will become clearer later. First let me reproduce the Miller derivation

R : Relevance

t_i : index terms

$\underline{t} = \{t_1, \cdots, t_k\}$

$$P(Rt_1 \ldots t_k) = P(R)P(t_1 \mid R) \ldots P(t_k \mid Rt_1 \ldots t_{k-1}) \tag{1}$$

$$P(t_1 \ldots t_k R) = P(t_1)P(t_2 \mid t_1) \ldots P(R \mid t_1 \ldots t_k) \tag{2}$$

$$\frac{P(R\underline{t})}{P(\underline{t}R)} = 1 = \frac{P(R)}{P(R \mid \underline{t})} \left[\frac{P(t_1 \mid R)}{P(t_1)} \cdots \frac{P(t_k \mid Rt_1 \ldots t_{k-1})}{P(t_k \mid t_1 \ldots t_{k-1})} \right] \tag{3}$$

$$P(t_i \mid t_j) = P(t_i) \qquad P(t_i \mid Rt_j) = P(t_i \mid R) \tag{4}$$

$$P(t_i \mid t_j \ldots) = P(t_i) \qquad P(t_i \mid Rt_j \ldots) = P(t_i \mid R) \tag{5}$$

$$P(R \mid \underline{t}) = P(R) \prod_{i=1}^{k} \frac{P(t_i \mid R)}{P(t_i)} \tag{6}$$

$$\log P(R \mid \underline{t}) = \sum_{i=1}^{k} \delta_{is} \log \frac{P(t_i \mid R)}{P(t_i)} + \log P(R) \tag{7}$$

The mathematics for Model I$\frac{1}{2}$ is summarised in the box above. The aim of the model is to compute the probability of relevance (event R) of a document conditional on the occurrence of index terms 1 to k, the entire term population, given by (6). The calculation is rather neatly done by writing out the total probability function for the joint probability function in two ways, (1) and (2), and then taking the ratio (3). Equations (4) and (5) make up the independence assumptions, unrestricted and restricted to the set of relevant documents. Using those assumptions in (3) it can be rewritten as (6). The equation (7) is derived from (6) by taking logs and restricting the product, and hence the sum, to just the search terms, this is achieved by setting $\delta_{is} = 1$ if for a document the ith index term occurs as one of the s search terms, and zero otherwise. Thus only the *presence* of a search term in a document contribute to the overall weight, *absent* search terms are not considered. The prior probability $P(R)$ is taken as constant for one search. The $P(t_i \mid R)$ is estimated. Miller recommends that it is estimated by the user possible with help from a professional searcher. $P(t_i)$ is obtainable from system data. The weighting formula (7) thus arrived at is a variant of the F_1 formula in Robertson and Sparck Jones(1976). An important difference is the estimation method adopted. One could say that Miller's approach was the first attempt at an incomplete probabilistic formulation of Model II.

In their earlier papers Sparck Jones (1975) and Robertson (1974) arrived at an incomplete version of Model II through statistical considerations. The starting point for this approach was probably Sparck Jones' 1972 paper on a statistical interpretation of term specificity and its application in retrieval. There she mooted that the weight of a search term should be proportional to $f(N) - f(n) + 1$, for N the number of documents in the collection, n the number of times the term occurs, and where $f(x) = y$ such that $2^{y-1} < x \le 2^y$; a log function for f satisfies this condition, which gives rise to the well known inverse document frequency weighting function. What was missing from this early formulation was any information about the distribution of terms in the relevant documents and how it differed from the distribution in the non-relevant documents or in all the documents in the collection. This was remedied in Sparck Jones (1975) by presenting the F_1 weighting formula, and in Robertson (1974) the F_2 formula (see below). Independently, Yu and Salton (1976) defined a precision weight which was monotone with respect to F_4, more precisely it was F_4 without the log.

To help to describe the subsequent development of Model II we will need some standard notation. The symbols and formulae that follow are the same as those used in Robertson and Sparck Jones (1976).

	Document Relevance		
	+	-	
Document Indexing +	r	$n-r$	n
-	$R-r$	$N-n-R+r$	$N-n$
	R	$N-R$	N

The symbols in the above table have the following meaning, for each term t with respect to a given query q.

N	the number of documents in the collection
R	the number of relevant documents for q
N	the number of documents having t, and
r	the number of relevant documents having t

This notation with the 2×2 table has now become standard, for example, it is used in Van Rijsbergen (1979) for a standard exposition of Model II. The various weighting functions, $F_1 - F_4$, can now be defined readily in terms of the variables, which we now do.

$$w_1 = \log\left(\frac{\frac{r}{R}}{\frac{n}{N}}\right) \tag{F_1}$$

$$w_2 = \log\left(\frac{\frac{r}{R}}{\frac{n-r}{N-R}}\right) \tag{F_2}$$

$$w_3 = \log\left(\frac{\frac{r}{R-r}}{\frac{n}{N-n}}\right) \tag{F_3}$$

$$w_4 = \log\left(\frac{\frac{r}{R-r}}{\frac{n-r}{N-n-R+r}}\right) \tag{F_4}$$

It must be emphasised that the motivation for these formulae was statistical, but a probabilistic explanation was given in the Appendix of Robertson and Sparck Jones (1976). Estimating these weights, $F_1 - F_4$, was recognised as a difficult problem. For example, if the weights are to be used predictively, it is likely that the basis would be a very small sample, and that some of the variables would be zero leading to the log function being undefined. Various techniques for dealing with these situations were available derived from the work of Cox (1970), however, IR research standardised on adding ½ to each of the four components in the expression. For example F_4, would become

$$w_4 = \log \left(\frac{\dfrac{r+\frac{1}{2}}{R-r+\frac{1}{2}}}{\dfrac{n-r+\frac{1}{2}}{N-n-R+r+\frac{1}{2}}} \right).$$

By doing this, the problem could be largely ignored, and in this way extensive experimentation could proceed as was demonstrated in Sparck Jones and Bates (1977), and Sparck Jones and Webster (1980).[1] As is often the case, common sense ad hoc assumptions turn out eventually to have good theoretical backing[2]. This case is no exception, there is now extensive theory for these kinds of estimation problems, see below in the section on estimation.

It is interesting that the empirical approach to establishing Model II was very much in the forefront, the account based on probability theory was slow to emerge. Underlying the statistical account were assumptions and conditions which were more easily understood in terms of probability theory and to this day continue to be discussed. We will now look briefly at some of these assumptions and conditions. There are four types,

1. Independence assumptions.
2. Ordering principles.
3. Optimality conditions.
4. Estimation.

As one would expect these all interact, but in the context of this paper we will discuss them separately.

To facilitate discussion we will define the following probabilities for random variables D and Q to denote a document and a query, R a binary random variable to denote relevance. R[3] can have values r and $\bar{r}$ representing relevance and non-relevance, D and Q are vectors of binary variables T_i representing presence or absence of attributes usually, but not always, index terms. All the probabilities are conditional on a specific query and in general this dependence can be left out in the notation, however, we will need that dependence later at which point it will be

---

[1] Croft, W.B. and D.J. Harper(1979) found a way of approximating Model II, and implementing it, that did not require relevance information.

[2] One of the most famous examples is Planck's constant.

[3] A third use of R, now a binary variable.

reintroduced explicitly. For the moment our discussion will be in the context of Model II although similar comments will apply to the other models.

$P(R|D)^4$ can be instantiated to $P(r|D)$or $P(\bar{r}|D)$, the probability of relevance or non-relevance for a random document. The inverse probabilities are therefore $P(D|r)$ and $P(D|\bar{r})$, the likelihood of observing a document D given that it is relevant. If $D = (t_1,\ldots,t_k)$ for k terms we can also express this as the probability that a document contains the terms t_1 to t_k, where $t_i = 1$ or 0 indicating presence or absence, so, the occurrence of t_i when it is zero actually means the absence of term i.

Independence

Even before the probabilistic models were completely formulated independent assumptions were made simply to reduce the complexity of the calculations and estimations. Almost every probabilistic model, with some notable exceptions, for example Goffman (1969), has assumed that the relevance judgement of one document is not affected by the same judgement for any other document. Independence of index terms has come as pairs of linked assumptions. There are three possible events or sets on which independence can be required (a) the set of relevant documents, (b) the set of non-relevant documents, and (c) the whole collection. In general these assumptions themselves cannot be specified independently, for example assumptions (a) and (b) can imply a violation of (c). Formally these pairs of assumptions can be expressed as

$$P(t_1,\ldots,t_k|r)= \prod_1^k P(t_i|r) \qquad\qquad (\mathrm{I_a})$$

$$P(t_1,\ldots,t_k|\bar{r}\vee r)= \prod_1^k P(t_i|\bar{r}\vee r) \qquad\qquad (\mathrm{I_c})$$

$$P(t_1,\ldots,t_k|r)= \prod_1^k P(t_i|r) \qquad\qquad (\mathrm{I_a})$$

$$P(t_1,\ldots,t_k|\bar{r})= \prod_1^k P(t_i|\bar{r}) \qquad\qquad (\mathrm{I_b})$$

Let us agree to call the pair $\{\mathrm{I_a}, \mathrm{I_c}\}$, $\mathrm{I_{ac}}$, and the second pair $\mathrm{I_{ab}}$. Miller (1971) in specifying Model $\mathrm{I}\frac{1}{2}$ clearly made assumptions $\mathrm{I_{ac}}$ whereas Robertson and Sparck

---

[4] If we were to introduce Q as well we should to be explicit, $P(R|D)$ would read $P(R|D,Q)$.

Jones have argued for the superiority of I_{ab}. It is now common practice to assume I_{ab}. See Cooper (1995) for an interesting discussion on why the independence assumptions made are less severe than might appear at first sight. Many attempts to have been made to replace the independence assumptions with assumptions for dependence between terms, but although intuitively this should lead to better models, to date no conclusive empirical evidence has emerged that relaxing the independence assumptions will lead to more effective retrieval (see Van Rijsbergen, 1977, Harper and Van Rijsbergen, 1978, and Yu et al, 1983, for some early attempts).

Ordering

Ranking of the output of a retrieval strategy was either explicit or implicit in many of the early retrieval techniques. A notable exception to this was the common Boolean strategy that simply output an unordered set. Even the traditional evaluation parameters, such as Precision and Recall, were mostly presented as a pair of numbers that varied as the value of a control parameter thus giving rise to the well known precision-recall graph. But, there was little consensus on what control parameters to use, or, to put it differently, what information pertaining to a query and document should be used to calculate such a parameter. It was mostly a matter of experimental investigation using the results of the precision-recall evaluation to suggest one control parameter over another; for example, it might be claimed that cosine correlation is better than co-ordination level matching. With advent of the probabilistic accounts, the situation changed somewhat. In 1965 Maron already claimed that the ranking in his model was optimal.

In Model II a similar but more detailed claim is made by Robertson and Sparck Jones (1976). It is important to emphasise that these claims are with respect to a given model. In that paper they propose two possible ordering strategies,

i. The probability of relevance of a document should be calculated from the terms present in the document only.

ii. The probability of relevance of a document should be calculated from the terms present in the document and from those absent.

The strong claim is that within Model II, ordering strategy (ii) is correct and strategy (i) is incorrect. This is in contradistinction to Miller (1976) who used strategy (i), but of course in Model $I\frac{1}{2}$ as set up by Miller, strategy (i) is correct. In Model II given the probabilities as defined above and the fact that one is computing the probability of relevance conditional on a random variable D, which is a vector of binary variables taking values 1 and 0 corresponding to the presence and absence of terms, it follows naturally within the model that strategy (ii) applies. It becomes a matter of empirical test which model is better, and there is no doubt that Model II won out in the end. The combination of I_{ab} and ordering strategy (ii) led to the derivation of weighting formula F_4. Paradoxically although matching between documents and a query is restricted to absence/presence of query terms, F_4 is evaluated and summed for only the query terms *present* in the document; this is achieved by a mathematical rearrangement of the matching function; implicit in F_4 is the absence information (see Van Rijsbergen, 1979, p.118-119, for a simple derivation).

Optimality

One of the strengths of Model II is that there are theoretical results showing that the probability ordering principle optimises performance. A proof of this is possible because we can define the performance parameters such as precision and recall in probabilistic terms. For example, recall is the probability of retrieval given relevance and precision is the probability of relevance given retrieval. To be entirely correct one should state that recall (precision) is an *estimate* of the probability thus defined[5]. It has been shown that retrieving with respect to a single query in order of the probability of relevance based on all the available data is the best that is obtainable on the basis of that data. This result is now enshrined in the Probability Ranking Principle which was formulated in detail by Robertson (1997), although it was first justified in this form in Robertson (1975).

There is a decision-theoretic version of this principle which is formulated in terms of the loss associated with retrieving a non-relevant document and not retrieving a relevant document. The decision to be made for each document, is to retrieve or not retrieve; by taking the decision corresponding to the smaller expected loss one minimises the overall risk. By choosing a particularly simple 0/1 loss function one recovers the decision theoretic equivalent of the Probability Ranking Principle. This was well-known in the mid-seventies and explained in detail in Robertson (1975) and Van Rijsbergen (1979).

There is an even earlier version to be found in Harter (1974). He made his argument in terms of expected recall and expected precision, which are other names for the estimates of the probabilistically defined precision and recall. Harter on page 81 of his thesis claims (as definition) that;

> An **optimal indexing strategy** is a strategy which for each value of expected recall,
>
> achieves the maximum possible value of expected precision.

Harter then goes on to prove that the decision-theoretic described above is optimal. Note that this was for indexing and not retrieval, but it is easy to convert one into the other, as was done in Van Rijsbergen, *et al* (1980).

Estimation

If one looks at the 2×2 table above, it is immediately obvious that problems arise in the case where some of the cell values are zero and thereby makes the *log* function in one of the weights ($F_1 - F_4$) undefined. This is most likely to occur in the case

---

[5] One of the first people to make this translation from ratios to probabilities, albeit for recall and fallout, was Swets (1967); his aim was to define a composite effectiveness measure based on recall and fallout. He used decision theory to motivate its construction.

where r is zero which leaves us with the problem of handling $log(0)$, which is usually $-\infty$. As mentioned earlier the way to handle this is to add $\frac{1}{2}$ to each entry in the inner cells, thereby avoiding any one cell becoming zero. So what is the problem here? Let us look at one example, r/R, this is an estimate for the probability of occurrence of a particular index term in the set of relevant document, it is normally estimated by taking a biased sample and counting the number of times the term occurs in the documents judged relevant in the sample. When $r=0$ it means that the particular term does not occur in the sub-sample of relevant documents. The question now is does that imply that it will not occur in any further relevant documents? It is rightly assumed that this is not so.

This problem is equivalent to the following problem for black and white balls. Let us suppose that we have a bag of black and white balls of unknown mixture. We start to sample the bag and we get a run of white balls, let us say m of them. Now, the next time we choose a ball from the bag what is the probability p of choosing a black one. So far there are zero black balls in the sample, and we do not know the composition of the bag; should we assume p=0? Laplace in 1774, proposed and justified what has become known as the *Laplace's law of succession*[6], namely

$p = \dfrac{r+1}{n+2}$. But, in the Robertson Sparck Jones approach $p = \dfrac{r+\frac{1}{2}}{n+1}$. How to reconcile these two? It turns out that there is an estimation theory couched in terms of the prior distribution one can assume on the parameter p of the form $\propto p^{a-1}(1-p)^{b-1}$ where a and b are numerical parameters which lead to a Bayesian estimate $p = \dfrac{r+a}{n+a+b}$. Now with $a=1$ and $b=1$ we get Laplace's rule, with $a=\frac{1}{2}$ and $b=\frac{1}{2}$ we get the Robertson and Sparck Jones estimate. The important point here is that it is the type of prior distribution that leads to the form of estimate, a different prior gives a different estimate. The ultimate choice of parameters a and b is a matter for experimentation. For more details and further references, see Steinhaus (1957), Good (1965), Van Rijsbergen (1977), and Orlitsky, *et al* (2003).

2. UNIFIED MODEL

Robertson, Maron and Cooper (1982) attempted to unify Models I and II, the result we will call Model III (Maron,1984). From a theoretical point of view this was a very interesting piece of research but it did not lead to any significant experimentation. It highlighted the differences between the two models. Model I was seen as grouping users together in order to compute a probability of relevance for a *given document*, whereas Model II groups document documents together in order to compute a probability of relevance for a *given user*. In essence Model III is based on an event space which is the Cartesian product of the class of uses of a system and the class of documents in the systems. The probability of relevance is

---

[6] Keynes (1929, p.368) gives a lucid historical account of Laplace's law.

now conditioned on an individual use and document. It is hard to see what is to be gained by gluing Models I and II together like this, which perhaps explains the lack of experimentation with it. Fuhr (1986) attempted a different combination of probabilistic indexing with search term weighting for this he used Croft's extension of the binary independence model (Croft, 1981) which by then had become a standard name for Model II.

Thompson (1986) went on to generalise Model III. In his approach different models are seen as expert opinions which are then combined probabilistically. His framework is not just restricted to combining probabilistic retrieval engines, but is able to combine any number of search engines. Moreover, unlike Model III, it also was able to incorporate relevance feedback.

3. AI AND IR

Although Model II was mainly seen as a ranking model by the IR community, it is clear from the above that there is an equivalent decision-theoretic formulation, let us call this Model IV. This approach has a history of its own, eventually converging with Model II in the IR literature. One of the earliest exposition of the construction of an optimum linear discriminate function to discriminate patterns of one class (relevant) from patterns in another class (non-relevant) was given by Nilsson (1965). In his book (section 3.5) a detailed example is given of how to solve this problem for patterns that have attributes independently distributed conditional on each class (assumption I_{ab} above). Nilsson states the problem as follows:

'Suppose that we wish to design a machine to categorize patterns each consisting of d binary components. (Each $x_i = 1$ or 0). Let us assume that $R = 2$; that is , there are two categories, labelled category 1 and category 2.'

Nilsson proceeded to derive the optimum classifier, and I quote verbatim,

$$g(X) = \sum_{i=1}^{d} x_i \log\left[\frac{p_i(1-q_i)}{q_i(1-p_i)}\right] + \sum_{i=1}^{d} \log\left(\frac{1-p_i}{1-q_i}\right) + \log\left[\frac{p(1)}{1-p(1)}\right]$$

This is a discriminant function to discriminate category 1, with prior probability $p(1)$ from category 2, with prior probability $1-p(1)$. The p_i and q_i are now the familiar conditional probabilities $P(x_i = 1|1)$ and $P(x_i = 1|2)$. If we now think of category 1 as the relevant category, and category 2 as the non-relevant one, then the first summation gives as the F_4 weighting function from Model II. This is the optimum function assuming complete knowledge of the parameters p's and q's. Without such knowledge these parameters require estimation, just as in IR, and indeed Laplace's law is given as a candidate estimation rule. A similar derivation was given by Minsky (1961). The Nilsson derivation was repeated in Duda and Hart (1973).

From an experimental point of view, the classifier $g(X)$ can be used to separate the relevant from the non-relevant documents iteratively. This requires the estimation of p and q from whatever information is available, substituting those values into g and using it do a trial separation of the documents. On the basis of that result the p's and q's can be re-estimated and one can go around again. There is a theorem called the Perceptron Convergence Theorem (Nilsson, 1965, Minsky, 1969) that under some mild conditions ensures that if the documents are linearly separable, the iterative procedure will converge resulting in a separation of the two classes. This process is reminiscent of the adaptive procedure proposed by Rocchio (1966), and indeed not surprisingly the above iterative decision process can be transformed into Rocchio's algorithm, thus giving a nice probabilistic interpretation of the Rocchio procedure (Van Rijsbergen, 1979).

Model IV, although having its beginnings in the AI and Pattern recognition literature evolved as a probabilistic approach to IR. It can be viewed as a special case of Model II, if the loss function is a binary one, or alternatively as a more general approach if one allows the user to specify the loss function. A summary of this situation was captured nicely in the Robertson and Sparck Jones (1976) paper.

4. LANGUAGE MODELLING

The last probabilistic approach to IR that we wish to describe is part of what has now become known as the Language Modelling approach – we will call it Model V. A potted history for this approach can be found in Hiemstra (2000) and a good overview of the extent of current research is readily available in Croft and Lafferty (2003). Although Ponte and Croft (1998) were the first to suggest the use of language models in information retrieval, there is a relevant pre-history. A language model is a probabilistic mechanism for generating text. A good source to early references in this area are Edmundson (1963), and Herdan (1964), where one will find citations for the early work of Mandelbrot, Markov, and Simon. What distinguishes this earlier work from the current research on language models in IR, is that in IR the generative models are used to rank or classify documents.

Lafferty and Zhai (2003) have made a good case for treating Model II[7] and Model V as equivalent from a probabilistic point of view, but different statistically[8]. We will now show this.

The aim is to calculate the probability of relevance conditional on a query and document, $P(r|D,Q)$[9], this is done indirectly via Bayes' rule:

$$P(R = r|D,Q) = \frac{P(D,Q|R = r)P(R = r)}{P(D,Q)}$$

---

[7] I will stick with Lafferty and Zhai's reference to Model II, although the comparison is really more transparent in terms of Model IV.

[8] Robertson, in commenting on an earlier draft, has pointed out to me that this so called equivalence is not as straightforward as it might appear. There is a subtle issue about Q appearing as a conditioning event, a particular instance of the query, and when Q appears as a random variable to the left of the conditioning stroke. This issue remains a matter for debate.

[9] See footnote 4, we are now including Q in the conditioning event.

It is the right side of this equation that is used to rank documents and usually by transforming it using into the log-odds ratio form which is a monotonic transformation not affecting the rank ordering. Thus we rank in terms of

$$\log\frac{P(r|D,Q)}{P(\bar{r}|D,Q)} = \log\frac{P(D,Q|r)P(r)}{P(D,Q|\bar{r})P(\bar{r})}$$

There are two ways of deriving the probabilistic equivalent versions of the weighting functions, one for Model II and one for Model V. They depend on which way one factors the joint probability $P(D,Q|R)$.

$$P(D,Q|R) = P(Q|R)P(D|Q,R) \qquad \text{for Model II}$$
$$= P(D|R)P(Q|D,R) \qquad \text{for Model V}$$

If one now does the expansion for the *log* function on the right-hand side of the above equation using first the expansion for Model II and then for Model V, one obtains the two equivalent weighting functions.

$$\log\frac{P(r|D,Q)}{P(\bar{r}|D,Q)} = \log\frac{P(D|Q,r)}{P(D|Q,\bar{r})} + \log\frac{P(r|Q)}{P(\bar{r}|Q)} \qquad \text{for Model II}$$

$$= \log\frac{P(Q|D,r)}{P(Q|D,\bar{r})} + \log\frac{P(r|D)}{P(\bar{r}|D)} \qquad \text{for Model V}$$

As they stand, ranking by either formula would give the same result, but the most striking difference is that for Model II the bias term does not depend on D, whereas for Model V it does. Note that $\log\dfrac{P(r|Q)}{P(\bar{r}|Q)} = \log\left[\dfrac{p(1)}{1-p(1)}\right]$ in the expansion for Model IV given by Nilsson. A bias term independent of a document can be safely ignored when ranking documents with respect to a given query. Doing this, one is left, after a little algebra, with the F_4 weighting function where specific statistical estimates are assumed for the component probabilities.

By making some further statistical assumptions about independence, one can derive a simpler weighting function for Model V (see Lafferty and Zhai, 2003, for details), namely,

$$\log \frac{P(r|D,Q)}{P(\bar{r}|D,Q)} \propto \log P(Q|D,r)$$

where $\propto$ stands for equivalent in rank ordering.

From a generative point of view Model II uses a probabilistic mechanism to generate a document from a query, whereas a language model does the reverse, generates a query from a document. Both queries and documents are represented by index terms, and to specify the generative process an assumption about the dependence, or independence, of these terms has to be made. Once this has been done assumptions about the form of the estimation rules for component probabilities are made, which will differ from model to model. Another difference is the use of relevance feedback information, one of the strengths of Model II is that such information is readily deployed iteratively. This is not so for Model V, it is not entirely clear yet how relevance feed-back information is deployed when in principle one has a different language model for each document.

5. CONCLUSIONS

We have summarised a number of approaches to information retrieval based on the use of probability theory and statistics from the early sixties through to the present. It is clear that a number disparate strands of development occurred culminating in successful models of retrieval. Without doubt Model II has been empirically the most successful, and owes its existence substantially to the early work of Spärck Jones when she invented the statistically motivated IDF and F1. This research was built on by the joint work with Robertson when they specified Model II in their joint paper in 1976. All the while Sparck Jones experimented heavily with these early ideas establishing an experimental basis for their acceptance. This experimentation continued to this day through her involvement with the TREC initiative. Her influence on TREC (Voorhees and Harman, in press) has been substantial. What is interesting is that despite the long history of these approaches they are still the subject of active research.

Keith van Rijsbergen was born in Holland in 1943. He was educated in Holland, Indonesia, Namibia and Australia. He took a degree in mathematics at the University of Western Australia. As a graduate he spent two years tutoring in mathematics while studying computer science. In 1972 he completed a Ph.D. in computer science at Cambridge University. After almost three years of lecturing in information retrieval and artificial intelligence at Monash University he returned to the Cambridge Computer Laboratory to hold a Royal Society Information Research Fellowship. In 1980 he was appointed to the chair of computer science at University

College Dublin; from there he moved in 1986 to the Glasgow University where he is now. Since about 1969 his research has been devoted to information retrieval, covering both theoretical and experimental aspects. He has specified several theoretical models for IR and seen some of them from the specification and prototype stage through to production. His current research is concerned with the design of appropriate logics to model the flow of information and the application of Hilbert Space theory to content-based IR . He is a fellow of the IEE, BCS, ACM, the Royal Society of Edinburgh, and the Royal Academy of Engineering. In 1993 he was appointed Editor-in-Chief of **The Computer Journal**, *an appointment he held until 2000. He is also the author of a well-known book on Information Retrieval. In1999, together with Crestani and Lalmas, edited a book entitled "Information Retrieval: Uncertainty and Logics", and most recently (2004) has published 'The Geometry of Information Retrieval', CUP.*

ACKNOWLEDGEMENTS

I would like to thank David Harper, Mounia Lalmas, and Stephen Robertson for helpful comments on an earlier draft of this paper.

REFERENCES[10]

Barkla, J.K. (1969). Construction of weighted term profiles by measuring frequency and specificity in relevant items, Presented at the Second Cranfield Conference on Mechanised Information Storage and Retrieval Systems, Cranfield, Bedford.

Cooper, W.S. (1995). Some inconsistencies and misidentified modelling assumptions in probabilistic information retrieval, *ACM Transactions on Information Systems*, **13**, 100-111.

Cox, D.R. (1970). *Analysis of binary data*, Methuen, London.

Croft, W.B. (1981). Document representation in probabilistic models of information retrieval, *Journal of the American Society for Information Science*, **32**, 451-457.

Croft, W.B. and J. Lafferty (2003). *Language modelling for information retrieval*, Kluwer, Dordrecht.

*Croft, W.B. and D.J. Harper (1979). Using probabilistic models of document retrieval without relevance information, *Journal of Documentation*, **35**, 285-95.

Duda, R.O. and P.E. Hart (1973). *Pattern classification and scene analysis*, Wiley, New York.

Edmundson, H. P. (1963). A statistician's view of linguistic models and language-data processing, In: P.L. Garvin (ed), *Natural language and the computer*, McGraw-Hill, New york.

Fuhr, N. (1986). Two models of retrieval with probabilistic indexing, *Proceedings 1986 – ACM conference on research and development in information retrieval*, Pisa, 249-257.

Fuhr, N. (1989). Models for retrieval with probabilistic indexing, *Information Processing and Management*, **25**, 55-72.

Goffman, W. (1969). An indirect method of information retrieval, *Information Storage and Retrieval*, 4, 361-373.

Good, I.J. (1965). *The estimation of probabilities: An essay on modern Bayesian methods*, MIT Press, Cambridge, Mass.

Harper, D.J. and C.J. van Rijsbergen (1978). An evaluation of feedback in document retrieval using co-occurrence data, *Journal of Documentation*, **34**, 189-216.

---

[10] A number of the references cited here can be found in K. Sparck Jones and P. Willett(eds.), Readings in Information Retrieval, Morgan Kaufmann, San Francisco, 1997. Those will be prefaced by an *.

Harter, S.P. (1974). *A probabilistic approach to automatic keyword indexing*, PhD Thesis, University of Chicago.

Herdan, G. (1964). *Quantitative linguistics*, Butterworths, London.

Hiemstra, D. (2000). *Using language models for information retrieval*, PhD Thesis, Universiteit Twente.

Keynes, J.M. (1929). *A treatise on probability*, MacMillan and Co, London.

Lafferty, J. and C.-X. Zhai (2003). Probabilistic relevance models based on document and query generation, In: Croft, W.B. and J. Lafferty(2003).

Laplace, P.S. (1774). Mémoire sur la probabilité des causes par les événements, *Mém. prés. à l'Acad. des Sc.*, Paris, **6**, 621-56.

Maron, M.E. (1965). Mechanized documentation: The logic behind a probabilistic interpretation, In: M. Stevens, *et al* (eds.), *Statistical Association Methods for Mechanized Documentation*, National Bureau of Standards Miscellaneous Publication 269, Washington, 9-13.

Maron, M.E. (1983) Probabilistic approaches to the document retrieval problem, In: G. Salton and H.-J. Schneider, Lecture Notes in Computer Science, **146**, 98-107.

Maron, M.E. (1984). Probabilistic retrieval models, In: Dervin, B. and M. Voigt (eds.), *Progress in Communication Sciences*, Ablex Publishing, Norwood, New Jersey, **5**, 145-176.

*Maron, M.E. and J.L. Kuhns (1960). On relevance, probabilistic indexing, and information retrieval, *Journal of the ACM*, 7, 216-44.

Miller, W.L. (1971). A probabilistic search strategy for Medlars, *Journal of Documentation*, 27, 254-66.

Minsky, M. (1961). Steps towards artificial intelligence, In: E. Feigenbaum and J. Feldman (eds.) *Computers and Thought*, McGraw-Hill, New York, 406-50.

Minsky, M. and S. Papert (1969). *Perceptrons: an introduction to computational geometry*, MIT Press, Cambridge, Mass.

Nilsson, N.J. (1965). *Learning machines*, McGraw-Hill, New York.

Orlitsky, A., N.P. Santhanam, and J. Zhang (2003). Always Good Turing: asymptoticall optimal probability estimation, *Science*, 302, 427-31.

Ponte, J. and W.B. Croft (1998). A language modelling approach to information retrieval, In: Proceedings of the 21st International Conference on Research and Development in Information Retrieval, 275-81.

Robertson, S.E. (1974). Specificity and weighted retrieval, *Journal of Documentation*, 30, 40-46.

Robertson, S.E. (1975). *A theoretical model of the retrieval characteristics of information retrieval systems*, PhD Thesis, University College London.

*Robertson, S.E. (1977). The probability ranking principle, *Journal of Documentation*, 33, 294-304.

Robertson, S.E. and K. Sparck Jones (1976). Relevance weighting of search terms, *Journal of the American Society for Information Science*, **27**, 129-146.

Robertson, S.E., M.E. Maron, and W.S. Cooper (1982). Probability of relevance: a unification of two competing models for document retrieval, *Information Technology: Research and Development*, 1, 1-21.

Rocchio, J.J. (1966). *Document retrieval systems*, PhD Thesis, Harvard University.

Sparck Jones, K. (1972) A statistical interpretation of term specificity and its application in retrieval, *Journal of Documentation*, **28**, 11-21.

Sparck Jones, K. (1975). A performance yardstick for test collections, *Journal of Documentation*, **31**, 266-72..

Sparck Jones, K. and R.G. Bates (1977). *Research on automatic indexing 1974-1976*, Computer Laboratory Technical Report, Vol. I: Text, University of Cambridge.

Sparck Jones, K., S. Walker, and S.E. Robertson (2000). A probabilistic model of information retrieval: development and comparative experiments, *Information Processing and Management*, **36**, Part 1 779-808; Part 2 809-840.

Sparck Jones, K. and C.A. Webster (1980). *Research on relevance weighting 1976-1979*, British Library R&D Report 5553.

Steinhaus, H. (1957). The problem of estimation, *The Annals of Mathematical Statistics*, 28, 633-48.

Swets, J.A. (1967). *Effectiveness of information retrieval methods*, project No. 8668, Scientific Report No. 8, Bolt, Beranek, and Newman, Cambridge, Mass.0

Thompson, P. (1986). *Subjective probability, combination of expert opinion, and probabilistic approaches to information retrieval*. PhD Thesis, University of California, Berkeley.

Van Fraassen, B.C. (1980). *The scientific image*, Clarendon Press, Oxford.

Van Rijsbergen, C.J. (1977). A theoretical basis for the use of co-occurrence data in information retrieval, *Journal of Documentation*, 33, 106-119.

Van Rijsbergen, C.J. (1979). *Information retrieval*, Second Edition, Butterworths, London.
Van Rijsbergen, C.J., S.E. Robertson, and M.F. Porter (1980). *New models in probabilistic information retrieval*, British Library R&D Report 5587.
Voorhees, E. and D. Harman (in press). TREC: Experiment and Evaluation in Information Retrieval, MIT Press, Cambridge, Mass.
Yu, C.T., D. Buckley, K. Lam, and G. Salton (1983). A generalised term dependence model in information retrieval, *Information Technology: Research and Development*, **2**, 129-54.
Yu, C.T. and G. Salton (1976) Precison weighting – an effective automatic indexing method, *Journal of the ACM*, **23**, 76-88.

MARTIN F. PORTER

LOVINS REVISITED

1. PREAMBLE

This is a festschrift paper, so I am allowed to begin on a personal note. In 1979 I was working with Keith van Rijsbergen and Stephen Robertson on a British Library funded IR project to investigate the selection of good index terms, and one of the things we found ourselves having to do was to establish a document test collection from some raw data that had been sent to us on a magnetic tape by Peter Vaswani of the National Physical Laboratory. I was the tame programmer in the project, so it was my job to set up the test collection.

On the whole it did not prove too difficult. The data we received was a collection of about 11,000 documents (titles and short abstracts), 93 queries — in a free text form, and relevance judgements. All the text was in upper case without punctuation, and there were one or two marker characters to act as field terminators. By modern standards the data was really very small indeed, but at the time it was considerably larger than any of the other test collections we had. What you had to do was to cast it into a standard form for experimental work. You represented terms and documents by numbers and created flat files in text form corresponding to queries, relevance assessments and a term to document index. One process however was less straightforward. On their way to becoming numeric terms, the words of the source text were put through a process of linguistic normalization called suffix stripping in which certain derivational and and inflectional suffixes attached to words were removed. There was a standard piece of software used in Cambridge at that time to do this, written in 1971 by Keith Andrews (Andrews, 1971). One of the courses in Cambridge is the one year post-graduate Diploma in Computer Science. Each student on the course is required to do a special project, which includes writing a significant piece of software — significant in the sense of being both useful and substantial. Keith's piece of software was more useful than most, and it continued to be used as a suffix stripping program, or stemmer, for many years after it was written.

Now by an odd chance I was privy to much of Keith's original thinking at the time that he was doing the work. The reason for this was that in 1971 I was looking for a house in Cambridge, and the base I was operating from was a sleeping bag on the living room floor of an old friend called John Dawson, who was Keith's diploma supervisor. Keith used to come round and discuss stemming algorithms with him, while I formed a mute audience. I learnt about the Lovins stemming algorithm of 1968 (Lovins, 1968), and must I think have at least looked at her paper then, since I

John I. Tait (ed.), *Charting a New Course: Natural Language Processing and Information Retrieval. Essays in Honour of Karen Spärck Jones.* 39–68

know it was not new to me when I saw it again in 1979. Their view of Lovins' work was that it did not go far enough. There needed to be many more suffixes, and more complex rules to determine the criteria for their removal. Much of their discussion was about new suffixes to add to the list, and removal rules. It was interesting therefore to find myself needing to use Andrews' work eight years later, and questioning some of its assumptions. Did you need that many suffixes? Did the rules need to be so complicated? Perhaps one would do better to break composite suffixes into smaller units and remove them piecemeal. And perhaps syllables would be a better count of stem length than letters. So I wrote my own stemmer, which became known as the Porter stemmer, and which was published in 1980 (Porter, 1980).

I must explain where Karen Sparck Jones fits into all of this. Keith Andrews' piece of work was originally suggested by Karen as a Diploma student project, and she was able to use the Andrews stemmer in her IR experiments throughout the seventies. In 1979 however Karen had moved much more into the field of Natural Language Processing and Artificial Intelligence, and by then had two or three research students in that field just writing up their PhDs (only one of whom I really got to know — John Tait, the editor of this volume). So we were in contact, but not working together. That again was an odd chance: that Karen had been my research supervisor in a topic other than IR, and that when later I was doing IR research at Cambridge I was not working with Karen. While I was engaged on writing the stemmer, Karen showed some justifiable irritation that I had become interested in a topic so very remote from the one for which we had received the British Library funding. Nevertheless, she came into my room one day, said "Look, if you're getting interested in stemming, you'd better read this", and handed me the 1968 issue of Mechanical Translation that contains the Lovins paper. I still have this issue with Karen's name across the top. (And I hope she didn't expect it back!)

Another 20 years have gone by, and I have been studying the Lovins stemmer again, really because I was looking for examples to code up in Snowball, a small string processing language I devised in the latter half of 2001 particularly adapted for writing stemming algorithms. Lovins' stemmer strikes me now as a fine piece of work, for which she never quite received the credit she deserved. It was the first stemmer for English set out as an algorithm that described the stemming process exactly. She explained how it was intended to be used to improve IR performance, in just the way in which stemmers are used today. It is not seriously short of suffixes: the outstanding omissions are the plural forms *ements* and *ents* corresponding to her *ement* and *ent*, and it is easy enough to add them into the definition. It performs well in practice. In fact it is still in use, and can be downloaded in various languages from the net[1]. The tendency since 1980 has been to attach the name "Porter" to any language stemming process that does not use a dictionary, even when it is quite dissimilar to the original Porter stemmer (witness the Dutch Porter stemmer of Kraaij and Pohlmann[2](Kraaij, 1994 and Kraaij, 1995),

---

[1] The Lovins stemmer is avaliable at
      `http://www.cs.waikato.ac.nz/~eibe/stemmers`
      `http://sourceforge.net/projects/stemmers`
[2] See `http://www-uilots.let.uu.nl/~uplift/`

but the priority really belongs to Lovins. It also has one clear advantage over the Porter algorithm, in that it involves fewer steps. Coded up well, it should run a lot faster.

A number of things intrigued me. Why are the Lovins and Porter stemmers so different, when what they do looks so similar? Could the stemmer, in some sense, be brought up-to-date? Could the Porter stemmer be cast into the Lovins form, and so run faster?

This paper is about the answers for these questions. In discovering them, I have learned a lot more about my own stemmer.

2. WHY STEM?

It may be worth saying a little on what stemming is all about. We can imagine a document with the title,

Pre-raphaelitism: A Study of Four Critical Approaches

and a query, containing the words

PRE-RAPHAELITE CRITICISM

We want to match query against title so that "Pre-raphaelitism" matches "PRE-RAPHAELITE" and "Critical" matches "CRITICISM". This leads to the idea of removing endings from words as part of the process of extracting index terms from documents, a similar process of ending removal being applied to queries prior to the match. For example, we would like to remove the endings from

critical
critically
criticism
criticisms
critics

so that each word is reduced to "critic". This is the *stem*, from which the other words are formed, so the process as a whole is called *stemming*. It is a feature of English morphology that the part of the word we want to remove is at the end — the suffix. But the same is broadly true of French, German and other languages of the Indo-European group. It is also true of numerous languages outside Indo-European, Finnish for example, although there is a boundary beyond which it is not true. So Chinese, where words are simple units without affixes, and Arabic, where the stem is modified by prefixes and infixes as well as suffixes, lie outside the boundary. As an IR technique it therefore has wide applicability. In developing stemmers two points were recognised quite early on. One is that the morphological regularities that you find in English (or other languages) mean that you can attempt to do stemming by a purely algorithmic process. Endings *al*, *ally*, *ism* etc. occur throughout English vocabulary, and are easy to detect and remove: you don't need access to an on-line dictionary. The other is that the morphological irregularities of English set a limit to the success of an algorithmic approach. Syntactically, what look like endings may not be endings (*offspring* is not *offspr* + *ing*), and the list of endings seems to extend indefinitely (*trapez-oid, likeli-hood, guardian-ship, Tibet-an, juven-ilia, Roman-*

esque, ox-en ...) It is difficult to gauge where to set the cut-off for these rarer forms. Semantically, the addition of a suffix may alter the meaning of a word a little, a lot, or completely, and morphology alone cannot measure the degree of change (*prove* and *provable* have closely related meanings; *probe* and *probable* do not.) This meant that stemming, if employed at all, became the most challenging, and the most difficult part of the indexing process.

In the seventies, stemming might be applied as part of the process of establishing a test collection, and when it was there would not usually be any attempt to make the stemming process well-defined, or easily repeatable by another researcher. This was really because the basis for experiment replication was the normalised data that came out of the stemming process, rather than the source data plus a description of stemming procedures. Stemming tended to be applied, and then forgotten about. But by the 1980s, stemming itself was being investigated. Lennon and others (Lennon, 1981) found no substantial differences between the use of different stemmers for English. Harman (Harman, 1991) challenged the effectiveness of stemming altogether, when she reported no substantial differences between using and not using stemming in a series of experiments. But later work has been more positive. Krovetz (Krovetz, 1995), for example, reported small but significant improvements with stemming over a range of test collections.

Of course, all these experiments assume some IR model which will use stemming in a particular way, and will measure just those features that tests collections are, notoriously, able to measure. We might imagine an IR system where the users have been educated in the advantages and disadvantages to be expected from stemming, and are able to flag individual search terms to say whether or not they are to be used stemmed or unstemmed. Stemming sometimes improves, occasionally degrades, search performance, and this would be the best way of using it as an IR facility. Again stemming helps regularise the IR vocabulary, which is very useful when preparing a list of terms to present to a user as candidates for query expansion. But this advantage too is difficult to quantify.

An evaluative comparison between the Lovins and later stemmers lies in any case outside the scope of this paper, but it is important to bear in mind that it is not a straightforward undertaking.

3. THE LOVINS STEMMER

Structurally, the Lovins stemmer is in four parts, collected together in four Appendices A, B, C and D in her paper. Part A is a list of 294 endings, each with a letter which identifies a condition for whether or not the ending should be removed. (I will follow Lovins in using "ending" rather than "suffix" as a name for the items on the list.) Part A therefore looks like this:

.11.

alistically	B
arizability	A
izationally	B

.10.
antialness   A
arisations   A
arizations   A
entialness   A
.09.
allically   C
antaneous   A
antiality   A
.....

.01.
a   A
e   A
i   A
o   A
s   W
y   B

Endings are banked by length, from 11 letters down to 1. Each bank is tried in turn until an ending is found which matches the end of the word to be stemmed and leaves a stem which satisfies the given condition, when the ending is removed. For example condition C says that the stem must have at least 4 letters, so *bimetallically* would lose **allically** leaving a stem *bimet* of length 5, but *metallically* would not reduce to *met*, since its length is only 3.

There are 29 such conditions, called A to Z, AA, BB and CC, and they constitute part B of the stemmer. Here they are (* stands for any letter):

A	No restrictions on stem
B	Minimum stem length = 3
C	Minimum stem length = 4
D	Minimum stem length = 5
E	Do not remove ending after *e*
F	Minimum stem length = 3 and do not remove ending after *e*
G	Minimum stem length = 3 and remove ending only after *f*
H	Remove ending only after *t* or *ll*
I	Do not remove ending after *o* or *e*
J	Do not remove ending after *a* or *e*
K	Minimum stem length = 3 and remove ending only after *l, i* or *u*e*
L	Do not remove ending after *u, x* or *s*, unless *s* follows *o*
M	Do not remove ending after *a, c, e* or *m*
N	Minimum stem length = 4 after *s**, elsewhere = 3
O	Remove ending only after *l* or *i*
P	Do not remove ending after *c*
Q	Minimum stem length = 3 and do not remove ending after *l* or *n*
R	Remove ending only after *n* or *r*

S	Remove ending only after *dr* or *t*, unless *t* follows *t*
T	Remove ending only after *s* or *t*, unless *t* follows *o*
U	Remove ending only after *l, m, n* or *r*
V	Remove ending only after *c*
W	Do not remove ending after *s* or *u*
X	Remove ending only after *l, i* or *u*e*
Y	Remove ending only after *in*
Z	Do not remove ending after *f*
AA	Remove ending only after *d, f, ph, th, l, er, or, es* or *t*
BB	Minimum stem length = 3 and do not remove ending after *met* or *ryst*
CC	Remove ending only after *l*

There is an implicit assumption in each condition, A included, that the minimum stem length is 2.

This is much less complicated than it seems at first. Conditions A to D depend on a simple measure of minimum stem length, and E and F are slight variants of A and B. Out of the 294 endings, 259 use one of these 6 conditions. The remaining 35 endings use the other 23 conditions, so conditions G, H ... CC have less than 2 suffixes each, on average. What is happening here is that Lovins is trying to capture a rule which gives a good removal criterion for one ending, or a small number of similar endings. She does not explain the thinking behind the conditions, but it is often not too difficult to reconstruct. Here for example are the last few conditions with their endings,

Y (*early, ealy, eal, ear*). *collinearly, multilinear* are stemmed.
Z (*eature*). *misfeature* does not lose *eature*.
AA (*ite*). *acolouthite, hemimorphite* lose *ite*, *ignite* and *requite* retain it.
BB (*allic, als, al*). Words ending *metal, crystal* retain *al*.

CC (*inity*). *crystallinity* ⟹ *crystall*, but *affinity, infinity* are unaltered.

Part C of the Lovins stemmer is a set of 35 transformation rules used to adjust the letters at the end of the stem. These rules are invoked after the stemming step proper, irrespective of whether an ending was actually removed. Here are about half of them, with examples to show the type of transformation intended (letters in square brackets indicate the full form of the words),

1)	bb	⟹	b	rubb[ing]	⟹ rub
	ll	⟹	l	controll[ed]	⟹ control
	mm	⟹	m	trimm[ed]	⟹ trim
	rr	⟹	r	abhorr[ing]	⟹ abhor
2)	iev	⟹	ief	believ[e]	⟹ belief
3)	uct	⟹	uc	induct[ion]	⟹ induc[e]
4)	umpt	⟹	um	consumpt[ion]	⟹ consum[e]

5)	rpt	$\Rightarrow$	rb	absorpt[ion]	$\Rightarrow$ absorb
6)	urs	$\Rightarrow$	ur	recurs[ive]	$\Rightarrow$ recur
7a)	metr	$\Rightarrow$	meter	parametr[ic]	$\Rightarrow$ paramet[er]
...					
8)	olv	$\Rightarrow$	olut	dissolv[ed]	$\Rightarrow$ dissolut[ion]
...					
11)	dex	$\Rightarrow$	dic	index	$\Rightarrow$ indic[es]
...					
16)	ix	$\Rightarrow$	ic	matrix	$\Rightarrow$ matric[es]
...					
18)	uad	$\Rightarrow$	uas	persuad[e]	$\Rightarrow$ persuas[ion]
19)	vad	$\Rightarrow$	vas	evad[e]	$\Rightarrow$ evas[ion]
20)	cid	$\Rightarrow$	cis	decid[e]	$\Rightarrow$ decis[ion]
21)	lid	$\Rightarrow$	lis	elid[e]	$\Rightarrow$ elis[ion]
....					
31)	ert	$\Rightarrow$	ers	convert[ed]	$\Rightarrow$ convers[ion]
....					
33)	yt	$\Rightarrow$	ys	analytic	$\Rightarrow$ analysis
34)	yz	$\Rightarrow$	ys	analyzed	$\Rightarrow$ analysed

Finally, part D suggests certain relaxed matching rules between query terms and index terms when the stemmer has been used to set up an IR system, but we can regard that as not being part of the stemmer proper.

4. THE LOVINS STEMMER IN SNOWBALL

Snowball is a string processing language designed with the idea of making the definition of stemming algorithms much more rigorous. The Snowball compiler translates a Snowball script into a thread-safe ANSI C module, where speed of execution is a major design consideration. The resulting stemmers are pleasantly fast, and will process one million or so words a second on a high-performance modern PC. The Snowball website[3] gives a full description of the language, and also presents stemmers for a range of natural languages. Each stemmer is written out as a formal algorithm, with the corresponding Snowball script following. The algorithm definition acts as program comment for the Snowball script, and the Snowball script gives a precise definition to the algorithm. The ANSI C code with the same functionality can also be inspected, and sample vocabularies in source and stemmed form can be used for test purposes. An essential function of the Snowball script is

---

[3] See http://snowball.sourceforge.net

that it should be fully understood by the reader of the script, and Snowball has been designed with this in mind. It contrasts interestingly in this respect with a system like Perl. Perl has a very big definition. Writing your own scripts in Perl is easy, after the initial learning hurdle, but understanding other scripts can be quite hard. The size of the language means that there are many different ways of doing the same thing, which gives programmers the opportunity of developing highly idiosyncratic styles. Snowball has a small, tight definition. Writing Snowball is much less easy than writing Perl, but on the other hand once it is written it is fairly easy to understand (or at least one hopes that it is). This is illustrated by the Lovins stemmer in Snowball, which is given in Appendix 1. There is a very easy and natural correspondence between the different parts of the stemmer definition in Lovins' original paper and their Snowball equivalents. For example, the Lovins conditions A, B ... CC code up very neatly into routines with the same name. Taking condition L:

L   Do not remove ending after *u, x* or *s*, unless *s* follows *o*

corresponds to

```
define L as ( test hop 2 not 'u' not 'x' not ('s' not 'o') )
```

When `L` is called, we are the right end of the stem, moving left towards the front of the word. Each Lovins condition has an implicit test for a stem of length 2, and this is done by `test hop 2`, which sees if it is possible to hop two places left. If it is not, the routine immediately returns with a false signal, otherwise it carries on. It tests that the character at the right hand end is not *u*, and also not *x*, and also not *s* following a letter which is not *o*. This is equivalent to the Lovins condition. Here is not of course the place to give the exact semantics, but you can quickly get the feel of the language by comparing the 29 Lovins conditions with their Snowball definitions.

Something must be said about the `among` feature of Snowball however, since this is central to the efficient implementation of stemmers. It is also the one part of Snowball that requires just a little effort to understand.

At its simplest, `among` can be used to test for alternative strings. The `amongs` used in the definition of condition AA and the `undouble` routine have this form. In Snowball you can write

```
'sh' or 's' or 't'   'o' or 'i'   'p'
```

which will match the various forms *shop, ship, sop, sip, top, tip*. The order is important, because if `'sh'` and `'s'` are swapped over, the `'s'` would match the first letter of ship, while `'o'` or `'i'` would fail to match with the following `'h'` — in other words the pattern matching has no backtracking. But it can also be written as

```
among('sh' 's' 't') among('i' 'o') 'p'
```

The order of the strings in each among is not important, because the match will be with the longest of all the strings that can match. In Snowball the implementation of among is based on the binary-chop idea, but has been carefully optimised. For example, in the Lovins stemmer, the main among in the endings routine has 294 different strings of average length 5.2 characters. A search for an ending involves accessing a number of characters within these 294 strings. The order is going to be $K\log_2 294$, or $8.2K$, where K is a number that one hopes will be small, although one must certainly expect it to be greater than 1. It turns out that, for the successive words of a standard test vocabulary, K averages to 1.6, so for each word there are about 13 character comparisons needed to determine whether it has one of the Lovins endings.

Each string in an among construction can be followed by a routine name. The routine returns a true/false signal, and then the among searches for the longest substring whose associated routine gives a true signal. A string not followed by a routine name can be thought of as a string which is associated with a routine that does nothing except give a true signal. This is the way that the among in the endings routine works, where indeed every string is followed by a routine name.

More generally, lists of strings in the among construction can be followed by bracketed commands, which are obeyed if one of the strings in the list is picked out for the longest match. The syntax is then

```
among ( S₁₁  S₁₂  ...  (C₁ )
        S₂₁  S₂₂  ...  (C₂ )
        . . .

        Sₙ₁  Sₙ₂  ...  (Cₙ )
      )
```

where the S_{ij} are strings, optionally followed by their routine names, and the C_i are Snowball command sequences. The semantics is a bit like a switch in C, where the switch is on a string rather than a numerical value:

```
switch(...) {
    case S₁₁ : case S₁₂ : ... C₁ ; break;
    case S₂₁ : case S₂₂ : ... C₂ ; break;
    . . .

    case Sₙ₁ : case Sₙ₂ : ... Cₙ ; break;
}
```

The among in the respell routine has this form. The full form however is to use among with a preceding substring, with substring and among possibly separated by further commands. substring triggers the test for the longest matching substring, and the among then causes the corresponding bracketed command to be obeyed. At a simple level this can be used to cut down the size of the code, in that

```
substring C among ( S₁₁  S₁₂  ...  (C₁ )
                     S₂₁  S₂₂  ...  (C₂ )
                     . . .

                     Sₙ₁  Sₙ₂  ...  (Cₙ )
                   )
```

is a shorter form of

$$\text{among} (\begin{array}{llll} S_{11} & S_{12} & \ldots & (C \ C_1 \ ) \\ S_{21} & S_{22} & \ldots & (C \ C_2 \ ) \\ \ldots & & & \\ S_{n1} & S_{n2} & \ldots & (C \ C_n \ ) \\ ) & & & \end{array}$$

More importantly, substring and among can work in different contexts. For example, substring could be used to test for the longest string, matching from right to left, while the commands in the among could operate in a left to right direction. In the Lovins stemmer, substring is used in this style:

    [substring] among (...)

The two square brackets are in fact individual commands, so before the among come three commands. [sets a lower marker, substring is obeyed, searching for the strings in the following among, and then] sets an upper marker. The region between the lower and upper markers is called the slice, and this may subsequently be copied, replaced or deleted.

It was possible to get the Lovins stemmer working in Snowball very quicky. The Sourceforge versions could be used to get the long list of endings and to help with the debugging. There was however one problem, that rules 24 and 30 of part C conflicted. They are given as

24)　　　end $\Rightarrow$ ens except following s

...

30)　　　end $\Rightarrow$ ens except following m

This had not been noticed in the Sourceforge implementations, but immediately gave rise to a compilation error in Snowball. Experience suggested that I was very unlikely to get this problem resolved. Only a few months before, I had hit a point in a stemming algorithm where something did not quite make sense. The algorithm had been published just a few years ago, and contacting one at least of the authors was quite easy. But I never sorted it out. The author I traced was not *au fait* with the linguistic background, and the language expert had been swallowed up in the wilds of America. So what chance would I have here? Even if I was able to contact Lovins, it seemed to me inconceivable that she would have any memory of, or even interest in, a tiny problem in a paper which she published 33 years ago. But the spirit of academic enquiry forced me to venture the attempt. After pursuing a number of red-herrings, email contact was finally made.

Her reply was a most pleasant surprise.

> ... The explanation is both mundane and exciting. You have just found a typo in the MT article, which I was unaware of all these years, and I suspect has puzzled a lot of other people too. The original paper, an MIT-published memorandum from June 1968, has rule 30 as
>
> ent $\Rightarrow$ ens except following m

and that is undoubtedly what it should be ...

5. AN ANALYSIS OF THE LOVINS STEMMER

It is very important in understanding the Lovins stemmer to know something of the IR background of the late sixties. In the first place there was an assumption that IR was all, or mainly, about the retrieval of technical scientific papers, and research projects were set up accordingly. I remember, being shown, in about 1968, a graph illustrating the "information explosion", as it was understood at the time, which showed just the rate of growth of publications of scientific papers in various different domains over the previous 10 or 20 years. Computing resources were very precious, and they could not be wasted by setting up IR systems for information that was, by comparison, merely frivolous (articles in popular magazines, say). And even in 1980, when I was working in IR, the data I was using came from the familiar, and narrow, scientific domain. Lovins was working with Project Intrex (Overhage, 1966), where the data came from papers in materials science and engineering.

Secondly, the idea of indexing on every word in a document, or even looking at every word before deciding whether or not to put it into an index, would have seemed quite impractical, even though it might have been recognised as theoretically best. In the first place, the computing resources necessary to store and analyse complete documents in machine readable forms were absent, and in the second, rigidities of the printing industry almost guaranteed that one would never get access to them. A stemmer therefore, would be seen as something not applied to general text but to certain special words, and in the case of the Lovins stemmer, the plan was to apply it to the subject terms that were used to categorize each document. Subsequently it would be used with each word in a query, where it was hoped that the vocabulary of the queries would match the vocabulary of the catalogue of subject terms.

This accounts for:—

1. The emphasis on the scientific vocabulary. This can be seen in the endings, which include *oidal, on, oid, ide,* for words like *colloidal, proton, spheroid, nucleotide*. It can be seen in the transformation rules, with their concern for Greek *sis* and Latin *ix* suffixes. And also it can be seen in in the word samples of the paper (*magnesia, magnesite, magnesian, magnesium, magnet, magnetic, magneto* etc. of Fig. 2).
2. The slight shortage of plural forms. The subject terms would naturally have been mainly in the singular, and one might also expect the same of query terms.
3. The surprising shortness of the allowed minimum stems — usually 2 letters. A controlled technical vocabulary will contain longish words, and the problem of minimum stem lengths only shows up with shorter words.

If we take a fairly ordinary vocabulary of modern English, derived from non-scientific writing, it is interesting to see how much of the Lovins stemmer does not actually get used. We use vocabulary V, derived from a sample of modern texts from Project Gutenberg[4]. It contains 29,401 words, and begins

a   aback   abandon   abandoned   abandoning   abandonment   abandons abasement   abashed   abate   abated ...

We find that 22,311, or about 76%, of the words in V have one of the 294 endings removed if passed through the Lovins stemmer. Of this 76%, over a half (55%) of the removals are done by just five of the endings, the breakdown being,

s (13%)   *ed* (12%)   *e* (10%)   *ing* (10%)   *es* (6%)   *y* (4%)

If, on the other hand, you look at the least frequent endings, 51% of them do only 1.4% of the removals. So of the ones removed, half the endings in V correspond to 2% of the endings in the stemmer, and 1.4% of the endings in V correspond to half the endings in the stemmer. In fact 62 of the endings (about a fifth) do not lead to any ending removals in V at all. These are made up of the rarer "scientific" endings, such as *aroid* and *oidal*, and long endings, such as *alistically* and *entiality*.

This helps explain why the Porter and Lovins stemmers behave in a fairly similar way despite the fact that they look completely different — it is because most of the work is being done in just a small part of the stemmer, and in that part there is a lot of overlap. Porter and Lovins stem 64% of the words in V identically which is quite high. (by contrast, an erroneous but plausibly written Perl script advertised on the web as an implementation of the Porter stemmer still proves to stem only 86% of the words in V to the same forms that are produced by the Porter stemmer.)

A feature of the Lovins stemmer that is worth looking at in some detail is the transformation rules. People who come to the problem of stemming for the first time usually devote a lot mental energy to the issue of morphological irregularity which they are trying to address.

A good starting point is the verbs of English. Although grammatically complex, the morphological forms of the English verb are few, and are illustrated by the pattern *harm, harms, harming, harmed*, where the basic verb form adds *s*, *ing* and *ed* to make the other three forms. There are certain special rules: to add *s* to a verb ending *ss* an *e* is inserted, so *pass* becomes *passes*, and adding *e* and *ing* replaces a final *e* of the verb (*love* to *loves*), and can cause consonant doubling (*hop* to *hopped*), but apart from this all verbs in the language follow the basic pattern with the exception of a finite class of irregular verbs. In a regular verb, the addition addition of *ed* to the basic verb creates both the past form ("I harmed") and the p.p. (past participle) form ("I have harmed"). An irregular verb, such as *ring,* forms its past in some other way ("I rang") and may have a distinct p.p. ("I have rung"). It is easy to think up more examples.

---

[4] See http://promo.net/pg/ The vocabulary may be viewed at http://snowball.sourceforge.net/english/voc.txt

stem	past	p.p.
ring	rang	rung
rise	rose	risen
sleep	slept	slept
fight	fought	fought
come	came	come
go	went	gone
hit	hit	hit

How many of these verbs are there altogether? On 20 Jan 2000, in order to test the hypothesis that the number is consistently over-estimated, I asked this question in a carefully worded email to a mixed group of about 50 well-educated work colleagues (business rather than academic people). Ten of them replied, and here are the guesses they made:

20, 25, 25, 50, 180, 200, 426, 25000, 10%, 20%

The last two numbers mean 10% and 20% of all English verbs. My hypothesis was of course wrong. The truth is that most people have no idea at all how many irregular verbs there are in English. In fact there are around 135 (see section 3.3. of Palmer, 1965). If a stemming algorithm handles suffix removal of all regular verbs correctly, the question arises as to whether it is worth making it do the same for the irregular forms. Conflating *fought* and *fight*, for example, could be useful in IR queries about boxing. It seems easy: you make a list of the irregular verbs and create a mapping of the past and p.p. forms to the main form. We can call the process English verb respelling. But when you try it, numerous problems arise. Are *forsake, beseech, cleave* really verbs of contemporary English? If so, what is the p.p. of *cleave*? Or take the verb *stride* which is common enough. What is its p.p.? My *Concise Oxford English Dictionary* says it is *stridden*[5], but have we ever heard this word used? ("I have stridden across the paving").

To compose a realistic list for English verb respelling we therefore need to judge word rarity. But among the commoner word forms even greater problems arise because of their use as homonyms. A *rose* is a type of flower, so is it wise to conflate *rose* and *rise*? Is it wise to conflate *saw* and *see* when *saw* can mean a cutting instrument?

We suddenly get to the edge of what it is useful to include in a stemming algorithm. So long as a stemming algorithm is built around useful rules, the full impact of the stemmer on a vocabulary need not be studied too closely. It is sufficient to know that the stemmer, judiciously used, improves retrieval performance, But when we look at its effect on individual words these issues can no longer be ignored. To build even a short list of words into a stemmer for special treatment takes us into the area of dictionary-based stemmers, and the problem of

---

[5] In looking at verbs with the pattern *ride, rode, ridden,* Palmer (1965), notes that "we should perhaps add STRIDE with poast tense *strode,* but without a past participle (there is no *stridden).*

determining, for a pair of related words in the dictionary, a measure of semantic similarity which tells us whether or not the words should be conflated together.

About half the transformation rules in the Lovins stemmer deal with a problem which is similar to that posed by the irregular verbs of English, which ultimately goes back to the irregular forms of second conjugation verbs in Latin. We can call it Latin verb respelling. Verbs like *induce, consume, commit* are perfectly regular in modern English, but the adjectival and noun forms *induction, consumptive, commission* that derive from them correspond to p.p. forms in Latin. You can see the descendants of these Latin irregularities in modern Italian, which has *commettere* with p.p. *commesso*, like our *commit* and *commission*, and *scendere* with p.p *sceso* like our *ascend* and *ascension* (although *scendere* means "to go down" rather than "to go up").

Latin verb respelling often seems to be more the territory of a stemmer than English verb respelling, presumably because Latin verb irregularities correspond to consonantal changes at the end of the stem, where the stemmer naturally operates, while English verb irregularities more often correspond to vowel changes in the middle. Lovins was no doubt particularly interested in Latin verb respelling because so many of the words affected have scientific usages.

We can judge that Latin verb respellings constitute a small set because the number of second conjugation verbs of Latin form a small, fixed set. Again, looking at Italian, a modern list of irregular verbs contains 150 basic forms (nearly all of them second conjugation), not unlike the number of forms in English. Extra verbs are formed with prefixes. Corresponding English words that exhibit the Latin verb respelling problem will be a subset of this system. In fact we can offer a Snowball script that does the Latin verb respelling with more care. It should be invoked, in the Porter stemmer, after removal of *ive* or *ion* endings only (see Figure 1).

The script means that if *suas*, for example, is preceded by one of the strings in `prefix`, and there is nothing more before the prefix string (which is what the `atlimit` command tests), it is replaced by *suad*. So *dissuas(ion)* goes to *dissuad(e)* and *persuas(ive)* to *persuad(e)*. Of course, *asuas(ion), absuas(ion), adsuas(ion)* and so on would get the same treatment, but not being words of English that does not really matter. The corresponding Lovins rules are shown in brackets. This is not quite the end of the story, however, because the Latin forms *ex + cedere* ("go beyond") *pro + cedere* ("go forth"), and *sub + cedere* ("go after") give rise to verbs which, by an oddity of English orthography, have an extra letter *e*: exceed, proceed, succeed. They can be sorted out in a final respelling step:

```
define final_respell as (
    [substring] atlimit among(
        'exced'     (<-'exceed')
        'proced'    (<-'proceed')
        'succed'    (<-'succeed')
        /* extra forms here perhaps */
    )
)
```

```
define prefix as (
    among (
        'a' 'ab' 'ad' 'al' 'ap' 'col' 'com' 'con' 'cor' 'de'
        'di' 'dis' 'e' 'ex' 'in' 'inter' 'o' 'ob' 'oc' 'of'
        'per' 'pre' 'pro' 're' 'se' 'sub' 'suc' 'trans'
    ) atlimit
)

define second conjugation form as (
    [substring] prefix among (
        'cept'     (<-'ceiv')    //-e    con de re
        'cess'     (<-'ced')     //-e    con ex inter pre re se suc
        'cis'      (<-'cid')     //-e    de (20)
        'clus'     (<-'clud')    //-e    con ex in oc (26)
        'curs'     (<-'cur')     //      re (6)
        'dempt'    (<-'deem')    //      re
        'duct'     (<-'duc')     //-e    de in re pro (3)
        'fens'     (<-'fend')    //      de of
        'hes'      (<-'her')     //-e    ad (28)
        'lis'      (<-'lid')     //-e    e col (21)
        'lus'      (<-'lud')     //-e    al de e
        'miss'     (<-'mit')     //      ad com o per re sub trans (29)
        'pans'     (<-'pand')    //      ex (23)
        'plos'     (<-'plod')    //-e    ex
        'prehens'  (<-'prehend') //      ap com
        'ris'      (<-'rid')     //-e    de (22)
        'ros'      (<-'rod')     //-e    cor e
        'scens'    (<-'scend')   //      a
        'script'   (<-'scrib')   //-e    de in pro
        'solut'    (<-'solv')    //-e    dis re (8)
        'sorpt'    (<-'sorb')    //      ab (5)
        'spons'    (<-'spond')   //      re (25)
        'sumpt'    (<-'sum')     //      con pre re (4)
        'suas'     (<-'suad')    //-e    dis per (18)
        'tens'     (<-'tend')    //      ex in pre (24)
        'trus'     (<-'trud')    //-e    ob (27)
        'vas'      (<-'vad')     //-e    e (19)
        'vers'     (<-'vert')    //      con in re (31)
        'vis'      (<-'vid')     //-e    di pro
    )
)
```

Figure 1 Verb Conjugation

As you might expect, close inspection of this process creates doubts in the same way as for English verb respelling. (Should we really conflate *commission* and *commit*? etc.)

The other transformation rules are concerned with unusual plurals, mainly of Latin or Greek origin, *er* and *re* differences, as in *parameter* and *parametric*, and the *sis/tic* connection of certain words of Greek origin: *analysis/analytic, paralysis/paralytic* ... (rule 33), and *hypothesis/hypothetic, kinesis/kinetic* ... (rule 32). Again, these irregularities might be tackled by forming explicit word lists. Certainly rule 30, given as,

ent $\Rightarrow$ ens except following *m*,

goes somewhat wild when given a general English vocabulary (*dent* becomes *dens* for example), although it is the only rule that might be said to have a damaging effect.

6. A LOVINS SHAPE FOR THE PORTER STEMMER

The 1980 paper (Porter, 1980) may be said to define the "pure" Porter stemmer. The stemmer distributed at[6] can be called the "real" Porter stemmer, and differs from the pure stemmer in three small respects, which are carefully explained. This disparity does not require much excuse, since the oldest traceable encodings of the stemmer have always contained these differences. There is also a revised stemmer for English, called "Porter2" and still subject to slight changes. Unless otherwise stated, it is the real Porter stemmer which is being studied below.

The Porter stemmer differs from the Lovins stemmer in a number of respects. In the first place, it only takes account of fairly common features of English. So rare suffixes are not included, and there is no equivalent of Lovins' transformation rules, other than her rule (1), the undoubling of terminal double letters. Secondly, it removes suffixes only when the residual stem is fairly substantial. Some suffixes are removed only when at least one syllable is left, and most are removed only when at least two syllables are left. (One might say that this is based on a guess about the way in which the meanings of a stem is related to its length in syllables[7].) The Porter stemmer is therefore "conservative" in its removal of suffixes, or at least that is how it has often been described. Thirdly, it removes suffixes in a series of steps, often reducing a compound suffix to its first part, so a step might reduce *ibility* to *ible*, where *ibility* is thought of as being *ible* + *ity*. Although the description of the whole stemmer is a bit complicated, the total number of suffixes is quite small — about 60.

The Porter stemmer has five basic steps. Step 1 removes an inflectional suffix. There are only three of these: *ed* and *ing*, which are verbal, and *s*, which is verbal (*he sings*), plural (*the songs*) or possessive (*the horses' hooves*), although the rule

---

[6] See http://www.tartarus.org/~martin/PorterStemmer
[7] Lovins (1968), p. 25, mentions that a stemming algorithm developed by James L. Dolby in California used a two-syllable minimum stem length as a condition for most of the stemming.

for *s* removal is the same in all three cases. Step 1 may also restore an *e* (*hoping* ⇒ *hope*), undouble a double letter pair (*hopping* ⇒ *hop*), or change y to i (*poppy* ⇒ *poppi*, to match with *poppies* ⇒*poppi*.) Steps 2 to 4 remove derivational suffixes. So *ibility* may reduce to *ible* in step 2, and *ible* itself may be removed in step 4. Step 5 is for removing final *e*, and undoubling *ll*.

A clear advantage of the Lovins stemmer over the Porter stemmer is speed. The Porter stemmer has five steps of suffix removal to the Lovins stemmer's one. It is instructive therefore to try and cast the Porter stemmer into the shape of the Lovins stemmer, if only for the promise of certain speed advantages. As we will see, we learn a few other things from the exercise as well.

First we need a list of endings. The Lovins endings were built up by hand, but we can construct a set of endings for the Porter stemmer by writing an ending generator that follows the algorithm definition. From an analysis of the suffixes in steps 2 to 4 of the Porter stemmer we can construct Figure 2. This is not meant to be a linguistic analysis of the suffix structure of English, but merely to show how the systems of endings works in the stemming algorithm. Suffixes combine if their boxes are connected by an arrow. So *ful* combines with *ness* to make *fulness*.

$$ful + ness \Rightarrow fulness$$

The combination is not always a concatenation of the strings however, for we have,

$$able + ity \Rightarrow ability$$
$$able + ly \Rightarrow ably$$
$$ate + ion \Rightarrow ation$$
$$ible + ity \Rightarrow ibility$$
$$ible + ly \Rightarrow ibly$$
$$ize + ate + ion \Rightarrow ization$$

The path from *ize* to *ion* goes via *ate*, so we can form *ization*, but there is no suffix *izate*. Three of the suffixes, *ator*, *ance* and *ence*, do not connect into the rest of the diagram, and *ance, ence* also appear in the forms *ancy, ency*. The letter to the left of the box is going to be the condition for the removal of the suffix in the box, so

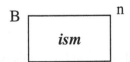

means that *ism* will be removed if it follows a stem that satisfies condition B. On the right of the box is either *n, v* or hyphen. *n* means the suffix is of noun type. So if a word ends *ism* it is a noun. *v* means verb type. hyphen means neither: *ly* (adverbial) and *ful, ous* (adjectival) are of this type. If a suffix is a noun type it can have a plural form (*criticism, criticisms*), so we have to generate *isms* as well as *ism*. Again, the combining is not just concatenation,

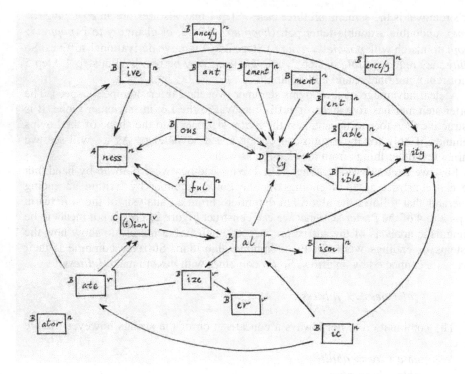

Figure 2: Lovins Porter Stemmer

> *ity* + *s* ⟹ *ities*
>
> *ness* + *s* ⟹ *nesses*

If a suffix has *v* type, it has *s*, *ed* and *ing* forms,

> *ize* + *s* ⟹ *izes*
>
> *ize* + *ed* ⟹ *ized*
>
> *ize* + *ing* ⟹ *izing*

Type *v* therefore includes type *n*, and we should read this type as "verb or noun", rather than just "verb". For example, *condition*, with suffix *ion*, is both verb ("They have been conditioned to behave like that") and noun ("It is subject to certain conditions").

Figure 2 is therefore a scheme for generating combined derivational suffixes, each combination possibly terminated with an inflectional suffix. A problem is that it contains a loop in

$$ize \Rightarrow ate \Rightarrow ion \Rightarrow al \Rightarrow ize \Rightarrow ...$$

suggesting suffixes of the form *izationalizational*... We break the loop by limiting the number of joined derivational suffixes of figure 2 to four. (Behaviour of the Porter stemmer shows that removal of five combined derivation suffixes is never desirable, even supposing five ever combine.) We can then generate 181 endings, with their removal codes. But 75 of these suffixes do not occur as endings in V, and they can be eliminated as rare forms, leaving 106. Alphabetically, the endings begin,

> *abilities ability able ables ably al alism (alisms) alities
> ality alization (alizationed) (alizationing) (alizations) alize
> alized (alizer) (alizered) (alizering) (alizers) (alizes)
> (alizing) ally alness (alnesses) als ance ances ancies
> ancy ...*

The eliminated rare forms are shown bracketed.

The 106 endings are arranged in a file as a list of strings followed by condition letter,

```
'abilities'          B
'ability'            B
'able'               B
'ables'              B
'ably'               B
'al'                 B
....
```

and this file is called in by the `get` directive in the Snowball script of Appendix 2, which is the Porter stemming algorithm laid out in the style of the Lovins algorithm. In fact, precise equivalence cannot be achieved, but in V only 137 words stem differently, which is 0.4% of V. There are 10 removal conditions, compared with Lovins' 29, and 11 transformation or respelling rules, compared with Lovins' 35. We can describe the process in Lovins style, once we have got over a few preliminaries.

We have to distinguish y as a vowel from y as a consonant. We treat initial y, and y before vowel, as a consonant, and make it upper case. Thereafter *a, e, i, o, u* and y are vowels, and the other lower case letters and Y are consonants. If [C] stands for zero or more consonants, C for one or more consonants, and V for one or more vowels, then a stem of shape [C]VC has length 1s (1 syllable), of shape [C]VCVC length 2s, and so on.

A stem ends with a short vowel if the ending has the form *cvx*, where c is a consonant, v a vowel, and x a consonant other than w, x or Y. (Short vowel endings with *ed* and *ing* imply loss of an *e*, as in *removing = remove + ing* from the stem.)

Here are the removal conditions,

A   Minimum stem length = 1s

B   Minimum stem length = 2s
C   Minimum stem length = 2s and remove ending only after *s* or *t*
D   Minimum stem length = 2s and do not remove ending after *m*
E   Remove ending only after *e* or *ous* after minimum stem length 1s
F   Remove ending only after *ss* or *i*
G   Do not remove ending after *s*
H   Remove ending only if stem contains a vowel
I   Remove ending only if stem contains a vowel and does not end in *e*
J   Remove ending only after *ee* after minimum stem length 1s

In condition J the stem must end *ee*, and the part of the stem before the *ee* must have minimum length 1s. Condition E is similar.

Here are the respelling rules, defined with the help of the removal conditions. In each case, the stem being tested does not include the string at the end which has been identified for respelling.

1)   Remove *e* if A, or if B and the stem does not end with a short vowel

2)   Remove *l* if B and the stem ends with *l*

3)   *enci/ency* ⇒ *enc* if A, otherwise ⇒ *enci*

4)   *anci/ancy* ⇒ *anc* if A, otherwise ⇒ *anci*

5)   *ally* ⇒ *al* if A, otherwise ⇒ *alli*

6)   *ently* ⇒ *ent* if A, otherwise ⇒ *entli*

7)   *ator* ⇒ *at* if A

8)   *logi/logy* ⇒ *log* if A, otherwise ⇒ *log*

9)   *bli/bly* ⇒ *bl* if A, otherwise ⇒ *bli*

10)   *bil* ⇒ *bl* if stem ends vowel after A

11)   *y/Y* ⇒ *i* if stem contains a vowel

The 106 endings are distributed among conditions A to E as A(5), B(87), C(8), D(3) and E(1). F to J deal with the purely inflectional endings: F with *es*, G with *s*, H with *ing* and *ings*, I with *ed* and J with *d*. There is however one point at which the Lovins structure breaks down, in that removal of *ed* and *ing(s)* after conditions I and H requires a special adjustment that cannot be left to a separate transformation rule. It is to undouble the last letter, and to restore a final *e* if the stem has length 1s and ends with a short vowel (so *shopping* loses a *p* and becomes *shop*, *sloping* gains an *e* and becomes *slope*.)

The Porter stemmer cast into this form runs significantly faster than the multi-stage stemmer — about twice as fast in tests with Snowball.

We will call the Porter stemmer P, the Lovins stemmer L, and this Lovins version of the Porter stemmer LP. As we have said, P and LP are not identical, but stem 137 of the 29,401 words of *V* differently.

A major cause of difference is unexpected suffix combinations. These can be subdivided into combinations of what seem to be suffixes but are not, and rare combinations of valid suffixes.

The first case is illustrated by the word *disenchanted*. P stems this to *disench*, first taking of suffix *ed*, then removing *ant*, which is a suffix in English, although not a suffix in this word. P also stems *disenchant* to *disench*, so the two words *disenchant* and *disenchanted* are conflated by P, even though they make an error in the stemming process. But *ant* is a noun type suffix, and so does not combine with *ed*. *anted* is therefore omitted from the suffix list of LP, so LP stems *disenchanted* to *disenchant*, but *disenchant* to *disench*.

This illustrates a frequently encountered problem in stemming. S_1 and S_2 are suffixes of a language, but the combination S_1S_2 is not. A word has the form xS_1, where x is some string, but in xS_1 S_1 is not actually a suffix, but part of the stem. S_2 is a valid suffix for this word, so xS_1S_2 is another word in the language. An algorithmic stemmer stems xS_1 to x in error. If presented with xS_1S_2 it can either (*a*) stem it to xS_1, knowing S_1 cannot be a suffix in this context, or (*b*) stem it to x, ignoring the knowledge to be derived from the presence of S_2. (*a*) gives the correct stemming of at least xS_1S_2, although the stemming of xS_1 will be wrong, while (*b*) overstems both words, but at least achieves their conflation. In other words (*a*) fails to conflate the two forms, but may achieve correct conflations of xS_1S_2 with similar forms xS_1S_3, xS_1S_4 etc., while (*b*) conflates the two forms, but at the risk of additional false conflations. Often a study of the results of a stemming strategy on a sample vocabulary leads one to prefer approach (*b*) to (*a*) for certain classes of ending. This is true in particular of the inflectional endings of English, which is why the removals in step 1 of P are not remembered in some state variable, which records whether the ending just removed is verb-type, noun-or-verb-type etc. On balance you get better results by throwing that information away, and then the many word pairs on the pattern of *disenchant/disenchantment* will conflate together.

Other examples from *V* can be given: in *misrepresenting*, *ent* is not a suffix, and *enting* is not a valid suffix combination; in *witnessed*, *ness* is not a suffix, and *nessed* not a valid suffix combination.

This highlights a disadvantage of stemmers that work with a fixed list of endings. To get the flexibility of context-free ending removal, we need to build in extra ending which are not grammatically correct (like *anted* = *ant* + *ed*), which adds considerably to the burden of constructing the list. In fact L does not include *anted*, but it does include for example *antic* (*ant* + *ic*), which may be serving a similar purpose.

For the second case, the rare combinations of valid suffixes, one may instance *ableness*. Here again the multi-step stemmer makes life easier. P removes *ness* in step 3 and *able* in step 4, but without making any necessary connection. L has *ableness* as an ending, dictionaries contain many *ableness* words, and it is an easy matter to make the connection across from *able* to *ness* in diagram 1 and generate extra endings. Nevertheless the ending is very rare in actual use. For example, Dickens' *Nicholas Nickleby* contains no examples, *Bleak House* contains two, in the same sentence:

> I was sure you would feel it yourself and would excuse the reasonableness of MY feelings when coupled with the known excitableness of my little woman.

reasonableness is perhaps the commonest word in English of this form, and *excitableness* (instead of *excitability*) is there for contrast. Thackeray's *Vanity Fair*, a major source in testing out P and Porter2, contains one word of this form, *charitableness*. One may say of this word that it is inevitably rare, because it has no really distinct meaning from the simpler *charity*, but that it has to be formed by adding *ableness* rather than *ability*, because the repeated *ity* in *charity* + *ability* is morphologically unacceptable. Other rare combinations are *ateness*, *entness*, and *eds* (as in *intendeds* and *beloveds*). *fuls* is another interesting case. The *ful* suffix, usually adjectival, can sometimes create nouns, giving plurals such as *mouthfuls* and *spoonfuls*. But in longer words *sful* is a more "elegant" plural (*handbagsful*, *dessertspoonsful*).

These account for most of the differences, but there are a few others.

One is in forms like *bricklayers* ⟹ *bricklai* (P), bricklay (LP). Terminal *y* is usefully turned to *i* to help conflate words where *y* is changed to *i* and *es* added to form the plural, but this does not happen when *y* follows a vowel. LP improves on P here, but the Porter2 algorithm makes the same improvement, so we have nothing to learn. There is also a difference in words endings *lle* or *lles*, *quadrille* ⟹ *quadril* (P), *quadrill* (LP). This is because *e* and *l* removal are successive in step 5 of P, and done as alternatives in the respelling rules of LP. In LP this is not quite correct, since Lovins makes it clear that her transformation rules should be applied in succession. Even so, LP seems better than P, suggesting that step 5*b* of P (undouble *l*) should not have been attempted after *e* removal in step 5*a*. So here is a possible small improvement to Porter2. Another small, but quite interesting difference, is the condition attached to the *ative* ending. The ending generator makes B the removal condition by a natural process, but in P its removal condition is A. This goes back to step 3 as originally presented in the paper of 1980:

$(m>0)$ ICATE ⟹ IC

$(m>0)$ ATIVE ⟹

$(m>0)$ ALIZE ⟹ AL

$(m>0)$ ICITI ⟹ IC

$(m>0)$ ICAL ⟹ IC

$(m>0)$ FUL ⟹

$(m>0)$ NESS ⟹

$(m>0)$ corresponds to A. With removal condition B, the second line would be

$(m>1)$ ATIVE ⟹

which looks slightly incongruous. Nevertheless it is probably correct, because we remove a half suffix from *icate, alize, icity* and *ical* when the stem length is at least s1, so we should remove the full *ate* + *ive* suffix when the stem length is at least s2.

We should not be influenced by *ful* and *ness*. They are "native English" stems, unlike the other five, which have a "Romance" origin, and for these two condition A has been found to be more appropriate. In fact putting in this adjustment to Porter2 results in an improvement in the small class of words thereby affected.

6. CONCLUSION

You never learn all there is to know about a computer program, unless the program is really very simple. So even after 20 years of regular use, we can learn something new about P by creating LP and comparing the two. And in the process we learn a lot about L, the Lovins stemmer itself.

The truth is that the main motivation for studying L was to see how well the Snowball system could be used for implementing and analyzing Lovins' original work, and the interest in what she had actually achieved in 1968 only came later. I hope that this short account helps clarify her work, and place it the context of the development of stemmers since then.

Martin Porter read maths at Cambridge, and later studied Computer Science, taking a Ph.D. (1967-1969), with Karen as his supervisor. Until 1984 he held a variety of University posts in the computing/IR field. After 1984 he worked freelance, developing IR software. In Muscat he produced the first commercially available IR system with query expansion and relevance feedback based on the probabilistic model pioneered by Stephen Robertson and Karen. He worked with John Tait on the BBC Domesday Project. After Muscat, Martin directed the Xapian project, and is now working on a new IR system, Grapeshot. He is best known, however, for his work on stemming algorithms, and his stemmer for English, done in 1980, is always called the Porter stemmer. He was the Strix award winner for 2000, and is currently a Visiting Research Fellow of City University, London.

NOTE

The web addresses noted in the text have a "last visited" date of December 2001.

REFERENCES

Andrews K (1971) The development of a fast conflation algorithm for English. Dissertation for the Diploma in Computer Science, Computer Laboratory, University of Cambridge.

Harman D (1991) How effective is suffixing? *Journal of the American Society for Information Science*, **42**: 7–15.

Kraaij W and Pohlmann R. (1994) Porter's stemming algorithm for Dutch. In Noordman LGM and de Vroomen WAM, eds. Informatiewetenschap 1994: Wetenschappelijke bijdragen aan de derde STINFON Conferentie, Tilburg, 1994. pp. 167–180.

Kraaij W and Pohlmann R (1995) Evaluation of a Dutch stemming algorithm. Rowley J, ed. *The New Review of Document and Text Management*, volume 1, Taylor Graham, London, 1995. pp. 25–43,

Krovetz B (1995) *Word sense disambiguation for large text databases*. PhD Thesis. Department of Computer Science, University of Massachusetts Amherst.

Lennon M, Pierce DS, Tarry BD and Willett P (1981) An evaluation of some conflation algorithms for information retrieval. *Journal of Information Science*, **3**: 177–183.

Lovins JB (1968) Development of a stemming algorithm. *Mechanical Translation and Computational Linguistics*, **11**: 22–31.

Overhage, CFJ (1966) Plans for project Intrex. *Science*, **152**: 1032–1037.

Palmer, FR (1965) *A linguistic Study of the English Verb*. Longmans, London,

Porter MF (1980) An algorithm for suffix stripping. *Program*, **14**: 130–137.

APPENDIX 1

```
stringescapes {}

routines (
  A B C D E F G H I J K L M N O P Q R S T U V W X Y Z AA BB CC

  endings

  undouble respell
)

externals ( stem )

backwardmode (

  /* Lovins' conditions A, B ... CC, as given in her Appendix B, where
     a test for a two letter prefix ('test hop 2') is implicitly
     assumed. Note that 'e' next 'u' corresponds to her u*e because
     Snowball is scanning backwards. */

  define A  as ( hop 2 )
  define B  as ( hop 3 )
  define C  as ( hop 4 )
  define D  as ( hop 5 )
  define E  as ( test hop 2 not 'e' )
  define F  as ( test hop 3 not 'e' )
  define G  as ( test hop 3 'f' )
  define H  as ( test hop 2 't' or 'll' )
  define I  as ( test hop 2 not 'o' not 'e' )
  define J  as ( test hop 2 not 'a' not 'e' )
  define K  as ( test hop 3 'l' or 'i' or ('e' next 'u') )
  define L  as ( test hop 2 not 'u' not 'x' not ('s' not 'o') )
  define M  as ( test hop 2 not 'a' not 'c' not 'e' not 'm' )
  define N  as ( test hop 3 ( hop 2 not 's' or hop 2 ) )
  define O  as ( test hop 2 'l' or 'i' )
  define P  as ( test hop 2 not 'c' )
  define Q  as ( test hop 2 test hop 3 not 'l' not 'n' )
  define R  as ( test hop 2 'n' or 'r' )
  define S  as ( test hop 2 'dr' or ('t' not 't') )
  define T  as ( test hop 2 's' or ('t' not 'o') )
  define U  as ( test hop 2 'l' or 'm' or 'n' or 'r' )
  define V  as ( test hop 2 'c' )
  define W  as ( test hop 2 not 's' not 'u' )
  define X  as ( test hop 2 'l' or 'i' or ('e' next 'u') )
  define Y  as ( test hop 2 'in' )
  define Z  as ( test hop 2 not 'f' )
  define AA as ( test hop 2 among ( 'd' 'f' 'ph' 'th' 'l' 'er' 'or'
                                    'es' 't' ) )
```

```
define BB as ( test hop 3 not 'met' not 'ryst' )
define CC as ( test hop 2 'l' )


/* The system of endings, as given in Appendix A. */

define endings as (
  [substring] among(
  'alistically' B 'arizability' A 'izationally' B

    'antialness' A  'arisations' A  'arizations' A  'entialness' A

    'allically' C   'antaneous' A   'antiality' A   'arisation' A
    'arization' A   'ationally' B   'ativeness' A   'eableness' E
    'entations' A   'entiality' A   'entialize' A   'entiation' A
    'ionalness' A   'istically' A   'itousness' A   'izability' A
    'izational' A

    'ableness' A    'arizable' A    'entation' A    'entially' A
    'eousness' A    'ibleness' A    'icalness' A    'ionalism' A
    'ionality' A    'ionalize' A    'iousness' A    'izations' A
    'lessness' A

    'ability' A     'aically' A     'alistic' B     'alities' A
    'ariness' E     'aristic' A     'arizing' A     'ateness' A
    'atingly' A     'ational' B     'atively' A     'ativism' A
    'elihood' E     'encible' A     'entally' A     'entials' A
    'entiate' A     'entness' A     'fulness' A     'ibility' A
    'icalism' A     'icalist' A     'icality' A     'icalize' A
    'ication' G     'icianry' A     'ination' A     'ingness' A
    'ionally' A     'isation' A     'ishness' A     'istical' A
    'iteness' A     'iveness' A     'ivistic' A     'ivities' A
    'ization' F     'izement' A     'oidally' A     'ousness' A

    'aceous' A      'acious' B      'action' G      'alness' A
    'ancial' A      'ancies' A      'ancing' B      'ariser' A
    'arized' A      'arizer' A      'atable' A      'ations' B
    'atives' A      'eature' Z      'efully' A      'encies' A
    'encing' A      'ential' A      'enting' C      'entist' A
    'eously' A      'ialist' A      'iality' A      'ialize' A
    'ically' A      'icance' A      'icians' A      'icists' A
    'ifully' A      'ionals' A      'ionate' D      'ioning' A
    'ionist' A      'iously' A      'istics' A      'izable' E
    'lessly' A      'nesses' A      'oidism' A

    'acies' A       'acity' A       'aging' B       'aical' A
    'alist' A       'alism' B       'ality' A       'alize' A
    'allic'BB       'anced' B       'ances' B       'antic' C
    'arial' A       'aries' A       'arily' A       'arity' B
    'arize' A       'aroid' A       'ately' A       'ating' I
    'ation' B       'ative' A       'ators' A       'atory' A
    'ature' E       'early' Y       'ehood' A       'eless' A
    'elity' A       'ement' A       'enced' A       'ences' A
    'eness' E       'ening' E       'ental' A       'ented' C
    'ently' A       'fully' A       'ially' A       'icant' A
    'ician' A       'icide' A       'icism' A       'icist' A
    'icity' A       'idine' I       'iedly' A       'ihood' A
    'inate' A       'iness' A       'ingly' B       'inism' J
```

'inity'CC	'ional' A	'ioned' A	'ished' A
'istic' A	'ities' A	'itous' A	'ively' A
'ivity' A	'izers' F	'izing' F	'oidal' A
'oides' A	'otide' A	'ously' A	

'able' A	'ably' A	'ages' B	'ally' B
'ance' B	'ancy' B	'ants' B	'aric' A
'arly' K	'ated' I	'ates' A	'atic' B
'ator' A	'ealy' Y	'edly' E	'eful' A
'eity' A	'ence' A	'ency' A	'ened' E
'enly' E	'eous' A	'hood' A	'ials' A
'ians' A	'ible' A	'ibly' A	'ical' A
'ides' L	'iers' A	'iful' A	'ines' M
'ings' N	'ions' B	'ious' A	'isms' B
'ists' A	'itic' H	'ized' F	'izer' F
'less' A	'lily' A	'ness' A	'ogen' A
'ward' A	'wise' A	'ying' B	'yish' A

'acy' A	'age' B	'aic' A	'als'BB
'ant' B	'ars' O	'ary' F	'ata' A
'ate' A	'eal' Y	'ear' Y	'ely' E
'ene' E	'ent' C	'ery' E	'ese' A
'ful' A	'ial' A	'ian' A	'ics' A
'ide' L	'ied' A	'ier' A	'ies' P
'ily' A	'ine' M	'ing' N	'ion' Q
'ish' C	'ism' B	'ist' A	'ite'AA
'ity' A	'ium' A	'ive' A	'ize' F
'oid' A	'one' R	'ous' A	

'ae' A	'al'BB	'ar' X	'as' B
'ed' E	'en' F	'es' E	'ia' A
'ic' A	'is' A	'ly' B	'on' S
'or' T	'um' U	'us' V	'yl' R
'{'}s' A	's{'}' A		

'a' A	'e' A	'i' A	'o' A
's' W	'y' B		

```
        (delete)
    )
)

/* Undoubling is rule 1 of appendix C. */

define undouble as (
  test substring among ('bb' 'dd' 'gg' 'll' 'mm' 'nn' 'pp' 'rr' 'ss'
                        'tt')
  [next] delete
)

/* The other appendix C rules can be done together. */

define respell as (
  [substring] among (
    'iev'   (<-'ief')
    'uct'   (<-'uc')
    'umpt'  (<-'um')
    'rpt'   (<-'rb')
```

```
'urs'   (<-'ur')
'istr'  (<-'ister')
'metr'  (<-'meter')
'olv'   (<-'olut')
'ul'    (not 'a' not 'i' not 'o' <-'l')
'bex'   (<-'bic')
'dex'   (<-'dic')
'pex'   (<-'pic')
'tex'   (<-'tic')
'ax'    (<-'ac')
'ex'    (<-'ec')
'ix'    (<-'ic')
'lux'   (<-'luc')
'uad'   (<-'uas')
'vad'   (<-'vas')
'cid'   (<-'cis')
'lid'   (<-'lis')
'erid'  (<-'eris')
'pand'  (<-'pans')
'end'   (not 's' <-'ens')
'ond'   (<-'ons')
'lud'   (<-'lus')
'rud'   (<-'rus')
'her'   (not 'p' not 't' <-'hes')
'mit'   (<-'mis')
'ent'   (not 'm' <-'ens')
   /* 'ent' was 'end' in the 1968 paper - a typo. */
'ert'   (<-'ers')
'et'    (not 'n' <-'es')
'yt'    (<-'ys')
'yz'    (<-'ys')
    )
  )
)

define stem as (

  backwards (
    do endings
    do undouble
    do respell
  )
)
```

APPENDIX 2

```
integers ( p1 p2 )
booleans ( Y_found )

routines (
```

```
        endings respell
        shortv
        undouble
        A B C D E F G H I J
)

externals ( stem )

groupings ( v v_WXY )

define v          'aeiouy'
define v_WXY      v + 'wxY'

backwardmode (

    define shortv as ( non-v_WXY v non-v )

    define undouble as (
        among ('bb' 'dd' 'ff' 'gg' 'mm' 'nn' 'pp' 'rr' 'tt')
        and ([next] delete)
    )

    define A as $p1 <= cursor
    define B as $p2 <= cursor
    define C as (B 's' or 't')
    define D as (B not 'm')
    define E as ('e' or 'ous' A)

    define F as ('ss' or 'i')
    define G as not 's'
    define H as gopast v
    define I as (not 'e' gopast v)
    define J as ('ee' A)

    define endings as (

        [substring] among (

            'ed'    I
            'ing'   H
            'ings'  H

                    (delete
                     undouble or (atmark p1  test shortv  <+ 'e')
                    )

            'd'     J
            'es'    F
            's'     G

            get '/home/martin/Snowball/festschrift/endings'
                    (delete)
        )
    )

    define respell as (
        [substring] among (
            'e'     (B or (A not shortv) delete)
            'l'     (B 'l' delete)
            'enci'
            'ency'  ((A <- 'enc') or <- 'enci')
            'anci'
            'ancy'  ((A <- 'anc') or <- 'anci')
            'ally'  ((A <- 'al') or <- 'alli')
            'ently' ((A <- 'ent') or <- 'entli')
            'ator'  (A <- 'at')
```

```
            'logi'
            'logy'   ((A <- 'log') or <- 'logi')
            'bli'
            'bly'    ((A <- 'bl') or <- 'bli')
            'bil'    (v A <- 'bl')
            'y' 'Y'
                     (gopast v  <-'i')

        )
      )
 )

define stem as (
     test hop 3
     unset Y_found
     do ( ['y'] <-'Y' set Y_found)
     do repeat(goto (v ['y']) <-'Y' set Y_found)

     $p1 = limit
     $p2 = limit
     do(
         gopast v  gopast non-v  setmark p1
         gopast v  gopast non-v  setmark p2
     )

     backwards (
         do endings
         do respell
     )
     do(Y_found  repeat(goto (['Y']) <-'y'))

 )
```

APPENDIX 3

The list of 181 endings included by the `get` directive in the program of Appendix 2, set out here in two columns. The numbers to the right show their frequency of occurrence in the sample vocabulary. The 75 rare endings are shown commented out.

	ending					ending			
	'abilities'	B /*	(3)	*/	//	'alnesses'	B /*	(-)	*/
	'ability'	B /*	(14)	*/		'als'	B /*	(46)	*/
	'able'	B /*	(293)	*/		'ance'	B /*	(93)	*/
	'ables'	B /*	(4)	*/		'ances'	B /*	(30)	*/
	'ably'	B /*	(68)	*/		'ancies'	B /*	(2)	*/
	'al'	B /*	(285)	*/		'ancy'	B /*	(18)	*/
	'alism'	B /*	(5)	*/		'ant'	B /*	(92)	*/
//	'alisms'	B /*	(-)	*/		'ants'	B /*	(29)	*/
	'alities'	B /*	(7)	*/		'ate'	B /*	(261)	*/
	'ality'	B /*	(24)	*/		'ated'	B /*	(208)	*/
	'alization'	B /*	(1)	*/		'ately'	B /*	(38)	*/
//	'alizationed'	B /*	(-)	*/		'ates'	B /*	(73)	*/
//	'alizationing'	B /*	(-)	*/		'ating'	B /*	(119)	*/
//	'alizations'	B /*	(-)	*/		'ation'	B /*	(356)	*/
	'alize'	B /*	(2)	*/		'ational'	B /*	(4)	*/
	'alized'	B /*	(4)	*/	//	'ationalism'	B /*	(-)	*/
//	'alizer'	B /*	(-)	*/	//	'ationalisms'	B /*	(-)	*/
//	'alizered'	B /*	(-)	*/	//	'ationalities'	B /*	(-)	*/
//	'alizering'	B /*	(-)	*/	//	'ationality'	B /*	(-)	*/
//	'alizers'	B /*	(-)	*/	//	'ationalize'	B /*	(-)	*/
//	'alizes'	B /*	(-)	*/	//	'ationalized'	B /*	(-)	*/
//	'alizing'	B /*	(-)	*/	//	'ationalizes'	B /*	(-)	*/
	'ally'	B /*	(78)	*/	//	'ationalizing'	B /*	(-)	*/
	'alness'	B /*	(2)	*/		'ationally'	B /*	(2)	*/

```
//  'ationalness'     B /*  (-)  */        'icative'          B /*   (2)  */
//  'ationalnesses'   B /*  (-)  */    //  'icatively'        B /*  (-)  */
//  'ationals'        B /*  (-)  */    //  'icativeness'      B /*  (-)  */
//  'ationed'         B /*  (-)  */    //  'icativenesses'    B /*  (-)  */
//  'ationing'        B /*  (-)  */    //  'icatives'         B /*  (-)  */
    'ations'          B /* (139) */    //  'icativities'      B /*  (-)  */
    'ative'           B /*  (40) */    //  'icativity'        B /*  (-)  */
    'atively'         B /*   (4) */        'icities'          B /*   (1)  */
//  'ativeness'       B /*  (-)  */        'icity'            B /*   (5)  */
//  'ativenesses'     B /*  (-)  */        'ics'              B /*  (21)  */
    'atives'          B /*   (7) */        'ion'              C /* (383)  */
//  'ativities'       B /*  (-)  */        'ional'            C /*  (18)  */
//  'ativity'         B /*  (-)  */    //  'ionalism'         C /*  (-)  */
    'ator'            B /*  (25) */    //  'ionalisms'        C /*  (-)  */
    'ators'           B /*  (10) */        'ionalities'       C /*   (1)  */
    'ement'           B /*  (70) */        'ionality'         C /*   (1)  */
//  'emently'         B /*  (-)  */    //  'ionalize'         C /*  (-)  */
    'ements'          B /*  (31) */    //  'ionalized'        C /*  (-)  */
    'ence'            B /* (100) */    //  'ionalizer'        C /*  (-)  */
    'ences'           B /*  (25) */    //  'ionalizered'      C /*  (-)  */
    'encies'          B /*   (9) */    //  'ionalizering'     C /*  (-)  */
    'ency'            B /*  (41) */    //  'ionalizers'       C /*  (-)  */
    'ent'             D /* (154) */    //  'ionalizes'        C /*  (-)  */
    'ently'           D /*  (53) */    //  'ionalizing'       C /*  (-)  */
    'ents'            D /*  (25) */        'ionally'          C /*  (12)  */
    'er'              B /* (613) */        'ionalness'        C /*   (1)  */
    'ered'            B /*  (44) */    //  'ionalnesses'      C /*  (-)  */
    'ering'           B /*  (31) */        'ionals'           C /*   (1)  */
    'ers'             B /* (281) */        'ioned'            C /*  (13)  */
    'ful'             A /* (163) */        'ioning'           C /*   (3)  */
    'fulness'         A /*  (31) */        'ions'             C /* (192)  */
//  'fulnesses'       A /*  (-)  */        'ism'              B /*  (33)  */
    'fuls'            A /*   (5) */        'isms'             B /*   (5)  */
    'ibilities'       B /*   (2) */        'ities'            B /*  (62)  */
    'ibility'         B /*  (10) */        'ity'              B /* (236)  */
    'ible'            B /*  (53) */        'ive'              B /* (132)  */
    'ibles'           B /*   (2) */        'ively'            B /*  (34)  */
    'ibly'            B /*  (14) */        'iveness'          B /*  (14)  */
    'ic'              B /* (142) */    //  'ivenesses'        B /*  (-)  */
    'ical'            B /*  (91) */        'ives'             B /*  (12)  */
//  'icalism'         B /*  (-)  */    //  'ivities'          B /*  (-)  */
//  'icalisms'        B /*  (-)  */        'ivity'            B /*   (1)  */
//  'icalities'       B /*  (-)  */        'ization'          B /*   (4)  */
    'icality'         B /*   (1) */    //  'izational'        B /*  (-)  */
//  'icalize'         B /*  (-)  */    //  'izationals'       B /*  (-)  */
//  'icalized'        B /*  (-)  */    //  'izationed'        B /*  (-)  */
//  'icalizer'        B /*  (-)  */    //  'izationing'       B /*  (-)  */
//  'icalizered'      B /*  (-)  */        'izations'         B /*   (1)  */
//  'icalizering'     B /*  (-)  */        'ize'              B /*  (32)  */
//  'icalizers'       B /*  (-)  */        'ized'             B /*  (32)  */
//  'icalizes'        B /*  (-)  */        'izer'             B /*   (3)  */
//  'icalizing'       B /*  (-)  */    //  'izered'           B /*  (-)  */
    'ically'          B /*  (59) */    //  'izering'          B /*  (-)  */
//  'icalness'        B /*  (-)  */        'izers'            B /*   (1)  */
//  'icalnesses'      B /*  (-)  */        'izes'             B /*   (6)  */
    'icals'           B /*   (2) */        'izing'            B /*  (30)  */
    'icate'           B /*   (9) */        'ly'               E /* (135)  */
    'icated'          B /*   (7) */        'ment'             B /* (105)  */
//  'icately'         B /*  (-)  */    //  'mently'           B /*  (-)  */
    'icates'          B /*   (4) */        'ments'            B /*  (50)  */
    'icating'         B /*   (3) */        'ness'             A /* (428)  */
    'ication'         B /*  (23) */        'nesses'           A /*  (21)  */
//  'icational'       B /*  (-)  */        'ous'              B /* (340)  */
//  'icationals'      B /*  (-)  */        'ously'            B /* (130)  */
//  'icationed'       B /*  (-)  */        'ousness'          B /*  (22)  */
//  'icationing'      B /*  (-)  */    //  'ousnesses'        B /*  (-)  */
    'ications'        B /*   (8) */
```

DONNA HARMAN

THE HISTORY OF IDF AND ITS INFLUENCES ON IR AND OTHER FIELDS

1. INTRODUCTION

Once upon a time there were no web search engines, there was no web, and there were few computers. Yet people still needed to find information. They did this, in a much more limited way than now, by using indices to books and journals. These indices could be card catalogs, listing the titles, authors, and some "metadata" for books, or they could be specific published indices for given fields, such as *Index Medicus* for medicine, or *The Engineering Index* for various engineering fields. These indices were all built by hand, employing thousands of librarians and others. Note that many of these services are still ongoing today.

How were these indices built? They started with a controlled vocabulary, that is an *indexing language* that contains all the words available to the indexer. This indexing language was often presented as a thesaurus, with one or more levels of nesting---the MeSH thesaurus that is used in MEDLARS is a prime example of this type of controlled vocabulary. There are usually indexing rules that direct how many terms should be assigned, how those terms should be selected, etc.

As is often the case, there developed many theories of how to best build thesauri, and how to best assign index terms. In terms of building thesauri, there is the issue of term *specificity* that deals with how detailed to make terms. Using an example from Lancaster's (1972) book, one could use the term "welding" or "arc welding" or "argon arc welding". Alternatively one could have "animals" or "dogs" or "spaniels" (or all of them). Obviously the more precise the indexing vocabulary, the higher the precision of the results (assuming perfect indexing and searching). Correlated with this was term *exhaustivity* which deals with how many terms to assign any given article and how many terms to include in a search request. The more terms assigned, the higher the recall.

Starting in the mid 1960s, Cleverdon of the Cranfield Institute of Technology ran a series of experiments (Cleverdon, Mills & Keen 1966, Cleverdon 1997). to determine the best way to index a collection, i.e., what is the best type of indexing language. He used three types of manually-produced indices: a selection of the actual terms in the collection (unigrams), a combination of these terms into concepts (phrases) that represent a more specific idea, and a combination of concepts that are grouped into specific areas called themes. There were 1400 abstracts from aerodynamics papers that were indexed, and he collected 225 search requests which

John I. Tait (ed.), *Charting a New Course: Natural Language Processing and Information Retrieval. Essays in Honour of Karen Spärck Jones.* 69–79

could be then used to create queries. Searching was done by hand using each of the indexing methods on the search requests to build queries and complete relevancy decisions were made across the set.

What he found surprised the library community. As Cleverdon reported:

> Quite the most astonishing and seemingly inexplicable conclusion that arises from the project is that the single term indexing languages are superior to any other type...unless one is prepared to say that the whole test conception is so much at fault that the results are completely distorted, there is no course except to attempt to explain the results which seem to offend against every canon on which we were trained as librarians.

Meanwhile, outside the library community, people using the new computers had been working on the creation of indices and abstracts automatically, as this was one of the first applications for the computer.

Luhn (1957) proposed producing indices by examining the occurrence of "notions", i.e., single words or phrases that represent particular ideas within a given technical area. These notions would be created automatically by counting their occurrence within the same paragraph, or within adjacent paragraphs. Alternatively he suggested the counting of notions by the positional occurrence, such in the title or section headings or abstracts. These notions would then be gathered, based on some thresholding device, and used as the index for a given article. He envisioned the use of a thesaurus to expand specificity.

Edmundson and Wyllys (1961) were interested in automatically producing both indices and abstracts and therefore considered both word significance measures and sentence significance measures. In addition to considering word frequency within a given document, they also proposed in 1961 the use of "reference" frequency, which measured both the frequency in the document and also its relative frequency within a document collection. In particular they presented four ways of measuring this based on two frequency functions.

$$f_{wd} = N_{wd} / N_d$$
$$r_{wc} = N_{wc} / N_c$$

$$S_1 = f_{wd} - r_{wc}$$
$$S_2 = f_{wd} / r_{wc}$$
$$S_3 = f_{wd} / (f_{wd} + r_{wc})$$
$$S_4 = log(f_{wd} / r_{wc})$$

where N_{wd} is the frequency of term$_{wd}$ in the document d, N_d is the number of terms in document d, N_{wc} is the frequency of term$_{wd}$ in the collection, and N_c is the number of terms in the collection. Although they ran no experiments, they selected S_1 and S_2 as the favorites, commenting that S_4 was too time-consuming a computation.

A paper by Carroll and Roeloffs (1969) actually reported on some experiments, albeit with only 19 documents. They removed 300 different stopwords, and did some minimal stemming. They then experimented with five different types of measures. These included the raw frequency counts, the first two measures (S_1 and

S$_2$) from Edmundsen and Wyllys, plus two more complex combinations of these called the Poisson Standard Deviate and the Standard Deviate. These measures were all used to produce ranked lists of index terms, which were then compared using the Kendall sum-of-ranks method with a list of carefully created manual index terms. The raw requency count was the major winner, with the more complex combinations doing the worst.

But indexing is only one part of the process. Assuming it is possible to index using only the terms in a document, how are the searches to be made? This gets back to the exhaustivity vs specificity issue. If there are many terms in the search (high exhaustivity), then the recall will be high, but with low precision. If the terms are very specific, the precision improves, but at the expense of recall. Luhn had envisioned very long queries to be used in his early paper, but Cleverdon had done some investigation in his 1966 experiment to show that using full abstracts as queries were too long and using titles as queries were too short.

2. EARLY SEARCHING USING TERM WEIGHTS

The papers cited in the introduction cover only some of the work that was done; likewise this section will follow only two of the paths that investigated searching in the early days. Stevens (1965) presents a survey of both the early automatic searching and indexing work.

One of the issues in automatic indexing was how to determine if one index was better than another. One method was to compare to manual indexing, but since the point of indexing articles was to allow better searching for information, a natural question to ask would be if one index allowed better searching than another. This was the question asked by Cleverdon in his previously mentioned Cranfield testing. Salton at Harvard and later Cornell University was also building test collections, and investigating co-citations and thesaurus use in these smaller collections. Salton's interest lay more in the searching end of the operation than in the automatic indexing end, and he quickly moved into the use of the natural language terms occurring in the text.

Salton and Lesk (1968) tested various ways of using the document terms in three test collections, including a subset of the Cranfield collection (200 documents and 42 requests). This paper presented many results, but in particular it was shown that significant improvements could be found by weighting the terms by their frequency within a given document (Luhn's method), and that using a cosine correlation between the document and query terms was better than just a straight overlap of the matching terms. Additionally they tested the use of the Cranfield manual index terms (average 30 per document) versus the terms in the abstract (average 91 per document after stopwords removed) and found that the manual index terms performed slightly better than the automatic ones. This improvement was more notable when a thesaurus was also used.

A second path investigating searching was taken at the University of Cambridge Computer Laboratory. This group appears to have been more interested initially in the automatic indexing side of the operation, but used searching as the evaluation method. In 1972 Karen Spärck Jones published a paper (Sparck Jones, 1972) examining the relationship of the exhaustivity of indexing to the specificity of the index terms, and in particular performed some experiments in statistically determining the specificity of a given term. She redefined exhaustivity and specificity as

> exhaustivity of a document description is the number of terms it contains, and the specificity of a term is the number of documents to which it pertains

She performed experiments with three test collections, including the Cranfield 200 collection. For this collection she was using the manually-selected single terms. The first experiment was to reduce the number of terms available for indexing by removing the most frequent terms; this reduced search performance in all three collections. The second experiment was a weighting scheme in which the terms were weighted by a type of relative frequency, in particular the term distribution curve for the whole collection. This curve has a Zipfian distribution and therefore the weight of term$_i$ is

$$weight_i = \log n_i - \log N + 1$$

where n is the number of documents in the collection containing term$_i$ and N is the total number of documents in the collection. Performance using this weighting function on the three collections was significantly improved over using no weighting.

Note that weighting by collection frequency is an independent variable with respect to weighting by document frequency. So combining the two seemed the obvious next step. Salton and Yang (1973) compared the collection frequency measure, which they called *inverse document frequency* or IDF, with the document term frequency weighting method and with a term discrimination measure that they had previously been trying. They used these various weights in two ways, i.e., either as ways of removing terms with high document frequency (using IDF), or as term weights, which were multiplied by the existing document term frequency weights (tf) they had been using earlier. For the Cranfield 424 collection (a subset with 424 documents from Cranfield) they found the most improvements in performance using the multiplying strategy, thus producing the now famous tf*idf weighting.

Sparck Jones (1973) explored the differences between document term frequency weighting and collection frequency weighting, along with an examination of document length effects (but not combinations of these). She produced more formalized versions of the various weighting schemes, contrasting the differences that would be expected, and then performed experiments to check out these hypotheses. Again she was using the manual index terms from Cranfield (and two other collections) and found that the collection frequency weighting always helped performance, whereas the term frequency did not always help and the length had little effect (note however that there were not many terms involved--an average of 32 for Cranfield, with likely few duplicate terms).

3. THE USE OF IDF OVER THE YEARS IN IR

The early work using IDF was further built on with the introduction of models for IR. Use of the cosine correlation in Salton's SMART system was formalized into a vector space model. Although a model of probabilistic indexing had been proposed and tested by Maron and Kuhns (1960), the major probabilistic model in use today was developed by Robertson and Spärck Jones in 1976 (Robertson & Sparck Jones, 1976). This model is based on the premise that terms that appear in previously retrieved relevant documents for a given query should be given a higher weight than if they had not appeared in those relevant documents. This of course required relevance judgments to be made, but Sparck Jones (1979) used this method in a typical online session using relevance feedback and found that adding the relevance weighting from only the first couple of relevant documents retrieved by a ranking system still produced performance improvements.

Work up to this point using probabilistic indexing required the use of at least a few relevant documents, making this model more closely related to relevance feedback than to term weighting schemes of other models. Croft and Harper (1979) presented a theoretical motivation for the model and detailed a series of experiments using probabilistic indexing without any relevance information. They assumed that all query terms have equal probability of occurring in relevant documents and derived a term weighting formula that combined a weight based on the number of matching terms and on a term weighting similar to the IDF measure.

$$similarity_{jk} = \sum_{i=1}^{Q} (C + \log(N - n_i) / n_i)$$

where Q is the number of matching terms between document j and query k, C is a constant for tuning the similarity function, n_i is the number of documents having term i in the collection, and N is the number of documents in the collection.

Experimental results showed that this term weighting produced somewhat better results than the use of the IDF measure alone. Being able to provide different values to C allowed this weighting measure to be tailored to various collections. Setting C to 1 ranked the documents by IDF weighting within number of matches, a method that was suitable for the manually-indexed Cranfield collection used in this study (because it can be assumed that each matching query term was very significant). C was set much lower in tests with the UKCIS2 collection (Harper, 1980) because the terms were assumed to be less accurate, and the documents were very short (consisting of titles only).

Croft (1983) expanded his combination weighting scheme to incorporate within-document frequency weights, again using a tuning factor K on these weights to allow tailoring to particular collections. The results show significant improvement over both the IDF weighting alone and the combination weighting, with the scaling factor K playing a large part in tuning the weighting to different collections.

$$similarity_{jk} = \sum_{i=1}^{Q} (C + IDF_i) * f_{ij}; \quad f_{ij} = K + (1 - K) * (freq_{ij} / max\ freq_i)$$

where Q is defined as before, IDFi is the IDF weight for term i in the collection, freqij is the frequency of term i in document j, K is a constant for adjusting the relative importance of the two weighting schemes, and *max freq_j* is the maximum frequency of any term in document j. The best value for K proved to be 0.3 for the automatically indexed Cranfield collection, and 0.5 for the NPL collection, confirming that within-document term frequency plays a much smaller role in the NPL collection with its short documents having few repeating terms.

Salton and Buckley (1988) summarized twenty years of SMART experiments in automatic term weighting by trying 287 distinct combinations of term weighting assignments, with or without cosine normalization, on six of the existing standard collections. Besides confirming that the best document term weighting is provided by a product of the within-document term frequency and the IDF, normalized by the cosine measure, they showed performance improvements using enhanced query term weighting measures for queries with term frequencies greater than one.

A different approach was taken by Harman (1986). She selected four term weighting factors proven important in past research and tried different combinations in order to arrive at an "optimum" term weighting scheme. The four factors investigated were: the number of matches between a document and a query, the distribution of a term within a document collection, the frequency of a term within a document, and the length of the document. Various combinations, including log combinations, were tried and two different measures for the distribution of a term within a document collection were used, the IDF measure by Spärck Jones and a revised implementation of the "noise" measure (Dennis, 1964, Salton & McGill, 1983). Note that the use of noise here refers to how useful a term can be considered for retrieval versus being simply a "noisy" term, and examines the concentration of terms within documents rather than just the number of postings or occurrences. The noise measure consistently slightly outperformed the IDF (however with no significant difference).

The noise measure was used again by Lochbaum and Streeter (1989), but with better normalization (and called entropy). The formula was as follows.

$$entropy_k = \sum_{i=1}^{N} ((freq_{ik} / totfreq_i) * \log_2(totfreq_i / freq_{ik}))$$

where $freq_{ik}$ is the frequency of term i in document k and $totfreq_i$ is the frequency of term i in the collection of N documents.

The 1986 Harman experiment was repeated by Smith and Dimmick (1997) with both the older collections and two of the new TREC collections. Table 1 shows the average precision performance on four collections: the full 1400 Cranfield collection (abstracts), the NPL collection, and two subsets of the TREC collection, *AP 88-90* and *FR 94*. The various weighting factors are binary (no weighting), the variations used in Harman, including length normalization, and the BM25 measure from OKAPI to show the improvements for a more modern measure.

Table 1. *Average precision for four collections and 10 weighting measures*

Weighting function	Cranfield	NPL	AP 88-90	FR 94
BINARY	0.2465	0.2144	0.0568	0.0189
tf	0.1425	0.1187	0.0173	0.0083
log (tf + 1)	0.2298	0.1839	0.0642	0.0155
IDF	0.2937	0.2487	0.1033	0.0371
noise	0.3062	0.2466	0.1134	0.0416
log (tf+1) * IDF	0.3187	0.2356	0.1391	0.0324
log (tf+1) * noise	0.3335	0.2416	0.1524	0.0361
log (tf+1) *IDF/log(length+1)	0.3880	0.2685	0.1668	0.0458
log(tf+1)*noise/log(length+1)	0.3966	0.2742	0.1778	0.0514
BM25	0.4097	0.2757	0.2371	0.2079

Several trends can be noted from the table. First, the longer the document, the more important it is to "normalize" document term frequency by using the log of the term frequency. This also applies to document length normalization. The small collections are abstracts of approximately 91 words; by contrast the *AP* has a median of over 400 words and the *FR* has a median of 588 words, with many very long documents. The modern methods such as BM25 improve greatly over the log of the term, and this is particularly notable for the *FR* collection.

Second, note that the IDF measure is about twice as important as the document frequency factor for the longer documents in the new collections, and only somewhat less for the short documents in the older collections.

As a final comment, the noise measure is always somewhat better than the IDF measure. Looking beneath the averages, however, Smith and Dimmick reported that the difference was skewed. When noise outperformed IDF, the difference is small (15% on AP and 14.5% on FR), whereas when the IDF was better, it was better by 79.5% on AP and 58% on FR. This erratic behavior would create an unstable system and therefore the use of IDF instead of noise is recommended.

In 1992 a new very large test collection became available and a forum (TREC) was created to encourage the various retrieval groups to use this collection in a focused evaluation at NIST (Harman, 1993). The TREC test collections (subsets are used in Table 1) presented several major challenges to the term weighting algorithms developed up until then. The first was the vast scale-up in terms of number of documents to be searched, from several megabytes of documents to 2 gigabytes of documents.   The second challenge was that these documents are mostly full-text and therefore much longer than most algorithms were designed to handle.

For TREC-1, groups concentrated on the scale-up in the number of documents. Groups such as SMART, OKAPI and the University of Massachusetts at Amherst (UMass) re-engineered their systems for speed, but basically used the old term weighting algorithms. This worked reasonably well for groups like SMART and UMass because they were working with combinations of IDF and document term frequencies already and therefore the growth from abstract to full text was not a critical problem. However systems like the OKAPI system from City University, London, had no document term frequency component, only the IDF component, and performance suffered greatly from the longer documents. This of course resulted in work by all participants to deal with the document length factor. In particular, the OKAPI team for TREC-2 became involved in both the theoretical and experimental work for adding document frequency information to their system (Robertson, Walker, Hancock-Beaulieu & Gatford, 1994, Robertson & Walker, 1994). This eventually resulted in the now famous BM25 term weighting formula. The BM25 measure contains both the IDF measure and a complex document term frequency measure normalized for document length. It should also be noted that this formula contains four adjustable parameters to allow tuning to specific collections (similar to the earlier UMass term weighting work). For details and further experiments concerning the BM25 measure, see Sparck Jones, Walker & Robertson (2000).

Over successive TRECs, the other groups such as SMART and UMass made further adjustments to their document frequency and document length weighting formulas, but the IDF measure was basically kept intact. Even the new language modeling systems such as LEMUR have variations of IDF buried in their models (see Hiemstra & de Vries, 2000).

4. OTHER USES OF IDF

Today the IDF measure appears in almost every IR system in some form and is critical to good performance, even for languages other than English. Savoy (2003) tested various retrieval models on four European languages and found that the BM25 model worked as well in French, Italian, and German as it worked in English. He not only used the German words for indexing but also used 5-grams; in all cases the IDF term distribution measure performed correctly. More surprisingly, the IDF measure has been successfully used in languages without word boundaries. The NTCIR workshop for cross-language retrieval in Japanese, Chinese, and Korean (Chen & Chen, 2001) confirmed that both BM25 and the SMART vector space model using tf*idf both produced excellent results using both words and bi-gram models.

An obvious use of IDF is in summarization for location of the best sentences for extraction (as visualized by the Edmundson and Wyllys early work). Much of the early summarization work used IDF, along with positional information. McKeown *et al* (1999) reported on the use of tf*idf as one of the measures in a multi-document summarization system; here the use was in finding similar sentences to allow clustering of different themes across the documents. These themes were used in the planning stage of the summarization to create the "infrastructure" for text generation. Tzoukermann (reported in Tzoukermann, Muresan & Klavans, 2001) used the IDF extensively in measuring the importance of noun phrases in email for the purposes of gisting email. She weighted all parts of noun phrases and used the results as features for machine learning algorithms to build the gists. A final example of the use of IDF in summarization is its use by Zechner and Waibel (2000) in summarization of spontaneous dialogs in speech. Here they used the tf*idf to locate the most important terms in the dialogs; this was combined with MMR (Maximal Marginal Relevance) to identify the speech segments containing highly weighted terms that are dissimilar to previous segments.

The IDF measure (usually in combination with tf) has been used in many other applications as part of a similarity measure. One such application is speech retrieval, another is filtering, and a third is question answering. The BBN group used this similarity function in TREC-2003 (Xu, Licuanan & Weischedel, 2003) as a way of selecting which of many "kernel" facts to return in answer to questions involving people or things. They extracted those facts using appositives and copulas, propositions, structured patterns and relations, but used both reliability of the extraction method and the similarity of the facts to the question to rank the likely candidates.

IDF has also been used on non-textual applications. Downie used the IDF to measure distributional properties of music, in particular interval-only representations of monophonic melodies that had been broken into n-grams (Downie & Nelson, 2000). The IDF was successfully used (with tf) to retrieve these n-gram representations in almost 1000 international folksongs. It has also been used in image retrieval as a scoring function for features such as local and global color and local and global texture (Muller, Squire, Muller & Pun, 1999).

5. CONCLUSION

The surprisingly simple IDF measure developed in 1972 by Karen Spärck Jones has continued to dominate the term weighting metrics used in information retrieval, despite several efforts to develop more complex measures of term distribution. It has been incorporated in (probably) all information retrieval systems, and used in languages other than English. As other fields start to use information retrieval techniques, they are adopting the IDF measure, with or without document term frequency measures, as part of their measures. Undoubtedly, there will be further work on both other measures of term distribution and other ways of using IDF, but the development of the IDF measure has made an immeasurable contribution to human language technology.

Donna Harman graduated from Cornell University with a degree in electrical engineering. She has worked on search engine technologies and their evaluation for many years and currently leads a group in the US National Institute of Standards and Technology active in this field. She received the 1999 Strix Award from the U.K Institute of Information Scientists for her initiation of the Text Retrieval Conferences (TREC), which focus on the evaluation of retrieval techniques. A similar forum for automatic summarization, called the Document Understanding Conference (DUC) was started in 2000. Karen Spärck Jones has been active in both TREC and DUC since their inception.

REFERENCES

Lancaster, F. (1972). *Vocabulary control for information retrieval*. Washington, D.C.: Information Resources Press.

Cleverdon, C., Mills, J. & Keen, E. (1966). *Factors determining the performance of indexing systems*, vol. 1: design, vol. 2: test results. Cranfield, England: Aslib Cranfield Research Project

Cleverdon, C. (1997) The Cranfield tests on indexing language devices. In K. Sparck Jones & P. Willett (Eds.), *Readings in information retrieval (pp. 47-59)*. San Francisco: Morgan Kaufmann Publishers, Inc.

Luhn, H. (1957). A statistical approach to mechanized encoding and searching of literary information. *IBM Journal*, 309-317.

Edmundson, H. & Wyllys, R. (1961). Automatic abstracting and indexing--survey and recommendations. *Communications of the ACM*, 4, 226-234.

Carroll, J. & Roeloffs, R. (1969). Computer selection of keywords using word-frequency analysis. *American Documentation*, 227-233.

Stevens, M. (1965). *Automatic indexing: a state-of-the-art report*. NBS Monograph 91. Washington, D.C.

Salton, G. & Lesk, M. (1968). Computer evaluation of indexing and text processing. *Journal of the Association of Computer Machinery*, 15, 8-36.

Sparck Jones, K.S. (1972). A statistical interpretation of term specificity and its application in retrieval. *Journal of Documentation*, 28(1), 11-21.

Salton, G. & Yang, C. (1973). On the specification of term values in automatic indexing. *Journal of Documentation*, 29(4), 351-372.

Sparck Jones, K.S. (1973). Index term weighting. *Information Storage and Retrieval*, 9, 619-633.

Maron, M. & Kuhns, J. (1960). On relevance, probabilistic indexing and information retrieval. *Journal of the Association of Computer Machinery*, 7, 216-244.

Robertson, S. & Sparck Jones, K.. (1976). Relevance weighting of search terms. *Journal of the American Society for Information Science*, 27(3), 129-146.

Sparck Jones, K. (1979). Search term relevance weighting given little relevance information. *Journal of Documentation*, 35(1).30-48.

Croft, W. & Harper, D. (1979). Using probabilistic models of document retrieval without relevance information. *Journal of Documentation*, 35(4), 285-295.

Harper, D. (1980). Relevance feedback in document retrieval systems: an evaluation of probabilistic strategies. (Doctoral dissertation, Jesus College, Cambridge, England (1980).

Croft, W. (1983). Experiments with representation in a document retrieval system. *Information Technology: Research and Development*, 2(1), 1-21.

Salton, G. & Buckley, C. (1988). Term-weighting approaches in automatic text processing. *Information Processing and Management*, 24(5), 513-523.

Harman, D. (1986). An experimental study of factors important in document ranking. In *Proceedings of the ACM conference on research and development in* information retrieval, 186-193.

Dennis, S. (1964). The construction of a thesaurus automatically from a sample of text. In *Proceedings of the statistical association methods for mechanized documentation*. National Bureau of Standards Miscellaneous Publication 269.

Salton, G. & McGill, M. (eds). (1983). *Introduction to modern information retrieval*.. McGraw-Hill, New York, NY: McGraw-Hill.

Lockbaum, K. & Streeter, L. (1989). Comparing and combining the effectiveness of latent semantic indexing and the ordinary vector space model for information retrieval. *Information Processing and Management*, 25(6), 665-676.

Smith, M. & Dimmick, D. (1997) A study of factors important in document ranking (revisited). (unpublished report of work done at NIST) Harman, D. (1993). Overview of the first Text REtrieval Conference (TREC-1). In *Proceedings of the first Text REtrieval Conference (TREC-1)*, 1-20.

Robertson, S., Walker, S., Hancock-Beaulieu, & Gatford, M. (1994). Okapi and TREC-2. *In Proceedings of the Second Text REtrieval Conference (TREC-2)*, 21-34.

Robertson, S. & Walker, S. (1994). Some simple effective approximations to the 2-poisson model for probabilistic weighted retrieval. In *Proceedings of the 17th annual international ACM SIGIR conference on research and development in information retrieval*, 232-241.

Sparck Jones,.K., Walker, S. & Robertson, S. (2000). A probabilistic model of information retrieval: development and comparative experiments, parts 1 and 2. *Information Processing and Management*, 36(6), 779-840.

Hiemstra, D. & de Vries, (2000) A. Relating the new language models of information retrieval to the traditional retrieval models. Technical Report TR—CTIT—00—09, Centre for Telematics and Information Retrieval.

Savoy, J. (2003). Cross-language information retrieval: experiments based on CLEF 2000 corpora. *Information Processing and Management*, 39(1), 75-116.

Chen, K. & Chen, H.(2001). Cross-language Chinese text retrieval in NTCIR Workshop-towards cross-language multilingual text retrieval. *SIGIR Forum* 32(2), 12-19.

McKeown, K., Klavan, J., Hatzivassiloglou, V., Barzilay, R. & Eskin, E. (1999) Towards multidocument summarization by reformulation: progress and prospects. In *Proceedings of the 17th national congress on artificial intelligence (AAAI-99)*.

Tzoukermann, E., Muresan, S. & Klavans, J. (2001). GIST-IT summarizing email using linguistic knowledge and machine learning. In Proceedings of the ACL 2001 Workshop on Evaluation Methods for Language and Dialog Systems.

Zechner, K. & Waibel, A. (2000). DIASUMM: flexible summarization of spontaneous dialogues in unrestricted domains. In *Proceedings of COLING 2000*, 968-974.

Xu, J., Licuanan, A. & Weischedel, R. (2003). Evaluation of an extraction-based approach to answering definitional questions. In *Proceedings of the 27th annual international ACM SIGIR conference on research and development in information retrieval*, 418-424

Downie, S. & Nelson, M. (2000). Evaluation of a simple and effective music information retrieval method. In *Proceedings of the 23th annual international ACM SIGIR conference on research and development in information retrieval*. 73-80.

Muller, H., Squire, D., Muller, W. & Pun, T. (1999). Efficient access methods for content-based image retrieval with inverted files. In *Proceedings of the SPIE Symposium on Voice, Video and Data Communication*. 461-472.

GARETH J. F. JONES

BEYOND ENGLISH TEXT: MULTILINGUAL AND MULTIMEDIA INFORMATION RETRIEVAL

1. INTRODUCTION

In common with many areas of language processing, the origins of information retrieval (IR) research are to be found in the exploration of techniques for electronic English language text archives. The adoption of this research strategy arose, I suspect, from the general competence in the English language of scientific researchers internationally, and more particularly due to the availability of standard English text collections for comparative experimental research. A number of successful models for information retrieval were, and continue to be, developed using these test collections as their primary research focus.

English language document collections, and electronic text documents in any language, represent only a minority of the information sources that a user may wish to search to satisfy their information need. The need to expand the scope of IR research beyond English text has been recognised in the last 10 years. Increasing amounts of work are now being reported which explore non-English IR, cross-language information retrieval (CLIR), multilingual information retrieval (MLIR) and multimedia information retrieval (MIR).

When these efforts to expand the horizons of IR began, it was not at all clear what approaches should be adopted for these new tasks in order to achieve the greatest IR effectiveness. However, as we shall see in this chapter, the techniques of probabilistic information retrieval and the approaches to automatic indexing, developed by Karen Spärck Jones and her various collaborators over the last 30 years, have stood up remarkably well to the new challenges. Indeed at the time of writing, the comment from many researchers seeking to develop novel more effective IR methods for these and other tasks, continues to be *"... it's good, but it still isn't really any better than Okapi ... "*. The reason for this result should perhaps not be too surprising given the rigor and care taken over the years to ground these models in sound theoretical analysis, and the extensive experimental evaluations that have characterized this work (Sparck Jones, Walker, & Robertson, 2000a) (Sparck Jones, Walker, & Robertson, 2000b).

This chapter continues in Section 2 with a brief review of the relevant details and indexing assumptions of the probabilistic model of IR. Section 3 describes experimental work with non-English test collections, this is extended in Section 4 which gives results for cross-language and multilingual IR. Section 5 introduces

John I. Tait (ed.), *Charting a New Course: Natural Language Processing and Information Retrieval. Essays in Honour of Karen Spärck Jones.* 81–97

multimedia IR and highlights some relevant experimental work. Finally, Section 6 draws conclusions from existing work and looks toward future applications and challenges.

2. PROBABILISTIC MODELS AND FEATURE INDEXING

IR systems seek to satisfy a user's *information need*. Current IR systems attempt to do this by locating *relevant* documents from within which the user themself extracts the required information. Potentially relevant documents are selected and returned to the user based on a retrieval model. This model can make use of whatever information is made available about the documents from among which it is seeking to locate the relevant ones. Document retrieval models fall into two broad classes of Boolean and best-match, the latter is the most dominant in current IR research and is the only approach considered here. Over the years many best-match or ranked retrieval models have been proposed and evaluated. The most popular models being: the vector-space approach (Salton & Buckey, 1988), the probabilistic model (Robertson & Sparck Jones, 1976), and more recent methods based on statistical language modelling (Ponte & Croft, 1998). For reasons of its demonstrated effectiveness, and Karen Spärck Jones's strong association with its development, this discussion focuses only on the probabilistic approach.

The probabilistic model seeks to evaluate a simple quantity *P(relevance|document)*, the probability of relevance given this document for a *specific* search request. Using this model documents can be returned to the user in decreasing order of probability of relevance. This is more formally stated in the Probability Ranking Principle (Robertson, 1977) (Sparck Jones et al., 2000a):

> P1: If retrieved documents are ordered by decreasing probability of relevance on the data available, then the system's effectiveness is the best to be gotten for the data.

If we had a complete model of each document, describing all potentially important features, with a corresponding model of the information need expressed by the search request, we might expect perfect retrieval with all relevant documents having higher probabilities than non-relevant documents. Alas such document models do not currently exist, and retrieved ranked document lists interleave relevant and non-relevant documents. Even if it were possible to compute *P(relevance|document)* perfectly, the under specification of information need often found in expressed search requests may cause an unavoidable ambiguity in document relevance. In any case, the objective of research in probabilistic IR is to improve the reliability of these imperfect relevance probability estimates.

Every document can be assumed to be a unique event, and in general, we take it that the description of each document used for retrieval is similarly unique. A problem arises with this modelling assumption, since it is difficult to assign probabilities to unique events. A solution comes in the form of decomposing document descriptions into their non-unique components or attributes, whose association with relevance can be estimated. These attributes can be used in combination to synthesise a relevance probability estimate for each unique document. The derivation of the early form of this practical probabilistic model (the "binary independence model") is described in van Rijsbergen (1979), and the more recent extended form of the model (well known as the "Okapi BM25'" model) in Sparck Jones et al. (2000a). In the BM25 model the likelihood of relevance for a document *j* is computed based on the sum of the *combined weights cw(i,j)* of the independent attributes *i* which occur in both the document and the current search request. *cw(i,j)* values are computed based on the classic IR attribute weighting features of across document collection frequency (the *collection frequency weight cfw(i)*) of attributes *i*, the *within document frequency* of an attribute *i* in the document *j*, and an adjustment of the weight to compensate for document length (Robertson & Walker, 1994).

of-words" which lists the attributes occurring within the document and their frequency of occurrence. The degree of match between a document *j* and the search request is then simply computed as a matching score *ms(j)* of the number of attributes in common between the request and the document. A list of documents ranked by matching score is then returned to the users. Documents are thus represented within the IR system as (assumed) independent attributes. The theory of the probabilistic model tells us nothing about the language of these attributes or even the media of the documents. Of course, much of the experimental work that established the effectiveness of this model was carried out using English text collections, but in theory there should be no reason why it cannot be used for other languages or media.

Several well established techniques are typically applied for automatic indexing of English language text documents. These include removal of frequent *stop words*, such as those in van Rijsbergen's list (van Rijsbergen 1979), *suffix stripping*, using a method such as the Porter algorithm (Porter 1980), standardisation of spelling, and conflation of synonyms. Whatever preprocessing is applied, the features used for retrieval are still independent attributes derived from the document. Combined with enhancements such as relevance feedback and pilot searching using large additional document collections, BM25 has shown consistently good effectiveness in comparative retrieval evaluation exercises such as TREC (Robertson, Walker, & Beaulieu, 1998) (Sparck Jones et al., 2000b).

The following sections look at the adaptations required for the application of probabilistic retrieval to non-English documents, cross-language and multilingual information retrieval, and its effectiveness for multimedia information retrieval.

3. NON-ENGLISH INFORMATION RETRIEVAL

A key consideration when developing an IR system for a new language is the selection of the most suitable set of attributes to be used to index the documents. The lexical and structural differences between languages mean that the distributions of attributes within individual documents and across collections will vary between different languages. However, since the probabilistic model makes no explicit language dependent assumptions about these distributions, there is no reason to suppose that, with appropriately selected indexing units, it should not work effectively for any language.

From a linguistic perspective English actually provides a good starting point for the investigation of indexing methods and retrieval models. The basic word units of the language are easily identified, and the types and degrees of inflection of individual words are relatively simple compared to those of many other languages. There are of course many exceptions to these apparently simple rules of inflexion, and ongoing debate over the basic units of meaning, but generally these concerns can be safely ignored or handled by explicit exception lists for the purposes of IR indexing. Some other languages have similar properties to English while others introduce new issues which must be addressed for effective retrieval. This discussion outlines some of the features relating to indexing and retrieval of a range of representative languages.

From an IR perspective, languages such as French, Italian and Spanish can be addressed using adaptations of the techniques used for English. Thus for each language, we need to develop a suitable set of high frequency stop words that can be removed safely without affecting retrieval effectiveness, suffix stripping algorithms to conflate words to common stems, and appropriate synonym dictionaries (Wechsler, Sheridan, & Schäuble, 1997). Probabilistic IR methods using this approach have been shown to be effective in comparative evaluations of non-English IR tasks, for example within the Cross-Language Evaluation Forum (CLEF) workshop series (Savoy, 2004).

More complex issues are introduced by languages such as German and Dutch which are highly declensional with a rich system of inflections and cases (Braschler & Ripplinger, 2004). In addition, in common with other Germanic languages, such as Swedish, and other languages such as Finnish, there is free compounding of words to express concepts developed from the component words. In these cases, although words are still the building blocks of the language, they are frequently combined into noun compounds without spaces. If one of these noun compounds appears in a search request and a document, there is a very good chance that this is a relevant document. However, the generative nature of the compounds means that often no match will be found for a search compound within the document set. This can lead to many potentially relevant documents being missed, since they don't contain the compound in exactly the form used in the request. The general approach to this problem is to develop methods for compound splitting; these techniques may rely on the use of a compound dictionary or language specific rules for identifying word units within compounds, or a combination of both methods (Braschler & Ripplinger, 2004). Of course, in addition to the decompounding of these concatenated words, indexing of these languages also benefits from the application of effective stemmers and removal of stop words.

Different issues arise in the case of east Asian languages such as Chinese and Japanese. The written form of these languages uses ideograms of Chinese origin. There are many thousands of these characters which usually have some meaning associated with them. Most words are formed by bringing two characters together. The meaning of the word is usually related to those of its constituent characters. Shorter words consisting of one character can express simple concepts and occasional longer words more complex ones. While Chinese is restricted to a single character set, in the case of Japanese three additional character sets are in common usage: *hiragana* whose role is similar to function words and verb suffices in English, *katakana* which are used to transliterate Western concepts, e.g. *computer* appears phonetically in Japanese katakana as *ko n pu ta*, and *romaji*, for Western characters sometimes used for numbers and proper nouns. The major concern when indexing languages of this type is the observation that there are no spaces between the words of each sentence. The text must thus be segmented into suitable representative units prior to indexing. Further since the ideogram character set is itself so rich, there is a question of what the best units for retrieval actually are.

A number of approaches have been explored for indexing these languages. The most basic method is simply to take each character as an indexing unit, a slightly more elaborate one is to use overlapping n-grams of characters of varying lengths, while the most complex strategy is to apply morphological analysis to identify the most likely word break points. A number of experiments using various Chinese and Japanese test collections exploring different approaches to segmentation have been carried out with inconclusive results, for example Huang & Robertson (1997) and Jones, Sakai, Kajiura, & Sumita (1998). Regardless of the indexing units selected, the probabilistic IR model has achieved consistently good retrieval performance with these languages. This was demonstrated recently for Japanese by the very good performance of the Toshiba BRIDJE system, which is based on BM25, at the NTCIR-4 Asian language evaluation workshop (Sakai, Koyama, Kumano, & Manabe, 2004).

4. CROSS-LANGUAGE AND MULTILINGUAL INFORMATION RETRIEVAL

Another topic moving IR beyond English language text collections, which has received considerable attention in recent years, is retrieval applications working with more than one language. This subject is broadly classified into two areas: cross-language information retrieval (CLIR), and multilingual information retrieval (MLIR). CLIR is concerned with the retrieval of documents in one language using search requests in another language, e.g. French requests used to retrieve Chinese documents. MLIR extends this to retrieval from a collection where documents are uniquely present in one language, but the collection overall covers documents in multiple languages, e.g. using a Japanese request to retrieve from a collection with documents in English, French, German, Spanish, Finnish and Russian. In practice, more complex situations are clearly possible. A single document may contain material in more than one language, and individual documents may be repeated in different languages within a collection. From these definitions it can be argued that CLIR is really a subset of MLIR. This section introduces research questions posed by CLIR amd MLIR, and outlines the main solutions that have been proposed and explored to date.

4.1. Cross-Language Information Retrieval

The principal question that arises in the context of CLIR is: how should the language barrier between the search requests and documents be crossed? Should search requests be translated into the language of the documents, should the documents be translated into the language of the request, or both? Further, what is the best approach to carrying out this translation?

4.1.1 Request translation vs document translation

There are well rehearsed arguments for and against request or document translation, with the main issues relating to translation cost, at what stage it is carried out, its effectiveness for retrieval, the available translation and computational resources, and the storage implications.

Generally it is held that translating requests when they are entered will be fast enough, since they are likely to short, not to interfere with interactive searching. Unfortunately, short requests often have minimal formal linguistic structure, and further because they are short, there is little information of the context in which the request words have been selected by the user. These factors mean that it will often be difficult to perform reliable deep linguistic analysis when attempting to perform translation of the request. One consequence of this is that it can be difficult to select the contextually appropriate translation of polysemous words. A further implication of attempting to translate short requests is that the mistranslation of individual words can have a significant impact on retrieval effectiveness. However, since the document collection to be searched will not have been translated, and is therefore accurate, redundancy effects are often found to help to ameliorate translation errors even for short requests. It is further frequently argued that, since deep linguistic analysis of request may not be possible (or if possible may not be desirable, if it is likely to be unreliable), and since we are only seeking to transfer the words into another language, shallower translation methods may be better for request translation CLIR.

Consider now the alternative approach of document translation. Documents are generally much longer than search requests, and the content will generally be linguistically well structured with large amounts of contextual information available. Thus translation of documents using formal linguistic analysis is potentially more accurate than it is for requests. While they may generally be translated more accurately then short requests, translated documents will nevertheless contain a number of errors arising from incorrect analysis of the source text and limitations of the translation dictionaries. These errors will inevitably impact adversely on retrieval accuracy for CLIR. However, adopting document translation does mean that no translation has to take place when the search request is entered, so the retrieval stage itself is computationally faster and cheaper. Also, the search request is now accurate, with no possibility of translation error. A major disadvantage of document translation is the very high cost of translating all the documents. Although, since translation is done in advance of retrieval and only has to be done once, it can really be regarded as part of a very expensive indexing process.

However, there are storage implications which arise from the need to maintain a separate search collection in each request language into which the documents are translated.

Experimentally both request and document translation have been shown to be effective, with at least one study showing that combining the retrieval output of both methods used independently can produce the best overall retrieval effectiveness (McCarley, 1999).

One way to address the problem of storage is to translate all documents into a single "pivot" language, most probably English, and then to translate the requests into this same language when they are entered. This has the disadvantage that since both the requests and documents are being translated, translation errors will be compounded with a consequential impact on retrieval effectiveness. Pivot languages can also be used when resources are not available to translate directly between the request and document languages (Gollins & Sanderson, 2001). In this case they can be used for translation of both requests and the documents into the pivot language, or for sequential translation of either the requests or documents into the language of the other.

4.1.2 Translation methods for CLIR

Another widely debated issue in CLIR is how the translation should be carried out. The issues here relate both to the actual best means of translation for CLIR, were a perfect translation resource to be available, and the most appropriate method, where technical and resourcing limitations mean that real translation systems are currently far from perfect. Broadly speaking the three translation strategies that have been explored for CLIR can be categorised as: dictionary-based, comparable corpora, and machine translation.

Most early work in CLIR advocated the use of bilingual dictionaries for topic translation, with a variety of elaborations to improve their effectiveness for this task (Hull & Grefenstette, 1996). In its simplest form, this approach replaces each word in the search request with all possible translations of the word in the document language appearing in a bilingual dictionary. As well as including the appropriate translation, if it is available in the dictionary, this simple method often introduces many contextually inappropriate translations of this word. These incorrect translations have been shown to significantly degrade CLIR retrieval effectiveness relative to monolingual IR for the same set of requests and documents. It has been demonstrated that dictionary-based CLIR performance can be improved by using careful phrase translation, and relevance feedback both prior to and after translation of the request (Ballesteros & Croft, 1998).

Given the problems with ambiguity arising from the use of bilingual dictionaries, and the gaps which occur with regard to their coverage of domain specific vocabulary items, alternative methods have been explored which align comparable corpora in the different languages (Sheridan & Ballerini, 1996). Related terms appearing in this aligned content are used to translate requests in a context specific way. One of the problems with this strategy is that suitable related corpora are often not available for alignment. A widely explored way to overcome this problem is to use content from the internet (Nie, Simard, Isabelle, & Durand, 1999). In this approach large numbers of web pages are collected and aligned, and then used for request translation. Nie et al. demonstrated that an improvement in retrieval effectiveness can be obtained by using the aligned web documents in combination with a bilingual dictionary.

Perhaps the most obvious solution to crossing the language barrier between requests and documents is to use a standard commercial machine translation system. Indeed for CLIR using document translation, machine translation would appear to be the only realistic option given the huge amount of ambiguity that the other translation methods would introduce. Certainly I'm not aware of work which attempts to translate whole document collections using a different method. The arguments in favour of machine translation for CLIR centre on the potential for accurate translation of the words, appearing in the request or the document, which can be achieved by bringing sophisticated translation resources to bear on the task. Current machine translation systems often produce rather unnatural prose output. However this is not a problem for CLIR where we are only interested in the reliable translation of words with good relevance selectivity. The arguments against machine translation for CLIR are based on the previously stated issues of poor linguistic structure in search requests, which can render them difficult for formal linguistic analysis using machine translation, with consequential translation failures and inappropriate translation of words. Dictionary limitations can also result in translation problems with domain specific words for both requests and documents.

My former colleagues and I at Toshiba performed a comparative evaluation of progressively more sophisticated request translation strategies ranging from simple bilingual dictionary lookup, to part-of-speech tagging, sense disambiguation, and full machine translation for an English - Japanese CLIR task (Jones, Sakai, Collier, Kumano, & Sumita, 1999). Perhaps surprisingly given the arguments against machine translation for CLIR, the best retrieval effectiveness was found using full machine translation. This result was observed for both natural language request statements, and requests modified to disrupt the linguistic structure by removing the function words prior to translation. More recent experiments have shown that a combination of machine translation and the Okapi BM25 probabilistic model combined with relevance feedback produces among the best reported effectiveness for the CLEF CLIR tasks (Jones & Lam-Adesina, 2001) (Lam-Adesina & Jones, 2003). Analysis of the retrieval behaviour of individual requests showed that there is sensitivity to the failure to translate important words, usually previously unseen proper nouns. For example, failure to translate phonetic loan word proper nouns rendered in katakana in Japanese if they are not present in the translation dictionary, significantly degrades retrieval effectiveness. This will often be a problem for bilingual dictionaries as well; although, its impact on retrieval performance may be masked by translation ambiguity issues. However comparable corpora should be able to capture these domain specific translations, as long as they include documents covering the appropriate related topics in their training set.

Many papers have been published describing CLIR results in recent years. The references included here are generally those which first introduced or advocated a particular translation approach for CLIR, in each case subsequent work has often extended these methods. While machine translation shows good results when available, bilingual dictionaries and aligned corpora remain an important translation resource for CLIR with language pairs for which well developed machine translation tools are not available. There are direct bilingual dictionaries available between most major languages pairs, and even for minority languages there are bilingual dictionaries to major languages such as English, while the expanding amounts of electronic text available from many sources mean that corpus-based methods will become an increasingly important resource.

4.2. Multilingual Information Retrieval

In MLIR the IR system is expected to respond to a search request in one language by generating a ranked list of potentially relevant documents in multiple languages. Similar to CLIR, MLIR can be approached using either a request or document translation strategy. The challenges of MLIR include similar translation issues to CLIR; however it also introduces a significant new problem which arises because the documents in each language will often be in separate collections. In a practical system document collections may be geographically distributed with no option to merge them into a single collection. However, even if the documents can be combined into a single physical collection, the fact that they are in different languages means that semantically related search terms cannot be conflated, and effectively it will still behave as separate, language specific, sub-collections. The major difficulty that arises for the MLIR is how to take the separate outputs from searching individual collections and merge them into a single output list for delivery to the user, which reliably ranks relevant documents higher than non-relevant ones. For this reason, MLIR is often seen as being akin to monolingual distributed IR, where separate search collections are stored and searched independently for practical or commercial reasons (Callan, 2000).

The merging problem arises since ranked lists from the separate collections will be generated using different indexing strategies, and, as discussed earlier, the features will have varied distributions for the individual languages. This means that the document matching scores from the retrieved ranked document lists will generally be incompatible. For example, documents retrieved from a collection with higher average matching scores will tend to be favoured in the merged list. Thus the list may be biased towards certain collections regardless of the actual relative likelihood of documents retrieved from these collections being relevant. If this problem is overcome, a further concern is that the matching score profiles of the lists may be different. Hence the lists cannot be merged in a simple reliable way. In general for distributed IR, difficulties of list merging vary depending on the number of differences between the IR systems used to compute the separate lists, and potentially the cooperation between the maintainers of the separate search engines (Callan, 2000). If the separate retrieval systems use different retrieval ranking algorithms then the scores will clearly be incompatible, but even if an identical retrieval strategy is used for all the collections, the matching scores will be incompatible due to the different values used to estimate the term weights or other ranking parameters. In MLIR, these issues are compounded by problems arising from the variations in the properties of the languages. For document translation MLIR, if the document index data are located physically together, the index files can be combined to form a single search collection. This removes the need for merging of separate lists. However, if the collections are distributed or request translation is being used, some method of merging must be adopted.

A variety of list merging algorithms of varying complexity have been proposed for distributed IR. A number of these have been applied for MLIR with varying degrees of success. The simplest approach involves ignoring the score incompatibility problem, and simply merging the ranked lists using their raw scores. More complex methods involve ranking the separate collections in terms of their estimated likelihood of containing relevant documents, combining these collection matching scores with the matching scores of individual documents to form a composite score, and using this combined score to generate the final merged document list. These methods have been shown to effective for monolingual distributed IR (Callan, 2000). Unfortunately, they have not proved so successful for MLIR, where it has been difficult to improve performance beyond that achieved using the simplest methods (Lam-Adesina & Jones, 2003) (Savoy, 2004).

In our experiments for the CLEF workshop MLIR task in 2003, we translated all the documents from their original languages of French, German and Spanish into English using machine translation. We then compared retrieval effectiveness of various list merging strategies with that for a single collection formed from the translated documents. Overall we found that the single collection method worked best indicating that all the merging strategies fell short of the performance that could potentially be achieved using these document sets (Lam-Adesina and Jones, 2003). Once again our results showed that the BM25 Okapi probabilistic model produced among the best retrieval effectiveness for this task. Of course it will not always be possible to translate the entire retrieval collections and then combine them, and thus merging is an important ongoing concern for MLIR requiring further investigation.

5. MULTIMEDIA INFORMATION RETRIEVAL

The current expansion in archives of digital multimedia content is creating the need for tools to automatically search and retrieve material from these collections. Similar to the work on multilingual text documents, recent years have seen a rapid increase in research exploring Multimedia Information Retrieval (MIR). Multimedia archives comprise material in one or more of audio or visual media, often accompanied by some form of electronic text annotation. Retrieval from these collections raises a number of issues with respect to both the indexing and retrieval processes. Multimedia content can be either static, in case of individual digitised images such photographs or paintings, or temporal, comprising audio and/or video content. The static or temporal nature introduces various concerns with respect to the presentation to the user and browsing of retrieved content.

Indexing and retrieval methods for MIR depend on the media under consideration. Let us consider these in order of increasing complexity. Electronic text material available for MIR can either take the form of metadata or direct transcription of content. Metadata may describe the content in some way, e.g. the names or roles of the characters appearing in an image, or the events taking place in a video. Transcriptions of linguistic content may be generated manually or automatically. For example, the close captioning often broadcast with TV sources can be captured and used as a high quality transcription of the content for the purpose of retrieval and browsing.

Existing IR research has focussed very much on linguistic content, and so can in general be applied directly to manually annotated material associated with multimedia content. The usefulness of manually entered descriptive metadata will depend on the quality of the data, and its relevance to an individual request. Thus, while the visual content of an image may make it relevant to a particular request, if the descriptive metadata is not pertinent to the aspect of this item which makes it relevant, then the MIR system will fail to locate it. Thus the effectiveness of MIR will clearly be affected by the accuracy and richness of the annotation. Additionally, the complexity of the retrieval methods used for textual annotations may be influenced by their complexity; if the annotations are highly structured, this may be taken into account in the retrieval algorithms adopted.

Of more interest within recent and current research, is MIR based on automated annotation of the content. The following sections consider indexing and retrieval for first spoken documents, and then image and video data.

5.1. Spoken Document Retrieval

In many situations it is uneconomic or impractical to manually transcribe the spoken contents of multimedia documents, and thus transcriptions must be generated automatically using speech recognition technologies. Forming transcriptions in this way using current speech recognition tools has a number of limitations. The most significant issue is that, like machine translation systems used for CLIR, these tools make mistakes; incorrect words can be inserted into the transcription, correct words deleted, or one word incorrectly substituted for another one. These errors arise for a number of reasons relating to both the natural language data and the tools themselves. Speech recognition is inherently challenging for a number of reasons including the following: the speech may be poorly articulated, it may not follow expected linguistic patterns, it may be captured using poor quality equipment, there may be high levels of background or environmental noise, or there may be crosstalk where more than one speaker is talking at the same time. The accuracy of a speech recognition system is limited by the effectiveness of its acoustic models to accurately recognise the sound patterns of the current speaker, and of its language models to predict their use of word patterns. Current speech recognition transcription systems are also correctly described as "large vocabulary", where only the words within a predefined vocabulary can be recognised correctly; other so called "out-of-vocabulary" words will be transcribed incorrectly by definition. In general, the overall accuracy of an automatically generated document transcript will depend on the extent to which the speech deviates from the trained parameters of the speech recognition system and the quality of the input speech signal.

The effect of recognition errors is to produce a "noisy" transcription which will have some similarities to the output of a machine translation system. The characteristics of the errors however are likely to be somewhat different. A machine translation system can determine its output, although it may experience problems with the naturalness of the word patterns generated, or be subject to limitations in the richness of the available vocabulary or linguistic structures. By contrast, a speech recognition system must do its best to transcribe the data presented to it. Automatic transcriptions often include apparently random insertion and deletion errors. A potential problem for both machine translation and speech recognition though is how to appropriately handle input words outside their vocabulary.

Research into spoken document retrieval (SDR) began with a number of projects in the early 1990's. These examined various approaches to automatically indexing the spoken contents and were evaluated using locally developed test collections (Glavitsch & Schäuble, 1992) (Jones, Foote, Sparck Jones, & Young, 1996). When these projects started, the potential of IR techniques derived from experience with electronic text documents to transfer successfully to errorful spoken document index files was very much an open question.

Video Mail Retrieval using Voice (VMR) at Cambridge University was one of these early SDR projects. Karen Spärck Jones and myself worked with others to investigate the impact on retrieval effectiveness of several approaches to spoken document recognition. The VMR project used a small test collection of 300 voice mail messages to explore SDR effectiveness. We used the BM25 model to compare retrieval behaviour for manually created message transcriptions with those generated using a 20,000 word large vocabulary system and an alternative technique known as *phone lattice spotting (PLS)* (Jones et al., 1996). In neither case was the recognition system specifically adapted for the indexing of these messages. The transcription system was trained for a broadcast news recognition task, and achieved an average word error rate of 47%. PLS uses subword level speech recognition to form a phone lattice structure. The lattice is scanned for phone strings corresponding to possible occurrences of words appearing in a search request, as such it is an open-vocabulary indexing method able to recognise any word appearing in a message. Experiments using the VMR test collection demonstrated retrieval effectiveness of around 70-75% of that for manual transcriptions for both these recognition techniques, rising to around 85% when they were used in combination.

It is a feature of speech recognition that the hardest words to recognise accurately are often short function words. Of course, these are generally not useful for retrieval, and hence SDR systems can still operate with good reliability in the presence of relatively high word recognition error rates. A further issue is that since important words within a document are often repeated, even if the word is recognised incorrectly when it occurs in one place, it may be correctly recognised elsewhere in the document. Whilst errors of this type will degrade the overall quality of term weights, the documents will still be retrieved. This distortion of term weights can result in some distortion of the ranked retrieval list, relative that to that which would be achieved with a perfect document transcription, but overall high levels of retrieval effectiveness can still be achieved.

Interest in SDR increased significantly in the mid-1990's and a track was introduced at the annual TREC series in 1997. For the first time researchers were able to work with a common SDR test collection. The SDR track ran for 4 years, each conference increased the document collection size or the complexity of the retrieval task. During this time speech recognition technologies continued to advance. Using the best available transcription systems, achieving recognition average word errors rates of around 20% with a vocabulary of around 65,000 words, together with the BM25 model and retrieval enhancement techniques, such as relevance feedback and merging with in-domain large contemporaneous text collections, TREC SDR participants demonstrated similar overall retrieval effectiveness for manual and automatic document transcriptions (Johnson, Jourlin, Sparck Jones, & Woodland, 2001) (Garafolo, Auzanne, & Voorhees, 2000). The success of the TREC SDR track indicated, at least for a task where the transcription system can be well trained for the domain of the document collection, in this case broadcast news, that SDR is effective using current speech recognition technologies. Most MIR research interest has now moved to the new challenges of image and video retrieval.

5.2. Image and Video Retrieval

Whereas it is natural to use the same indexing units for spoken content and written linguistic content, the appropriate mechanism for indexing and retrieving from visual media is much less clear. Visual content can include natural scenes either in static images or moving video, as well as other image content, for example scanned or overlaid textual material.

Considering first the more straightforward case of textual content in images. The first stage in automatically indexing this material is to identify zones or regions in the image containing text. The text in these zones is then recognised using an optical character recognition (OCR) process. After this, it can be indexed using a standard retrieval approach derived from experience with electronic text documents. Unfortunately, similar to speech recognition systems, OCR systems make mistakes; although the errors in this case are often of a different form. Instead of making whole word recognition errors, as is the case for speech recognition, OCR systems typically make errors in the recognition of individual characters. Each of these errors will usually introduce a new word into the indexing vocabulary of the collection. These words will not be useful indexing terms, since they will not match correctly with terms appearing in typed search requests, and they will also have disproportionately high collection frequency weights, since they are very rare within the document collection. A simple way to resolve this problem might be to attempt to correct automatically the spelling of these words using a dictionary. However, it is not always clear what the correct word should be. Indeed sometimes a word not present in the dictionary will actually have been correctly recognised by the OCR system, and attempting to correct OCR errors in this way may replace these accurately recognised words with incorrect words taken from the dictionary. As a consequence of this problem, "correcting" the OCR output with a dictionary may lead to a degrading of retrieval effectiveness. Another issue, similar to spoken document recognition, is that the accuracy of the output of an OCR system will be related to the difficulty of the recognition task. OCR accuracy will depend on the quality of the printing, the fonts used, and the contrast between the print and the paper. For example, modern laser printed output with a simple font is easier to recognise than older mechanically printed documents for which the paper may be yellowing with age. Significantly more difficult to recognise accurately is handwritten text, for which accuracy will obviously depend on how clearly it has been written, as well as the other factors affecting printed text.

Experimental exploration of scanned text image retrieval has demonstrated that the BM25 model once again performs well for this task with printed data (Jones & Lam-Adesina, 2002). To the best of my knowledge its effectiveness for more difficult hand written documents has at present not been examined, although work using a statistical relevance model for retrieval of handwritten historical documents is reported by Rath, Manmatha, & Lavrenk (2004). Interestingly, while relevance feedback has been shown to be very effective for SDR (Johnson et al., 2001), the differences in error types encountered between OCR and speech generated transcripts, mean that it does not transfer to scanned text documents in a simple way (Jones & Lam-Adesina, 2002).

A much less well defined task is the retrieval of multimedia documents based on non-linguistic visual content. When examining a visual scene, we might want to identify any number of different features. For example, we may wish to recognise the individuals appearing in the image, the place where the scene is taking place, the objects in the picture, or perhaps the events being depicted. Identifying these features is very difficult. Indeed doing this in a robust way outside a very narrow pre-defined domain is currently not possible. Much visual media can be interpreted in a seemingly unlimited, often subjective, number of ways. This type of intelligent analysis will be beyond analysis of visual features alone, often requiring knowledge outside that available in the visual content itself. Of course, texts can frequently be interpreted in many ways as well, but for retrieval purposes, word level indexing has generally been shown to be effective without needing to determine any particular interpretation of the text. In the case of images, not only are attempts at recognising features unreliable, there is no obvious parallel means of selecting indexing units for open domain retrieval. Current video media retrieval systems either focus on very narrow domains, for example identifying pictures of predefined named individuals, or seek to index images using low-level features, such as colour or texture. Indexing images using such low-level features is perhaps comparable to identifying the letters in a text document without determining what the words are.

The difficulty in indexing images and of specifying search queries for them means that retrieval of visual media inherently requires more user interaction than text retrieval. A user will typically initiate a search either using a text request which will locate some potentially relevant images or video based on their textual annotation, or they will select a sample image and request the retrieval system to "find me more like this", in response to which the system returns images with similar colour and texture profiles to those of the example. The user is then able to provide feedback on the images retrieved using this initial query, after which further searches are carried out, with feedback after each one, until the user's information need has been satisfied.

Since 2001 the TRECVID workshop has provided standard document collections for researchers to explore indexing and retrieval tasks for video data (Smeaton, Kraaji, and Over, 2004). Tasks undertaken in TRECVID include: automated shot boundary detection, visual feature recognition, locating named individuals or events in video, and interactive searching of a video archive. TRECVID is proving instructive in the development and evaluation of MIR technologies, but perhaps the clearest message so far is the large amount of work that remains to be done to achieve mature MIR systems.

6. CONCLUDING THOUGHTS AND FUTURE CHALLENGES

This chapter has demonstrated how fundamental work on English language text information retrieval has been successfully applied for multilingual and multimedia documents. In each case the underlying probabilistic model has contributed to an effective IR system. For text retrieval in a new language it has been illustrated that the need is for the selection of appropriate indexing units and development of automatic indexing methods, including morphological processing, stop word lists, and suffix stripping algorithms. Research issues for CLIR relate primarily to translation methods to cross the language barrier between search requests and documents. For MLIR issues of translation are compounded with the need for effective merging of the document lists retrieved from different language collections. Speech and scanned text document retrieval have been shown to be remarkably robust to indexing errors in automatic recognition of their content. It is only in the area of visual media where Karen Spärck Jones's work in IR has not been fully explored. It is perhaps interesting to speculate as to whether the probabilistic model might be successfully adapted for indexing and retrieval of visual media. The ongoing issues of defining and recognising visual indexing features continue to be the focus of much research in visual media retrieval. However, the lessons from spoken and scanned text document retrieval suggest that a probabilistic IR model applied for visual retrieval would be robust to considerable degrees of indexing errors. However, there is already research underway exploring the use of the alternative language modelling approach to IR in visual retrieval (Westerveld and de Vries, 2004).

Solution of the problems of multilingual and multimedia information retrieval explored in this chapter does not represent the end of the story for research into information access technologies for this data. Research interest continues to evolve to embrace more challenging tasks. For example, work is currently being established in the areas of retrieval from multilingual collections of image and video archives, retrieval from multilingual web collections, and question-answering methods for multilingual and multimedia data.

Gareth J. F. Jones obtained a B.Eng in Electrical and Electronic Engineering from the University of Bristol, and a PhD examining the Application of Linguistic Models in Continuous Speech Recognition from the same institution. Subsequently he worked with Karen Spärck Jones on the Video Mail Retrieval using Voice (VMR) project at the University of Cambridge, and was then appointed as a Lecturer in Department of Computer Science at the University of Exeter. From 1997-98 he was a Toshiba Fellow at the Toshiba Corporation Research and Development Center in Kawasaki, Japan. In 2003 he was appointed as a Senior Lecturer in the School of Computing at Dublin City University.

REFERENCES

Ballesteros, L., & Croft, W. B. (1998). Resolving Ambiguity for Cross-Language Retrieval. In *Proceedings of the 21st Annual International ACM SIGIR Conference on Research and Development in Information Retrieval*, pp. 64-71, Melbourne, ACM.

Braschler, M., & Ripplinger, B. (2004). How Effective is Stemming and Decompounding for German Text Retrieval? *Information Retrieval*, 7(3-4), 291-316, Kluwer.

Callan, J. (2000). Distributed Information Retrieval. In W. B. Croft, editor, *Advances in Information Retrieval*, pp. 127-150. Kluwer.

Garafolo, J. S., Auzanne, C. G. P., & Voorhees, E. M. (2000). The TREC Spoken Document Retrieval Track: A Success Story. In *Proceedings of the RIAO 2000 Conference: Content-Based Multimedia Information Access*, pp. 1-20, Paris.

Glavitsch, U., & Schäuble. P. (1992). A System for Retrieving Speech Documents. In *Proceedings of the 15th Annual International ACM SIGIR Conference on Research and Development in Information Retrieval*, pp. 168-176. ACM.

Gollins, T., & Sanderson, M. (2001). Improving Cross Language Retrieval with Triangulated Translation, In *Proceedings of the 24th Annual International ACM SIGIR Conference on Research and Development in Information Rretrieval*, pp 90-95, New Orleans, ACM.

Huang, X., & Robertson, S. E. (1997). Application of Probabilistic Methods to Chinese Text Retrieval. *Journal of Documentation*, 53(1), 74-79.

Hull, D. A., & Grefenstette. G. (1996). Querying Across Languages: A Dictionary-Based Approach to Multilingual Information Retrieval. In *Proceedings of the 19th Annual International ACM SIGIR Conference on Research and Development in Information Retrieval*, pages 49-57, Zürich, ACM.

Johnson, S. E., Jourlin, P., Sparck Jones, K., & Woodland, P. C. (2001). Spoken Document Retrieval for TREC-9 at Cambridge University. In E. M. Voorhees and D. K. Harman, editors, *Proceedings of the Ninth Text REtrieval Conference (TREC-9)*, pp. 117-126. NIST.

Jones, G. J. F., Foote, J. T., Sparck Jones, K., & Young, S. J. (1996). Retrieving Spoken Documents by Combining Multiple Index Sources. In *Proceedings of the 19th Annual International ACM SIGIR Conference on Research and Development in Information Retrieval*, pp. 30-38, Zürich,. ACM.

Jones, G. J. F., Sakai, T., Kajiura, M., & Sumita, K. (1998). Experiments in Japanese Text Retrieval and Routing using the NEAT System. In *Proceedings of the 21st Annual International ACM SIGIR Conference on Research and Development in Information Retrieval*, pp. 197-205, Melbourne, ACM.

Jones, G. J. F., Sakai, T., Collier, N. H., Kumano, A., & Sumita, K. (1999). A Comparison of Query Translation Methods for English-Japanese Cross-Language Information Retrieval. In *Proceedings of the 22nd Annual International ACM SIGIR Conference on Research and Development in Information Retrieval*, pp. 269-270, San Francisco, ACM.

Jones, G. J. F., & Lam-Adesina, A. M. (2001). Exeter at CLEF 2001: Experiments with Machine Translation for bilingual retrieval. In *Proceedings of the CLEF 2001: Workshop on Cross-Language Information Retrieval and Evaluation*, pp. 59-77, Darmstadt, Springer Verlag.

Jones, G. J. F., & Lam-Adesina, A. M. (2002). An Investigation of Mixed-Media Information Retrieval. In *Proceedings of the 6th European Conference on Digital Libraries*, pp. 463-478, Rome, Springer Verlag.

Lam-Adesina, A. M., & Jones, G. J. F. (2003). Exeter at CLEF 2003: Experiments with Machine Translation for Monolingual and Bilingual and Multilingual Retrieval. In *Proceedings of the CLEF 2003: Workshop on Cross-Language Information Retrieval and Evaluation*, Trondheim, Springer.

McCarley, J. S. (1999). Should we Translate the Documents or the Queries in Cross-language Information Retrieval. In *Proceedings of the 37th Annual Meeting of the Association for Computational Linguistics (ACL 99)*, pp. 208-214, University of Maryland, MD, ACL.

Nie, J.-Y., Simard, M., Isabelle, P., & Durand, R. (1999). Cross-Language Information Retrieval Based on Parallel Texts and Automatic Mining of Parallel Texts from the Web. In *Proceedings of the 22nd AAnnual International ACM SIGI Conference on Research and Development in Information Retrieval*, pp. 74-81, San Francisco, ACM.

Ponte, J. M., & Croft, W. B. (1998). A Language Modelling Approach to Information Retrieval. In *Proceedings of the 21st Annual International ACM SIGIR International Conference on Research and Development in Information Retrieval*, pp275-281, Melbourne, ACM.

Porter, M. F. (1980). An algorithm for suffix stripping. *Program*, 14, 130-137.

Rath, T., Manmatha, R., & Lavrenko, V. (2004). A Search Engine for Historical Manuscript Images. In *Proceedings of the 27th Annual International ACM SIGIR International Conference on Research and Development in Information Retrieval*, pp369-376, Sheffield, ACM.

Robertson, S. E. (1977). The Probability Ranking Principle in IR. *Journal of Documentation*, 33, 294-304.

Robertson, S. E., & Sparck Jones, K. (1976). Relevance weighting of search terms. *Journal of the American Society for Information Science*, 27, 129-146.

Robertson, S. E., & Walker, S. (1994). Some simple effective approximations to the 2-Poisson model for probabilistic weighted retrieval. In *Proceedings of the 17th Annual International ACM SIGIR Conference on Research and Development in Information Retrieval*, pp. 232-241, Dublin, ACM.

Robertson, S. E., Walker, S. & Beaulieu, M. M. (1999). Okapi at TREC-7: automatic ad hoc, filtering, vls and interactive track. In E. Voorhees and D. K. Harman, editors, *Proceedings of the Seventh Text REtrieval Conference (TREC-7)*, pp. 253-264. NIST.

Sakai, T., Koyama, M., Kumano, A., & Manabe, T. (2004). Toshiba BRIDJE at NTCIR-4 CLIR: Monolingual/Bilingual IR and Flexible Feedback. In *Proceedings of NTCIR-4*.

Salton, G, & Buckley, C. (1988). Term-Weighting Approaches in Automatic Text Retrieval. Information Processing and Management, 24, 513-523, Elsevier.

Savoy, J. (2004). Combining Multiple Strategies for Effective Monolingual and Cross-Language Retrieval. *Information Retrieval*, 7(1-2), 121-148, Kluwer.

Sheridan, P. & Ballerini, J. P. (1996). Experiments in Multilingual Information Retrieval using the SPIDER system. In *Proceedings of the 19th Annual International ACM SIGIR Conference on Research and Development in Information Retrieval*, pp. 58-65, Zürich, ACM.

Smeaton, A. F., Kraaji, W., & Over, P. (2004). The TREC Video Retrieval Evaluation (TRECVID);' A Case Study and Status Report. In *Proceedings of RIAO 2004 – Coupling Approaches, Coupling Media and Coupling Languages for Information Retrieval*, pp. 25-37, Avignon.

Sparck Jones, K., Walker, S., & Robertson, S. E. (2000a). A probabilistic model of information retrieval: development and comparative experiments: Part 1. *Information Processing and Management*, 36(6), 779-808, Elsevier.

Sparck Jones, K., Walker, S., & Robertson, S. E. (2000b). A probabilistic model of information retrieval: development and comparative experiments: Part 2. *Information Processing and Management*, 36(6), 809-840, Elsevier.

van Rijsbergen, C. J. (1979). *Information Retrieval*. (2nd edition) Butterworths.

Wechsler, M., Sheridan, P., & Schäuble, P. (1997). Experiments in Multilingual Information Retrieval using the SPIDER System. In *Proceedings of the 5th RIAO Conference, Computer-Assisted Information Searching on the Internet*, Montreal.

Westerveld, T. & de Vries, A. P. (2004). Multimedia Retrieval Using Multiple Examples. In *Proceedings of the Third International Conference on Image and Video Retrieval*, pp. 344-352, Dublin, Springer.

MARK T. MAYBURY

KAREN SPÄRCK JONES AND SUMMARIZATION

1. INTRODUCTION

For someone whose speaking rate was rumoured to serve as a benchmark[1], Karen was probably in least need of summarization aids because she could communicate so much in so little time. But then again given how prolific Karen was communicatively, her listeners including her students, research assistants, conference attendees, colleagues, and friends probably would have paid well for such a spoken language summarization device. As in the others fields, text summarization has benefited from Karen's broad but at the same time direct and precise thoughts ranging from user and source issues, to algorithms, to scientific methodology.

2. EARLY INTEREST

Karen's early interest in summarization is quite possibly a result of her early research in the 1950's and 1960's in information retrieval. Faced with mounds of documents and an eye toward enhancing document access, Karen explored methods to enhance retrieval. Because of computing and storage limitations, research often took place on human generated abstracts of source documents, such as scientific paper abstracts. Her thesis research (Sparck Jones 1964) focused on the core idea that word classes could be derived by clustering based on lexical co-occurrence. From the lens of summarization, this can be viewed as an effort in the distillation and summarization of semantics from a corpus. Some of her subsequent information retrieval experiments demonstrated that keyword clustering could enhance retrieval (although she discovered it enhanced precision not recall, as expected). Term frequencies were a key aspect of this analysis.

Around the same period, Luhn (1958) at IBM explored the selection of salient information based on term frequency. Later, Edmundson (1969) compared term frequency with other features, including cue phrases (e.g., "significant", "impossible", "hardly"), title and heading words, and sentence location. Then a few

---

John I. Tait (ed.), *Charting a New Course: Natural Language Processing and Information Retrieval. Essays in Honour of Karen Spärck Jones*. 99-103

years later, Pollock and Zamora (1973) described an abstracting program at Chemical Abstracts Service that used cue-phrases specific to chemistry subdomains both as positive (bonus word) and negative (stigma word) tests for selection of sentences, which were then compacted based on shallow linguistic analyses.

3. KICK STARTING AN INTERNATIONAL COMMUNITY

In characteristic style, Karen was an instigator of the December 1993 Dagstuhl Seminar "Summarizing Text for Intelligent Communication". Karen and Brigitte Endres-Niggemeyer corralled the top summarization researchers along with some professional human abstractors across the world for about a week into the 18th century manor Schloss Dagstuhl, The International Conference and Research Center for Computer Science nestled in Wadern Germany, about an hour north of Saarbruecken. Here Karen helped shape an international focus on this important natural language research area. The Dagstuhl Seminar culminated in the first collection of papers related to document summarization which appeared in 1995 in a special issue on Text Summarization of the *Journal of Information Processing and Management* (Sparck Jones and Endres-Niggemeyer 1995). In her introduction to that special collection, Karen notes the combination of increasing amounts of electronic text combined with advancements in natural language processing as motivating "the first [Seminar] wholly devoted to automatic summarizing". She continues:

> However, the Seminar recognized that progress in automatic summarizing demands a multi- or inter-disciplinary approach drawing on relevant ideas and experience from several different subject areas ... The Seminar sought a more comprehensive view of the requirements, resources, and possibilities for summarizing, both to provide better motivation for medium-term implementation and a solid ground for longer-term research. This would, moreover, ensure that summarizing was correctly seen not only in its conventional role as providing fixed surrogates for stored documents, but as a dynamic activity as creating summaries in particular contexts to suit individual data and user needs. (p. 625).

Professional human abstractors had been invited to the seminar. Together with the researchers, they created abstracts, in part, to explore computational models inspired by human performance.

A few years later, Karen introduced the first book collection on automated summarization (Mani and Maybury 1999) with a position paper that outlined the challenges facing the field. This collection reported that modern summarization techniques could reduce by as much as 80% the material needed to be read without recall or precision loss. It also proposed a three-phased architecture including interpretation (i.e., analysis), transformation, and generation (i.e., synthesis).

Karen discussed challenges within this summarization framework. She stressed the need to carefully examine factors such as the nature of the input, output, and the purpose for which summaries are being used. She suggested a near-term strategy for the field of text summarization, aiming (conservatively) at the goal of producing "sufficient for the day" indicative summaries using a variety of linguistic processing methods. In her hallmark manner of perspicuously characterizing the nature and scope of a problem, Karen articulated the importance of distinguishing input factors (source form, subject type, unit), purpose factors (situation, audience, use), and output factors (material, format, style) with respect to summarization (Sparck Jones 1999).

4. DISCOURSE MODELING FOR SUMMARIZATION

Karen championed important ideas such as the move from purely surface level statistical approaches toward the use of rhetorical structure and/or discourse purpose segmentation to enhance extraction of relevant units from source texts. Karen (Sparck Jones 1993) noted how the process of summarization could exploit linguistic (i.e., thematic units), world (i.e., linked facts), and/or communicative (e.g., speech acts) units, either for content selection or content generalization. Thus, for bottom-up selection, a method could select the most mentioned entity (linguistic), the most novel or explanatory fact (world), or the most significant communicative function.

In a "deliberately restricted" comparative analysis using ten paragraphs (3 "noddy" texts and 7 newspaper articles) Karen simulated processing on three levels: linguistic, knowledge (e.g., scripts and frames), and communicative (e.g., discourse intentions and rhetorical structures). She found that all of these different kinds of structural information were needed to adequately represent the source and, thus, support effective summarization. Karen also pointed out, as evidenced by DeJong's (1979) FRUMP, that "reasonable and appropriate summaries may still be obtained for particular contexts by type-limited strategies" (p. 225).

5. TEXT SUMMARIZATION EVALUATION

Having a long background in creating ideal collections to support systematic comparative evaluations (e.g., Sparck Jones and Rijsbergen 1975), it was only natural that Karen would leverage her extensive experience when document summarization evaluation came to the fore. Interestingly, when specifying guidelines for the "ideal" retrieval test collection, she indicated that individual collection items should include, among other items: "(a) full text (b) abstract (c) title (d) free extracted keywords or keyword string, derived from full text, abstract, and title"(p. 65).

Karen provided leadership in this area in such formal roles as a member of the DARPA/NIST Text Retrieval Conferences Program Committee since 1994, and member of the DARPA Translingual Information Extraction Detection and Summarization (TIDES) Program Advisory Committee since 1999. Furthermore, as Donna Harman (2003) points out, in 2000 Karen was a major contributor to a summarization roadmap (Baldwin et al. 2000) to guide DARPA-sponsored summarization evaluation and the associated Document Understanding Conference (DUC). The first major evaluation in the Fall of 2001 directly (as opposed to within a particular task) evaluated generic summaries from English newswire and newspaper articles. While generic summaries (i.e., ones not focused on a particular situation, audience or use) may result in greater human judgment variability, they occur frequently in practice. Also, the task included summarization of individual documents and sets of documents (there were 60 sets of 10 documents). Over time, it is expected that deeper language understanding and task-and user-focused summarization will support more sophisticated summarization. Machine generated summaries were compared by human assessors to human created baselines.

15 groups participated in DUC-2001, with all but 3 pulling out extracts as opposed to generating abstracts. 17 groups participated in DUC-2002, with 13 focusing on single document summarization at 100 words, eight of them on a multidocument task. Two common evaluation metrics were used: a length adjusted coverage metric and brevity. Also, previously inconsistent judgments of grammaticality, coherence, and organization were improved by replacing these vague metrics with a series of specific measures of phenomena such as proper anaphora, subject/verb agreement, and dangling connectives. 21 groups participated in DUC-2003 which consisted of four tasks including very short "headline" summary (10 words) for 300 single documents (13 groups participated), short summaries (100 words) of 10 documents about an event (16 groups did this one), short summaries of 10 documents on a topic from a specific viewpoint (11 tried this), and short summaries of 10 documents relevant to a given question (9 tried this). Over these first three years, common tasks and common evaluations helped researchers identify real problems, learn from one another, and refine their research and evaluation strategies. This all is very much in the spirit of Karen's original motivations behind the "ideal" IR test collection several decades prior.

6. SUMMARY FUTURE

Human summarization already plays a crucial role in our daily lives, from newspaper headlines, to book digests, to movie reviews, to biographies and obituaries, to short wireless messages. Expanding volumes and availability of information promises automated summarization an increasingly important role. Already there exist practical demonstrations of capabilities such as medical patient record summarization, broadcast news video summarization, multilingual summarization, and even audio summarization. In summary, we are once again blessed with Karen's clarity of thought and communication in crucial topics encompassing user, source, methodology, and evaluation issues in summarization.

Dr. Mark Maybury is Executive Director of MITRE's Information Technology Division. Mark also serves as Executive Director of ARDA's Northeast Regional Research Center (nrrc.mitre.org). He serves on the Board of Directors of the Object Management Group. Mark has published over sixty refereed articles. He is editor of Intelligent Multimedia Interfaces (AAAI/MIT Press 1993), Intelligent Multimedia Information Retrieval (AAAI/MIT Press 1997), New Directions in Question Answering (AAAI/ MIT Press 2004), co-editor of Readings on Intelligent User Interfaces (Morgan Kaufmann Press 1998), Advances in Text Summarization (MIT Press 1999), Advances in Knowledge Management (MIT Press 2001) and

Personalized Digital Television (Kluwer Academic, 2004), and co-author of Information Storage and Retrieval (Kluwer Academic 2000). Mark received his B.A. in Mathematics from the College of the Holy Cross, an M. Phil. in Computer Speech and Language Processing from Cambridge University, England, an M.B.A. from Rensselaer Polytechnic Institute and a Ph.D. in Artificial Intelligence from Cambridge University.

REFERENCES

Baldwin, B., Donaway, R., Hovy, E., Liddy, E., Mani, I., Marcu, D., McKeown, K., Mittal, V., Moens, M., Radev, D., McKeown, K., Mittal, V., Moens, M., Radev, D., Sparck Jones, K., Sundheim, B., Teufel, S., Weischedel, R., and White, M. 2000. An evaluation roadmap for summarization research. http://duc.nist.gov/roadmapping.html.

DeJong, G. F. 1979. Skimming stories in real time: An experiment in integrated understanding. Ph.D. Thesis. Yale University.

Gladwin, P., Pulman, S. and Sparck Jones, K. 1991. Shallow processing and automatic summarising: a first study. Technical Report No. 223, University of Cambridge, Computer Laboratory.

Harman, D. 2003. The importance of focused evaluations: A Case Study of TREC and DUC. Invited paper in the Proceeedings of the NTCIR Workshop on Chinese and Japanese Text Retrieval and Text Summarization.

Mani, I. and Maybury, M. (eds.) 1999. *Advances in Automatic Text Summarization*. MIT Press. (mitpress.mit.edu/book-home.tcl?isbn=0262133598)

Maybury, M. in press. Universal Multimedia Information Access. In Carbonelle, N. (ed.) UAIS Special Issue on Multimodality in Universal Computer Access.

Sakai, T. and Spärck Jones, K. 2001. Generic Summaries for Indexing in Information Retrieval. In Croft, W. B., Harper, D. J., Kraft, D. H. and Zobel, J. (eds.) Proceedings of the 24th Annual International ACM SIGIR Conference on Research and Development in Information Retrieval (SIGIR 2001), September 9-13, 2001, New Orleans, Louisiana, USA. 190-198.

Spärck Jones, K. 1964. Synonymy and Semantic Classification. PhD thesis. University of Cambridge; with additional chapter, "Twenty years later: a review", Edinburgh: Edinburgh University Press, 1986.

Spärck Jones, K. and van Rijsbergen, C. 1975. Report on the need for and provision of an ideal information retrieval test collection. British Library Research and Development Report 5266, Computer Laboratory, University of Cambridge.

Spärck Jones, K. 1993a. Discourse modeling for automatic summarization. Computer Laboratory TR 290, University of Cambridge. Travaux du Cercle Linguistique de Prague, New Series, Vol 1, 1995, Amsterdam, John Benjamins, 201-227.

Spärck Jones, K. 1993b. What might be in a summary? In Knorz, G., Krause, J. and Womser-Hacker, C. (eds.). Information Retrieval 93: Von der Modellierung zur Anwendung. Konstanz: Universitätverlag Kongstanz, 9-26. http://www.cl.cam.ac.uk/ftp/papers/ksj/ksj-whats-in-a-summary.ps.gz

Spärck Jones, K. and Endres-Niggemeyer, B. (eds.) 1995. *International Journal of Information Processing and Management : Special Issue on Text Summarization.* 31(5).

Spärck Jones, K., 1997. Summarizing: Where are we now? Where should we go? In Mani, I., and Maybury, M. (eds.) Proceedings of the ACL/EACL'97 Workshop on Intelligent Scalable Text Summarization, Madrid, Spain, 11 July 1997.

Spärck Jones, K. 1999. Automatic summarising: factors and directions. In Mani, I. and Maybury, M. (eds.) *Advances in Automatic Text Summarization*, Cambridge, MA: MIT Press, pp. 1-12. (http://xxx.lanl.gov/cmp-lg/9805011).

Spärck Jones, K. 2001. Factorial summary evaluation. Workshop on Text Summarization. ACM SIGIR 2001 conference. (http://www-nlpir.nist.gov/projects/duc/duc2001/duc_papers/cambridge2.pdf).

ARTHUR W.S. CATER

QUESTION ANSWERING

1. INTRODUCTION

Karen Spärck Jones has for several decades been a researcher of leading international stature in the fields of Information Retrieval (IR) and Natural Language Processing (NLP). In IR in general, persons who seek information attempt to characterise the information they seek, and a system (which may have human as well as software components) tries to assist. In the branch of IR known as Document Retrieval, a system responds not with the information sought, but with citations of documents where that information is likely to be found. In the branch known as Passage Retrieval, a system responds with excerpts from such documents. In the branch known as Fact Retrieval, a person is expected to require an answer to a question, and a system responds with an answer. These three kinds of system are contrasted in Figure 1. The documents in which Document Retrieval deals, and the passages in which Passage Retrieval deals, consist largely of text written in a natural language; the concern with identifying documents or passages likely to be relevant to a user's need for information leads to a natural interest in NLP. Fact Retrieval may be concerned with extracting information from largely-textual documents, and/or from databases or even other sources.

It is very clear that Fact Retrieval involves seeking the answer to a question, though that does not imply that the question must be phrased in a natural language. Even in the cases of Document Retrieval and Passage Retrieval, the information need can still be phrased as a question in ordinary language: "What documents (or passages) contain information on …". When one imagines a person interacting with a purely-software system whose response is expected to come in the form of documents or passages, such a question appears unnatural. But if one imagines a person interacting with another human who is engaged to act as intermediary, it is more natural. Further, if one imagines a person interacting, directly and without an intermediary, with an information management system whose response could take many forms, drawing information out of diverse kinds of resource, such a question would be entirely appropriate if citations or excerpts were indeed the preferred form of response.

Sample Factoid Question: When was the city of Dublin founded?

John I. Tait (ed.), *Charting a New Course: Natural Language Processing and Information Retrieval. Essays in Honour of Karen Spärck Jones.* 105–128
© 2005 Springer.

Kind of system:	Interpretation of result:	Result returned.
1. *DOCUMENT* RETRIEVAL	If you look for these documents you should find the answer inside:	
2. *PASSAGE* RETRIEVAL	It says here that:	
3. *FACT* RETRIEVAL	YES, I CAN TELL YOU THAT:	Dublin was founded in 988 AD.

Figure 1: Three different kinds of retrieval system

An integrated information management system such as has been envisaged in Sparck Jones (1990) would combine resources of many kinds: document collections, both personal and globally available; dictionaries; databases; and others. Access to these resources requires some form or forms of indexing, as well as some means for a user to describe the information need. The question answering research community has now adopted as its medium-term goal (Burger et al., 2002) the development of systems which can produce complex answers through fusion of results retrieved from several heterogeneous (and often large-scale) resources.

The topic of natural language access to (isolated) databases was widely investigated during the 1970s and 1980s. It was generally presumed, optimistically, that natural language would prove an ideal medium of communication for untrained users to express their requirements, that the limited domains of practical databases would necessitate only rather small vocabularies, and that translation of natural language questions into formal database queries would not be especially demanding. Spärck Jones, with co-author Ann Copestake, challenges many of the early assumptions in their widely cited paper (Copestake and Sparck Jones, 1990). They do not dismiss database access as a task for natural language question answering, but they do demonstrate that a question answering system for this application cannot be based on significantly simplifying restrictions in matters of vocabulary, knowledge representation, ability to handle extended dialog, and robustness. Nowadays, the task of open-domain question answering in context is a particular focus of attention for the research community (Burger et al., 2002), where such simplifications are manifestly inappropriate.

With the advent of the World Wide Web, the field of IR became of much more widespread interest than before. Vast quantities of text are available to all comers, who need a technology for selecting a very small relevant fragment. In Sparck Jones (1997) it is argued that there is a role for both natural language processing, and also statistically based methods of indexing and retrieval, such as have been developed in mainstream IR research over decades and are found in most of today's search engines. Both kinds of techniques are used by web-based question answering systems, such as those listed in Table 1 accessible at the time of writing. The principal role envisaged in Sparck Jones (1997) for NLP is however not to process user questions, but rather to assist in indexing and to prepare gists of extended passages, document, or sets of documents. The "Vision Statement to Guide Research in Question and Answering (Q&A) and Text Summarization" (Carbonell et al., 2000) (Spärck Jones is among the authors) is concerned with NLP for question answering and for summarization, both individually and in combination.

Running through these writings of Spärck Jones is a common theme, namely that it is important that natural language processing systems should be subjected to quantitative evaluation. Such evaluation has been a commonplace in IR for decades. Methods for evaluation in NLP have been the focus of the more recent EAGLES project (among others), and the performance of natural language question answering systems has been systematically tested in a new specific track of the most recent sessions of the long-established TREC (Text REtrieval Conference) series. In 1999, two years after the TREC Q&A tracks began, US Government agencies promoting four large-scale research programmes concerned with information management brought into being two advisory committees. The first committee, on which Karen Spärck Jones served as one of six members, was responsible for the production in April 2000 of the "Vision Statement" on the future development of question answering and text summarization; the second was responsible for recommending in 2002 a five-year phased research agenda (a "Roadmap") for achieving some or all of the vision, with progress to be evaluated in a preplanned manner through Q&A tracks of successive TRECs. Themes that have emerged in the earlier writings of Karen Spärck Jones have clearly found wide recognition and support in the international NLP research community

The bulk of this paper is organised around five major themes which have surfaced over and again in the writings of Karen Spärck Jones. In §2, we trace her observations and arguments about the usefulness for question answering of shallow techniques for indexing and retrieval, based on the use of statistics about use of words in texts rather than on understanding of the language of texts. The topic of §3 is semantic processing, whether of questions or of information found in texts or other sources, and the use of knowledge by inference processes. In §4 we review the comments on the need for large-scale dictionaries and wide-coverage grammars, explaining why they are necessary resources not only for open-domain question answering systems but also for systems with very limited answering capabilities, such as database interfaces. §5 is concerned with the problems of, and desirability of, answering questions using information from disparate resources that are heterogeneous in scale, content, format, and granularity. In §6 we collect her claims for the evaluation of question-answering systems, particularly the intrinsic difficulty of evaluating the effectiveness of systems intended to assist in interactive refinement of a question. All these themes have been incorporated into the ambitious five-year Roadmap for research in question answering, as shown in §7, the conclusion. They will influence the field for a long time to come.

Table 1 Web-based Question Answering Systems

System	URL
AnswerBus	http://www.answerbus.com/
AskJeeves	http://www.askjeeves.com/
BrainBoost	http://www.brainboost.com/
ExtrAns	http://www.ifi.unizh.ch/CL/extrans/
Ionaut	http://www.ionaut.com:8400/
LAMP	http://www.comp.nus.edu.sg/~smadellz/lamp/lamp_index.html
Language Computer	http://languagecomputer.com/demos/question_answering/ internet_demo/index.html
Quasm	http://ciir.cs.umass.edu/~reu2/
	http://129.219.59.31/qademo.html
Start	http://www.ai.mit.edu/projects/infolab/
Wondir	http://www.wondir.com/

2. THE MERITS OF SHALLOW TECHNIQUES FOR FINDING ANSWERS

By the late 1980s, there had been twenty to thirty years of advance in two kinds of approach to the problem of locating information encoded in text. Traditional Information Retrieval had been developing methods based on measuring statistical properties of the distributions of words and the frequencies of their cooccurrences. Artificial Intelligence had been developing methods for extracting representations of meaning from texts and drawing inferences from them. Sparck Jones (1990) posed the question of whether sophisticated cataloguing and indexing would be rendered pointless by AI approaches. In that paper, the notion of an "intelligent library" was described, which might provide a context in which retrieving information might properly be viewed as being the same activity as answering questions; and beyond that, the "integrated information management system" (henceforth IIMS). The intelligent library would be capable of performing inferences, based only in part upon information contained in the documents it manages, in order to help researchers to answer the kinds of questions they are really interested in. The IIMS furthermore would handle a wide variety of information resources: document collections, databases, e-mail, dictionaries, and so forth.

A thoroughly hypothetical example is given to illustrate the intelligent library, of a researcher interested in evidence for a particular mineral deficiency (Tungsten) causing an imaginary disease (Snodgrass's disease). General knowledge about the relationship between diet and disease, specific information about the nature of the disease (probably found from the documents managed by the intelligent library), and possibly a chemical analogy (between Tungsten and other minerals) would be combined to produce the answer that the deficiency is a symptom and not a cause of the disease

There is discussion in Sparck Jones (1990) of whether an AI-style knowledge base might be used by the intelligent library. The conclusion is that this is not the correct way to treat information found in the library's documents, and that an "unintelligent wordmaster" is more appropriate. A strong-AI representation of document content is not logically workable, and a weak-AI representation would in fact be no more than a fancy indexing device. Indexing devices are intended to establish relationships amongst containers of information, and between those containers and the uses to which their content might be put. Language elements (words, and perhaps word senses) provide the only way to achieve this that offers the ability to capture commonality as well as specificity. There are problems besetting the automatic extraction of useful index keys and access relations that arise, most particularly when the library contains a variety of types of information container as in an IIMS. Sometimes, as with book titles, there is very little text to work with; sometimes, as with entire books, there is perhaps too much; sometimes, as with dictionary entries versus entire books, the differences in scale necessitate possibly irreconcilable procedures for indexing content and for extracting information in response to a question. Nevertheless it is argued in Sparck Jones (1990) that traditional IR methods, enhancing information on language elements with statistically derived data on occurrence and cooccurrence, provide the better indexing and accessing capabilities, for an IIMS in particular. The hallmark of such a system is perceived to be its interactivity, especially in elucidating the actual information need of a user. This, together with the quality of statistics gathered from the large volumes and rich variety of material with which an IIMS would work, makes such indexing more powerful than one might think.

The World Wide Web had come into public consciousness by the time of writing of Sparck Jones's 1997 paper. With it, large-scale resources were available both to be experimented upon by IR and AI researchers alike, and also to be searched by casual end users. Such searchers brought an unwelcome uncertainty and vagueness to the retrieval situation: queries were typically incomplete (averaging 1.8 words), phrasing of queries highly variable, and the users sought information they did not know from sources that they did not know. This was a far cry from the early situation where skilled and knowledgeable intermediaries assisted users in formulating precise queries using controlled vocabularies. Nevertheless, the quality of statistics that could be generated from such large-scale resources can combat this uncertainty, it is claimed. Help also comes from redundancy in discourse: in the typical retrieval situation, a user repeatedly refines a query, probably using synonymous or otherwise related terms, and being presented with partially overlapping result sets.

Clearly there are distinctions that are missed by shallow methods that perform no linguistic analysis: there is a real difference between a Venetian blind and a blind Venetian. The AI – or rather NLP (Natural Language Processing) – assumption is that some syntactic analysis is indispensable in order to identify proper conceptual units. Traditional manual indexing does deliver the sort of direct explicit representation of syntactic (and semantic) entities and relationships beloved of NLP, and experiments within the IR tradition have therefore been possible to determine the relative effectiveness of indexing with such data on the one hand, and shallow statistical (co-) occurrence data on the other. The conclusion of such experimentation has been twofold: really complex descriptions of content are too constraining, making it unlikely that any response to a query will be found; and moderately complex ones do not significantly outperform coordination of simple terms.

It was claimed in Sparck Jones (1997) that for extraction of answers from The Web, the need was for power and robustness with respect to the data, and for flexibility and friendliness with respect to the users. If indexing could be done at search time, rather than at time of acquisition of data, then it could exploit the instantaneous perspective of the particular user, and also exploit up-to-date statistics, and together these would make retrieval more powerful and responsive. Tuning of statistical methods, and exploiting the opportunity to identify sensible compound terms afforded by The Web's richer file data, offered more promise for retrieval from The Web than does Natural Language Question Answering. There was probably no starring role for NLP in Web document retrieval, and other IR tasks such as Passage Retrieval and Hypertext Link Generation could be done entirely without NLP, using statistical methods alone. Given that, in 1997, statistical methods proven effective for other kinds of collection were only partially adopted, and there was only minimal evaluation of the effectiveness of those methods in retrieval from The Web, there was no proven need for NLP. Further, given that user requests were so very fragmentary, averaging 1.8 words, there was hardly opportunity for meaningful NLP either. There were supporting roles NLP might play, for tagging texts prior to finding compounds, synonyms, collocates etc., and for multilingual retrieval, for example. Work was needed on combining linguistic and statistical methods.

Such work is now in progress. During the 1990s, as noted in the Vision Statement (Carbonell et al., 2000) and accepted in the Roadmap (Burger et al., 2002), "semantics was on the back burner". There are efforts such as Harabagiu et al. (2003) to *enhance* question-answering systems that answer the "Information Seeking" kinds of question, by using primarily statistical knowledge, with additional semantic and pragmatic knowledge to answer "Reading Comprehension" questions. There is no suggestion that semantic knowledge will supplant statistical information, which proves both effective and fast at identifying the needles of answer-containing texts in the haystacks of gigabyte collections.

3. KNOWLEDGE BASES AND INFERENCE

Documents are but one of the kinds of resource containing information that a person might wish to extract. Throughout the 1970s and 1980s there was much interest in providing access to databases through the medium of natural language, and there is review and critique of the work of this period in Copestake and Sparck Jones (1990). The process of translating requests for information into database queries is at the focus of most of that work, but there are other supporting functions too. It is shown that, for a variety of reasons, such an interface must possess inferential capabilities that must rest on some form of knowledge separate from the content of the database being accessed. The "intelligent library", besides needing to retrieve and correlate information contained in documents and other resources, would also require an ability to perform inferences based on knowledge separate from that information. While it is denied in Sparck Jones (1990) that what such a system does is answer questions, the concerns with inference and the form of a knowledge base are similar to those arising in the database interface context. Similarly, in a rather brief note (Sparck Jones, 1997) there is mention of information reduction tasks, such as the generation (in natural language) of gists or summaries, which would require kinds of inference using knowledge not explicit in the resources being reduced.

In their review of natural language interfaces to databases, Copestake & Spärck Jones illustrate their observations using a hypothetical database containing information about students, the courses they are offered, and the lecturers who teach those courses. They stress that the work of such an interface is not limited to the translation of a request into a query expressed in the formal language of a database system. An interface has a valuable role to play in handling metalevel questions, that is, questions about the structure of the database. It also should be able to respond to misguided questions using metalevel information. These aspects of their paper are reserved for §6 here, which deals with retrieval from disparate sources.

Even if we pretend for the moment that question translation is the only task of an interface, such translation is not straightforward but is beset by a host of problems. One such problem is that some questions cannot be translated into just one query, but need several queries, for example to discover the full (recursively defined) set of prerequisites for taking a given course. It may also be that some preliminary query of the database is required, to discover information needed by the interface just in order to translate the question correctly, or to resolve ambiguities in it. Some reasoning is required, using information that necessarily is represented by means outside of the database data itself, in order to apprehend the need for such multiple or preparatory queries, in order to formulate those queries, and in order to process the results of those queries.

General linguistic knowledge is clearly required, especially if an interface is to handle questions occurring in an extended dialogue, replete with ellipsis and anaphora and other dialogue phenomena. Specific lexical knowledge is necessary, particularly about proper names, abbreviations, and terms for database entity types and their attributes and relationships: there are opportunities for acquiring such knowledge from the database but difficulties with this too. But most salient here, extralinguistic knowledge is necessary too.

In general, an interface needs domain knowledge just in order to perform the core task of translating a question into a formal query. Even reasoning with such knowledge is not adequate in fact to resolve some ambiguities, for example the question "who takes the course on databases?" could arguably[1] be intended as a question about lecturers or about students. There are many sources of ambiguity, in questions just as much as in other constructions: lexical, structural, semantic, and referential ambiguities all need to be resolved if misunderstandings are to be avoided, and this is problematic. The inference required to avoid misunderstandings may be unreliable. Errors may have costly consequences: at best, wasted effort doing database processing of unintended queries, but possibly corrupting or destroying database data. The user might not be able to tell from the answer received that the question had been misunderstood. Due to error, an interface may miss the fact that there is an ambiguity. For these reasons, Copestake and Spärck Jones recommend that an interface should ask the user to confirm the interpretation of a question before executing the translated query, invasive though this may be. The interpretation the user is asked to confirm should be highly likely to be both reasonable and correct, and inference using domain knowledge and domain constraints is required to identify such an interpretation.

Copestake and Spärck Jones advocate the use of a database domain model, which is separate from a database schema and is presumably more like a knowledge base. The core task of translating questions into queries would involve first the generation of a domain-independent, underspecified logical form, in which many ambiguities are left unresolved: the sizeable part of the interface which accomplishes this could be highly portable between databases. This logical form representation would then be translated into domain terms. Most of the disambiguating inferences could be performed using the mix of general knowledge and database-specific (and hence non-portable) knowledge contained in the domain model: for example, selecting the different relationships linking terms in "Maths lectures" and "Smith's lectures". The selected interpretation should be communicated to the user and confirmed before being further translated into schema terms and executed.

The acknowledged problem with this interposition of a domain model between the domain-independent logical form and the domain-specific database schema is that there may be cases where access to database content is required for disambiguation of the question. This is hard to arrange if the domain model is a strict intermediate. In the special context of an interface to a database, there is a particular motivation for trying to distinguish data and knowledge, because the operation of retrieval performed on data in the database is clearly distinct from the operation of inference performed on knowledge in a domain model. But it is somewhat artificial to require that the domain model be a strict intermediate, and that inference be wholly concluded before retrieval is begun. In a wider context of answering questions using information other than from a database, there may still be reason for a conceptual distinction between data and knowledge but no rigid distinction between operations on them.

---

[1] In a context where the responsibilities of teaching staff are under review, it would be natural to use "takes the course" or indeed "does the course" to mean "teaches the course".

An IIMS ("integrated information management system", envisaged in Sparck Jones (1990) as a successor to the "intelligent library") is seen as requiring reasoning typical of AI. Such a system would have a variety of information sources, some large and some relatively small, some multi-user and some belonging to a single person. Certainly it would provide one or more users with access to the information in these varied sources, but furthermore it would exploit the information in those sources for system-internal purposes connected with better fulfilling that user-oriented function. While some activities might be simple and shallow, others might be imprecise and deep. To formulate plans of action to satisfy a user's information need, where the actions might be interrelated in complex ways, would require dynamic reasoning, and could not realistically be done using static devices such as scripts or hypertext links. The IIMS might even propose actions to its user, taking an initiative rather than merely responding to a direct request.

The IIMS would need to characterise its own world. The knowledge base it uses to do this might provide a means to answer some questions that a user might pose, though by no means all such questions. The main use of a knowledge base however would be to support inferential matching of information resources to the functional requirements of the tasks and subtasks that the system tries to perform.

It is mistaken, according to Sparck Jones (1990), to suppose that there is profit in encoding the entire content of the documents (and other sources) managed by an IIMS in its knowledge base. Text itself is the most economical way of representing all the kinds of information that one might wish to extract from text. A knowledge base could not supplant documents except by being greatly expanded, rather than condensed, compared to the documents themselves. The proper role of the knowledge base of an IIMS is not to provide answers to questions. It might perhaps be expected instead to act as an "intelligent catalogue", a superstructure with pointers to documents, supporting efficient searching and reasoning about the appropriateness of sources to tasks, and allowing the user to be directed to those sources for the information they seek. But Spärck Jones questions whether the knowledge base would then actually be doing anything useful at all, or whether it would merely be a fancy indexing mechanism.

It is also mistaken, according to Sparck Jones (1990), to suppose that information retrieval is the same thing as question answering, or that relevant answers to information requests can be produced by the AI model of reasoning using a knowledge base. It is not realistic to assume that either user need or document content can be known with sufficient definiteness, and this basic imprecision is compounded by the indirectness of descriptions of document content. Typically the user is not asking the answer to a question from the knowledge base, and the matching of descriptions that a system does is not giving the answer.

Another difficulty with an IIMS using a knowledge base to answer user questions arises from its essential property of managing varied types of information source. It is implausible, again according to Sparck Jones (1990), that varied resources will have types of information sufficiently in common to allow their information to be embodied in a common knowledge base. The only plausible commonality is at the level of natural language words and perhaps morphemes. Spärck Jones suggests an indexing and accessing device, based on words associated with one another in a network. There would be a high degree of redundancy, many words labelling many "first-order information objects". The network of associations might have both real and virtual links between words, and might be in part static and in part dynamic. Some associations between words would arise from the fact of their cooccurrence in the first-order information objects they collectively label, while others would arise from second-order information objects like dictionaries and thesauri. There is value then in having not just multiple sources of associative information, but also multiple types of source.

The idea of using associative networks as a knowledge representation medium was not novel, as Sparck Jones (1990) was at pains to point out. But the old idea could acquire new potency because of the greatly improved capacity and speed of modern machines, and the power of modern highly interactive interfaces. A research agenda was suggested, to explore issues in the construction and exploitation of associative networks for a variety of types of information object, a variety of system functions, and a variety of user need types.

Further items for a research agenda are found in Sparck Jones (1997). There, two particular kinds of system task are distinguished: content encapsulation, which involves identifying suitable labels for describing the content of information objects; and information reduction, which involves generating new information objects by selection from, and/or by generalisation over, the content of primary information objects. Content encapsulation may involve the representation of facts extracted from document texts, among other kinds of label. Some information reduction may be done at a shallow text level, but it may be done better if it involves processing document texts at a deep content level. The new reduced information objects may be used as intermediates in a system for interactive information management and retrieval, in which users ultimately obtain their information by inspecting the primary objects - in which case they could take any suitable form including associative networks or symbolic knowledge bases. Alternatively, the new derived objects may be gists, themselves texts, which will probably be viewed by human eyes and regarded by human users as legitimate sources of information. For this, NLP is required, both for parsing of original sources and for generation of derived objects. The NLP could be shallow, stitching together samplings of original texts, but deeper NLP would be better. Extracting predications from original texts, representing them in a manner that supports reasoning with them, and generating new text to convey a selection of those predications, would result in more succinct, more natural, more cohesive, and therefore more useful gists. Not only is such generation of new texts from representations of predications an ingredient of summarisation, it is also one of the core activities in constructing helpful and relevant natural language answers to questions.

4. WIDE-COVERAGE GRAMMARS AND LEXICONS

The information contained in a traditional database serves a limited range of purposes. Even for a large organisational database, there is a definite boundary to the set of topics covered by information in the database. It is tempting to conclude that users of such a database, whether using a natural language interface or not, will be concerned with a set of topics that can be delimited in advance, and that they will wish to carry out a predictable range of activities, seeking information according to various criteria, inserting and updating information of particular types. This predictability might allow simplifications of the lexicon and grammar needed by a natural language interface. Many words, even quite common ones, need not be known at all, and some senses of other words may be ignored because they do not relate to anything in the domain of the database. Certain grammatical constructions and distinctions may be excluded from the grammar, either because they do not naturally arise in the context of use of the database, or because users can be instructed to frame their questions in ways which the interface will understand. Simplifications such as these appear attractive not only because they might reduce the cost of producing an interface, but also because they might alleviate the problem of ambiguity, by reducing the likelihood that a parser will even detect unintended possible interpretations of questions and commands.

In their review of natural language interfaces to databases, Copestake and Spärck Jones warn against such simplifications. They acknowledge that large grammars and lexicons are hard to construct, and that their use does exacerbate problems of ambiguity. They argue however that those users who would most benefit from natural language interfaces are also those users who are most likely to have misunderstandings about the domain of a database, most likely to ask inappropriate questions, and most likely to have metalevel questions about the domain and structure of the database rather than about the data it contains. In their hypothetical database about students and courses and lecturers, a question asking who goes to a certain set of lectures might, in a spirit of cooperativeness, be treated as a question about enrolment. But this phrasing might also betray a misunderstanding about the scope of the database, a belief that the database records information that in fact it does not, about actual attendance at lectures rather than enrolment in courses.

Three reasons are given why a wide-coverage general-purpose grammar is desirable for a natural-language interface to a database. First, misunderstandings as mentioned above may be undetectable with a narrow grammar specialised to the anticipated range of questions. Second, a user may engage in a dialogue, in which for example a series of questions build upon previous answers. Phenomena such as tense, ellipsis, and anaphora will have to be handled. Third, and most important, casual users – those users most likely to get any benefit at all from natural language interfaces – will either need training in the limitations of an interface with restricted capabilities, or great patience in dealing with the frustration of dealing with an interface whose limitations they can sense but not understand. The cost of providing a wide-coverage general-purpose grammar is considerable, but ought not to be an issue since such a grammar could be used portably for interfaces to many different databases, and could also be put to many other uses than database interfaces.

Likewise, Copestake and Spärck Jones argue that the lexicon used by a natural language interface to a database should have wide coverage of general vocabulary, as well as having good treatment of proper names, domain-specific terms, abbreviations, and other specialised vocabulary. Some of the general vocabulary, though in widespread use across many domains, may nevertheless need domain-specific additions: the English verbs *be* and *have* being prime examples. Specialised vocabulary may be acquired semi-automatically, by a mixture of tools that mine the content of the database and tools that guide an installation specialist (or possibly a user) through a process of describing the behaviours of words. These tools have their problems, for example with verbs needing verbal or sentential complements. With the question "Which courses require students to take Basic Maths?" Copestake and Spärck Jones illustrate that, contrary to previous claims, such verbs may have perfectly natural uses in database-oriented questions and so should not be excluded from vocabulary.

The lexical knowledge required by a database interface has semantic as well as syntactic components. Copestake and Spärck Jones surmised that inference on word senses could be useful, for instance using the information that *algebra* is a kind of *mathematics* to answer questions about maths courses. Detailed selectional restrictions were seen as useful too, but also problematic because, unless so general as to be no longer useful, they always seem to exclude some meaningful sentences from analysis. For example, restricting the subject of *require* to be something human would exclude a question such as "Which courses require students to take Basic Maths?".

It was hard however to gather data to test experimentally the usefulness of such semantic information, because at the time large-scale resources such as WordNet were only just becoming available. Work on extracting lexical information from machine-readable dictionaries was under way, and was seen by Copestake and Spärck Jones as offering relief from the pain of constructing wide-coverage lexicons by hand. Even if it is deemed impractical to have the full range of syntactic and semantic information for each word of a large vocabulary, it may still be useful to have a big dictionary containing words not in the interface's lexicon[2]. This helps the interface to distinguish misspellings of known words from correctly-spelt unknown words, because it has a sufficiently large fund of valid but unknown words. Generally it is ill-advised and even counterproductive to coerce every word to a word in the lexicon, because it can lead to responses from a software system which are quite mystifying to the user. Patchy coverage of vocabulary, like patchy syntactic knowledge, can be most frustrating to a user. Copestake and Spärck Jones recommend that, even for a system such as a database interface which is intended to work in a restricted domain, there should be a wide-coverage grammar, and a big dictionary, derived perhaps from machine-readable forms of dictionaries published for use in the normal way by ordinary people. The software system's lexicon should contain syntactically and semantically rich information about all common senses of common vocabulary, in addition to domain-specific terms and names and abbreviations. In the years since, considerable research has taken place in many centres on topics of vocabulary acquisition from machine-readable dictionaries, and on "Named Entity Recognition".

---

[2] This use of a dictionary is quite separate from the use of dictionaries and thesauri as 2nd-order sources of information about word associations suggested in Sparck Jones (1990) (and mentioned in §4 above).

5. RETRIEVAL FROM DISPARATE RESOURCES

The task of a natural language interface to a database system, according to Copestake and Sparck Jones (1990), properly involves more than translating questions into formal queries (and presenting the results, whether using natural language or not). It is not obvious that such translation would really be useful. If the interface's abilities are restricted, it will not be a good substitute for an interpreter for a formal query language, and a menu system interface will be better at making apparent its limitations than an interface which appears to handle language but whose coverage is only patchy. If an interface is to be almost unrestricted, and to support a variety of needs of inexperienced users, it will be very costly to construct, and much of it will not prove portable to other databases in other domains. Nevertheless there are four reasons given why the attempt should be made to provide unrestricted natural language access to databases with support for inexperienced users. First, users need not learn a formal query language; and second, the questions that can be asked using a query language can potentially be asked using natural language too. These two reasons are commonplaces. The third reason is that metalevel questions, about the domain structure and the database constraints, can be accepted in the same way as questions about facts recorded in the database. The fourth is that dialogue can be possible, which would be especially useful for query refinement. These last two motivations could only be realised if the interface has relatively unconstrained coverage, but furthermore, they would require that it has access to resources other than the database content itself. Copestake and Spärck Jones see a need for a domain model, separate from both the database and the database's schema, both in the core task of translating single database-content questions and in fulfilling these further requirements.

A database is usually designed to be able to process efficiently a set of frequently required operations. Natural language access has the big advantage for inexperienced or infrequent users, or for any user with an ad-hoc query, that it can hide the actual structure of the database. The natural language form of a question can bear hardly any resemblance to its equivalent in the formal query language. The process of translating the question into the query can in the general case need knowledge of both the database structure and the database content. Copestake and Spärck Jones illustrate with the question "Who teaches Smith mathematics?", which requires knowing that two relations must be joined (one that record teachers of courses, one that records students enrolled on courses) and requires knowing which particular courses could be termed "mathematics". These two items of knowledge, about structure and about content respectively, would be provided by a domain model.

An ability to ask about the nature and organisation of the content of a database will be of value to infrequent or inexperienced users. Such questions should be answered by the interface using information from sources other than the database itself. Relational databases are in a sense self-describing, with catalog relations holding schema information - about the client relations , their attributes and their datatypes, their keys and foreign keys, and in some cases integrity constraints that must be enforced. But this self-description does not contain all the information about the database that an interface requires. It does not tell how words naming concepts and relationships map onto attributes, relations, and joins. It does not tell about cognate data that might plausibly have been represented in the database but was not (such as faculty affiliations, course durations, continuous assessment exercises, in the example database used by Copestake and Spärck Jones). An additional, explicit source of knowledge, which Copestake and Spärck Jones call a "domain model", should be available to an interface to allow it to respond to user questions about the form and scope of the database. It will be useful also to respond to some misguided questions that appear to ask about database content, but which betray some misunderstanding. For example, if a user asks for a list of courses with more than one lecturer and there is a constraint stating that courses can have only one, an answer referring to that constraint is much better than an answer that no such courses exist.

Another category of misunderstanding is to presume that the database contains types of information that actually it does not. With a domain model, which contains general world knowledge about the types of entities described in the database together with tie-ins to the database where appropriate, there is a chance to detect this kind of misunderstanding and respond to it in an appropriate and useful manner. Without it, there is a danger that a question may be answered with wrong data of the correct general type. For example, asking for the place where a lecturer teaches a course – which for the sake of argument is not stored in the database – might be "cooperatively" answered with information the database does store about a place (an office, say) that is associated in any way with the lecturer. This is misleading and potentially dangerous.

There is considerable scepticism in Copestake and Sparck Jones (1990) about the practicality or real usefulness of providing natural language interfaces to databases. The labour and skill required to tailor general-purpose interfaces would rule out their use for mass-market single-user systems. Large commercial systems are not much concerned with casual users anyway and are quite prepared to invest in training staff to use database query tools. Enabling database systems to answer natural language questions is more likely to incur costs in terms of skilled work than to save costs. But the point here is that such interfaces, if they were deployed, ought to access more sources of information than just one. Different kinds of question require different mixes of the information sources for producing their answers. Copestake and Spärck Jones go on to suggest that there may be significant advantages to natural language interfaces – and perhaps spoken language interfaces - providing access to other kinds of material also, specifically mentioning text bases and document bases. They conclude that research is required in more general contexts, interfacing databases and knowledge bases.

The "integrated information management system of the future" (IIMS) is predicted in Sparck Jones (1990) to make extensive use of AI in order to provide access to a much more varied collection of information sources. The IIMS may be used to perform - or to support its user in performing - a variety of tasks, such as tracking correspondence, assembling bibliographies, analysing experiment statistics. It will access - or provide its user with access to - a variety of information sources, such as internal reports, personal electronic mail, library catalogue, external and internal databases, dictionary, and others. In order to utilise the information in these sources, it will be necessary to compare them to each other and find points of connection between them, as well as determining what relationship exists between information in any resource and information required by the IIMS - or its user - for some purpose. Both of these types of comparison are expected to pose great difficulties, partly because the sources are heterogeneous in three ways: content, granularity, and scale. Difficulties also arise because of the heterogeneity of the tasks. A consequence is that the relevance relations that the IIMS has to apply, to connect sources to each other and to connect sources to requests for information, will be numerous and varied. To the extent that words are used in all sources, they may form a basis of comparison. But relevance will be hard to establish in the face of uncertainty. One of the causes of this uncertainty is inconsistency of expression: the different authors of different items of information – and the user, if there is one, seeking information - will use the same words to mean different things, and different words to mean the same thing. The extreme stylistic differences between a dictionary entry on one hand, and an e-mail on the other, only go to compound the effects of vocabulary diversity, making comparisons more uncertain still. Research is required in order to establish ways of comparing and connecting diverse types of information source so that users can gain access to them in as a unified whole. It is questionable whether such access is best seen as being done by a software system accepting a natural language question and answering it.

6. THE NEED FOR EVALUATION

In developing techniques for information management and retrieval, researchers have adopted standard methods for evaluating the performance of their document retrieval systems. Using test collections which record the "right answers" for certain questions made it possible to measure characteristics such as precision and recall, and this in turn made it possible to determine the impact - for good or ill – of any proposed technique. Measuring success made possible sustained and verifiable progress.

For natural language question answering, and for broader kinds of information management system too, there is similarly a need for evaluation. What needs to be evaluated however is not only effectiveness, but also usability. In a software system such as an interface to a database, there are some usability issues discussed in Copestake and Sparck Jones (1990) One such issue is that an interface must make its limitations obvious to its user. When presented with a software system that communicates reasonably well in natural language, people are too readily inclined to treat it as having normal human linguistic and cognitive abilities. This misunderstanding can lure people into using language that the system cannot handle correctly, and to ask it questions that lie outside its scope. (A different form of interface, based on menus for example, may be preferable because it makes no pretence to understand language and because it offers no means to ask questions other than those it is designed to answer.) If a software system has wide but nevertheless limited linguistic coverage, a user may unwittingly overstep the bounds of the system's competence. There is a danger that the system may then respond inappropriately, perhaps mistakenly recognising a kind of question it is designed to answer and answering it. This behaviour will strike the user as unintelligent and perhaps incomprehensible, and will make the system hard to use.

Users may be lured into asking questions outside the system's scope, either asking for information the system does not have, or more insidiously, inviting it to assume a role it is not designed to fulfil. In the example database of courses and students and lecturers, a user could ask an inappropriate question - seeking guidance - that nevertheless could be answered in a factual way using data about course prerequisites. If the user supposes that the system is able to act in the role of advisor, it would be both inappropriate and misleading for the system to do so, for to do so properly would require additional information outside the domain of the database.

Another kind of misunderstanding that can arise in the database interface arena concerns null results. Where a user expects to get data and none is produced, it is helpful for the interface to report which part of a complex question is responsible for the non-existence of matching data. It is especially useful if the reason is due to a constraint of which the user must not have been aware, for example that courses can only have one lecturer. This kind of misunderstanding can and should (usually[3]) be detected using a domain model, without accessing the database itself at all.

For usability, a natural language interface to a database should provide feedback in the form of paraphrase or other restatement of a question, not just when the system suspects a problem of interpretation or when null results are produced, but routinely, before the database is even consulted (Copestake and Sparck Jones, 1990). This will allow a user to confirm or alter the system's interpretation of a question, and will provide the only means for detecting a misinterpretation that arises due to system error.

The effectiveness of a question answering system should also be measured, in terms of precision and recall or other similar quantities, for similar reasons to those which motivate quantitative evaluation of document retrieval systems. Difficulties in doing this were anticipated (Sparck Jones, 1988; 1990), particularly in the case of an interactive system targeted at users who need to refine their question through a series of reformulations. Such a user approaches a system the first time in a state of ignorance about what the real question is. Once there has been a process of reformulation, the initial state of ignorance cannot be replicated. This makes it impossible to test alternative strategies in a strictly comparable way, with the same materials and the same questions and the same users: the users inevitably change. While a system may be very good at facilitating the restatement of need by a user, it will be impossible to determine which of two systems would be better at doing this for a particular user on a particular occasion because the occasion is irreproducible.

For the class of question answering systems in which interactive reformulation of questions is an important activity to be supported, a form of evaluation could be carried out by measuring user satisfaction with the system's performance. To the

---

[3] If an expert user wishes to check that a constraint has been satisfactorily enforced, the interface should of course not intercept the question to inform about the constraint. A user model is therefore needed, as well as a domain model.

extent that users indicate satisfaction with the accuracy and completeness of the results they eventually obtain, such a system succeeds. Sparck Jones (1990) expresses the hope and belief that a more rigorous form of evaluation is possible. If no better form of evaluation can be found, then attention should be devoted to determining what relationship there might be between the subjective levels of satisfaction that users express, and an objective notion of system effectiveness which cannot be measured except by indirection. While it is desirable that users be satisfied with system performance, and satisfaction measures are useful in that regard, it is regrettably possible that satisfaction measures do not give any particular guidance to system designers to help them improve effectiveness. In such an eventuality, what system designers should strive to do is to satisfice rather than satisfy: putting aside prejudices[4] about the form of interaction users desire, instead focusing on establishing what users require and then - perhaps minimally - meeting those requirements (Sparck Jones, 1997).

For the class of question answering systems which do not emphasise interactiveness, objective measures of effectiveness can be obtained directly. As with document retrieval, test collections can be established which pair sample questions with correct answers, and the precision and recall characteristics of systems can be established. In principle, systems being compared may use both private internal information sources, and public external knowledge sources, in any combination. The evaluations of question answering systems in the TREC series (TREC-8 through TREC-12) featured standardised questions, more-or-less standardised answers, and a 3-gigabyte collection of documents in which answers had to be found. This permitted evaluation of the effectiveness of the participating systems, allowing conclusions to be drawn about the efficacy of the techniques they employed and of any internal knowledge they utilised. The number of papers contributed to the track has shown an almost constant growth[5] as shown in figure 2.

The demands for response generation have evolved through the five occasions when TREC has featured a question-answering track. In TREC-8 and TREC-9, systems were expected to operate in two modes: giving long answers or short answers, of 50 or 250 bytes respectively, containing the desired verbatim text extracted from one of the 736,794 documents in a collection.

---

[4] It is possible that the desire for an ability to pose questions and receive answers through natural language is just a prejudice, and that other means of interaction are adequate and perhaps preferable. Copestake and Sparck Jones (1990) suggest that menu-based systems may in fact be better suited to interfaces with limited abilities because they make the limitations more readily apparent to users.

[5] Although there is a dip in the number of contributions to the QA track from TREC-11 to TREC-12, it was still the track with most contributions.

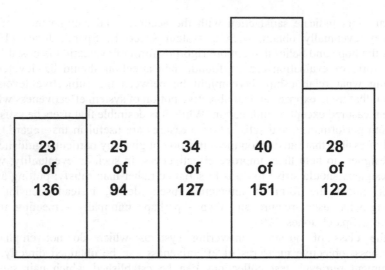

| 23 of 136 | 25 of 94 | 34 of 127 | 40 of 151 | 28 of 122 |

TREC-8   TREC-9   TREC-10 TREC-11 TREC-12

Figure 2: Number of papers contributed to QA tracks of TREC

Five candidate answer strings were permitted. In TREC-10, only short answers were permitted. By TREC-11, systems were evaluated on their ability to provide the exact required answer, regardless of length; and on their ability to distinguish questions for which answers were and were not known. For TREC-11, a distinction was drawn between "Information Seeking" questioning, where an answer to a single question is required from any of the documents in a collection, and "Reading Comprehension" questioning, in which a series of questions probe the system's ability first to identify one document and then answer subsequent questions on the basis of that document's text. This requires several additional abilities: to handle discourse phenomena such as anaphora and tense; to use pragmatic and semantic inferences, as was done in Lehnert's pioneering work on question answering as a means for testing comprehension (Lehnert, 1978)); and to generate novel text rather than merely reproduce a fragment of supplied text. These abilities nevertheless fall far short of those required for the vision of an Integrated Information Management System expounded in Sparck Jones (1990). It is thought desirable to combine the techniques that underpin Information Seeking question-answering systems with additional techniques for Reading Comprehension, as part of a move toward systems that approach the richness of the IIMS (Harabagiu et al., 2003).

In TREC-12 there were two tasks (Voorhees, 2003). In the "passages task", systems were required to identify 250-character strings containing answers to factoid questions, or to report their belief that there was no correct answer to be found. The AQUAINT Corpus of English News Text was used (as in TREC-11 before it), consisting of over a million documents and around 3 gigabytes of text. In the "main task", systems were encouraged to attempt exact answers to factoid questions, list questions, and definition questions. Correct answers to list questions contained – as it turned out – between 3 and 44 items, drawn from multiple sources. List questions were deliberately compiled by the assessors, while the factoid and definition questions were drawn from the AOL and MSNSearch logs of real-life questions from real users. The questions were tagged as to their type. The evaluation of list answers was done in terms of equally-weighted precision and recall of items in an ideal answer, that was composed by assessors partly on the basis of their own searches and partly on the basis of further items uncovered by the systems being evaluated. The evaluation of definition answers was done in terms of nuggets of desired information, some vital and some not, compiled again by a mix of assessors' search results and system-generated answers. Recall of nuggets in definition answers was treated as five times more important than precision, with precision being calculated according to a formula that penalised lengthy answers with few nuggets.

TREC-12 was the first occasion where there was significant participation in subtasks of answering list questions and definition questions. Not surprisingly, difficulties were encountered in evaluating systems' performance. There is noise: human assessors do not agree perfectly among themselves on what constitutes a perfect answer. The result of evaluation may perhaps be oversensitive to the mix of questions as well as the mix of question types. The fidelity of the evaluation is open to question too: the aspects of question answering that will matter to real users may not be being given appropriate weight by the scoring systems. Evaluation itself is the subject of evaluation.

There has been a general movement toward systematic evaluation of language processing systems, in the Question Answering track of the TREC series and elsewhere. This is very much in accordance with the spirit of recommendations contained in an extended series of the papers of Spärck Jones (1988; 1990; 1997).

7. CONCLUSIONS

Five major themes have been identified that Karen Spärck Jones has discussed over a series of papers spanning the decade 1987-1997. These themes have strongly influenced the ambitious Vision Statement to Guide Research in Question Answering and Text Summarization (Carbonell et al., 2000), agreed by a panel of six experts of whom Karen Spärck Jones was one. These themes among others are therefore also reflected in the recently promulgated Roadmap for Research in Question Answering (Burger et al., 2002), and so can be expected to receive still more research attention in the years ahead.

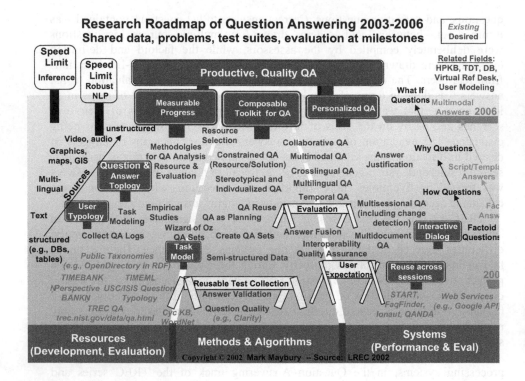

Figure 3: Question Answering Roadmap

The vision statement proposes that four levels of questioner sophistication should be considered, with the most sophisticated questioner type – the "Professional Information Analyst" – requiring a system very much like the "Integrated Information Management System" envisaged in Sparck Jones (1989). Constructing such a system is considered extremely ambitious, so much so that a series of milestones should be laid out as intermediates. The needs of the three less sophisticated and less demanding types of questioner should first be addressed by types of system with lesser capabilities. The roadmap makes concrete proposals for tasks that should be accomplished in order to realise these simpler systems and still build consistently towards the ultimate goal. Figure 3, reproduced here from Maybury (2002), illustrates the planned course of advances in three broad areas – Resources, Methods and Algorithms, and Systems.

The first of the five selected themes is the question of whether shallow processing has a role to play in question answering systems. The TREC evaluations have demonstrated that indexing and retrieval of documents using statistical information on word frequency and collocation frequency is a valuable and probably indispensable tool for locating documents wherein answers may be found. This is not to say that question answering can properly be done without any semantic or pragmatic analysis. In handling "Information Seeking" questioning, a categorisation of the question is required and candidate answers must be of an appropriate semantic type, and these activities need semantic information. Even then, rather shallow techniques based for instance on pattern matching have proved very useful. In handling "Reading Comprehension" questioning, richer semantic information and pragmatic information are both required. But traditional shallow techniques are required in order to identify the document(s) in which answers may be found, for each question individually in IS questioning, and for the initial scene-setting question in RC questioning. The Roadmap mentions "Real Time Question Answering" as an issue, with an associated subtask "Study Fast Models of Retrieval", and so seems to accept tacitly that shallow processing (which requires little time compared to deep processing) will continue to have a role in question answering systems.

The second theme is the use of knowledge bases and inference. With question answering systems having access to huge quantities of textual and other information, no credence is now given to the idea that those systems will answer questions by consulting a predigested representation of that information. Rather they will treat the document collections - or databases or whatever - as collections, in which elements must be first identified as potentially relevant and those elements must then be mined for answers. But knowledge bases may usefully contain information different to that contained in the collections, and inference of various kinds using it may be useful. The Roadmap illustrates this many times over, saying

- Accuracy [is important for real-world users,] "to be accurate a Q&A system must incorporate world knowledge and mechanisms that mimic common sense inference". [p2]
- Usability [is important for real-world users,] "special domain ontologies and domain-specific procedural knowledge must be incorporated". [p3]
- Completeness [is important for real-world users,] "world knowledge together with domain-specific knowledge must be combined and reasoned with, sometimes in complicated ways. A Q&A system must incorporate capabilities of reasoning and using high performing knowledge bases". [p3]
- Question Processing [is an issue], a related subtask is "Study models of question ambiguities for each class of question and for various degrees of complexity. Base the study on various ontologies and knowledge bases". [p10]
- Context and Q&A [is an issue], a related subtask is "Integration of contextual knowledge into and from world knowledge and special purpose ontologies as well as axiomatic knowledge". [p13]
- Answer extraction [is an issue], a related subtask is "Study NLP techniques that enhance answer extraction procession(sic): e.g. coreference resolution, incorporation of world knowledge". [p17]
- Answer formulation [is an issue], a related subtask is "develop inference mechanisms for fusion of answers in different formats". [p19]
- Advanced reasoning for Q&A [is an issue], the two related subtasks are "incorporate knowledge representation and reasoning mechanisms that

allow complex reasoning (e.g. reasoning by analogy)" and "incorporate models of common sense reasoning". [p21]

The third theme is the use of wide-coverage grammars and lexicons. For the English language, there are now lexical resources such as WordNet and FrameNet which are large and in widespread use. Similar resources have been developed and continue to be developed for languages other than English. Some high-scoring question-answering systems in TREC evaluations featured wide-coverage grammars, particularly for the Reading Comprehension task, while others used narrower grammars tuned for speed. Besides analysing the text of questions and the text of documents, a question-answering system may also need to formulate answers in natural language. The Roadmap recognises (as did Copestake and Sparck Jones (1990)) that multi-sentence answers may need to be generated, saying "Often more than one sentence needs to be generated as an answer, thus RST-based generation needs to be implemented to produce a coherent textual answer." [p18] The Roadmap also recognises multi-lingual question answering as an issue, and lists five related subtasks:

- Develop part-of-speech taggers, parsers and Named Entity recognizers for languages other than English
- Translate English questions in other languages. Translate the answer in English.
- Tools for answer retrieval in other languages.
- Develop knowledge bases and ontologies that contain concepts that are language-independent (interlingua type of hierarchies, linked to concepts or words in other languages than English).
- Develop multi-lingual retrieval engines. Generate parallel sets of answer paragraphs.

The fourth theme is retrieval from disparate sources. This theme is consistently evident throughout both the Vision Statement and the Roadmap from start to finish. Questioners may be less or more sophisticated, their questions less or more complex, and the answers too may be less or more complex. Complex answers are described as needing search of multiple sources (possibly in multiple media and/or multiple languages), fusion of information from multiple sources, adding interpretation and drawing conclusions. With multiple sources, there may be conflict to be resolved and there may be multiple alternatives. An entire section of the Roadmap is devoted to the issue of "Data sources for Q&A", laying out a need for more heterogeneous and larger data sources than used hitherto, and a need for several knowledge bases in different formats. All four related subtasks are germane:

- Collect heterogeneous data formats for Q&A that grow naturally over time
- Provide with databases in different formats and with heterogeneous data
- Provide access to several digital libraries
- Extract answers from multimedia data

The fifth and final theme, evaluation, lies at the heart of the Roadmap recommendations. Q&A tracks are expected to be held in subsequent TREC workshops, and the Roadmap has set out a five-year plan for the new requirements to be met at each workshop. The Q&A track of TREC-12 featured two tasks: while the "passages task" required document snippets containing answers to factoid questions, the focus of the "main task" was the exact answering of definition, list, and factoid questions. Five-year plans often do not survive the harsh contact with reality, and this focus is not in accordance with the plans laid out in the Roadmap. Nevertheless, the fact that TREC workshops are continuing to host a Q&A track, with test materials and evaluation methods and judgement criteria, reflects the fact that systematic evaluation is widely accepted as a means to coordinate and accelerate research in question answering. There are particular difficulties in felicitously and reliably evaluating answers to definition and list questions (Voorhees, 2003), which are themselves the subject of recommendations for future work.

The five major themes that have here been traced through a decade of the writings of Karen Spärck Jones may or may not be the ones she herself would pick out. Other themes that I have judged as relatively minor are certainly there to be found. In the opinion of the author however, it is these five that arise so persistently and are developed so consistently that they are the essence of Karen's gift to question answering research. The influence of her ideas will reverberate through the Q&A field for decades to come.

Arthur Cater has been a lecturer in the Computer Science Departmentat University College Dublin since 1980. He obtained his PhD for athesis entitled "Analysis and Inference for English" in 1981following three years of study under Karen Spark Jones inCambridge. He acted for three years in the1990s as Director of the Localisation Resources Centre at UCD. He is oneof the organisers of the Dublin Computational Linguistics Research Seminarseries, along with Josef van Genabith at Dublin City University and Carl Vogel at Trinity College Dublin. His current research interests are inaspects of computational linguistics, particularly interpretation of noun-noun compounds; and in game-playing from an artificial intelligence perspective,with particular emphasis on the game GO.

REFERENCES

Burger, J., Cardie, C., Chaudhri, V., Gaizauskas, R., Harabagiu, S., Israel, D., Jacquemin, C., Lin, C-W., Maiorano, S., Miller, G., Moldovan, D., Ogden, W., Prager, J., Riloff, E., Singal, A., Shrihari, R., Strzalkowski, T., Voorhees, E., & Weishedel, R. (2002). Issues, Tasks and Program Structures to Roadmap Research in Question and Answering (Q&A). Retrieved from the Web December 2003. http://www.ai.mit.edu/people/jimmylin/papers/Burger00-Roadmap.pdf

Carbonell, J., Harman, D., Hovy, E., Maiorano, S., Prange, J., & Sparck Jones, K. (2000). Vision Statement to Guide Research in Question and Answering (Q&A) and Text Summarization. Retrieved from the Web December 2003. http://www.ai.mit.edu/people/jimmylin/papers/Carbonell00.pdf

Copestake, A. and Sparck Jones, K. (1989). Natural Language Interfaces to Databases. *Knowledge Engineering Review, 5(4)*, 225-249.

Harabagiu, S. M., Maiorano, S. J., Pasca, M. A. (2003). Open-domain textual question answering techniques. *Natural Language Engineering, 9(3)*, 231-267.

Lehnert, W. (1978). *The Process of Question Answering*. Hillsdale, NJ: Lawrence Erlbaum.

Maybury, M. (2002). Toward a Question Answering Roadmap. Retrieved from the Web Sept. 2004. http://www.mitre.org/work/tech_papers/tech_papers_02/maybury_toward/maybury_toward_qa.pdf

Sparck Jones, K. (1988). A look back and a look forward. Address to ACM SIGIR upon acceptance of Distinguished Researcher Award.

Sparck Jones, K. (1997). The way forward in information retrieval. *ELSNET newsletter, 6(3),* 12-13.

Sparck Jones, K. (1989). Retrieving information or answering questions? 8th British Library Annual Research Lecture.

Voorhees, E.M. (2003) Overview of the TREC 2003 Question Answering Track. Retreived from the Web September 2004. http://trec.nist.gov/pubs/trec12/papers/OVERVIEW.12.pdf

A. COPESTAKE AND E.J. BRISCOE

NOUN COMPOUNDS REVISITED

1 INTRODUCTION

Over the past fifteen years or so, computational linguistics (CL) research, at least as published in the most prominent conferences and journals, has largely moved away from considering the problems of adapting systems to limited domains. While dialogue system research generally continues to make the assumption that domains will be of small size, the central research issues are in areas such as dialogue management and interfacing to speech recognition rather than the domain connection. Most other research in CL is aiming for broad coverage — even hand-coded grammars and lexicons are now frequently tested on relatively general corpora. Furthermore, there is a general realization that it is unrealistic to rely on representations of large amounts of world knowledge and on complex reasoning capabilities. Even for very limited domains, constructing axioms or equivalent knowledge representation structures is an extremely difficult and time-consuming task. This sort of detailed hand-coding has largely been replaced by attempts to use existing resources. Machine-readable dictionaries and encyclopedias have been exploited to some extent, but, for a variety of reasons, the use of corpora is more popular, often in conjunction with a large scale manually-constructed resource, especially WordNet (Fellbaum, 1998).

This development means that it is necessary to look again at some of the assumptions about the architecture of natural language processing systems. It has been usual to assume that analysers could leave certain information underspecified, on the assumption that it would be instantiated by subsequent domain reasoning (e.g., Hobbs et al, 1993). This approach now needs to be revisited: instead the question is how parsers and generators primarily dealing with syntax or compositional semantics can be integrated with statistical approaches, since these at least partially substitute for the domain knowledge assumed in earlier work.

This article investigates some issues in processing English noun compounds, since these offer particular challenges given their productivity in English, their high degree of inherent syntactic and semantic ambiguity, and their often specialised or idiomatic non-compositional interpretation. Indeed, it is partly an attempt to revisit some of the issues raised in Sparck Jones (1983) about the implications of noun compounds for processing architecture, although unlike that work, we make no attempt to address issues of psychological plausibility. As far as we are aware there is currently no general statistical approach to English noun compound semantics, although the systems developed by Lauer (1995) and Lapata (2002) both deal with

John I. Tait (ed.), *Charting a New Course: Natural Language Processing and Information Retrieval. Essays in Honour of Karen Spärck Jones.* 129–154

substantial subsets. But without consideration of the integration issues and the purposes of compound processing, any definition of a target for noun compound analysis is somewhat arbitrary.

Noun compound interpretation can be divided into three subtasks: identification of the compound, disambiguation of its internal structure (where the compound contains three or more nouns), and determination of the semantic relations which hold between its subconstituents. The rest of the article proceeds as follows. §2 contains a brief overview of some of the salient properties of English noun compounds, their standard treatment, and resultant problems. §3 gives some illustrative data of binary noun compounds in different frequency bands and estimates the distribution of longer compounds. §4, discusses an approach to the semantic representation and analysis of binary compounds. §5 considers how this approach might be extended to longer structurally ambiguous compounds. And §6 provides some tentative conclusions.

2 ENGLISH NOUN COMPOUNDS IN CL SYSTEMS

We will not consider here the internal structure of (noun) compounds involving bound morphemes (*pseudoscience, cytoplasm*) or formed from categories other than noun (*frying pan, pick-up*). Instead, we focus on binary-branching noun sequences of the general form in

(1)   a.   cat food
      b.   cat food container
      c.   cat food container label

(a) contains two nouns which can occur independently (i.e., free morphemes) and which combine productively and compositionally to form a compound in which the head noun is the right daughter. Informally, its interpretation is 'food for cat(s)'. (b) embeds (a) to create the larger (productive and compositional) compound with interpretation, 'container for food for cat(s)'. (c) embeds (b) to create one with the interpretation 'label for container for food for cat(s)', illustrating that the process of compound formation is fully productive and can result, in principle, in compounds of arbitrary size. Such compounds have been variously referred to in the literature as complex nominals, noun sequences, novel compounds, noun-noun compounds, and so forth. A complicating factor is that stucturally identical noun compounds may also be lexicalised and/or idiomatic, involving non-compositional or partially compositional, but semantically-specialised interpretations (e.g., *car park, home secretary*).

Structurally, in (b) *food* may either left-associate with *cat* or right-associate with *container* – the latter structure would be semantically plausible for a compound like *toy coffee maker*. Once a multiword subconstituent has been formed, it too can left/right-associate in the same fashion, so in (b) and (c) *container* and *label* left-associate with the previously-formed compound creating binary, left-branching compounds of increasing size. There is some evidence that left-branching is slightly preferred in such compounds, in contrast to a general preference for right-branching structures in most English syntax (e.g., Marcus, 1980). However, this is at most a marginal structural preference easily overridden by lexical choice: for example, in *law degree language requirement*, the plausible reading requires *language* to right-associate with *requirement*. Church and Patil (1982) noted that, in general, noun compounds of length n can have interpretations correlating with any possible binary-branching tree of length n. They demonstrate that the number of such trees rises exponentially, according to the Catalan series, resulting in considerable potential ambiguity. A three noun compound has two possible structural interpretations, a four word compound has five, whilst eight word compounds, which appear to be at the limit of those attested (e.g., Hirst, 1983) have 469. Church and Patil proposed precomputing the set of binary-branching trees of length n with nodes labelled 'N' and associating this set with a noun compound of length n. This delays the (exponential) complexity of processing noun compounds from syntactic analysis to interpretation.

Each structural left/right-association of a subconstituent in a normal English noun compound entails that some binary semantic relation holds between the syntactic head on the right and dependent to the left. This relation is usually one of semantic modification, paralleling the syntactic dependent-head structure, although there are compounds, such as *carbon paper* or *toy gun* in which the semantic type of the head changes. Earlier work debated the adequacy of utilising a fixed set of such relations, transforming them into a prepositional form (as in the paraphrases above), or leaving them unspecified to be resolved via a mixture of lexical and contextual information.

More recently, there has been some focus on identification of compounds in a partial parsing framework, such as that prevalent in information extraction systems, as compounds often identify (components of) named entities relevant to the extraction task (e.g., Rosario and Hearst, 2001). However, here we limit discussion to complete parsing CL architectures in which the identification of a compound is integrated with its structural analysis.

The LinGO English Resource Grammar (ERG: Copestake and Flickinger, 2000) incorporates a fairly standard approach to noun compound analysis in which binary-branching noun compound sequences are analysed with a doubly-recursive rule, N → N N, allowing for the productive, recursive combination of two or more nouns. A simplified version of the semantics for the ERG noun compound rule is as follows, where L_rel corresponds to the lexical relation associated with the leftmost element and R_rel with the rightmost:

$$L\_Rel(x) \wedge R\_rel(y) \wedge COMPOUND\_rel(x,y)$$

For instance, *polystyrene box* would be:

$$polystyrene\_rel(x) \wedge box\_rel(y) \wedge COMPOUND\_rel(x,y)$$

The actual semantic representation uses the Minimal Recursion Semantics (MRS) formalism (Copestake et al, in press) and includes quantification and scope, which are omitted here for the sake of simplicity. The main point is that the nature of the relationship between the two halves of the compound is left underspecified, as indicated by the COMPOUND_rel (which is a relation that is introduced by the grammar rule and is found only in noun compounds). An immediate consequence is that the potentially exponential ambiguity of such compounds is not constrained semantically.

This general approach has been tried in many systems, with the assumption being that the underspecified compound relation could be resolved by subsequent domain-specific processing. The theoretical justification is that it is impossible to list all the possible meanings of compounds, since cases are attested with meanings which can only be determined contextually. Downing (1977) discusses *apple juice seat*, uttered in a context in which it identifies a place-setting with a glass of apple juice. In fact, even for compounds with established meanings, context can force an alternative interpretation.

However, two problems arise. The first, as already discussed, is that the assumption of domain-specific processing is not available for broad coverage systems. The second is that full underspecification is known to be theoretically inadequate. Copestake and Lascarides (1997, henceforth C&L) discuss this in some detail, and we will only briefly recapitulate the main argument here. The problem is that the rule overgenerates: it implies that any two English nouns can be part of a compound, which is not the case. One easy way of seeing that even pragmatically plausible compounds are not always grammatical is to look at German-to-English translation, which reveals a variety of cases where German compounds are translated by a non-compound equivalent (e.g., *Terminvereinbarung/*date agreement/ agreement on a date* and further examples in C&L). Related evidence is that some classes of compound require a genitive marker (e.g., *blacksmith's hammer*, denoting a specific type of hammer, rather than its possession) and that stress patterns vary between (classes of) compounds (e.g., the more marked left-stress pattern can indicate a synthetic or argument-based, as opposed to modification or adjunct relation in productive, non-lexicalised compounds: *FRENCH teacher* 'teacher of French' vs. *French TEACHer* 'teacher who is French' or *TOY factory* 'factory which makes toys' vs. *toy FACTory* 'factory which is a toy'). Furthermore, the general ERG compound rule does not properly integrate with a treatment of lexicalised compounds: these should be listed in the lexicon, but then an ambiguity between productive and lexicalised interpretations results. This adds further lexically-based ambiguity to the high degree of inherent structural ambiguity.

In fact, different semantically-defined subclasses of noun-noun compounds have widely differing degrees of productivity. Potentially, this can be exploited to constrain both the ambiguity of the general ERG rule and the open-endedness of the interpretation process. This observation led C&L to propose an approach where compound classes were associated with a lexical rule hierarchy which could be expressed formally in terms of typed default feature structures. A portion of the hierarchy is reproduced in Figure 1 along with several illustrative schemata in Table 1: for details, please see C&L.

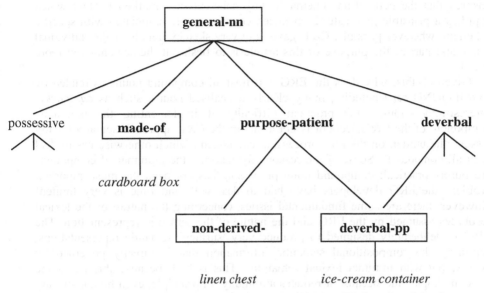

Figure 1: Fragment of hierarchy of noun compound schemata. The boxed nodes indicate actual schemata: other nodes are included for convenience in expressing generalisations. Reproduced from Copestake and Lascarides (1997).

Table 1 : Details of some schemata for noun compounds. / indicates that the value to its right is default information. Reproduced from Copestake and Lascarides (1997).

general-nn	N0 ->	N1	N2
	$\lambda x[P(x) \wedge Q(y) \wedge R(x,y)]$	$\lambda y[Q(y)]$	$\lambda x[P(x)]$
	R = /general-nn	anything /stressed	anything
made-of	R = made-of	substance	physobj /stressed
purpose-patient	R = TELIC(N2)	anything	artifact

In this approach, the grammar/lexicon delimits the range of compounds and indicates conventional interpretations, but some compounds may only be resolved by pragmatics (indicated by the general-nn schema corresponding to the ERG COMPOUND_rel). The other schemata encode conventional meanings. Probabilities are associated with schemata, ensuring that interpretations associated with productive patterns are preferred, and that the general-nn interpretation has a low probability. The highest probability rule that applies is preferred, but pragmatics may override interpretations in certain contexts. The pragmatic component also ensures that the general-nn schema is only coherent in a marked context which supplies a plausible predicate. Lexicalised compounds are associated with specific schemata wherever possible. C&L gave only very sketchy details of the individual schemata: part of the purpose of this article is to flesh out the semantics in more detail.

Given all this, why does the ERG still treat all compound nouns as related by COMPOUND_rel (including many clearly lexicalised nouns, such as *car park*)? Interestingly enough, the practical difficulty of implementing the pragmatic component of the C&L account is not a factor: the C&L approach actually greatly lessens the burden on the post-processing component, which otherwise has to deal with all compounds. Some of the reasons for ignoring the grammar of compounds are purely practical: compound noun processing has not been the most important problem the ERG developers have had to deal with and time is very limited! However, there are some fundamental issues, concerning the nature of the lexical resources assumed by the ERG and the nature of the semantic representation. The ERG is deliberately designed to produce very 'surfacy' semantic representations, capturing the compositional semantic information that is directly governed by syntax, but with minimal lexical semantics. This is both because this keeps the lexicon simple[1] and because it reduces ambiguity. In principle, even homonyms are not distinguished in the ERG if they have the same syntax. Although the different noun compound rules do not have to be applied during parsing in such a way as to increase ambiguity, they do imply a semantic categorisation of simplex nouns which would lead to more entries being required. The compounds themselves can only be analysed by the schemata if the components are at least partially disambiguated, but in a practical system, disambiguation of the elements and disambiguation of the compound as a whole should go hand-in-hand. Finally, the assumptions about productivity in C&L require that a large number of compounds be analysed in order to acquire the relevant frequencies: this is too time-consuming to do manually for fine-grained classes. Hence the C&L approach has not been fully tested, nor directly integrated with the ERG.

The two main pieces of work on corpus-based approaches to compound noun interpretation have already been mentioned. Lauer (1995) worked on bracketing compounds but also experimented with paraphrasing compounds with prepositional readings. Lapata (2002) develops a corpus-based approach to the interpretation of deverbal compound nominals which distinguishes between subject and object readings. The approach depends on an initial list of nominalisations extracted from available lexical resources. Lapata suggests that it could be extended to deal with some other types of compound.

Our aim in this article is to develop a general framework for integrating the ERG style approach to compounds with the corpus-based work. This is not a trivial problem. The systems should be regarded as separate modules, but the interface is relatively complex. Integration has to be at a semantic level, which means that the

---

[1] Even if in principle a semantically-oriented lexicon allows syntax to be predicted, at least defeasibly, to our knowledge nobody has yet demonstrated a practical simplification on a broad coverage grammar.

representations have to be compatible. While we do not want to significantly increase the complexity of lexical representation in the ERG by including lexical semantics, it is clear that compound noun interpretation requires information about noun argument structure, at least for the deverbal cases. Furthermore, as we will argue in more detail below, lexicalised compounds should be treated separately, thus both the ERG and the statistical component need to access a database of known compounds. It is also clear that compound noun disambiguation is only really useful in the context of a complete system, and that the issue of what lexical resources can be assumed is a crucial part of the integration.

3 ILLUSTRATIVE DATA

Before going on to describe and motivate a classification of compounds, we want to introduce some illustrative data from which we will draw examples. One of the problems with the discussion of compound nouns in the literature from the perspective of (statistical) language engineering has been the lack of discussion of frequency. We know that we will not achieve 100% performance on compound noun interpretation without full real world knowledge, reasoning power and contextual information. But since this is unobtainable, we need to get some idea of roughly what percentage of compounds we can expect to analyse to a given level of detail with realistic lexical resources. For instance, Downing's (1977) example of *apple juice seat* cannot be accurately analysed even by humans unless they have knowledge of the extra-linguistic context, but this does not mean that this is generally true for noun compounds. Conversely, the fact that some frequent compounds are very hard to analyse in any sort of compositional fashion is irrelevant for language engineering, since they can be listed in the lexicon.

Since we are not aware of an easily available source of English compound nouns organised by frequency, we will use small samples extracted from the BNC to illustrate the points we want to make here. The examples shown in Figure 2 comes from data automatically extracted by Mirella Lapata as described in Lapata and Lascarides (2003a). The compounds are all cases where a tagger has found two nouns separated by a space without a noun on either side (i.e., binary compounds). The data is organised into three groups according to frequency in the British National Corpus (BNC). All groups consist of 20 randomly selected compounds from a particular frequency band. The first set have frequency of over 500, the second contains compounds with a frequency of 5. In both cases, frequencies from singular and plural forms of the compound were aggregated, and compounds are given in singular form unless the data was so substantially skewed towards the plural that this seemed likely to be misleading. The third set contains compounds that only occurred once in the BNC. Since the automatic extraction procedure is not very reliable for these cases (see Lapata and Lascarides 2003a), the examples were manually checked and non-compounds were discarded. These hapax compounds are given in the form in which they are found in the corpus.

Frequency >500
blood pressure, case study, communist party, community care, county council, exchange rate, government department, government policy, health care, heart attack, home secretary, insurance company, interest rate, money supply, police force, power station, security forces, share price, subject area, telephone number
Frequency =5
abbey walls, birth spacing, building business, clutch bag, darts competition, dialysis bags, exhaust pollution, factory director, group winner, hygiene measures, jazz fan, league headquarters, oil town, polystyrene box, relaxation class, rose fertiliser, school course, silk backing, sugar mixture, tennis coach
Note that *dialysis bags* and *silk backing* were only found in a single section of the BNC.
Frequency =1
airshow accident, blight provisions, bracken tunnel, court manufacturers, demand issues, disk cylinder, earth lane, hotel boiler, installation team, intron RNA, listeria society, loss reserves, mob orator, plaster image, potato scoop, tax module, topic content, turf loam, university vice-rector, wholefood ingredients

Figure 2 Sample of English compound nouns in different frequency classes

Several compounds in the high frequency set would pose serious challenges for automatic analysis. Some are inherently non-paraphrasable (e.g., *home secretary*) while others, though basically compositional, carry additional meaning (e.g., *telephone number*). However, for a practical system, these high frequency lexicalised compounds are all unproblematic, since they can be listed. Indeed from a theoretical perspective, all the high-frequency compounds are established and it is plausible that most human readers treat them as though they were simplex words, even if they are in principle analysable.

Compound nouns of low frequency and hapaxes, in contrast, cannot be assumed to be listed in a broad-coverage system. However the smaller number of low-frequency lexicalised compounds makes this less problematic. In the sample of 20 compounds of frequency five given in Figure 3 perhaps only *clutch bag* and *dialysis bags* are inherently difficult to understand without lexical entries.[2] Some of the other examples are difficult to paraphrase but nevertheless comprehensible without context. For instance, *darts competition* does not have a good simple paraphrase involving a preposition or a single verb connecting the two nouns, but the meaning is straightforwardly deverbal: i.e., a semantics can be given which relates it to *compete at darts*. This is discussed in more detail in the next section. Of the other

---

[2] In fact *dialysis bag* is only used in one section, from a scientific paper, where it apparently means a bag made from some semi-permeable membrane that allows dialysis: i.e., the differential passage of small and large molecules.

examples, *birth spacing, exhaust pollution, group winner, rose fertiliser* and *tennis coach* have head nouns which are deverbal in a semantically straightforward way (though *coach* does not acquire the morphologically regular +*er* suffix) and where the left-hand element of the compound is an argument of the verb. Several of the other examples involve nouns which are inherently relational. For instance, in the relevant sense, *fan* is relational: one must be a fan of something. In general such nouns subcategorize for *of-* phrases. Relational nouns are not generally discussed in the compounds literature, but it make sense to treat them similarly to the deverbal cases: we will refer to relational and deverbal nominals generically as predicative nominals.

In principle, of course, many of these compounds could be ambiguous. For instance, *polystyrene box* might be paraphrasable as *box for polystyrene* rather than *box made of polystyrene*. However, the made-of pattern is highly productive and noun-noun compounds that fall into the pattern ⟨*substance,container*⟩ seem to generally be interpreted as made-of if that analysis is physically possible. Directly establishing that *polystyrene* is the sort of thing that can be used to construct boxes would take us into the real world knowledge trap that we wish to avoid for broad coverage systems. However, this knowledge can be approximated by corpus-derived information: for instance, Google returns more text snippets for *box made of polystyrene* than for *box for polystyrene*. We return to this point below.

In this collection of compounds, *listeria society* is the one example which is clearly 'pragmatic'. The full sentence is:

'We want to put behind us these tawdry, shabby years of the 1980s'; materialism, the salmonella, listeria society of Thatcher.' (quotation marks in original)

Trying to find a paraphrase which works here is difficult: in fact, understanding the compound properly requires a knowledge of UK history of the 1980s. This sort of compound is beyond the ability of currently envisaged broad-coverage systems to analyse, but luckily such examples are relatively rare.

Overall, within the low frequency compounds and the hapaxes, almost half are clear cases where the interpretation involves the left-hand noun acting as an argument to the right-hand noun, either because the right-hand noun is deverbal or relational. This implies that a complete separation of the lexical resources for the compound noun component of an integrated system would be suboptimal, since the subcategorization patterns of nouns are needed for the deep parser. Most of the remainder of the compounds could be paraphrased by a prepositional phrase (*accident at an airshow, course at school, tunnel in bracken* etc) or involve a made-of relation (*polystyrene box, silk backing, plaster image* and, perhaps more marginally, *turf loam* and *earth lane*). Obviously a far larger scale controlled study would have to be carried out to give accurate estimates of frequencies of the different compound types.

Although much of the earlier literature on noun compounds focussed on the structural ambiguity of three or more noun compounds, it is not clear to what extent this is an important practical problem for a broad-coverage system because of the lack of frequency data and data concerning the subconstituents of longer compounds. For example, Hirst (1983) noted that (2)) appeared on a sign at Gatwick Airport.

(2)   airport long-term car park courtesy vehicle pick-up point

However, it is unclear how often compounds of this length occur and the extent to which they are composed of familiar lexicalised subcompounds, such as *airport long-term car park*, allowing readers to circumvent the need for direct comparison of all 469 structural possibilities.[3]

We extracted all sentences containing two or more contiguous automatically-tagged nouns from the first 1.6 million sentences (approximately 29 million words) of the BNC (using a database constructed by Fabre Lambeau) and then used heuristic pattern matching rules to filter out spurious sequences resulting from problematic tokenisation, appositives, coordination, mistaggings, and so forth. The resulting (very approximate) estimated distribution of noun compounds of differing lengths is given below.

Table 2 Frequencies of different compound noun lengths

Length	Frequency
2	702,000
3	93,000
4	16,000
5	2000
6	300
7	40
8	7

The results imply a noun compound rate of occurrence in text considerably higher than that estimated by Leonard (1984) for a 1962 novel. Given that she also demonstrated that this rate of occurrence was increasing in modern English and that Lauer (1995) also reports higher rates of occurrence in more recent texts, this overall estimate, though still probably an overestimate, is not completely implausible. Note also that this sample of the BNC contains a high proportion of technical text where the noun compound rate is generally much higher than in fiction. Clearly, the estimated distribution is highly skewed in favour of shorter compounds and suggests that it would be appropriate for many applications to focus effort on interpretation of two and three noun compounds. However, many longer and more ambiguous

---

[3] The sign had disappeared by the time we made it to Gatwick Airport – possibly, because the familiarity-based strategy was not so accessible to non-native English speaking travellers.

compounds do occur in this relatively small sample, so an approach which generalised to them would be valuable.

Some representative examples of 4-8 word noun sequences discovered are given in (3) automatically lowercased and morphologically analysed, but bracketed manually according to our intuitive interpretation.

(3) a. ((science policy) (support group))
    b. ((whitby archive+s) (heritage centre))
    c. ((tourist board) ((car park) award+s))
    d. (((money advice) (support unit)) officer)
    e. (((world heritage) properties) (conservation bill))
    f. ((army (catering corps)) ((promotion selection) board))
    g. ((telephone (management system+s)) ((customer care) director))
    h. ((henley hall) ((gold (challenge cup)) (handicap hurdle)))
    i. (((lipid research) clinic+s) (coronary ((primary prevention) trial)))
    j. (eight-year ((((high speed) train) (power car)) (production line)))

These examples and the other examples we looked at mostly support the idea that longer compounds contain more frequent shorter ones as components. For instance, the five possible analyses of (a) are immediately reduced to one plausible analysis if *science policy* and *support group* are recognised as separate two noun compounds. In all the cases we have examined, the internal structure of the shorter compound is preserved under embedding into the larger one. However, there are still 'difficult' attachment decisions which intuitively require more careful comparison of the possible interpretations of the resultant larger compound. For instance, in (b) *tourist board* and *car park* are familiar subcompounds but the decision whether to left-associate *car park* with *tourist board* or right-associate it with *award+s* involves assessing the plausibility of awards being made for tourist board car parks over awards being made by the tourist board for car parks.

There is the suspicion with several of these examples that a more fine-grained analysis would uncover further structural factors constraining readings. For example, *Henley Hall, Whitby,* possibly *World Heritage,* and certainly *English Tourist Board* (from which (ex:3c) has been extracted as *English* was tagged as an adjective) are all proper names, at least partially tagged as such by the automatic tagger. Sequences of proper nouns most often constitute a multiword name, so there is a structural basis to prefer analyses which group them. Similary, the examples in (4) illustrate that many longer (often partly mistagged) noun sequences are not 'pure' noun-noun compounds, but contain adjective-like constituents, possessive nouns, appositive-like constituents, and so forth.

(4) a. Eastern Veterans' athletic association.
    b. Bechtel-Westinghouse standardise+ed nuclear unit power plant system (SNUPPS)

These introduce further structural constraints, or at least preferences, which either reduce the overall ambiguity or guide interpretation of such longer sequences. For example, in (a) *athletic* and in (b) *standardise+ed* are adjectival and must therefore right-associate. In (a) this means that the only real ambiguity is over the association of *Eastern* to *Veterans'* or to *(Veterans' (athletic association))*. The possessive marker creates a preference for the former attachment as it left-associates with noun phrases (although this is not absolute, as in *International Women's Javelin Competition*). In (b) most of the true ambiguity concerns the internal structure of *nuclear unit power plant system*, as adjective-like and parenthetical constituents tend to attach high to the entire compound and *Bechtel-Westinghouse* can only attach to the constituent created by attachment of *standardise+ed*.

We now consider the appropriate semantic representation of structurally unambiguous binary compounds, before returning to the issue of structural ambiguity resolution in larger compounds in section 5.

4 CLASSIFYING COMPOUNDS

The basic idea that we will advocate here is that compounds should either be given a semantics equivalent to that which would be assigned to a paraphrase or that, in the case of predicative heads (i.e., heads with associated non-unary predications), they should be related to an argument of the predication. This latter case covers derived deverbal heads and also relational heads. This approach is broadly consistent with Lauer (1995) and Lapata (2002), though we are proposing a more explicit semantic representation. Furthermore, we assume that lexicalised compounds may have arbitrary semantics. This approach contrasts with Levi's (1978) assumption of separate semantic primitives for compound relationships. Given the extensive nature of Levi's study, there have to be good arguments for adopting an alternative approach, and we will discuss this in some detail below.

To make the current proposal more concrete, if we assume that *airshow accident* can be paraphrased as *accident at (an) airshow*, the desired semantics is roughly:[4]

$$\text{airshow}(x) \wedge \text{at}(y,x) \wedge \text{accident}(y)$$

One assumption of the approach presented here is that specialisation relationships between the semantic representations for noun compounds can be efficiently computed, allowing for compounds to be incrementally instantiated. The nature of MRS, which is a flat semantic representation, is designed to facilitate this, although the details are too involved to describe here. However, for those readers who are already familiar with MRS, we should mention the complication that this representation is not syntactically directly analogous to the underspecified

---

[4] The issue of determining the appropriate determiner of the NP inside the PP is an interesting one, which is related to the issue of the quantification of the non-head noun in the compound semantics. We will however ignore these issues here.

representation which would be constructed by the ERG, due to the ordering of the arguments to COMPOUND:

$$airshow(x) \wedge COMPOUND(x,y) \wedge accident(y)$$

However, this problem can be avoided by using a robust variant of MRS (Robust MRS/RMRS: Copestake, 2003) which allowed the underspecification of argument position information.

The desired semantics for *jazz fan* is:

$$jazz(x) \wedge fan(y,x)$$

on the assumption that a relational noun, such as *fan* in this sense, corresponds to a two place relation. Again, it is possible to make this correspond to a syntactic specialisation of the COMPOUND relationship, but the details need not concern us.

We will now try and motivate this style of approach by discussing the four main considerations: expressive adequacy, compatibility with the ERG (or other grammar including semantics but underspecifying noun compound relations), computability/trainability and evaluation.

Expressive adequacy

The main question here is how detailed the semantic representation should be. The extent to which compound relations have to be specified is somewhat task-specific. For the predicative nouns, connecting up the non-head constituent of the compound to the head is a reasonable requirement. Paraphrasing with prepositions is more difficult to justify on formal grounds, since prepositions are themselves very underspecified or polysemous. Rather than claiming that this is fully adequate, we would simply argue that this puts nominal compounds into the same category as nouns modified by a PP, and thus means they no longer have to be treated as a special case. More practically, since in many languages noun compounds have to be translated by a prepositional phrase, specification of a preposition also corresponds reasonably well to a machine translation task, without the overhead of dealing with a full MT system or the idiosyncratic effects of dealing with a particular language pairing. In contrast, while semantic primitives might enable more determinate interpretations, in practice they would have to be linked up to lexical items for many tasks and defining the semantics of the primitives such as those used by Levi (1978) is non-trivial.

Compatibility

Compatibility with the ERG is rather straightforwardly assured by the paraphrase approach, since the semantic representations will correspond to those produced compositionally. The predicative cases are also obviously compatible, since all that is involved is linking up existing argument positions. Semantic primitives could also be incorporated however, so this is not a strong argument for paraphrasing.

Computability/trainability:

There are two possible approaches to developing a statistical approach to noun compound semantics. A supervised approach would involve labelling sample compounds with some set of predefined relations such as Levi's and using a learning algorithm to generalise to unseen compounds (e.g., Rosario and Hearst, 2001). The problem with this is the amount of training data that is required for the general case, although as with WSD, an aligned parallel corpus might be used so that the labels are, in effect, derived from the words of another language assuming that there is a good correlation. Unsupervised learning of compound relations relies on the observation that compounds can be paraphrased (e.g., by nouns modified by prepositional phrases) and that these alternative expressions turn up in corpora. This can be regarded as the corpus-driven analogue of the interpretation by abduction approach to noun compounds. Both Lauer's (1995) and Lapata's (2002) work fall into this latter category. The approach assumed here is intended to be compatible with their work, since although we assume an explicit semantic representation, this is directly related to the sort of structures which they extract.

Most approaches to the direct extraction of compounds (e.g., Lauer, 1995; Liberman and Sproat, 1992; Pustejovsky et al, 1993) have relied on a complete (sub)constituent heuristic in which the occurrence of a binary coordination is taken as evidence for some dependent-head relation and is often used as evidence that the two nouns should be bracketed together in larger compounds. This approach suffers badly from sparse data. Window-based extraction of non-adjacent nouns has generally lead to worse results because the additional data recovered has not compensated for noise introduced through spurious relations (e.g., Lauer, 1995).

The advent of practical statistical parsers capable of recovering grammatical relations offers a method for unifying the direct and paraphrase based approaches to extraction of noun-noun relation data and controlling for noise. For example, the RASP system (Briscoe and Carroll, 2002) can return weighted bilexical grammatical relations with precision of over 90% (Carroll and Briscoe, 2002). Relevant noun-noun relations could be recovered from RASP analysed data by extracting the grammatical relation, **ncmod** (non-clausal modifier), whenever this holds across nouns and a specified weight threshold is met. (5) shows some contexts in which this relation would be extracted. In (a) and (b) the _ indicates that the relation recovered corresponds closely to the unspecified relation of the generic ERG compound rule. In the other cases, the relation is further specified in a manner which should map fairly directly onto the proposed target representation.

(5)   a.   cat food (ncmod food cat)
        b.   cat's daily food (ncmod poss food cat)
        c.   food for the cat (ncmod for food cat)
        d.   cat (comfort food) (ncmod food cat)

To sum up, the advantage of a paraphrase approach for acquisition of noun compound relations is that paraphrases can be directly related to expressions in corpora and that thus an unsupervised learning approach is feasible.

Evaluation

This is one of the most difficult criteria to examine, and the remarks here are very preliminary. Lapata (2002) makes a binary distinction which can be checked manually without extensive training but the full problem of predicative compounds could be more challenging. Paraphrases can, in principle, be checked by humans who do not have extensive semantic training. Although the predicative compound semantics does not correspond quite so directly to paraphrases, alternative realisations can be generated, involving verbs rather than nominalizations. In contrast, evaluating semantic primitives objectively is very difficult.

One further point in favour of the paraphrase task is that it is inherently reversible: i.e., given a paraphrase, the system can be tested to see whether a compound can be generated. Although detailed discussion of this is beyond the scope of this article, a major reason for wanting to investigate this sort of approach is to allow flexible generation and regeneration. An example is in the generation of referring expressions, where a prepositional paraphrase may have to be substituted for a compound in a case where the non-head has to be modified. For instance, if a distinction has to be made between rare furs and common furs, the phrase *coat made from common furs* might be generated rather than the compound *fur coat*.

A detailed classification proposal

The current proposal is to classify compounds according to the categories listed below. In the case of multiple classifications being possible, the compound is to be interpreted as belonging to the first category that 'fits', since in general this will be the most informative.

      1.   Listed compounds. Ideally this would include all lexicalised compounds (e.g., *home secretary*), especially compounds where the elements are used in senses which are not found in isolation and compounds which are not semantically right-headed. To a first approximation, detecting that a compound is in this class simply involves checking a compound against a list of known high-frequency compound forms. Sense ambiguity is a potential problem, but although it is possible for a form which is established to be used in another sense, this is rare. The semantics for the compound is assumed to be listed. Copestake et al (2002) discuss a lexical database representation

of established compounds which is designed to be compatible with the ERG.

2. Hypernymic compounds: e.g., *tuna fish*, *oak tree*. On the basis of manual investigation of a sample of compounds from the BNC, this class seems to be fairly infrequent in general text.

3. Deverbal compounds. Ideally this would only include compound nominals where the rightmost noun is more-or-less regularly semantically derived from a verb as opposed to having idiosyncratic semantics. For instance, *factory director* probably should not be counted as a deverbal nominal, because one would not talk about 'directing a factory'. However, in practice, there is currently no good listing of deverbal nominals which draws this distinction and Lapata's experiments included both. This may not be too serious a practical problem if we are primarily concerned with integrating compounds into an existing system such as the ERG, since we will simply use the ERG lexicon as the arbiter.

4. It is worth noting the possibility of underspecifying the subject/object distinction. Lapata (2002) reports only about 89% agreement between human annotators on deciding whether a deverbal compound should be analysed as involving the subject or the object. One example she discusses is *student briefing*, where either interpretation is plausible in isolation and only analysis of surrounding sentences enables an interpretation to be made. Although we will not go into details here, the RMRS semantic representation mentioned above allows the underspecification of such information, though this is only relevant if a suitable confidence metric exists.

5. Relational compounds. As with deverbal compounds, the initial problem is deciding which nouns are relational. In the integrated system, we would treat the lexicon as defining the set of relational nouns, although the current ERG lexicon is quite inadequate in this respect. Most idiosyncratic deverbal compounds would be treated as relational. A starting point for improving the lexicon could be the Alvey Natural Language Tools (ANLT) lexicon, which subcategorises about 700 relational nouns for 'of' complements (Boguraev et al, 1987). However, the issue of sorting out regular nominalisations from idiosyncratic deverbal nouns and from underived relational nouns remains.

6. Made-of compounds. Despite the general argument given above against using non-lexical relations, there are several reasons to treat made-of compounds as a separate class. Most importantly, although the compounds are to some extent paraphrasable with *of*, this use is highly marked: especially when the substance noun is unmodified. So while *sword of Spanish steel* is acceptable (though a little epic in tone), *sword of steel* is strange. *box of polystyrene* is at least as likely to be interpreted as 'box containing polystyrene' as 'box made of polystyrene'. Hence the approach of paraphrasing with a preposition

does not work well here. Other points are that the made-of relation is very common, forming compounds fully productively and that it has a characteristic stress pattern (Liberman and Sproat, 1992). Finally, as mentioned in Copestake and Lascarides (1997), it is possible to give made-of an independently-motivated formally-specified semantics.

7. Prepositional compounds. This category includes compounds which can be paraphrased as a noun followed by a PP. An example is *airshow accident*, paraphrased as *accident at (an) airshow*. This is the class examined by Lauer (1995), although his test data would also include compounds that we have assigned to other classes.

8. Non-deverbal verb compounds. Some compounds do not have a prepositional paraphrase but do have a simple verbal paraphrase. Some of these cases are telic compounds, which are are discussed in more detail below. Other examples are more idiosyncratic: for instance, *oil town* (a low frequency compound from the illustrative set) is not easily paraphrased with a prepositional phrase, but could be treated as *town producing oil*. This compound falls into a small class along with *cotton town, wool town, steel town* etc.[5] It remains to be seen whether it is possible to extract these non-deverbal verb compounds in general, since the extant statistical work has not addressed this class.

9. Non-paraphrasable compounds. This will include pragmatic compounds such as *listeria society*. An ideal classifier would simply mark these as non-paraphrasable, since the strategy for dealing with them depends on the application.

It is arguable that telic compounds (Johnson and Busa, 1996; Pustejovsky, 1995) should be included as a specific case of compounds with a verb relation, as they were in Copestake and Lascarides (1997). In this case, the telic class would come after deverbal compounds in the classification order above. For instance, the compound *relaxation class*, in the low frequency compounds listed in the previous section, could be analysed as *class that teaches relaxation*, on the assumption that the verb *teach* fills the telic role of class. Many telic compounds can be paraphrased by the preposition *for*, but this is a rather uninformative paraphrase and does not always work, so a verbal paraphrase would be preferable. Furthermore, in some cases, a deverbal noun and a semantically similar but non-deverbal one will be given very different paraphrases if the telic role is not taken into consideration. Consider for instance *tin* and *container*. Because *container* is deverbal, a compound such as *paint container* will be analysed as relating to the verb *contain*, while *paint tin* would be treated as equivalent to *tin for paint*, thus obscuring the essential similarity between the expressions. The problem is that including telic compounds as a separate category make the definition of classes and their extraction more problematic, since it is not generally possible to recover a unique verb, although the

---

[5] Interestingly, the corresponding compounds with *city* don't occur as often, though this may reflect real world facts about concentration of manufacturing. *oil city* is found 6 times in the BNC, but 4 instances refer to Kirkuk: *cotton city* and *wool city* do not occur.

results for logical metonymy reported by Lapata and Lascarides (2003b) suggest that some form of verb extraction might be viable.

5 STRUCTURAL AMBIGUITY RESOLUTION

We primarily address three intertwined architectural issues in this section: firstly, at what point should ambiguity be resolved, secondly, what types of information should be deployed in its resolution, and thirdly, to what extent does the disambiguation process need to be specialised to noun compounds?

Earlier work on parsing typically assumed that the set of syntactic possibilities should be efficiently computed in advance of semantic interpretation. In frameworks such as chart parsing (e.g., Kay, 1973) or generalised LR parsing (Tomita, 1987), this meant that noun compounds exhibit worst-case complexity behaviour requiring at least polynomial (cubic) resources to efficiently compute a parse forest of analyses. Church and Patil's (1982) proposal to precompute sets of binary-branching trees and to associate these directly with compounds of a given length circumvents this cost at runtime but still just postpones the need for comparison of the analyses in order to derive an interpretation. In more recent work on statistical parsing, this assumption has (implicitly) been abandoned in favour of statistical models which condition the application of a syntactic rule at a certain point in a derivation on a variety of lexical and syntactic factors (e.g., Charniak, 2000; Collins, 1999). These models are compatible with either the chart or generalised LR parsing frameworks, but introduce the possibility of immediate selection or ranking amongst competing rules at any given point in a derivation as well as best-first search for the most probable analyses based on using the statistical model to incrementally compute a figure-of-merit for a derivation at any given point (e.g., Carabello and Charniak, 1998). Thus, they, at least implicitly, return the interpretation(s) compatible with the top-ranked analyses. These models use a uniform approach for the resolution of all structural ambiguities (that is, for example, all rules are conditioned on the lexical head of the ancestor rule) and none has been evaluated specifically on noun compounds.

Lauer (1995) describes two specific models for resolution of structural ambiguity in noun compounds. In the adjacency model, given a three noun compound, $N_1 N_2 N_3$ the semantic plausibility of left-associating N_2 with N_1 is compared to the semantic plausibility of right-associating N_2 with N_3. In the dependency model, the semantic plausibility of treating N_1 as a dependent of N_2 is compared to that of treating N_1 as a dependent of N_3. If the latter is more plausible, the parse action in the dependency model is to right-associate N_2. In both models, he assumes a default preference for left-association of N_2 if there is no difference in the semantic plausibility judgements compared.

Lauer argues that the dependency model is superior because it involves comparison based on semantic dependencies entailed by constituency rather than constituency per se. For example, analysing (ex:1b), *cat food container*, the adjacency model would compare cat-food and food-container whilst the dependency model would compare cat-container and cat-food. In Lauer's somewhat implicit semantic framework, the correct left-branching constituency: ((cat food) container) corresponds to two (embedded) dependent→head relations between cat→food and food→container. Therefore, the correct model should compare cat food to cat container.

Lauer develops the models into probabilistic ones in which independence is assumed between dependencies and/or associations. The details of these models are too intricate to repeat here, but the assumption of independence means that the resolution of ambiguity can be factored into a set of independent modifications / associations and generalised to longer compounds. Simplifying somewhat, essentially the products of the probabilities of each dependency / association entailed by each derivation can be compared, and the maximum chosen. For example, the analysis of (ex:1b) in the dependency model requires computation of the maximum of:

Left-branching:	P(cat→food)	P(food→container)
Right-branching:	P(cat→container)	P(food→container)

which reduces to comparison of the probability of P(cat→food) to P(cat→container) as the other dependency relation is shared between the two alternative analyses. However, the five analyses of (ex:1c) *cat food container label* in the dependency model each involve three dependent-head relations, so the model requires computing the maximum of:

1)	P(cat→food)	P(food→container)	P(container→label)
2)	P(cat→container)	P(food→container)	P(container→label)
3)	P(cat→label)	P(food→container)	P(container→label)
4)	P(cat→food)	P(food→label)	P(container→label)
5)	P(cat→label)	P(food→label)	P(container→label)

In this case, the dependency relation in the last column is manifested in all analyses, so a decision between 1), 2) or 3), and 4) or 5) can be made by comparing P(food container) to P(food label), whilst a decision between 1), 2) and 3) involves comparing P(cat food), P(cat container) and P(cat label), and that between 4) and 5) involves comparing P(cat food) and P(cat label). Similar considerations apply to the adjacency model.

To compare the models, Lauer estimates their parameters from counts of ordered pairs of adjacent or nearby nouns extracted from a training corpus, where the counts are interpreted as contributing evidence for a dependency-head relation or an adjacency relation between the two nouns, respectively. Lauer demonstrates that the dependency model performs better than both the adjacency model and a left-branching baseline on a test set of three noun compounds, achieving a peak accuracy of around 80% when trained only on adjacent nouns (as compared to 81.5% for humans on a similar task and about 75% for the adjacency model).

As far as we know, no extant complete statistical parsing model implements Lauer's dependency model of noun compound ambiguity resolution. The various Penn Treebank, constituency-based models of Bod, Collins and Charniak (referenced above) typically condition rules on much more context and only model dependencies indirectly. This suggests that their performance on noun compound ambiguity resolution will be worse than Lauer's dependency model, and possibly the adjacency model too, as when Lauer trained his models using a wider window of nearby nouns performance degraded.

The probabilistic generalised LR parsing model (PGLR, Briscoe and Carroll, 1993) is capable of modelling a general left-branching preference (by systematically preferring the reduce action when faced with a shift-reduce ambiguity). However, directly overlaying the model with lexical information yields a model closer to Lauer's adjacency model than his dependency based one. Consider, for example, a PGLR parser analysing (b) again. Any of the five analyses can be obtained by choosing a sequence of shift or reduce actions. For instance, in the parse configuration shown in 0 in Figure 4, a decision to reduce results in the left-branching analysis of *cat food* and the configuration in R. After the required shift, a further choice between reduce or shift will result either in the totally left-branching or balanced analysis, respectively, shown in RSRSR and RSSRR.

	Stack	Lookahead	Input Queue
0	cat food	container	label
R	(cat food)	container	label
S	cat food container	label	
RSR	((cat food) container)	label	
RSRSR	(((cat food) container) label)		
RSS	(cat food) container label		
RSSRR	((cat food) (container label))		
SR	cat (food container)	label	
SRR	(cat (food container))	label	
SRRSR	((cat (food container)) label)		
SRS	cat (food container) label		
SRSRR	(cat ((food container) label))		
SS	cat food container label		
SSRRR	(cat (food (container label)))		

Figure 4: PGLR parsing of cat food container label

To approximate the adjacency model we would treat the choice R vs. S as the preference for cat-food vs. food-container, and RSR vs. RSS as food-container vs. container-label, on the basis that the probability of a parse action, given the PGLR model, can be conditioned on the top two cells of the stack and the lookahead item in the relevant configuration. The choice of S leads to the other three analyses via either a further shift which yields the totally right-branching derivation at SSRRR;

alternatively, choosing reduce at S yields SR, another shift at this point yields SRS from which *label* reduces (left-associates) with *food container* before *cat* can attach, while reduce yields SRR in which *cat* is reduced (right-associates) with *food container* first. The correspondending adjacency preferences are: SR (food-container) vs. SS (container-label), SRR (cat-container) vs. SRS (container-label)[6]. Given Lauer's analysis and results it would clearly be preferable to integrate the dependency model into this extant statistical parsing framework, if possible. Nevertheless, this simple extension, based on adding lexical adjacency to the unlexicalised PGLR model, proposed in Briscoe and Carroll (1993), might be of practical benefit for a shallow and fast analysis in which it is desirable to resolve attachment before attempting the depth of interpretation envisaged in the previous section.

The approach to compound interpretation described in section 4 depends on the estimation of probabilities for subrules of the general form, N Ø N N, conditioned on semantically-defined relations over subclasses of nouns. However such probabilities are estimated, selection of an analysis for binary compounds reduces to choosing the subrule with highest probability. And this corresponds closely to choosing the analysis with the most likely dependency-head relation, given the lexical items as head and dependent, in Lauer's dependency model. We can approximate the dependency model in the following manner, adopting a statistical chart parsing approach as a minimal extension of the edge weighting approach implemented in the LKB (Copestake, 2002). Each time an edge is constructed using a subrule of the general form above, its probability is computed as:

$$P(relation).P(head, dependent| relation)$$

The estimation of these probabilities extends the dependency model (as presented above) by assuming that the (hidden) relation can be inferred from corpus data, as briefly outlined in the previous section. An edge not only records this probability but also makes its lexical head available for computation of the probabilities of superordinate edges. For instance, for the three noun compound (a), *cat food container*, one approach to ranking overall structural and lexical interpretations would be to compute the probability of all subrules applying between vertices 0 and 2 and vertices 1 and 3 yielding a set of ranked edges for (cat food) and for (food container). Then, edges from 0 to 3 can be computed from the lexical edges from 0 to 1 and 2 to 3 combined with the ranked binary edges above by reapplication of the same set of subrules, in accordance with the fundamental rule of chart parsing. The probability of the resultant edges will be the product of the probability of the contained binary edge and of the application of the formula above to the lexical item projected by this edge and the other contained lexical edge. This method extends

---

[6] We call this an approximation of the adjacency model as neither Lauer or Marcus define its extension to four or more nouns. However, our interpretation is analogous to Lauer's definition of the dependency model in that we extend the notion of 'adjacency' to the head in a noun-dependent-head configuration such as that in SR.

straightforwardly to longer compounds and supports packing of ranked edges subsuming identical substrings and best-first search or Viterbi-like pruning which would ensure that the number of edges rises at most quadratically with the length of the compound. The method relies on the correspondence between an application of an ERG compound (sub)rule and the creation of a head-dependent relation by the associated semantics described in section 2. Implementing a default left-branching preference in this framework, however, would require conditioning rule applications on ancestor rule contexts in the derivation, so that left- and right-branching expansions of the compound rule could be probabilistically distinguished.

The greater efficiency of the integration of the adjacency model with the PGLR parser over the dependency model with a chart parser can be seen in Table 3, which summarises the major points concerning structurally ambiguous compounds discussed so far. Row 1 shows the number of sets of possible binary directed head-dependent relations which could be found for an unordered set of nouns of the given length (Factorial(n)). Row 2 shows the number of such possible sets of relations which can hold, or binary-branching trees which can be constructed, given that English compounds are ordered (Catalan(n)). Row 3 gives the number of complete edges to be computed assuming Viterbi-like pruning of all but the most probable edges spanning a given substring in the chart parsing approximation of Lauer's dependency model (n^2). Row 4 gives the range of the numbers of shift-reduce conflicts to be resolved to determine any given analysis in the PGLR approximation of the adjacency model (n).

Table 3: Comparative efficiency of noun compound analysis

Length:	3	4	5	6	7	8
Unordered:	6	24	120	720	5040	40,320
Compounds:	2	5	14	42	132	469
Edges:	6	16	25	36	49	64
SR Conflicts:	1	2-3	3-5	4-7	5-9	6-13

The disparity between rows 1 and 2 indicates that there is considerable structural constraint, in terms of the ordering and adjacency requirement imposed on relations by the restriction to binary-branching tree structure, inherent in English noun compound syntax. Nevertheless, both the chart-based and PGLR models achieve considerably more efficiency in the computation of the most probable analysis over an approach that requires enumeration of each set of consistent possibilities, as comparison of rows 2 and 3 or 4 indicate.

The more practical ranked or best-first search versions of the chart-based method would, in practice, need to compute the probability of m more (packed) edges representing the m possible (sub)rules encoding more specific relations for each edge over a distinct substring recorded in row 3 of Table 3. Ranking the PGLR adjacency model in a similar manner would be more efficient since it only requires associating a probability with each branch of a binary-branching tree representing the probability of each successive shift or reduce decision in each conflict configuration. Taking the product of these probabilities down any given path from the root configuration 0 to a leaf node gives the probability of one analysis of a compound. So, for compounds of length 4, $16m$ edges need to be computed but only 8 probabilities need to be computed for each distinct branch of the parse conflict decision tree, defining the five possible analyses given in Figure 4.

Embedding the dependency model in the PGLR framework in a manner which preserves these efficiency gains is not possible. Recall that the dependency container→label is common to all five analyses. The choice of R at 0 in Figure 4 corresponds to choosing cat→food, in the sense that all derivations reachable from R entail cat food. However, the three reachable from S entail either cat→label or cat→container. In configuration 0, the probability of R, P(cat→food), could be estimated in the same manner as the probability of an edge in the chart parsing approach above. However, this could only be compared to the P(cat→container) under the assumption that a 'checking' reduction be performed on the constituent at the top of the stack and the lookahead item. This would involve an inefficient extension of the definition of PGLR parsing and, in any case, would not resolve the problem that, in general, (as here) shift actions can be compatible with conflicting subsequent reductions and thus dependency-head relations. Nevertheless, the adjacency model is compatible with PGLR parsing if derivations are ranked according to the product of the probabilities of every parse action taken to yield a derivation (e.g., Briscoe & Carroll, 1993). In this case, computing the n-best derivations from the graph-structured stack is similar to, and of the same order of complexity as, computing the n-best derivations from a chart. However, the PGLR model provides an easy way to integrate a left-branching default structural preference as a preference for reduce in favour of shift in shift-reduce conflict configurations involving reduction with a compound rule and a noun lookahead item.

6 CONCLUSIONS

This article has been concerned with laying out a methodology for integrating the statistical processing of compounds with a symbolic grammar and lexicon and with extant probabilistic parsing models. The approach suggested here has been designed to allow modularity, with compositional semantics being enhanced with lexical semantic information as it becomes available. We have attempted to show that an essentially semantic approach to compound representation is consistent with current work on automatic extraction from corpora (including the web). Integration is facilitated by the flat semantic representation adopted in the ERG. Ultimately, the availability of larger quantities of analysed data should allow incremental refinement of the classification of noun compounds, coupled with approximation of the productivity of noun compound patterns, which should lead to better and more constrained analyses.

Although we have been specifically discussing a hand-built grammar in this article, we think that this general discussion also has some relevance for interfacing to automatically constructed grammars. There seems to be a growing realization that providing a single statistical model for parsing or machine translation is not optimal, simply because of the problem of data sparsity. Noun compounds can be acquired from a tagged corpus, hence improving their analysis does not require having a huge treebank. The essential problem of finding a meaningful and extensible classification scheme for noun compounds applies equally to fully statistical approaches.

One point which we have not been able to discuss here, but which we think has quite serious implications for processing architecture, is the generally low human performance found on many compound processing tasks. Performance on the subject/object distinction has already been mentioned, but Lauer (1995) also found quite low human agreement on bracketing and Lapata and Lascarides (2003a) report about 89% agreement for the task of deciding whether a noun-noun sequence that occurs just once in the BNC is in fact a compound. One explanation for this is just that these tasks are not natural to humans (which makes it an interesting issue as to whether human performance can really be considered as an upper bound) but it is also possible that humans are making use of the redundancy in text when interpreting a passage and thus do not have to be highly accurate on any subtask. If automatic approaches to compound processing have similarly limited performance on subtasks, it is ultimately going to be necessary to find a way of exploiting redundancy and preventing errors from multiplying.

ACKNOWLEDGEMENTS

An earlier version of part of this article was presented at the Second International Workshop on Generative Approaches to the Lexicon, Geneva, 2003.

This research was supported by the Research Collaboration between NTT Communication Science Research Laboratories, Nippon Telegraph and Telephone Corporation and CSLI, Stanford University via a subcontract to the University of Cambridge, and by the EPSRC grant, (RASP) 'Robust Accurate Statistical Parsing' to University of Cambridge. We are very grateful to Mirella Lapata for providing us with her compound data, to Fabre Lambeau for allowing us to use his database of RASP-analysed BNC sentences, and to Tim Baldwin, John Carroll and colleagues at the Workshop on Generative Approaches to the Lexicon for insightful comments on earlier versions.

*Ann Copestake is a Reader in Computational Linguistics at the University of Cambridge Computer Laboratory. She has been involved in research in Computational Linguistics since 1985: she moved back to Cambridge in 2000 after having spent six years at Stanford University. Her research is on computational semantics, formal approaches to representation and grammar engineering. She is the editor of the CSLI Publications series, **Studies in Computational Linguistics.***

Ted Briscoe is Reader in Computational Linguistics at the Compute rLaboratory, University of Cambridge. From 1990 until 1996 he was an EPSRC Advanced Research Fellow undertaking research at Macquarie University in Sydney, University of Pennsylvania in Philadelphia and Xerox European Research Centre in

*Grenoble, as well as at the Computer Laboratory. His specific research interests include statistical androbust parsing techniques, acquiring lexical information from electronic textual corpora and dictionaries, defaults and constraint-based approaches to linguistic description, exploiting prosody and punctuation during parsing, models of human language learning and parsing, and evolutionary simulations of language variation and change. He has published over 50 research articles, edited three books, and been Principal/Co-Investigator or Coordinatorof twelve EU and UK funded projects since 1985. He is joint editor **of Computer Speech and Language** and is book review editor for **Natural Language Engineering**.*

REFERENCES

Boguraev, B., Briscoe, E., Carroll, J., Carter, D., and Grover, C. (1987). The derivation of a grammatically indexed lexicon from the Longman Dictionary of Contemporary English. *Proceedings of the 25th Annual Meeting of the Association for Computational Linguistics (ACL87)*, Stanford, CA: 193–200.

Briscoe, E. and Carroll, J. (2002). Robust accurate statistical annotation of general text. *Proceedings of the 3rd Int. Conference on Language Resources and Corpora (LREC02)*, Las Palmas, Gran Canaria: 1499–1504.

Carabello, S. and Charniak, E. (1998). New figures of merit for best-first probabilistic chart parsing. *Computational Linguistics* 24.2: 275–298.

Carroll, J. and Briscoe, E. (2002). High precision extraction of grammatical relations. *Proceedings of the 19th Int. Conference on Computational Linguistics (Coling02)*, Taipei, Taiwan: 134–140.

Charniak, E. (2000). A maximum entropy inspired parser. *1st Annual Meeting Nth. American Association for Computational Linguistics* Morgan Kaufmann, San Mateo, CA: 132–139.

Church, K. and Patil, R. (1982). Coping with syntactic ambiguity or how to put the block in the box on the table. *Computational Linguistics* 8: 139–149.

Collins, M. (1999). *Head-driven statistical models for natural language parsing*. PhD Dissertation, Computer and Information Science, University of Pennsylvania.

Copestake, A. and Lascarides, A. (1997). Integrating symbolic and statistical representations: the lexicon-pragmatics interface. *Proceedings of the 35th Annual Meeting of the Association for Computational Linguistics and 8th Conference of the European Chapter of the Association for Computational Linguistics (ACL-EACL 97)*, Madrid: 136–143.

Copestake, A. and Flickinger, D. (2000). An open-source grammar development environment and broad-coverage English grammar using HPSG. *Proceedings of the Second conference on Language Resources and Evaluation (LREC-2000)*, Athens, Greece: 591–600.

Copestake, A. (2002). *Implementing Type Feature Structure Grammars*. CSLI Publications.

Copestake, A., Lambeau, F., Villavicencio, A., Bond, F., Baldwin, T., Sag, I.A., Flickinger, D. (2002). Multiword expressions: linguistic precision and reusability. *Proceedings of the Third conference on Language Resources and Evaluation (LREC-2002)*, Las Palmas, Canary Islands: 1941–1947.

Copestake, A. (2003). "Report on the design of RMRS." Deliverable 1.1a: DeepThought — Hybrid Deep and Shallow Methods for Knowledge-Intensive Information Extraction.

Copestake, A., Flickinger, D., Sag, I.A. and Pollard, C. (in press). "Minimal Recursion Semantics: An Introduction." Journal of Research in Language and Computation.

Downing, P. (1977). On the Creation and Use of English Compound Nouns. *Language* 53(4): 810–842.

Fellbaum, C. (editor) (1998). *Wordnet, An Electronic Lexical Database*. MIT Press.

Hirst, G. (1983). *Semantic interpretation against ambiguity*. TR-CS-83-25, Dept .of Computer Science, Brown University.

Hobbs, J.R., Stickel, M., Appelt, D., and Martin, P. (1993). Interpretation as Abduction. *Artificial Intelligence* 63.1: 69–142.

Johnston, M. and Busa, F.. (1996). Qualia structure and the compositional interpretation of compounds. *Proceedings of the ACL SIGLEX workshop on breadth and depth of semantic lexicons*, Santa Cruz, CA.

Kay, M. (1973). "The MIND system." In *Natural Language Processing*, edited by R. Rustin, R.. Algorithmics Press, New York, 155–188.

Lapata, M. (2002). The disambiguation of nominalisations. *Computational linguistics* 28:3: 357-388.

Lapata, M. and Lascarides, A. (2003a). Detecting novel compounds: the role of distributional evidence. *Proceedings of the 10th conference of the European Chapter of the Association for Computational Linguistics (EACL-03)*, Budapest: 235–242.

Lapata, M. and Lascarides, A. (2003b). A probabilistic account of logical metonymy. *Computational Linguistics* 29(2) 263-317.

Lauer, M. (1995). *Designing Statistical Language Learners: Experiments on Compound Nouns*. Ph.D. thesis, Macquarie University, Sydney.

Leonard, R. (1984). *The Interpretation of English Noun Sequences on the Computer*. North-Holland, Amsterdam.

Levi, J. (1978). *The syntax and semantics of complex nominals*. Academic Press, New York.

Liberman, M. and Sproat, R. (1992). "The stress and structure of modified noun phrases in English." In *Lexical matters*, edited by I.A. Sag and A. Szabolsci. CSLI Publications, 131–182.

Marcus, M. (1980). *A Theory of Syntactic recognition for Natural Language*. MIT Press, Cambridge, MA.

Pustejovsky, J. (1995). *The Generative Lexicon*. MIT Press, Cambridge, MA.

Rosario, B. and Hearst, M.. (2001). Classifying the semantic relations in noun compounds via a domain-specific lexical hierarchy. *Proceedings of the Empirical Methods in Natural Language Processing*, Pittsburgh.

Sparck Jones, K. (1983). "So what about parsing compound nouns? ." In *Automatic natural language parsing*, edited by K. Sparck Jones and Y. Wilks. Ellis Horwood, Chichester, England, 164–168.

Tomita, M. (1987). An efficient augmented-context-free parsing algorithm. *Computational Linguistics* 13.1: 31–46.

STEPHEN G. PULMAN

LEXICAL DECOMPOSITION: FOR AND AGAINST

1. INTRODUCTION

This paper is about a problem in lexical semantics. The problem is this: to capture the validity of a variety of inferences that seem to be part of the semantic competence of a native speaker, words appear to need to be analysed as if they had internal structure. But what is the nature of this internal structure? There are at least two popular answers to this, both unsatisfactory: the first is that they are words themselves; the second that they are abstract semantic entities of some kind. The first answer is unsatisfactory because on this account we do not get all the right syntactic or semantic properties coming out. The second answer is unsatisfactory because there seem to be no empirically or philosophically satisfactory account of what these entities are.

Some influential writers, notably Jerry Fodor, have argued that the failure to find satisfactory answers to these questions shows that words do not after all have any internal structure, and maintain that in any case, the kind of inference we are trying to capture is not part of the semantic competence of the native speaker. However, while the range of meaning-constitutive inferences may be smaller than a traditional textbook on semantics might claim, I nevertheless maintain that there are some, and that some means should be found to capture them in a way that avoids objections to 'semantic primitives' accounts. I go on to explore a line of analysis that derives ultimately from the philosophy of action, and which sees some kinds of events as having internal structure of a kind consonant with the inference patterns we are interested in. However, although in some ways an improvement on the 'lexical decomposition' approach, my conclusion will be that this account is still not wholly satisfactory.

2. THE DESCRIPTIVE PROBLEM

We will begin with a brief historical review of linguistic treatments of this phenomenon. Within generative linguistics, Fillmore (1966) was perhaps the first to point out that there was a semantic regularity involving the verbs 'come' and 'bring' that was also found in a variety of other groups of verbs:

Bill brought John.	→	John came.
Bill brought the problem up.	→	The problem came up.
Bill brought John to.	→	John came to.
He brought the truth out.	→	The truth came out.

155

John I. Tait (ed.), *Charting a New Course: Natural Language Processing and Information Retrieval. Essays in Honour of Karen Spärck Jones.* 155–173
© 2005 Springer.

He was brought to trial.	→	He came to trial.
? He brought the toy apart.	→	The toy came apart.
He was brought up a Mormon.	→	? He came up a Mormon.

As the latter two examples illustrate, not every verb-particle combination involving 'bring' and 'come' works this way, and there are typically some aspects of the interpretation of each member of the pair which makes us hesitate to say that the relation is one of straightforward entailment: if Bill brought John to the party unconscious in a sack, does it follow that John came to the party? or that John came to the party unconscious in a sack? I feel happier about the latter than the former, which without modification has a suggestion of voluntary agency that the circumstances do not support. This seems to be a general phenomenon with this type of inference and so from now on I shall assume that any relevant modification (temporal, locative, etc) is held constant from the implicans to the implicandum.

This 'causative' inference is of course widely observed in other contexts:

X killed Y	Y died
X melted$_{transitive}$ Y	Y melted$_{intransitive}$
X put Y in/on/near Z	Y is in/on/near Z

(but NB prepositions like 'into')

X persuaded Y to leave	Y intends to leave
X persuaded Y that Z will leave	Y believes Z will leave
X forced Y to leave	Y left

Although there are some exceptions, these verbs all display roughly the same pattern, and thus in order to 'capture a generalisation', as we used to say, it would be good to find some systematic way of deriving these inferences rather than just listing them. The earliest theory within generative linguistics, and still in many ways the dominant paradigm, is the 'lexical decomposition' approach, which tries to account for these inference patterns by assuming that verbs are semantically complex and can be decomposed into their component meanings. Different verbs may nevertheless share some meaning components. Note that there is an unexamined methodological linguistic assumption here that the only way to express a generalisation is by encoding it into the linguistic representations assigned to sentences.

This approach begins with the generative syntax/semanticists like McCawley (1971), Lakoff (1972), through to other 'interpretive' generative semanticists like Jackendoff 1990, and through to more recent and fashionable syntactic theories (Hale and Keyser, 1993, 1997). Within natural language processing and artificial intelligence this approach to lexical semantics has also been widely adopted in one or another form: Wilks (1975), Schank (1975), and of course many of the relevant issues were discussed in Spärck Jones (1986).

X killed Y	X caused [Y died]
X melted$_{trans}$ Y	X caused [Y melted$_{intrans}$]
X put Y Prep Z	X caused (by ...) [Y Prep Z]
X persuaded Y to Z	X caused (by ...) [Y intends to Z]
X persuaded Y that Z	X caused (by ...) [Y believes that Z]
X forced Y to Z	X caused (by ...) [X Zed]

(The (by ...) components are the place where what is specific to the action of putting, persuading etc. is meant to be detailed.) Now we can have just one inference rule capturing what these inferences have in common:

$$X \text{ cause } Y \text{ (at time t)} \rightarrow \quad Y \text{ holds (at t+1)}$$

This rule 'captures the generalisation' since it applies to a natural semantic class of verbs, rather than stating similar properties over and over again for each verb.

3. FOR AND AGAINST LEXICAL DECOMPOSITION

Of course, such an analysis presupposes that we can give satisfactory answers to several questions:

> Is there any independent evidence for (mono-morphemic) words having internal structure, given that prima facie they should be atomic? This internal structure might be covertly syntactic, or purely semantic. (I shall refer to this as the 'internal structure' question.)

> What is the status of 'cause', 'melt$_{intrans}$', 'intends', 'believes', etc. in the right hand side of the analysis? Are they English words, or some abstract theoretical construct? If the latter, what is their independent justification? (The 'ontological' question.)

> Is it possible to fill in the (by ...) component so as to give a complete analysis of the left hand side? (By 'a complete analysis' we mean one in which the = is interpreted as a biconditional, i.e. that the right hand side gives necessary and sufficient conditions for the truth of the left hand side, and vice versa.) (The 'definitional' question.)

Note in passing that this kind of lexical decomposition is rather different from that which was proposed in the days of structuralist linguistics, where words constituting lexical fields were analysed in terms of a set of n-ary features. For example, kinship terminology or folk taxonomies across languages were frequently analysed in terms of features like +/-male, +/-parent, +/-sibling etc. (e.g. Nida 1951) For this type of analysis, there is a perfectly good answer to the second question, because the features in question were generally those that could be identified in a relatively language-neutral way, since they were perceptual, biological or social properties invariant across cultures. The first and third questions do not arise, because - at least for some of these scholars - these were not intended to be analyses of the meanings of the words involved. The intention was rather to be able to compare how different languages carved up the same 'semantic space' in partially different ways. For this of course it is essential that the dimensions of classification should be identifiable independently of any particular language, but there needs to be no claim that the words are composed of the dimensions in question.

4. THE INTERNAL STRUCTURE QUESTION

A variety of arguments have been offered suggesting that internal structure in these verbs can be discerned by using traditional syntactic tests for ambiguity. For example, it has been claimed (Lakoff, McCawley) that pronouns and ellipsis seem to be able to access the different components of a verb:

(1)   The sun melted the glass and that surprised me.

The claim is that this has two readings, one on which 'that' refers to, roughly, 'the sun melted the glass' and one on which it refers to 'the glass melted'.

(2)   The sun melted the glass and I was surprised that it did.

Similarly, here the ellipsis is supposed to be interpreted as either 'surprised that it (the sun) melted the glass', or 'surprised that it (the glass) melted'. These judgments are highly variable: I personally do not share them. Nor do they extend easily to other pairs of verbs putatively involving a similar relationship. Whereas I can just about interpret 'that' as the proposition that 'Bill died' in the first example,

(3)   a.   John killed Bill and that surprised me.
      b.   John killed Bill and I was surprised that he did.

I find it difficult to interpret the second conjunct of the b example as meaning 'I was surprised that Bill died'.

A more convincing set of arguments for internal structure are those based on adverbial modification, it seems to me:

(4)   a.   John almost killed Bill.
      b.   John almost did something that would have killed Bill.
      c.   John did something that almost killed Bill.

Example a. has two interpretations, paraphrasable as b. and c. If 'killed' has the internal structure suggested above then there is a nice explanation for this in terms of differing scopes for the adverb, suggested informally by:

X almost caused [Y died]
X caused [Y almost died]

A somewhat similar argument is based on adverbs like 'again':

(5) a.   John closed the door again
     b.   John closed the door before
     c.   The door was closed before

The a example is ambiguous in that what is asserted to be happening for the second time is either John's action of closing the door, or the door being closed (not necessarily by John on the earlier occasion). Again we can describe this by scope:

again [X cause [Y closed]]
X cause [again [Y closed]]

Note also that independently of the causal properties of these particular verbs, there are more general arguments for verbal predications having a complex denotation consisting of various subevents, from the literature on aspectual modification.

(6) a.   Joe was building a house
     b.   Joe hired a car for a day

In the 'imperfective paradox' type sentences as in (a), the VP 'building a house' is interpreted as describing a process which will result in a state, but when combined with the progressive only the preliminary process is asserted to hold. In the (b) example, the temporal modification most plausibly holds of the resulting state (i.e. Joe had the car for a day), but with a strange context and an iterative interpretation could hold of the initial event or process that results in that state. Either way these observations have typically been taken to show that the events these sentences describe have internal structure. (However, some more argumentation is perhaps required to show that this is associated with the verb independently of its arguments and modifiers.)

5. THE ONTOLOGICAL QUESTION

The most carefully argued answer to the ontological question was perhaps that given by Lakoff and the 'Generative Semanticists': the view argued for by Lakoff (1972) is that the abstract components 'cause', 'die', 'intend' (traditionally rendered in upper case: CAUSE, INTEND, DIE etc.) are abstract arbitrarily named predicates in a 'natural logic'. They may look just like English words in capital letters, but could instead be written 'ABC123' or '21s98j', or any other distinct symbol. They correspond to universal concepts, frequently realised as affixes or auxiliaries in other languages (i.e. they are readily grammaticalised: this point presumably applies more to notions like 'cause' than 'die').

Words are derived from them by processes analogous to syntactic rules:

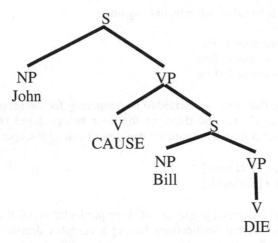

is transformed to:

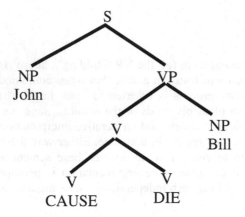

Then a process of 'lexical insertion' replaces the complex [CAUSE DIE] by 'kill'.

A more recent adherent of this type of theory, without the syntactic claims, is Jackendoff (e.g. 1990), for whom semantics is the study of the internal mental representations that constitute 'conceptual structure' and the formal relations between this level and other levels of representation. Jackendoff assumes a set of what we might call 'conceptual parts of speech': Thing, Event, State, Action, Place, Path, Property, Amount... etc. Syntactic constituents translate into things of these types. Particular words add extra more detailed 'concepts' which are taken as primitives of our internal mental representations. Thus an apparently simple example like:

(7)   Joe drank the wine

involves an analysis of 'drink' as constituted of the complex:

$[Event$ CAUSE($[Thing]i,$
    $[Event$ GO($[Thing$ LIQUID$]j$
    $[Path$ TO($[Place$ IN($[Thing$ MOUTH OF ($[Thing]i$)])])])])]

'Inference rules' can be defined which will be triggered by such structures:

At the termination of $[Event$ GO(X,$[Path$ TO(Y)])]
it is the case that $[State$ BE(X,$[Place$ AT(Y)])]

Jackendoff gives no explicit answer to the question of how GO, AT etc are to be interpreted. He says they are theoretical constructs that help to explain our intuitions about meaning. Elsewhere he claims that meaning postulate based theories like those of Lakoff are 'notational variants' of his, so presumably he would subscribe to the view expressed by Lakoff much earlier. (More on meaning postulates below.)

More recent theories that endorse abstract lexical components as part of the 'abstract syntax' of verbs, notably Hale and Keyser 1993, typically do not even address the question of the status of the 'words' (or perhaps 'concepts') they are dealing with. Fodor and Lepore (1998) point out that their invocation of more sophisticated syntactic models does not absolve them from an account of their primitives and suggests that they are subject to the same criticisms as earlier lexical decompositionalists.

There are several well known problems with the Lakoff/Jackendoff/Hale-Keyser view of the status of the abstract predicates invoked by their theories. Let us take the various options one by one: firstly, of course, we could just interpret things like 'CAUSE', 'LIQUID', etc. as what they appear to be, namely English words in capital letters. Lakoff and Jackendoff do not do this, presumably because of Fodor's (1973) arguments against this position. If these things are really just English words in capital letters, then 'John killed Bill' ought to be roughly synonymous with 'John caused Bill to die'. But this is not obviously so:

(8) a.   John caused Bill to die on Sunday by poisoning him on Saturday.
     b.   John killed Bill on Sunday by poisoning him on Saturday.
     c.   John caused Bill to die by swallowing cyanide.
     d.   John killed Bill by swallowing cyanide.

Example (a) seems easily interpretable, whereas (b) seems almost contradictory: at the very least, it needs some special accommodation to interpret, unlike (a). Example (c) is ambiguous, in that although Bill is the more likely cyanide swallower, it is linguistically possible to interpret the sentence with John swallowing cyanide (thereby dying and releasing the handle of the trapdoor through which Bill plummeted to his death). But example (d) cannot be interpreted with Bill as the swallower of cyanide. One would pre-theoretically expect (c) and (d) to have identical linguistic properties if they are alternative realisations of the same abstract structure.

It is quite clear that there are few, if any, completely convincing cases of the synonymy that we should expect to find. Note, however (we shall return to this later) that there is no question that 'John killed Bill' entails 'John caused Bill to die': it is the reverse entailment that seems to be problematic.

The second option would be to accept Jackendoff's assertion that these predicates are theoretical constructs that (by implication) need no other justification than that they account for our intuitions. But I do not find this view acceptable, on several grounds. To begin with, Jackendoff's analysis of 'drink' above, does NOT actually account for my own intuitions about the meaning of drink, for it seems to entail that sentences like 'some reptiles drink through their pores' would be logically contradictory. But more importantly, even if your intuition is that part of the meaning of 'drink' is that liquid should enter a mouth, then unless there is some explicit connection between the construct MOUTH and the meaning of the English word 'mouth', that intuition is not accounted for. Otherwise the analysis of 'drink' above would be equally applicable to a concept which involved ingesting liquid through the ears. Unless that connection can be supplied, in a non-circular way, then the 'theoretical construct' claim is just a roundabout way of saying that the meaning of drink is whatever it has to be to satisfy your intuitions about its meaning, which does not advance things very far.

There is another way of making Jackendoff's 'theoretical construct' claim, and another way of rebutting it, which is, I find, illuminating of the issues. (See Evans and McDowell 1976). I repeat it here because it does not seem to be an argument that many linguists are familiar with - at least, their continued adherence to upper-case-ese suggests not.

On this construal, notions like 'CAUSE', 'LIQUID', 'MOUTH' etc are terms of a semantic metalanguage constituting part of the theory of meaning (for English).

Any theory has to be stated in some language, preferably formal enough to see the consequences of it, and this is that language. It provides an account of the semantic intuitions of the native speaker in something like the way the theory of syntax does for intuitions of grammaticality, ambiguity, etc, since the speaker is claimed to have tacit knowledge of this theory.

Now, many people have found the notion of 'tacit knowledge' problematic. But surely one test of the adequacy of a claim that some kind of tacit knowledge of a theory underlies an ability is that explicit, non-tacit knowledge of that theory should be sufficient to exercise the ability in question. In the case of most theories of syntax, at least where they are formalisable, this condition is satisfied: if you could explicitly memorise and manipulate the various processes and representations involved, then when presented with various sentences from the language in question you can say whether it is grammatical, ambiguous, etc. But in the case of a theory like Jackendoff's, if you were able to memorise the various representations and processes, then all that you would be able to do when presented with a sentence is to translate it into the appropriate expression of the metalanguage. Given some of the 'inference' rules that Jackendoff provides, you might be able to check that the representation of one sentence was derivable from that of another. But what you would not be able to do is to determine whether a sentence was true or false, or even describe the conditions under which it would be true or false. To do this you would have to know what the truth conditions of the semantic metalanguage expressions were, and the 'theoretical construct' claim does not provide this. (Notice also that although the inference rules look as if they enable you to check for entailments, in fact, they do not, for the semantic correlate of one representation being derivable from another is not made explicit via such rules, strictly speaking. The sample rule given is quite consistent with the two representations being synonymous, for example. To make these distinctions reference has to be made to the properly semantic properties of the representations using notions like 'truth', so that synonymy can be distinguished from entailment).

To summarise, then, unless we have some independent idea of what these 'theoretical constructs' mean, all that is achieved by a theory like Jackendoff's is a translation from representations whose semantics we have intuitions about (namely English sentences) to representations for which we have no interpretation, not even an intuitive one. As many have remarked, this just replaces one mystery by a deeper one.

The third option, Lakoff's, is that the meanings of these predicates are fixed by definitions or meaning postulates. Meaning postulates, as introduced by Carnap, were expressions of first order logic of the form $\forall x.P(x) \rightarrow Q(x)$, i.e. universal quantification over a material conditional. The meanings of P and Q are assumed to be known already (in the unenlightening way that predicates are interpreted in first order logic, via an assumed interpretation function that associates predicates with the appropriate sets, sets of tuples, etc.) and the function of the meaning postulate is to restrict the class of models to be considered as possible for the first order theory in question, namely those models which were consistent with the postulates. Meaning postulates do not define new concepts, they relate existing ones. So for the claim that concepts like 'CAUSE' and 'INTEND' etc are defined by meaning postulates to make sense, what must be meant is that these concepts are defined (somehow, presumably via some biconditionals) and then related by postulates.

But how are these concepts to be defined? When we give a definition of one concept in terms of another, we presuppose the defining concept to be antecedently understood. For example, if we understand addition (+) and subtraction (-), we can define multiplication (*):

$$N*1 = N \text{ (base case), and } N*M = N+(N*(M-1)) \text{ (recursive case)}$$

We can also define concepts to have certain properties even if it is difficult to attach intuitive significance to them: e.g.

$$\text{infinity} + n = \text{infinity, for any } n.$$

But how would we get started in defining ABC123 in terms of other similar predicates? At least one of these predicates would have be understood already, otherwise we would have a completely free-floating structure of concepts linked to each other but not connected to anything external. For a predicate to be understood already, it would presumably have to correspond to a word or a phrase of a language (for that is all we have semantic intuitions about) but that would make it rather difficult to claim that the defined predicates correspond to universal, language-independent concepts.

Finally, note that Dowty 1979 does make an attempt to provide truth conditions for abstract predicates like CAUSE in terms of concepts in interval logic. This makes the relation between CAUSE and `cause' rather more complex, but is at least the right thing to try to do, since we are now relating CAUSE to something that is independently understood.

6. THE DEFINITIONAL QUESTION

In a lexical decomposition analysis, the assumption must be that the components jointly constitute a definition of the meaning of the decomposed word. If the components are themselves words, then we should have full-blown synonymy.
But as many have remarked, most persistently in recent years Jerry Fodor, full synonymy is exceedingly difficult to find, even if we are careful to observe distinctions like use and mention, object- and meta-language. The general form of counterexamples follows those quoted from Fodor earlier: given a putative definition of the form A is B, we find a situation of which B plausibly holds, but of which it would be at best strange, at worst false, to say that A holds.

(Actually, those given earlier from Fodor were running together two distinct issues: synonymy, and isomorphism of presumed underlying syntactic structure with an overt counterpart syntactic structure.)

For people like Lakoff and Jackendoff, these counterexamples presumably have little force, because CAUSE is not the same as 'cause'. They can always appeal to the extra content in the (by ....) clause, or the difference between CAUSE and 'cause' etc to explain the apparent lack of synonymy, much as the scientist can always accommodate small tolerances between predicted and observed measurements due to the imperfections of instrumentation. One might also observe that it is a tendency for forms similar in meaning to drift apart. Given that choice of one over the other will be apparent to the hearer (as a competent speaker) that choice will tend to have an informational value in itself, perhaps for Gricean or simply for information-theoretic reasons. That extra informational value can become conventionally attached to the relevant form, leading it to become semantically distinct.

Note again that (if there is a one-to-one correspondence between CAUSE and 'cause') although these are good arguments for non-synonymy, they do not challenge the observation that there is a relation of entailment: if X is a bachelor, then X is unmarried; if X killed Y, then X caused Y to die; if X persuaded Y that P, then X caused Y to believe that P, etc. It is the entailment in the other direction that is the doubtful one.

7. FODOR ON CONCEPTS

On Fodor's Representational Theory of Mind (see, for example, Fodor 1998), mental representations are syntactic objects, expressions of a 'language of thought', but with a semantics that ensures some kind of connection with things 'out there'. Mental representations of this type play a causal role in behaviour, and any putative psychological laws governing human behaviour will quantify over them. Thought is a kind of computation: syntactic processes operating on symbols, but in a way that preserves and respects the semantic properties of these symbols. The question of how these symbols get their semantic properties is thus crucial for Fodor: computation has to be more than just the shuffling of symbols. Fodor considers and rejects several different types of theory of content. The one which corresponds to one version of the lexical decomposition tradition is essentially that on which complex concepts are built up of simpler atomic ones, which are perceptually based if you are a traditional empiricist, or innate in some other way if you are a rationalist. Fodor rejects this theory on the grounds that if any version of it were true, there would be more compelling examples of adequate definitions, analyticity, full synonymy etc, than there actually are, as we have already seen.

Fodor likewise rejects what he calls 'inferential role' theories; theories that would see concepts as deriving their content from their role in a network of inferentially related concepts (perhaps via meaning postulates), something like Quine's 'web of belief'. The concepts are partially learned empirically in some way, but their full content is derived from their place in the inferential network. Again, he maintains, on this theory one would expect to see more examples of satisfactory definitions and analyticity.

Fodor has other more ideological reasons for rejecting this latter kind of theory: if the content of concepts is defined via their place in a network, and if this network derives even in part from empirical experience, then there is no guarantee that networks or concepts will be identical across individuals. Thus mental representations across people will not be type-identical, and so there will be no psychological laws quantifying over them. Since Fodor is committed to there being a level of explanation for behaviour which is irreducibly psychological or cognitive, this is not a conclusion he can accept. Furthermore, if there are no cross-person identities stable enough to support nomic generalisations, the door will be open to the worst varieties of relativism: one person's way of carving up the world will be no more privileged or 'correct' than any other person's. But while it is a reassuring fact that no two people see the world in exactly the same way, it is still the case that the similarities are vastly more striking than the differences, pathologies aside (if relativism is true, we have no basis for calling them pathologies). Notice that neither of these objections apply to the 'semantic primitives' theory, at least if the primitives are perceptually based, or innate, because we can then be sure that there are some points of identity across people independently of their exposure to the empirical world.

Fodor eventually arrives at a rather radical position concerning concepts (i.e. word meanings). The lack of convincing examples of definitions, etc. leads him to the claim that all (mono-morphemic) concepts are atomic. The ideological requirement to maintain that psychological laws exist and to avoid relativism leads him to the view that, in some sense therefore, all atomic concepts must be innate, since they have no more primitive components to be constructed out of. However, the actual sense in which all concepts are innate turns out to be rather weak. Faced with the absurd possibility that concepts like 'doorknob' or 'spade' might be innate, Fodor claims instead that what is innate is the ability to form concepts of that kind on the basis of rapid and variable exposure to instances. 'Concepts of that kind' means concepts that are identified via properties that depend on us - as opposed to natural kind terms (water, tiger, etc.), the content of which is semantically perceived to depend on some 'essence' particular to that kind. The latter are innate in an analogous way: the claim (see Laurence and Margolis, 2002) is that this semantic perception of shared 'essence' as the basis for membership of a kind is hard-wired in us.

The claim that concepts are atomic also requires Fodor to claim that whatever inferences might be associated with concepts (linking them to other concepts), they are not part of their meaning, but something that is learned separately and which is not necessary for possession of the concept. For example, he argues, the number two is both even and prime, but surely neither of these properties need be known for the concept 'two' to be understood. Or, more radically, if X is a dog then X is an animal. But surely, he says, someone could understand 'dog' and 'animal' perfectly well without making this connection, and once the connection was made, we would not want to say our concepts had changed. (Consider the proposition that 'dinosaurs were reptiles', a proposition firmly instilled in me by my children's encyclopedia many years ago. I now believe that dinosaurs were warm-blooded and perhaps the ancestors of birds. But I am still talking about the same creatures in these two semantically incompatible sentences.)

Here, then, is our dilemma. While I find many of Fodor's arguments against meaning-constitutive inferential relations convincing, I also find that there are many examples where the argument is dramatically less so. It seems to me that many inferences (although perhaps fewer than we used to think before Kripke and Putnam) are just not like the 'two' or 'dog' examples. If you don't know that 'X killed Y' implies 'Y died', or that 'X persuaded Y to/that P' implies 'Y intends to/believes that P', or that 'X melted the chocolate' implies 'the chocolate melted', then you simply won't be able to use these words properly. You will assent to the consistency of sentences or exchanges like:

A: X killed Y, you know.
B: But Y is alive!
A: Yes, I know that.

Whereas it may be just about conceivable to discover that our taxonomies of the natural world are so wrong that 'dogs are animals' has to be regarded as false (and hence cannot be partly constitutive of the meaning of 'dog') it just does not seem so plausible that we could empirically discover that it was after all possible to persuade someone that P without them coming to believe that P, that we could discover that someone could melt the chocolate without the chocolate melting. Notice that the 'dogs are animals' cases actually need a lot of work: how plausible is it that we could go on to discover that even 'dogs are things' was false? If there are some meaning-constitutive relations between words, then there are some analytic inferences, although there need not be any definitional equivalences. Although all persuadings of X that P involve communicating something that causes believings by X that P, it is not the case that all communications causing such believings count as persuadings. Fodor writes as if he believes that any kind of meaning-constitutive inference must imply the existence of definitional equivalences, but this is not so unless further assumptions are made. For example, any hierarchical taxonomy offers an example of a system of inferences that without further adornment supports no definitions. The inferences are all one way (transitive 'is a' inferences). It is only when logical vocabulary like 'not' and 'or' and a closed world assumption are added that we can go on to construct equivalences or definitions.

8. HORNSBY'S ANALYSIS

In the course of the development of a theory of action, Hornsby (1980: Appendix A) offers an account of inferences similar to some of those we have been discussing which avoids many of the problems of the lexical decomposition approach. In Hornsby's analysis, the transitive and intransitive versions of verbs like 'break', 'melt' etc are related by an equivalence of the form:

$$(9) \quad \exists e.V_{trans}(Subj,Obj,e) \leftrightarrow \exists e \exists f .action(Subj,e) \land cause(e,f) \land V_{intrans}(Obj,f)$$

where e and f are Davidsonian event variables. (Subj and Obj are placeholders for the corresponding variables or constants). The predicates 'action' and 'cause' are to be interpreted as the corresponding English words. (Note that this makes causation a relation between events: a position argued against very persuasively by Mellor (1987), but we will ignore that large question here).

Of course, this equivalence immediately falls foul of the Fodorean non-synonymy objection: Hornsby adds to the right hand side the further requirement:

$$(10) \quad \forall g \forall x.g \neq e \land action(x,g) \land cause(g,f) \rightarrow cause(g,e)$$

i.e. ... if every event other than e which causes f also causes e. The idea of this is to reduce the length of the causal chains which can count as instances of the transitive form. If John sank the boat, then the boat sank. But if John did some action A that caused the boat to sink, it will only be the case that John sank the boat if everything else that caused the boat to sink also caused A. So if John told Bill to make a hole in the boat, it will not follow that John sank the boat, even though he caused the boat to sink, because Bill making a hole did not cause John to tell him to do that. But if John hit a nail with a hammer, and via this made a hole in the boat, and this hole caused the boat to sink, then John did sink the boat, because hitting the nail caused the hole.

It is not quite clear how to interpret Hornsby's theory as a piece of linguistics.

There is little hope of deriving logical forms like those above while observing any reasonable version of compositionality. It is best to regard something like 9 as a second-order schema which will produce equivalences for each of the relevant class of verbs allowing the inferences we want to go through. This strikes me as an equally good way of 'capturing a generalisation' without encoding it directly in the logical form of the sentences.

9. ARE EVENTS ATOMIC? PIETROSKI'S ANALYSIS.

However, as many people have noted, most recently Pietroski (1998), causative analyses like these suffer from a problem. If we take examples like:

(11) a   Booth pulled the trigger (with his finger, on April 13th)
     b   Booth shot Lincoln (with a pistol, on April 13th),

it seems plausible that these sentences are both made true by the same event, the event that would be the action in Hornsby's analysis. And this event will be what the modifiers 'with NP' and 'on NP' are predicated of. But the pattern of entailments does not display the extensionality one would expect if this were so: it does not follow that:

(12) a   Booth pulled the trigger with a pistol.
     b   Booth shot Lincoln with his finger.

Pietroski restricts his discussion to cases like 'X boiled/melted Y, so Y boiled /melted' (although he also includes non-homonymous pairs like 'raise' and 'rise', and even 'kill' and 'die', the latter on etymological grounds). The main claim that Pietroski makes is that we should see the events described by sentences like these as complex: while in the Booth-Lincoln cases above there is in some sense only one action, different events can be 'grounded' by the same action. Furthermore, one event may be the beginning part of another: it may be possible to discern several different 'culminations' of the same action. The relations of grounding and culminating are defined by assuming a notion of
causation, and a mereological structure on events using the notion 'part of'.
     Event A 'grounds' event B iff A and B occur, A is a (possibly improper) part of B, and A causes every event that is a proper part of B but not a part of A (1998: 81).
     Event B 'culminates' event A iff A and B occur, B is a (perhaps improper) part of A, and B is an effect of every event that is a proper part of A but not a part of B. (1998:86) (Every event grounds itself, and every event terminates itself, on these definitions, for (say) in the first definition, if A is an improper part of B (i.e. A = B), there will be no events that are proper parts of B but not parts of A for A to cause, and so the second conjunct will be vacuously true: analogously for the second definition.)

But one subevent may ground different culminating events, allowing Pietroski to give an analysis of what is happening in sentences like:

(13) a   Booth pulled the trigger (with his finger, on April 13th).
     b   Booth shot Lincoln (with a pistol, on April 13th).
     c   Booth killed Lincoln (on April 13th?)
     d   Lincoln died (on April 14th).

On Pietroski's analysis, the same subevent (an action of Booth) can ground (at least) three relevant distinct events, with different culminating subevents. So the modifiers are not predicated of the same events, and the entailment puzzle concerning the a and b examples goes away. Furthermore, if 'Booth shot Lincoln on Tuesday' is true, but Lincoln did not die until Wednesday, it will not be true that 'Booth killed Lincoln on Tuesday' or that 'Booth killed Lincoln on Wednesday', because there will not be an event containing the right grounding and termination wholly temporally contained in either of those days. Note that this analysis requires it to be a property of events that given a cause and a related effect, there is not necessarily a single event containing both. Otherwise, if John burned the house down, and during this event, a pan of water boiled, it would be true that 'John boiled the water', which does not seem to reflect intuition (although 'John caused the water to boil' or 'John caused something to boil the water' would both be true).

Returning to our causative inferences, the neo-Davidsonian logical forms that Pietroski assigns to the melt$_{trans}$/melt$_{intrans}$ sentences are:

(14) a   Nora melted the chocolate.
     b $\exists$ e.melting$_{trans}$ (e) $\wedge$ Patient(e,the chocolate) $\wedge$ Agent(e,Nora)
     c   The chocolate melted.
     d $\exists$ f.melting$_{intrans}$(f) $\wedge$ Patient(f,the chocolate)

The notions of Agent and Patient (partly) are defined in terms of grounding and culmination:

(15) a $\forall$ e. $\forall$ x.Agent(e,x) $\leftrightarrow$ $\exists$ a.grounds(a,e) $\wedge$ action(a,x)
     b $\forall$ e. $\forall$ x.Patient(e,x) $\leftrightarrow$ $\exists$ f.culminates(f,e) $\wedge$ Patient(f,x)

Substituting in these definitions, the logical form for 'Nora melted the chocolate' will now be equivalent to:

(16) $\exists$ e.melting$_{trans}$(e) & $\exists$ f.culminates(f,e)
                 & Patient(f,the chocolate) & $\exists$ a. grounds(a,e) & action(a, Nora)

Pietroski takes the intransitive form of the verb to be basic and defines the transitive form

(17) $\forall$ e.melting$_{trans}$ (e) $\leftrightarrow$ $\exists$ f.melting$_{intrans}$ (f) & culminates(f,e)

Given this definition the logical form of 'the chocolate melted' is now entailed by that of 'Nora melted the chocolate'.

10. EVENT ONTOLOGY

Pietroski's analysis gives us an account of the entailment relations between sentences involving transitive and intransitive forms of a verb, without committing us to abstract causative morphemes. Could we extend this approach to our 'persuade/intend' or 'kill/die' examples? To try to do this we need to get a little clearer about what model theory is presupposed by the logical forms above.

What exactly now are the denotations of verbs like 'break$_{trans}$' and 'break$_{intrans}$'? On Pietroski's analysis, any event which culminates in a 'break$_{intrans}$' event will count as a 'break$_{trans}$' event. But every event culminates itself, and so every 'break$_{intrans}$' will count as a 'break$_{trans}$' (1998:105). Pietroski makes use of this fact to deal with cases where the 'break$_{trans}$' does not have an agent in the usual sense, but for now the important point is that the transitive denotations (properly) include the intransitive denotations.

To put a little more detail on this we will adopt the model theory proposed for events in Kamp and Reyle (1992) DRT, where the denotation of an n-place verb is given in terms of an n+1 tuple of individuals in the domain, of which the first (conventionally) is an event. So the denotation of 'snore' is a set of <Event,Individual> pairs such that the first member of the pair is an event of snoring by the second member, and so on for transitive and ditransitive verbs.

Under a version of this proposal, a sentence like 'The water boiled' is made true by the existence of an intransitive boiling event of which the patient is 'the water'.

A sentence like 'John boiled the water' is made true by the existence of a complex event including two subevents, the grounding event which is some action by John (which does not necessarily correspond to a linguistic denotation), and the culminating event, which is a boiling$_{intrans}$ event. Let the notation 'event$_{grnd/culm}$' mean an event which is a grounding or a culmination event, and let the notation 'event$_{<grnd...culm>}$' mean an event which contains both a grounding and a culmination event. 'Ind' means a non-event individual which will subscripted by agent or patient. So the denotation D of intransitive and transitive 'boil' etc. will be:

D(boil$_{intrans}$) = a set of <event$_{culm}$,ind$_{pat}$> pairs
D(boil$_{trans}$) = a set of <event$_{<grnd...culm>}$,ind$_{ag}$,ind$_{pat}$> triples, with the constraint that the extractable tuples <event$_{culm}$,ind$_{pat}$> are in D(boil$_{intrans}$)

It is straightforward to see how this would extent to the 'kill/die' cases:

D(die$_{intrans}$) = a set of <event$_{culm}$,ind$_{pat}$>pairs
D(kill$_{trans}$) = a set of <event$_{<grnd...culm>}$,ind$_{ag}$,ind$_{pat}$> triples,

with the constraint that the extractable tuples $<\text{event}_{culm}, \text{ind}_{pat}>$ are in $D(\text{die}_{intrans})$

Notice that in these definitions, the culminating events are constrained to be in the denotation of the intransitive verbs. The grounding events, by contrast, are not. There is no requirement in these verbs for the set of grounding events characteristic of killing or melting to correspond to the denotation of any other word or phrase. But perhaps for other classes of verb, there is: perhaps we could extend this analysis to our 'persuade' cases by requiring the grounding events to be of a particular kind. Verbs like 'persuade', for example, seem to require that whatever it is brings about the beliefs or intentions of the persuadee, it has to be some event of communication. Analogously, the culminating events need to be included in the denotation of the relevant propositional attitude. So on this kind of analysis, 'persuade' would denote a complex event containing at least two subevents, one, the grounding action by the agent being constrained to be in the denotation of 'verbs of communication', and the culminating event being constrained to be in the denotation of 'believe' or 'intend' events, depending on whether there is a finite or an infinitival complement.

$D(\text{persuade}_{trans})$ = a set of $<\text{event}_{<grnd...culm>}, \text{ind}_{ag}, \text{ind}_{pat}, \text{proposition}>$ tuples, with the constraint that tuples $<\text{event}_{grnd}, \text{ind}_{ag}>$ are in $D(\text{'verbs of communication'})$ and $<\text{event}_{culm}, \text{ind}_{pat}, \text{proposition}>$ are in $D(\text{believe})$ or $D(\text{intend})$

Now the entailments that we want will follow directly from the denotation of the verbs: we do not need to posit abstract 'believe' or 'intend' morphemes in the lexical representation or logical form for 'persuade': the relevant information is there in the denotation. In this particular case we could perhaps go on to tell a plausible developmental story about the acquisition of concepts like 'persuade'. We would predict that until you have learned which events count as acts of communication, and which count as beliefs or intentions, you will not be able to learn which events are in the denotation of 'persuade' since this includes both of the other types of event.

However, while moving responsibility for the validity of inferences from the representational level to the denotational level, we have ironically enough now got a story about the relevant entailments that is rather parallel to that we would tell for the 'dogs are animals' cases. Consider how our model theory would capture the 'dogs are animals' intuition. It would do so by stipulation that in every valid model for English, the set of dogs is to be a subset of the set of animals. Model theory for our analysis of causative verbs is of a similar nature, but using 'part of' rather than 'member of': 'X melted Y' entails 'Y melted' because whenever there is an event making 'X melted Y' true, there is a culminating sub-event making 'Y melted' true. 'X persuaded Y to leave' entails 'Y intends to leave' because the denotation of 'persuade' includes complex events whose culminations are 'intendings' by the patient. Unless we were to argue that mereological relations like 'part of' somehow are intuitively 'more necessary' than those like membership or set inclusion, we no longer have a formal basis for our intuition that there is a difference between the 'dogs are animals' cases, and the 'persuade/intend' ones. So that as well as acknowledging that with some effort you could imagine it turning out that we had misplaced dogs in our system of classification, we are also apparently acknowledging that we could discover that, after all, you could persuade someone to do something without them thereby intending to do it, since learning the meaning of 'persuade' is now just a question of learning its place in our ontology of different kinds of composite events. But this is not a conclusion that I am happy with.

Stephen Pulman graduated in English from London University, and his PhD in formal semantics was from the University of Essex. After teaching linguistics for several years he joined the University of Cambridge Computer Laboratory in 1984 as a lecturer, subsequently reader, in Natural Language Processing with Karen Spärck Jones. From 1988 to 1997 he was also Director of SRI International's Cambridge Computer Science Research Centre. In 2000 he was appointed to the Chair of General Linguistics at Oxford University, where he leads a group in computational linguistics currently working on the acquisition of domain knowledge from texts, large scale grammar engineering, computational semantics, and various practical applications such as automated examination grading. He was elected a Fellow of the British Academy in 2001.

ACKNOWLEDGEMENTS

Earlier versions of this paper have been presented to audiences at the University of Edinburgh, and the University of Oxford, and I am grateful to these audiences for their comments. I have also benefitted from comments on a draft by Ted Briscoe, Nicholas Shea, and Yorick Wilks.

REFERENCES

Dowty, D. (1979). *Word meaning and Montague grammar*. Dordrecht. D. Reidel.

Evans G. and McDowell, J. (Eds) (1976). Editors' introduction to *Truth and meaning: essays in semantics*. Oxford University Press.

Fillmore, C. J. (1966). Deictic categories in the semantics of 'come'. In *Foundations of Language*. 2, 219-227.

Fodor, J. A. (1970). *Three reasons for not deriving 'kill' from 'cause to die'*. Linguistic Inquiry 1:4, 429-438.

Fodor, J. A. (1998). *Concepts*. Oxford University Press.

Fodor, J. A. and Lepore, E. (1998). *The emptiness of the lexicon. Linguistic Inquiry* 29:2 269-288.

Hale, K. and Keyser, S. J. (1993). On argument structure and the lexical representation of semantic relations. In *The view from Building 20*. . S. J. Keyser, and K. Hale, (Eds) Cambridge, MA, Massachusetts Institute of Technology Press.

Hale, K and Keyser, S. J. (1997). On the complex nature of simple predicators. In *Complex predicates*. A. Alsina, J. Bresnan, and P. Sells. (Eds). Stanford, Center for the Study of Language and Information Publications: 29-65.

Hornsby, J. (1980). *Actions*. London: Routledge.

Jackendoff, R. (1990). *Semantic structures*. Massachusetts Institute of Technology Press

Kamp H. and Reyle, U. (1992).From *Discourse to logic*. Kluwer Academic Publishers.

Lakoff, G. (1972). Linguistics and Natural Logic. In *Semantics of natural language*. D. Davidson and G. Harman, (Eds). Dordrecht. D. Reidel.

Lawrence S. and Margolis, E. (2002). Radical Concept Nativism. In *Cognition* 86, 25-55.

Lepore, E. and Fodor, J. (1998). *Morphemes matter.* (with J. Fodor), forthcoming; RuCCS Tech Report .

McCawley, J. D. (1971) Prelexical Syntax. reprinted in *Semantic syntax..* P. Seuren, (Ed) (1974). *Oxford readings in philosophy.* Oxford University Press.

Mellor, D. H. (1987). The singularly affecting facts of causation. In *Metaphysics and morality: essays in honour of J. J. C. Smart.* P. Pettit, et al., (Eds). Oxford, Blackwell: 111-136.

Nida, E. A. (1951). *A system for the description of semantic elements.* Word 7, 1-14.

Pietroski, P. (1998). *Actions, adjuncts and agency. Mind,* 107 pp 73-112.

Spärck Jones, K. (1986). *Synonymy and semantic classification.* Edinburgh: Edinburgh University Press.

DONNA HARMAN

THE IMPORTANCE OF FOCUSED EVALUATIONS: A CASE STUDY OF TREC AND DUC

1. INTRODUCTION TO TREC

Evaluation has always been an important part of scientific research. A simplistic breakdown of research such as that done in language technology could be as follows: perform preliminary investigations in a particular area of interest, develop hypotheses about some issue in this area, devise a method of evaluating those hypotheses, perform the necessary experiments and evaluations, analyze the results, feed those results back into further experiments, and, at some point, determine a stopping point and report results in a scientific paper. The evaluation piece of this breakdown is critical because it determines what new investigations need to be made and also when significant findings are worth reporting.

Using the field of information retrieval as an example, we can see a long history of evaluation in areas such as weighting of single terms, use of phrases, development of stemming or segmentation algorithms, and more recently, retrieval of information across languages. In all these cases there has been extensive evaluation, and that evaluation has often used test collections.

The test collection paradigm in information retrieval was given a major boost by Cyril Cleverdon's Cranfield project in the early 1960's (Cleverdon, Mills & Keen, 1966). To evaluate the differences among manual indexing techniques, he built a large (for that time) test collection containing 225 questions and 1400 abstracts. He also devised some metrics based on recall and precision for systematic evaluation of results across indexing methods. Both the test collections and the metrics were quickly taken up by the various groups working on the "automatic indexing" systems that could retrieve text based solely on the content of that text. The Cornell SMART project, led by Professor Gerard Salton, and the University of Cambridge projects worked on by Dr. Karen Spärck Jones and others, used the Cranfield test collections and various subsets of the metrics. Additional test collections were built, especially in the SMART project, where test collections were created using articles from TIME magazine, abstracts from the MEDLINE collection (Salton, 1972), and abstracts from the *Communications of the Association of Computing Machinery* (CACM) (Fox, 1983). These various test collections, along with others such as the National Physical Laboratory (NPL) collection from Britain served as major evaluation vehicles for 30 years in the field of information retrieval.

John I. Tait (ed.), *Charting a New Course: Natural Language Processing and Information Retrieval. Essays in Honour of Karen Spärck Jones.* 175–194

In the middle 1970's, Spärck Jones and van Rijsbergen (1975) proposed the creation of a large test collection. This collection was not only to be many magnitudes larger than the then-current test collections, but was to be carefully designed to allow controlled experimentation. There were many factors to be considered in selecting the documents, selecting the test topics, and creating the relevance judgments, and these were discussed in detail in a later survey (Sparck Jones & van Rijsbergen, 1976) They pointed out the need for different text populations (e.g. various styles of writing), different document populations (e.g. general newspapers versus scientific articles), different request populations (e.g. precise vs. non-precise requests), etc., all to be measured and controlled to allow the various factors of the retrieval environment to be correlated with the various search parameters used in retrieval systems. Unfortunately this ideal test collection was not built due to lack of funding, forcing researchers to continue to use the small test collections.

But in addition to the problems with the size of the collections, there was no way of focusing the testing: groups used different subsets of the collections, different metrics, and different infrastructures in their series of isolated experiments. In 1981, Spärck Jones wrote

> Yet the most striking feature of the test history of the past two decades is its lack of consolidation. It is true that some very broad generalizations have been endorsed by successive tests: for example...but there has been a real failure at the detailed level to build one test on another. As a result there are no explanations for these generalizations, and hence no means of knowing whether improved systems could be designed (Sparck Jones, 1981, p. 245).

2. INITIAL DESIGN OF TREC

In 1992 a new test collection was built at the National Institute of Standards and Technology (NIST) as part of TIPSTER (Merchant, 1994), a large project for improvement in text retrieval and extraction sponsored by the U.S. Government. This test collection was larger than the older collections by a factor of 1000, i.e. instead of 2 megabytes of abstracts, this collection contained 2 gigabytes of documents.

Whereas NIST could have just released this collection to researchers, it seemed a good chance to address Spärck Jones's call for consolidation of results. This consolidation is more likely if groups can compare results across the same data, using the same evaluation method, and then meet to discuss openly how methods differ. The importance of a cross-system comparison is not to determine the best system but to give researchers some basis for understanding the strengths and weaknesses of the various techniques developed by others. This encourages the transfer of good ideas, and the identification of appropriate performance benchmarks for new approaches to match.

This was the genesis of the Text REtrieval Conference (TREC) (Harman, 1993), a focused evaluation to use this collection. This evaluation has been running for 13 years now, with over 100 participants in the current round of evaluation. (Complete details of TREC, including twelve years of proceedings and information on how to obtain the test collections can be found at http://trec.nist.gov).

The success of focused evaluations depends on several factors. First, the task design needs to strike a good balance between clear specification of the task and enough flexibility to allow a wide variety of experiments. Second, the data used for evaluation needs to be sufficiently focused, but still reflect a realistic environment. Third, there needs to be a reasonably large set of research groups interested in the task and data. And fourth, the various metrics and evaluation protocols should encourage broad experimentation by emphasizing diagnostic measures rather than just "competitive" scores.

The obvious starting point for focused evaluation was the basic core retrieval task, that of *ad hoc* retrieval from static collections. This task reflected the traditional test collection approach that researchers were familiar with, and came with evaluation protocols that were already accepted by the community. The first year NIST worked with the sponsoring agencies to create 50 complex descriptions of information needs (called topics in TREC), and asked participants to retrieve a ranked list of documents from the 2 gigabytes of data as an answer to each topic. Over the eight years that the ad hoc task was run, the topic design evolved to less complex topics, but the main task was the same.

Note that the systems used the same 50 topics, the same document set and were evaluated with the same metrics, so that cross-system comparison was valid. Starting in TREC-1 there were 18 systems, and this number grew to over 40 before the ad hoc task was halted. In the eight years of this task in TREC, each year built on previous work, much as Spärck Jones had called for. As a consequence there was a significant amount of technology transfer across systems, resulting in a doubling of retrieval effectiveness in the first five years of TREC. Techniques such as the OKAPI term weighting algorithms (Sparck Jones, Walker & Robertson, 2000) and pseudo-relevance (blind) feedback have been widely adopted by both researchers and commercial systems as a result of their comparative success in TREC. Benchmarks of performance for the various test collections each year are also of critical importance for those groups currently working on new ideas in retrieval systems.

Although the ad hoc task was designed to be a high-recall task, using mean average precision as the main metric, it is useful to also look at the high precision end of the curve as measured by the precision of the search at a cutoff of 30 documents. Spärck Jones provided annual summaries of the data (published as appendices in each proceedings) that showed performance increases across TRECs such that by the end of the eight years over 40% of the documents retrieved at rank 30 were relevant.

3. FOCUSED EVALUATIONS IN THE TREC TRACKS

An equally important role of focused evaluations is the ability to target specific problems in language technology and to design tasks for evaluation such that issues can be studied concurrently by multiple groups. The fact that groups usually take different approaches to solving the problem allows for a major multiplying factor in what is learned. Specific problems beyond the core ad hoc retrieval task have been investigated in TREC in "tracks" starting in 1994.

Two types of tracks have been run at TREC; tracks that are some type of modification of the ad hoc task, and tracks that work in new research areas. Examples of the first type are the running of the ad hoc task in Spanish, where both the topics and the documents were in Spanish, but the task was the same as the English ad hoc, or the speech retrieval track where the input documents were the results of speech recognition for news broadcasts. Here it was possible to explore the robustness of the core retrieval technology as it is transferred to a new language, or to a new media. Examples of the second type of track would be the cross-language track, and the QA track, both of which open new research areas and involve joining diverse communities of researchers (from the machine translation community and from the natural language processing community).

Table 1. Number of participants per track and total number of distinct participants in each track

Track	TREC											
	1992	1993	1994	1995	1996	1997	1998	1999	2000	2001	2002	2003
Ad Hoc	18	24	26	23	28	31	42	41	—	—	—	—
Routing	16	25	25	15	16	21	—	—	—	—	—	—
Interactive	—	—	3	11	2	9	8	7	6	6	6	—
Spanish	—	—	4	10	7	—	—	—	—	—	—	—
Confusion	—	—	—	4	5	—	—	—	—	—	—	—
DB Merging	—	—	—	3	3	—	—	—	—	—	—	—
Filtering	—	—	—	4	7	10	12	14	15	19	21	—
Chinese	—	—	—	—	9	12	—	—	—	—	—	—
NLP	—	—	—	—	4	2	—	—	—	—	—	—
Speech	—	—	—	—	—	13	10	10	3	—	—	—
Cross-Language	—	—	—	—	—	13	9	13	16	10	9	—
High Precision	—	—	—	—	—	5	4	—	—	—	—	—
VLC	—	—	—	—	—	—	7	6	—	—	—	—
Query	—	—	—	—	—	—	2	5	6	—	—	—
QA	—	—	—	—	—	—	—	20	28	36	34	33
Web	—	—	—	—	—	—	—	17	23	30	23	27
Video	—	—	—	—	—	—	—	—	—	12	19	ᵉ
Novelty	—	—	—	—	—	—	—	—	—	—	13	14
Genome	—	—	—	—	—	—	—	—	—	—	—	29
HARD	—	—	—	—	—	—	—	—	—	—	—	14
Robust	—	—	—	—	—	—	—	—	—	—	—	16
Total participants	22	31	33	36	38	51	56	66	69	87	93	93

ᵉ The video track was spun off as a separate evaluation effort in 2003.

Table 1 shows the various tracks that have been run over the 12 years of TREC and the number of participants in those tracks. Some of the tracks have been long-running, usually in areas of major research such as filtering or interactive retrieval. Other tracks have run for much shorter times, either because the track task was not sufficiently focused to allow interesting research or because the problem being addressed was quickly solved. Each track has taken advantage of the focused evaluation in different ways, but all have benefited from the concentration of multiple researchers on specific problems in information

3.1 The Cross-Language Track

The TREC-9 cross-language track provides an excellent example of successful design for a focused evaluation in a new research area. The task was the traditional information retrieval task: given an information need expressed in natural language, retrieve a list of documents ranked by the likelihood that they fill that need. In this case the topic was expressed in English, and the documents to be searched were in Chinese (encoded in BIG5). No restrictions were made on how to do this task: groups could automatically translate the English topic to Chinese, and then do Chinese to Chinese retrieval, or they could work directly with the original languages, such as by incorporating translation probabilities into the retrieval algorithms. All groups were asked to submit both cross-lingual and monolingual runs to allow for comparisons of various components.

The data consisted of about 250 megabytes of articles donated by Wisers, Ltd. from the 1998 and 1999 *Hong Kong Commercial Daily*, *Hong Kong Daily News*, and *Takungpao*. Twenty-five topics were generated in English for this task, and were translated into Chinese for the monolingual task by a native speaker. Four issues should be noted about the data used for evaluation. First, the documents were part of a general purpose collection that realistically would be searched for information. Second, both the collection and the individual documents were large enough to challenge the various algorithms. Third, there were a sufficient number of topics to allow for statistical variation of results (Buckley & Voorhees, 2000) and for stable comparison of the performance averages. And fourth, appropriate care was taken during the topic translation process to allow for comparison of results across the monolingual and cross-lingual runs. In particular, it was critical to have a native Chinese speaker translate the English topics, with specific instructions to express the information need *as it would naturally have been expressed in Chinese*.

The cross-language task attracted a wide variety of groups including five companies[1] from the U.S. (BBN Technologies; IBM Yorktown Heights, MNIS-TextWise Labs, Telcordia Technologies, Inc., and Trans-EZ Inc.), one company and two universities from China (Microsoft Research, China; Chinese University of Hong Kong and Fudan University), five universities from the U.S. (Johns Hopkins University; Queens College,CUNY; University of California, Berkeley; University of Maryland and the University of Massachusetts), and three other groups from Asia (KAIST from Korea, RMIT University/CSIRO from Australia, and National Taiwan University). These 16 groups not only brought many diverse approaches to the problem, but had access to different types of resources, such as local dictionaries, word lists, name extraction algorithms, etc.

---

[1] The identification of any private company in this paper does not imply endorsement by NIST.

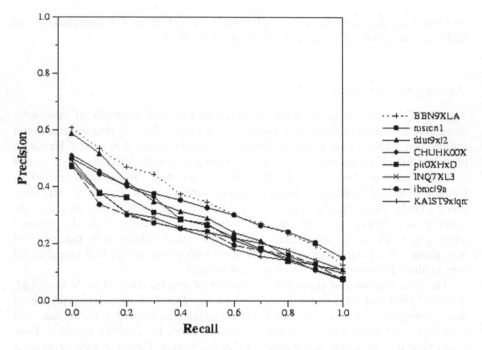

Figure 1. Results of the cross-language task, English to Chinese

Figure 1 shows the recall and precision for the cross-language task for the top 8 systems. The results are generally quite high, with three systems standing out for particular notice. The BBN system (Xu & Weischedel, 2001) achieved excellent results over all ranges of recall and precision. The system from Microsoft Research, China (Gao *et al*, 2001) did particularly well in the high recall range, whereas the system from Fudan University (Wu *et al*, 2001) excelled at the high precision end of the graph.

The particular value of this track was the incredible range of experiments that were performed. These ranged from full investigations of the use of different n-gram systems vs. word-based systems, to the development of a complete language modeling system by BBN. Since the task was so focused, this large set of experiments can be compared across systems, and serves as a major guidepost for further research and commercialization of Chinese cross-language retrieval.

3.2 The Web Track

A second example of the usefulness of a focused evaluation is the web track, which is now in its ninth year. This track was originally started by David Hawking (Hawking & Crasswell, 1999) as an efficiency track in TREC-7, with a corpus of 100 Gigabytes taken from the 1997 Brewster Kahle web archive and with an emphasis made on performance only at the high precision end, using the measure of precision at 20 documents retrieved. By TREC-8 it had been decided to start a small web collection that would parallel the ad hoc test collections (unstructured text, mostly newspapers and newswires), so 2 gigabytes of the 100 gigabyte collection were selected as the documents for searching. The results of TREC-8 showed that little difference existed between these ad hoc and web collections if the web documents were treated as unstructured documents, i.e. without the link structure. However, this assumption ignores a major component of the web (the links), and therefore in TREC-9 a true web track was created.

The 100 gigabyte collection from TREC-7 was used to create a special 10 gigabyte subsample (Bailey, Crasswell & Hawking, 2003) for TREC-9, with the link structure preserved as much as possible within that subset. The topics were taken from logs of search engines, and were therefore very short. The ad hoc style evaluation was modified by asking the NIST judges for a three-level decision: highly relevant, relevant, and non-relevant and also recording a "best" answer document (Voorhees, 2001). However, even with multiple degrees of relevance, there was no demonstrated advantage in using the link methods over the normal ad hoc methods used in TREC-8. Additionally the best answer documents showed no preferred pattern of link structure.

For the next TREC (TREC-2001), the web track repeated (for verification) the task in TREC-9, but added a new task taken directly from the web community. This task involved homepage finding, i.e. there were 145 queries looking for the homepages of specific projects or persons. This task, unlike the topic relevance task, showed major improvements for using links, with groups using either links or the url depth of a page scoring well above those groups using only the content of the pages.

TREC-2002 moved completely away from the familiar topic relevance task, working only with homepage/namepage finding and a new "bookmarking" task. Additionally a natural subset from the web, the *.gov domain, was used for testing. These tasks were again repeated in TREC-2003 with minor modifications.

The value of the focused evaluation for the web track differs from that for the cross-language track. Clearly there are some system features in the better performing systems that can be incorporated in other systems. More importantly, however, there was a focused effort by many groups to investigate how searching on web data differs from that on non-web data. This systematic common evaluation on web data gives researchers a solid ground on which to evolve more practical ways of dealing with the web. It also triggered the first trial of a 3-level (highly relevant/relevant/non- relevant) judgment system in TREC, since this seemed particularly critical for web search evaluation.

3.3 The Question-Answering Track

The question-answering track has been run since TREC-8. The purpose of the track is to encourage research into systems that return actual answers, as opposed to ranked lists of documents.

There have been many enthusiastic participants in this track, even in its first year, as the track is of interest both to groups that specialize in information retrieval and to groups that have a more general natural language processing (NLP) orientation. In order for the track to be effective, however, the focusing factors of task, data, and evaluation protocols needed to be carefully considered.

The task was initially defined to be simple question answering, where the answer could be found within a single document and could be answered by an answer-string of 50 bytes. Additionally groups could return a longer string (250 bytes), which is similar to passage retrieval, and is the easiest task for participants with little NLP background.

In TREC-8, the questions were solicited from participants and also provided by NIST. But this was deemed too artificial, and for TREC-9 the track used 693 short-answer questions taken from query logs of Encarta and Excite as testing material. It was guaranteed that each of these questions had a document that answered the question in the 2 gigabyte collection that was to be searched (this was verified by NIST before distributing the questions). An example of a question is "How tall is the Empire State Building"?

For evaluation, there were two obvious choices of methodology. The first, and the most traditional method in the NLP community, was to create answer keys during the question formation process. Then systems could be automatically graded against these keys. However, NIST chose to follow the tradition in information retrieval, where the right answers (relevant documents) are determined by a human reader. The NIST judges read all the submitted answers to each question and determined if they were correct or incorrect. Whereas this provided a level of subjectivity to the evaluation, it proved to be the best way of dealing with all the unforeseen problems of ambiguity and proper granularity of the answers (Voorhees & Tice, 2000). There were 28 groups worldwide that participated in the TREC-9 track, with the best system (Harabagiu, 2001) finding correct answers for more than 69% of the questions within the top five 50-byte answer strings that they returned. Figure 2 shows the results of the top 8 groups. The histogram heights measure the mean reciprocal rank (MRR) of the correct answers. An individual question received a score equal to the reciprocal of the rank at which the first correct response was returned, or 0 if none of the five responses contained a correct answer. The score for a submission was then the mean of the individual questions' reciprocal ranks. The line plotted in the figure shows the percent of the questions in which a given system did not return any correct answer.

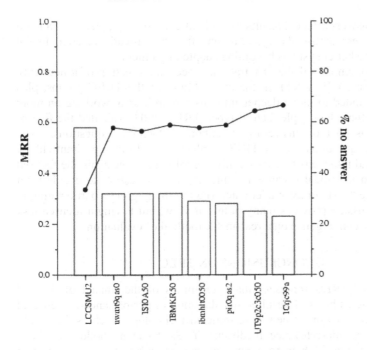

Figure 2. Results of systems for TREC-9 QA

For TREC-2001, the track used the same task, with the answer strings limited to 50 bytes and with some questions having no known answers in the data (the systems were supposed to return NIL for these questions). There were 500 questions taken from Microsoft and AskJeeves logs. A second task, that of list questions was added, where systems were asked to return lists of unique answers, often taken from different documents. An example of these questions is "Name 8 Chuck Berry songs".

TREC-2002 also evaluated the simple factoid questions, but this time required a single answer (not the ranked list of 5 returned in earlier TRECs) and required that this answer not be a 50-byte snippet of text but be an exact answer. By this time the systems were sophisticated enough to do this and the results were excellent (the best system getting 415 out of 500 answers correct). The list task was continued.

There have been several important consequences of the focused evaluation in factoid question-answering. First, it demonstrated that it is possible to answer simple questions automatically in an unlimited domain, and this has encouraged a whole new line of research both in the IR community and the NLP community. Second, it allowed many NLP groups working in this area to concentrate on a common, well-defined problem, with the evaluation effort done by an unbiased outside group (NIST). Several years of workshops at various NLP conferences have been devoted to the QA task. Many interesting research issues have arisen, such as how to automatically categorize the questions in order to properly assign algorithms. There were also important evaluation issues to be examined, such as how the granularity of the answers affected results. As a final consequence, there was a large spread in effectiveness across the systems, and this has already resulted in the methodologies of the better systems becoming adopted by others.

A separate major impact of the QA track has been the creation of a new U.S. government program (AQUAINT) in this area. Many of the TREC groups, plus others, have been funded to move deeper into this research area, working on more complex questions than the simple factoid type. TREC-2003 evaluated the first of these complex areas--that of answering definition or "who is" questions. The evaluation of these questions moves TREC further away from the Cranfield IR evaluation model and into areas that are mainly unexplored. Once again the focused model of evaluation is critical because for this task it is necessary to decide what kinds of answers are "best" or even adequate. Having many groups participating in the testing and discussion provides many points of view, but having a focused task will hopefully allow convergence on a reasonable method of evaluation

4. CONCLUSIONS ON TREC

The twelve years of TREC represent many examples of the impact of focused research. The basic ad hoc task resulted in a doubling of performance for retrieval systems, and the introduction of new core retrieval technology, such as the BM25 term weights, and pseudo-relevance feedback. These basic methodologies have been adopted worldwide, both in research and commercial systems. The use of tightly-focused tasks in the various tracks provided proof of the robustness of core retrieval methodologies across multiple languages and media and introduced new areas of information retrieval research, such as question-answering and cross-language retrieval.

The impact of TREC on the retrieval community extends far beyond the results of the various evaluations. The online proceedings of the various TREC conferences are one of the more heavily referenced publications for the community, and the test collections built for the various evaluations are not only publicly available, but are the collections of choice for appropriate tasks. A final impact has been the introduction of new people to information retrieval, both in the core area of retrieval research and in related areas such as natural language processing.

5. INTRODUCTION TO DUC

Research in summarization was one of the first efforts to use computers to understand language. Work was done back in the 1950s (Mani & Maybury, 1998) by many groups, including commercial services, to automatically produce abstracts or lists of pertinent keywords for documents. The interest in automatic summarization of text has continued, and currently is enjoying increased emphasis as demonstrated by the numerous summarization workshops held during the last five years.

Along with the research came efforts to evaluate automatic summarization performance. Two major types of evaluation have been used: *intrinsic* evaluation where the emphasis is on measuring the quality of the created summary directly, and *extrinsic* evaluation where the emphasis is on measuring how well the summary performs within a given task. But evaluation of summarization is extremely difficult to do well. Intrinsic evaluation implies that there is some standard on which to judge summarization quality and usually this standard is operationalized by finding an existing abstract/text data set or by having humans create an "ideal" summary (even though no such ideal exists). The inherent human variability in doing a summarization task requires complex experimental design and analysis to accurately measure differences in machine performance in this task. This problem occurs both for situations using existing abstracts with text (Marcu, 1999) and for situations where ideal summaries are created (Jing *et al*, 1998).

Extrinsic evaluation requires the selection of a task that could use summarization and then measuring the effect of using summaries (usually created automatically) instead of the original text. Critical issues here are the task selection and the metrics for measurement. For example the tasks should be time-consuming enough that summaries could be useful, such as deciding whether to read a document based on reading its summary. They also must be sensitive enough to the quality of a summary that differences among a set of well-constructed summaries will show a difference in performance of the task. For examples of extrinsic evaluations, see the TIPSTER SUMMAC evaluation (Mani *et al*, 1998, Firmin & Chrzanowski, 1998) and the Japanese NTCIR evaluation (Fukusima & Okomura, 1998, Nagao, 1998).

In 2000, Spärck Jones was a major contributor to a roadmap (Baldwin *et al*, 2000) to guide a new summarization evaluation sponsored by DARPA. This roadmap provided guidance for the new Document Understanding Conference (DUC), with a pilot run in 2000, and the first major evaluation in the fall of 2001.

The roadmap called for evaluation of generic summaries of both single documents and sets of multiple documents, at specified levels of text compression. Summaries can be classified based on characteristics of their input and output and DUC-2001 used largely domain-independent monolingual English newswire and newspaper articles as input with the task of creating fluent extracts or abstracts. The summaries were to be generic, i.e., minimally constrained with respect to their purpose: situation, audience (educated adult newspaper readers), and use. Whereas this may result in greater variability in human judgments, generic summaries are heavily in use and were felt to be an appropriate first target for evaluation.

The roadmap suggested that the initial evaluation was to be intrinsic, with extrinsic evaluation to be phased in over time, along with requirements of deeper text understanding techniques that can lead to more complicated summaries.

6. INITIAL DESIGN OF DUC

NIST went about the design of the first evaluation in a similar manner to TREC, i.e., design a well-defined task that is focused but realistic and come up with some way of measuring performance. The task was as follows:

1. Sixty sets of approximately 10 documents each were provided as system input. Given such a set of documents, the systems were to automatically

create 100-word generic summaries   for each document. Additionally
they were to create generic summaries of the entire set, one summary at
each of four target   lengths (approximately 400, 200, 100, and 50 words).
2.   The sets of documents were created at NIST by 10 retired information
analysts. Each person created six document sets, and then created 100-word
manual abstracts for each document, and for the entire document set at the
400, 200, 100 and 50 word lengths.   Thirty of the sets (documents and
manual abstracts) were distributed   as training data and the remaining
thirty sets of documents (without abstracts) were distributed as test data.
NIST then performed manual evaluation of the results.

The evaluation plan as specified in the roadmap was for NIST to concentrate on
manual comparison of the system results with the humanly-constructed abstracts.
Manual evaluation was considered critical because there was a general concern that
automatic evaluation would not be adequate to deal properly with linguistic devices
such as paraphrasing, or with abstracting methods that produce results differing
greatly from simple extracts of the initial text. Additionally there was a desire to
measure the coherence and organization of generated summaries.

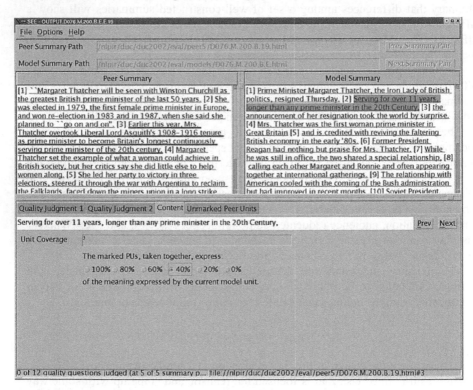

Figure 3. SEE interface for judging per unit coverage

Central to the manual comparison was a new tool developed by Chin-Yew Lin at the Information Sciences Institute, University of Southern California (http://www.isi.edu/~cyl/SEE). This tool allows pair-wise comparison of two summaries, and a modified version was used at NIST. Figure 3 shows one example of this interface. Human evaluation was done at NIST using the same personnel who created the manual abstracts (called model summaries). These people did pair-wise comparisons between their "model" summaries and the "peer" summaries. Peer summaries include system-generated summaries, additional manual abstracts generated by others, and baseline summaries.

The additional manual abstracts came from two other analysts who were asked to generate "duplicate" manual abstracts. The baseline summaries were defined to be the first 100 words for single documents and the first 50, 100, 200 or 400 words of the most recent document in the document set for the multi-document summaries. An additional baseline of concatenated first, second, etc. sentences from a chronological sequence of documents in the set was also used in the multi-document summaries.

Two specific areas of evaluation were examined using the SEE interface. The first area involved the quality of the summary. Each system-generated summary, baseline summary, and "duplicate" manual summary was judged for grammaticality, cohesion and organization using a five-point scale.

1. *Grammaticality*--[All, most, some, hardly any, or none] of the syntactic units (e.g., sentences, clauses, phrases, etc.) follow the rules of English grammatical form (independent of content).
2. *Cohesion*-- [All, most, some, hardly any, or none] of the sentences fit in as they should with the surrounding sentences.
3. *Organization/coherence*-- [All, most, some, hardly any, or none] of the summary is well-organized, i.e., the content is expressed and arranged in an effective way.

The second area of evaluation dealt with coverage, i.e., how well did the peer summaries cover the content of the documents (as expressed by the model summary). A pair-wise summary comparison was used in this part of the evaluation and judges were asked to do detailed coverage comparisons. SEE allowed the judges to step through predefined units of the model summary and for each unit of that summary, mark the sentences in the peer summary that expressed [all, most, some, hardly any or none] of the content in the current model summary unit.

The choice of units for the model and peer summaries involved practical as well as theoretical considerations. Researchers wanted units smaller than a sentence for better diagnostic information. Automatically determined units called elementary discourse units (EDUs) (Carlson *et al,* 2001) based on rhetorical structure theory were proposed. Because these required some human post-editing, it was only practical to use them for the model summaries, which are many fewer in number than the summaries produced by the research systems. The latter were automatically divided into sentences.

Note that some sentences in the peer summary could be marked as pertinent to multiple units in the model summary, and some sentences in the peer summary might not be marked as being pertinent to any units in the model summary.

This process is much more complex than doing a simple overall comparison, i.e., did the entire summary being judged (the peer summary) express [all, most, some, or hardly any] of the content in model summary. The decision to use this more complicated method sprung from a need for more detail about what parts of automatic summaries matched the model summaries and also because past evaluation experiences indicated that judges had more difficulty making an overall decision than they did making decisions at each unit.

7. DUC-2001

There were 15 groups that participated in DUC-2001, and an online proceedings (http://duc.nist.gov) contains papers from all the groups. The papers are a good sample of the 2001 state-of-the-art in summarization.

Most of the groups produced extracts rather than abstracts. Different techniques were used to select sentences for extraction, such as clustering documents or paragraphs or sentences to locate similarities, or locating important sentences using language modeling. Additionally various non-content features such as document length, sentence position, sentence length, cue word use, and document creation time were used in picking important sentences. Several groups also used these heuristics to improve coherence and organization. There was some effort to remove duplicate information by using the Maximal Marginal Relevance algorithm or by using overlap or similarities to other sentences.

The main significance of DUC-2001 is that it was the first large-scale intrinsic evaluation of summarization, both for single documents and across multi-document sets. It was large-scale both in the sense of realistic amounts of test data and in the fact that multiple groups participated in the same focused task. The use of human evaluators working with a well-defined mechanism (the SEE interface) to judge the summaries laid the groundwork for a more principled approach to intrinsic evaluation of summaries.

8. DUC-2002

DUC-2002 was designed and evaluated in much the same manner as DUC-2001 to allow continuity of research and evaluation. There were 60 more document sets with manual abstracts created in the same way as the first 60 sets. The target lengths of the summaries were shortened to eliminate the 400-word summary and to include a headline length summary. SEE was modified to replace the five-point intervals [All, most, some, hardly any, or none] with percentages [0, 20, 40, 60, 80, 100] to permit better score averaging and more consistent judgment by the evaluators.

The major shift for 2002 was in the quality evaluation. In particular the grammaticality, coherence and organization items, which were very difficult for NIST judges to score, were replaced by a series of questions about effective use of pronouns, dangling connectives, subject/verb agreement, etc. In addition to providing more consistent basis for quality assessment, they allowed the participants to more readily pinpoint text generation problems.

The final difference for DUC-2002 was the use of a common metric. DUC-2001 encouraged the researchers to try different metrics as this was the first time for the evaluation. Many groups investigated a coverage metric and it was decided to try a length-adjusted coverage metric for DUC-2002. In addition to measuring how well a peer summary covered the points in the model summary (the coverage metric), brevity would be rewarded.

There were 17 groups that took part in DUC-2002, with 13 of them tackling the single document summary task (at 100 words) and 8 of them working on the multi-document task. The participation of so many sites provided enough focus to allow some interesting conclusions to be drawn.

1. The use of the 12 peer quality questions rather than subjective scores for grammaticality, coherence and organization proved a success. The NIST judges were able to effectively handle these questions and the results hopefully provided useful diagnostic information for the participants. The scores varied widely across the questions, but in general most participants had higher quality summary scores than did the baselines.

2. The scores on the 100-word abstracts for single documents were within reasonable proximity to those of the human abstractors. Unfortunately they were also close to the baseline performance, which is very high for newspaper articles. It was decided to discontinue this task until genre other than newspaper articles became available.

3. The length-adjusted coverage metric worked very well and was accepted by the community.

4. The ranking of system scores across the four different compression rates (10, 50, 100 and 200 word lengths) for the multi-document summaries were similar, that is, systems that did well on one compression rate did equally well on all. This was a surprising outcome and means that testing at multiple compression rates is not necessary *if* there is a metric that normalizes for length.

5. The amount and nature of the human disagreements drew much discussion. There are two sources of disagreements here. The first is the disagreement among judges as to how well a system summary covers the model summary. This is similar to what is seen in relevance assessment for IR evaluations in that different judges are more lenient or strict in terms of their judging. This problem was handled to some degree by having the same judge look at all summaries for a given document set, and by having enough document sets to allow averaging to compensate. But in summarization there is a second source of disagreement and that is the model summaries themselves. Two people will write different models because they have different viewpoints of what is important in a document set and this has caused considerable concern in past evaluations. For this reason it was decided to attempt to lessen this type of disagreement in DUC-2003 by using some method of "constraining" the manual abstracts.

It should be noted that none of these conclusions could have been reached without a focused evaluation. Some of the conclusions needed multiple system results to allow the various trends to be seen, and others benefited from a large community discussion. It was critical to have a fixed task, with evaluation and metrics, to enable the researchers to have a common focus.

9. DUC-2003

DUC-2003 provided four different tasks for summarization.

1. Create a very short summary (10 words, no specific format other than linear) for 300 single documents. This task is a very real-world task in that these "headline" type summaries are often used as surrogates for the documents in applications like web search engines. NIST evaluated these summaries both intrinsically (similar to DUC-2002) and piloted a simulated extrinsic task of predicting their usefulness in selecting relevant documents.

2. Create short summaries (100-words) of 10 documents that are about a given event. The documents came from multiple sources and it was assumed that there would be significant amounts of similar information on the same event. The constraining factor here is this repetition. These summaries were evaluated intrinsically using SEE.

3. Create short summaries of 10 documents about a given topic but focused by a given viewpoint. The systems were given the viewpoint, but inadvertently, the other human abstractors were not. Again SEE was used for evaluation.

4. Create short summaries of 10 documents that were relevant to a given question. The question is the focusing factor here; note that these are query-specific abstracts rather than the generic abstracts produced in tasks 1-3. Both intrinsic evaluation using SEE and a trial extrinsic evaluation were done, with the extrinsic evaluation looking at how responsive the summary was to the question.

There were 21 groups that participated in DUC-2003, with 13 of them doing task 1, 16 doing task 2, 11 doing task 3 and only 9 trying task 4.

Task 1, the very short "headlines" for single documents, showed large performance differences between the humans and the baseline, but also that the systems were significantly different from each other (using a multiple comparisons test). One system was clearly best, with two in the next group, most in the middle, and two in the worst group. The extrinsic scores tended to track the intrinsic scores, implying that systems showing good coverage also provided useful summaries (or that the major component of usefulness was also being measured by coverage). There was less disagreement among human summaries, mostly because this was a highly constrained task.

Task 2 also showed significant performance differences between systems. Figure 4 shows the mean length-adjusted coverage score of the baselines (2 and 3), the 9 human judges (A-J), and the systems. The scores of the judges illustrates the level of disagreements of the models as they measure the coverage score comparing one human abstract against a second. The lines are the respective means of the manual, system, and baseline scores.

Both tasks 3 and 4 not only had fewer participants but also less stable results. These tasks were new to the summarization community and the results were not significantly different from the baselines.

Despite the attempts to constrain the human summaries in DUC-2003, the issue of human variability in constructing summaries, and therefore the difficulty in evaluation of system-generated summaries, has remained a major problem for intrinsic summary evaluation. It also affects the use of the test material for further training. Harman and Over (2004) studied these effects, showing that the large amount of human variability, both in the creation of the model summaries, and in the later comparison of these to system summaries, had little effect on the *relative ranking* of the various system/methods *if* enough instances of testing (document sets) were used to average out these effects. This however does not solve the training material issue, nor does it allow individual systems to examine results as easily on a per document set basis.

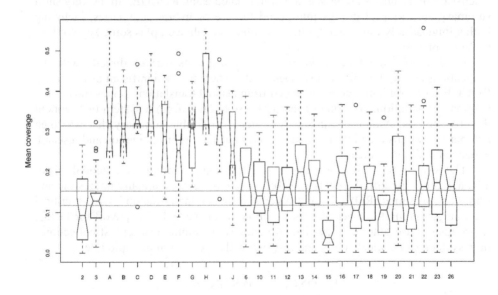

Figure 4. Task 2: Mean length-adjusted coverage by summary source

10. DUC-2004

DUC-2004 had five different tasks. Tasks 1 and 2 continued the research on very short summaries of single documents (75 bytes long), and short (665 bytes) summaries of multiple document sets. There were 50 new document sets created for these tasks. Tasks 3 and 4 were an important variation on this theme. In this case there were 24 document sets, each with around 10 documents. However the documents were in Arabic and the systems were asked to create both very short single document summaries and short multiple document summaries *in English*. Systems were asked to do this using a manual translation and then an automatic translation of the Arabic document.

Task 5 was also a multiple document summary task, with the documents all containing information about a given person and the summary to answer the question of "who is" that person. Note that this is a query-specific summary, a variation of task 4 in DUC-2003.

There were 23 groups that participated in DUC-2004, with 13 of them doing task 1, 16 doing task 2, 11 doing task 3, 10 doing task 4, and 14 trying task 5. NIST used the SEE system for coverage judgments on tasks 2 and 5, but the rest of the tasks were evaluated automatically using the new ROUGE metric (Lin, 2004) This was the first operational trial for this type of automatic evaluation.

The three important developments coming from DUC-2004 were some improved approaches to very short (headline) summary generation for single documents, some initial work in cross-language summarization, and some discussion of the new automatic evaluation method using ROUGE. In the very short summary area, several groups introduced the use of hybrid summaries, including both a linguistically motivated section (headline-like phrase), plus some keywords to provide context.

For the cross-language summarization, most groups worked directly with the translations as if they were English documents. There was a significant difference in ROUGE scores for summaries generated from manual translations versus those from automatic translations, but one of the best results came from a system that worked directly with the Arabic documents, producing an Arabic summary that was then automatically translated into English. Clearly much more investigation and research is needed in this new area.

The use of ROUGE for automatic evaluation represents a potential major advance for evaluation of summarization. While there remain many interesting and important questions, ROUGE (and other similar automatic methods) are a critical piece in generating the types of test collections that have had a big payoff for TREC. If groups can use automatic evaluation methods on summarization test collections, then systems can evaluate daily and research will move at a more rapid rate.

11. CONCLUSIONS ON DUC

The first four years of DUC represent the beginning of a community who are jointly tackling both better summarization techniques and better methods of evaluating summarization. Unlike TREC, this community is newly-formed, and this formation is a major result of having such a focused evaluation. By having a common set of tasks, and a common evaluation, researchers are able to see where the "real" problems occur, and can develop new research plans (and new evaluation plans) to solve these problems. This is easier to do when multiple groups are involved.

For further information on DUC, including online proceedings from every year and information on the data, see http://duc.nist.gov.

Donna Harman graduated from Cornell University currently heads a group at the National Institute of Standards and Technology working in the area of natural language access to full text, including both retrieval of that text, and processing of that text in terms of automatic question-answering and summarization. In 1992 she started the Text Retrieval Conference (TREC), an ongoing forum that brings together researchers from industry and academia to test their search engines against a common corpora involving over a million documents, with appropriate topics and relevance judgmentsfor this effort. A similar forum for automatic summarization, called the Document Understanding Conference (DUC) was started in 2000.

REFERENCES

Bailey, P., Craswell, N. & Hawking, D. (2003). Engineering a multi-purpose test collection for web retrieval experiments. *Information Processing and Management*, 39(6), 853-871.

Baldwin, B., Donaway, R., Hovy, E., Liddy, E., Mani, I., Marcu, D., McKeown, K., Mittal, V., Moens, M., Radev, D., Sparck Jones, K., Sundheim, B., Teufel, S., Weischedel, R. & White, M. (2000). An evaluation road map for summarization research. http://duc.nist.gov/roadmapping.html.

Carlson, L., Conroy, J., O'Leary, D., Marcu, D., Okurowski, M., Taylor, A. & Wong, W. (2001). An empirical study of the relation between abstracts, extracts, and the discourse structure of texts. In *Proceedings of the 2001 document understanding conference (DUC2001)*, 11-18.

Cleverdon, C., Mills, J. & Keen, E. (1966). Factors determining the performance of indexing systems, Vol. 1: design, Vol. 2: test results.} Aslib Cranfield Research Project. Cranfield, England.

Firmin,T. & Chrzanowski,M. (1998). An evaluation of automatic text summarization systems. In I. Mani & M. Maybury (Eds.), *Advances in Automatic Text Summarization* (pp. 325-340). Cambridge, Massachusetts: MIT Press.

Fox, E. (1983). Characteristics of two new experimental collections in computer and information science containing textual and bibliographic concepts. Technical Report TR 83-561. Cornell University: Computing Science Department.

Fukusima, T. & Okumura, M. (2001). Text summarization challenge: text summarization evaluation at NTCIR Workshop2. In *Proceedings of the second {NTCIR} workshop meeting on evaluation of Chinese and Japanese text retrieval and text summarization*, 9-14.

Gao, J., Xun, E., Zhou, M., Huang, C., Nie, J.-Y. & J.Zhang. (2001).TREC-9 CLIR experiments at MSRCN. In *Proceedings of the ninth Text REtrieval Conference (TREC-9)*,343-354.

Harabagiu, S., Moldovan, D., Pasca, M., Mihalcea, R., Surdeanu, M., Bunescu, R., Girju, R., Rus, V. & Morarescu, P. (2001). Falcon: Boosting knowledge for answer engines. In *Proceedings of the ninth Text REtrieval Conference (TREC-9)*,479-489.

Harman, D. (1993). Overview of the first Text REtrieval Conference (TREC-1). In *Proceedings of the first Text REtrieval conference (TREC-1)*, 1--20.

Harman, D. & Over, P. (2004). The effects of human variation in DUC summarization evaluation. In Proceedings of the text summarization workshop, ACL 2004, 10-17.Buckley, C. & Voorhees, E. (2000). Evaluating evaluation measure stability. In Proceedings of the 23th annual international ACM SIGIR conference on research and development in information retrieval, 33-40.

Hawking, D. & Craswell, N. (1999). Overview of the TREC-7 very large collection track. In *Proceedings of the seventh Text REtrieval Conference (TREC-7)*,91-104.

Jing,H., Barzilay,R., McKeown,K. & Elhadad,M. (1998). Summarization evaluation methods: experiments and analysis. In *Intelligent text summarization: Papers from the 1998 AAAI spring symposium*, 51-60.

Lin, C-Y. (2004). ROUGE: A package for automatic evaluation of summaries. In Proceedings of the text summarization workshop, ACL 2004, 74-81.

Mani,I., Firmin,T., House,D., Chrzanowski,M., Klein,G., Hirshman, L., Sundheim,B. & Obrst,L. (1998). The TIPSTER text summarization evaluation: final report. http://www.itl.nist.gov/iaui/894.02/related_projects/tipster_summac/final_rpt.html}.

Mani, I. & Maybury, M. (EdS). (1998).   *Advances in Automatic Text Summarization.Cambridge*, Massachusetts: MIT Press.

Marcu, D. (1999) The automatic construction of large-scale corpora for summarization research.   In Proceedings of the 22th annual international ACM SIGIR conference on research and development in information retrieval,137-144. Merchant, R. (1994).   TIPSTER phase I: Program overview. In R. Merchant(Ed, *Proceedings of the TIPSTER text program - phase I* (pp.1-2).   San Mateo, California: Morgan Kaufmann Publishing Co.

Nakao, Y. (2001).   How small distinction among summaries can the evaluation method identify.   In *Proceedings of the second NTCIR workshop meeting on evaluation of Chinese and Japanese text retrieval and text summarization*, 235-241

Salton, G. (1972).   A new comparison between conventional indexing (MEDLARS) and automatic indexing (SMART).   *Journal of the American Society for Information Science*, 23, 75-84.

Sparck Jones, K. (1981).   *Information retrieval experiment*. London, UK: Butterworths.

Sparck Jones, K. & van Rijsbergen, C. (1975). Report on the need for and provision of an "ideal" information retrieval test collection. British Library Research and Development Report 5266. University of Cambridge: Computer Laboratory.

Sparck Jones, K. & van Rijsbergen, C. (1976).   Information retrieval test collections.   *Journal of Documentation*, 32(1), 59-75.

Sparck Jones, K., Walker, S. & Robertson, S. (2000).   A probabilistic model of information retrieval: development and comparative experiments--parts 1 and 2.   *Information Processing and Management*, 36(6), 779--840.

Voorhees, E. (2001).   Evaluation by highly relevant documents.   In Proceedings of the 24th annual international ACM SIGIR conference on research and development in information retrieval, 74-82.

Voorhees, E. & Tice, D. (2000).   Building a question-answering test collection. In Proceedings of the 23th annual international ACM SIGIR conference on research and development in information retrieval, 200-207.

Wu, L., Huang, X., Guo, Y., Liu, B. & Zhang, Y. (2001). FDU at TREC-9: CLIR, filtering and QA tasks. In *Proceedings of the ninth Text REtrieval Conference (TREC-9)*, 189-202.

Xu, J. & Weischedel, R. (2001).   TREC-9 cross-lingual retrieval at BBN.   In *Proceedings of the ninth Text REtrieval Conference (TREC-9)*, 106.

ROBERT GAIZAUSKAS AND EMMA J. BARKER

MICE FROM A MOUNTAIN: REFLECTIONS ON CURRENT ISSUES IN EVALUATION OF WRITTEN LANGUAGE TECHNOLOGY

1. INTRODUCTION

One of the research topics of on-going concern to Sparck Jones and to which she has contributed significantly is *evaluation of natural language processing systems*. From her early concern with empirical experimentation in her thesis work (Spark Jones, 1964) to recent publications on evaluation for summarisation (Sparck Jones, 2001), including the only book yet published devoted solely to the subject of evaluation of natural language processing systems (Sparck Jones and Galliers, 1996), as well as several major papers reviewing IR system tests in the 60's and 70's (Sparck Jones, 1981b,a) and the TREC project (Sparck Jones, 1995,2000), evaluation has been a central theme of her research. Moreover, she has been a staunch advocate of and participant in efforts to organise and run evaluation programmes, as a member of the TREC programme committee and various NIST and DARPA advisory groups.

In this paper we would like to highlight Sparck Jones's contributions to this area, though not by producing an exhaustive review of what she has written on the subject, worthy as that enterprise would be. Rather, we would like to summarise and assess the conceptual framework for evaluation which Sparck Jones has developed, and then review parts of the TREC and DUC evaluation programmes from the perspective of this framework, with the primary aim of determining an informative and experimentally valid approach to evaluation for a research prototype question answering/summarisation system on which we are currently working. A secondary aim will be to shed light on the fruitfulness of current directions in TREC and DUC for the design and evaluation of end user systems that deploy technologies such as QA and summarization.

In a nutshell the research prototype, which we shall refer to as "Cub Reporter"[1], aims to investigate how question answering, summarization, and related written language technologies, can assist journalists in assembling background information from a news archive to contextualise breaking news stories. Specifically, we want to

---

[1] Cub Reporter is a research project funded by the UK EPSRC, grant reference: GR/R91465/01 and carried out as a collaboration between the Departments of Computer Science and Journalism at the University of Sheffield and with the UK Press Association. See: http://www.nlp.shef.ac.uk/cubreporter for further details.

John I. Tait (ed.), *Charting a New Course: Natural Language Processing and Information Retrieval. Essays in Honour of Karen Spärck Jones*. 195-238
© 2005 Springer.

address two questions: (1) what sort of evaluation would best serve the objectives of Cub Reporter? (2) are the question answering and summarisation evaluations currently being elaborated in the TREC and DUC programmes helpful in steering the development of and assessing QA and summarisation technology for the Cub Reporter scenario?

While the concern with a particular research project of our own might appear parochial, we believe that the Cub Reporter scenario is of more general interest for at least three reasons. First a scenario called "Cub Reporter" was first proposed as a challenge for language technology in a QA and summarization vision statement (Carbonell et al., 2000) and further elaborated in a QA Roadmap document (Burger et al., 2002), wherein it was proposed that this scenario should serve as an intermediate goal for the QA/summarization communities on the path towards the long term vision of a truly powerful professional information analyst tool. Secondly, question answering and summarisation evaluations are beginning to come together, perhaps due to the influence of the Roadmap on NIST. The TREC QA track is moving away from providing very short exact answers to simple factoid questions towards providing richer answers in the form of multiple relevant information "nuggets" pertaining to a question target. At the same time, the DUC summarisation evaluation now assesses summaries of multiple texts that are focussed on specific events and entities, rather than just generic summaries of single documents. This kind of merged QA/summarisation functionality appears to be what is required in the Cub Reporter scenario. Thus, Cub Reporter should provide confirmation that the general movement towards merging QA and summarisation is sensible, in that at least one "real world" application can utilise it. Thirdly, since Cub Reporter is a real scenario, not a laboratory exercise, there are users – reporters – carrying out the Cub Reporter scenario on a daily basis. Investigating their work environment, as a test setting for any QA or summarisation technology we may develop can help us to ascertain whether the measures being used in QA and summarisation evaluation are addressing the most important aspects of the technology

The rest of the paper is organised as follows. In the next section we present a set of concepts and definitions, influenced by Sparck Jones and Galliers (1996), which provide a framework for talking about evaluation. In Section 3 we review the tasks and methodologies adopted in TREC Question Answering track and the Document Understanding Conference summarization evaluations. In Section 4 the Cub Reporter scenario is presented and the relevance and utility of current evaluation programmes to it is discussed. Finally we conclude by summarising the principal results of our analysis. In essence our message is this: there are good reasons for believing that useful and fun as the NIST/DARPA exercises are in promoting technology development, there is an urgent need to consider the extrinsic evaluation of these technologies in real setups, a need with Sparck Jones has identified and emphasized for at least a decade.

2. A FRAMEWORK FOR EVALUATION

In the following we will lay out, as succinctly as possible, the conceptual framework for NL system evaluation presented in Sparck Jones and Galliers (1996), referred to as SJ&G in the following. Terms that SJ&G use with technical meaning are italicised. The general approach is to introduce a number key concepts, specifically, *system*, *user*, *setup* and *evaluation* and then to identify for each of these a set of descriptive features in terms of which these concepts are to be characterised. Specifying an evaluation then boils down to instantiating the features with particular values for particular instances of the concepts.

2.1 Systems

A *system* is "the entire software-hardware entity in the situation of interest" (SJ&G, p. 6). Much of what SJ&G say concerning evaluation pertains to the evaluation of any computer system. However, if we are interested in systems that include language technology we may want to distinguish the language part of the system, or *l-system*, from the non-language part of the system, or *n-system*. L- and n-systems are *subsystems*. Systems or subsystems maybe further described structurally in terms of *components*.

Systems may also be described functionally. A system has an *objective* – what the system is designed or intended to do – and what a system does or carries out is its *task*[2]. Viewed from the larger context, or *environment*, of the setup (see below) within which a system is embedded, the system has a *function* – the role of the system in the setup.

Finally, we may describe a system by observing its behaviour when it is run – what SJ&G call its *operation*. It is the operation of a system that we evaluate.

2.2 Users

A *user* is any human involved with a system's operation. This includes not only those who consume its intended output, but designers, operators, etc. Such different *roles* are one feature by which users are characterised. Others include *category* – whether a user is, e.g., an habitual or casual user; *activity* – what the user does (analogue of task for system); *aim* – what the user is trying to achieve through his or her activity in a setup (analogue of system objective); *behaviour* – what we observe (and evaluate) when a user in engaged in his or her activity (analogue of system operation).

---

[2] It is not entirely clear whether SJ&G are trying to make a substantive distinction between system task and objective, but it would appear so. To take a deliberately exaggerated example, a system might carry out the task of summarisation, when its objective was translation. Thus, the distinction, if we understand it correctly, is between *actual* and *intended* action.

2.3 Setups

A system operates within a larger context or setting, and in general a system cannot be evaluated effectively in isolation from this setting. SJ&G refer to the combination of setting, including users, and system as the *setup*. In addition to the system or systems it contains and its users, a setup is characterised by its own overall *purpose*. When a setup is operational we observe its *working* (analogue of system operation and user behaviour).

SJ&G illustrate these concepts of system, user and setup by means of a fictitious database enquiry system with a natural language interface deployed by a motorbike manufacturer. The purpose this hypothetical setup is decision support. Users fall into one of three categories: work organisers, managing work activities in the workshop, warehouse stock controllers, and financial analysts. However, in the setup they all have the same role which is as submitters of queries. The aim of these users is to obtain information from the DBMS and make sensible decisions. Within this setup there is a computer system whose function is to meet the data needs of its users and whose objective is to answer data queries. The system is a hybrid system, composed of an l-system, which is a NL interpreter/generator for handling NL queries and generating responses, and an n-system which handles data retrieval and database management. The l-system is composed of components such as a grammar and lexicon, domain and data models, a parser and a generator, a co-reference resolver and a dialogue manager.

2.4 Evaluation

According to SJ&G specifying an evaluation requires specifying its *remit* and its *design*. Together they constitute a *scenario* for evaluation.

Evaluation Remit Specifying an evaluation's remit requires first being clear about the *motivation* for the evaluation – why is the evaluation being carried out? Motivation is characterized by identifying the *perspective* being taken (e.g. financial, administrative, scientific), the *interest* prompting the evaluation (e.g. of a system developer, funder, etc.), and the *consumer* (e.g. manager, user, scientist, funder, etc.). Specifying the remit also requires specifying the *goal* of the evaluation – what is to be discovered? Further features of the remit are: *orientation* (intrinsic or extrinsic – see below); *kind* (investigation of an operational system or setup, or experiment to determine how a system might perform in certain circumstances); *type* (black box or glass box); *form of yardstick* (ideal performance, attainable performance, performance comparable with a given alternative); *style* (suggestive, indicative, exhaustive); and *mode* (quantitative/qualitative/hybrid).

Evaluation Design Specifying the evaluation design requires answering four classes of question. The first involves characterising the *subject* of evaluation, which may be a component, subsystem, system or setup. To be clarified are: the subject's *ends*, e.g. for a system its objective or function, the subject's *context*, e.g. for a system the setting, and the subject's *constitution*, as structure and process. This aspect of the design specification appears to be simply completing the characterisation, as given above, of the entities that form the subject of the evaluation, viz. systems and setups.

Once the characterisation of the subject of the evaluation is complete it becomes possible to identify the key *performance factors* whose variation needs to be investigated in carrying out the evaluation. These performance factors fall into two categories: *environment variables* and *parameter settings*. Environment variables are variable aspects of the system's setting, i.e. that part of the setup external to the system, whose alteration can be expected to affect system behaviour. They include the range of system inputs – data variables and their values – the system must process as well as other external constraints it must meet if it is to fulfil its function. Parameter settings are variable aspects of the system itself, or of its components. To take an example, in a multi-document summarisation system, environment variables might be document set and compression rate – these are givens for the system designer. Parameter settings might be, for example, whether to use stemming or not in analysing words before computing term frequency across the document set or comparing sentences for word overlap. These are choices for the designer. In passing it is worth noting that the distinction between environment variables and parameter settings is an extremely important one for Sparck Jones and figures centrally in everything she has written on evaluation since at least Sparck Jones (1981b). There the distinction appears, in a review of the twenty preceding years of IR system testing, in slightly different terms as that between *data variables* and *mechanism variables* (pp. 245-246). The environment variable/parameter setting distinction is a generalisation of this distinction, but the essential force of it is there already: any evaluation needs to separate clearly, and then vary systemically, those aspects of a setup which are external to the system being studied and those which are internal to it.

Given the characterisation of the subject of an evaluation, in particular the identification of relevant performance factors, the second set of questions that need to be addressed in evaluation design pertain to evaluation *criteria*. Criteria are divided into *extrinsic* criteria, those relating to a system's function and *intrinsic* criteria, those relating to a system's objective. Recall that a system's function is the role it plays in an embedding setup, while its objective is what it is designed to do[3]. SJ&G illustrate this distinction with reference to a machine translation (MT) system scenario in which intrinsic criteria would be those assessing the quality of the translation, while extrinsic ones might be those relating to the amount of post-editing required by human editors, assuming a setup of computer-assisted translation. Since criteria are frequently rather general, they need to be operationalised as *measures*. In the MT example, measures for the intrinsic criterion of translation quality could be things like readability score or percentage of lexical items translated with an incorrect sense; measures for the extrinsic criterion of amount of post-editing could be average number of substitutions/insertions/deletions per sentence. To specify fully an evaluation a *method* must also be specified for the

---

[3] The distinction between assessing a system's performance with respect to its objective versus its function is reminiscent of the distinction made in software engineering between *verification* ("Have we built the system right?") and *validation* ("Have we built the right system?) [Boehm, 1984]. If this parallel is exact then SJ&G's approach to NLP evaluation can be seen fitting smoothly into the broader tradition of testing within software engineering.

application of each measure. Thus, how many sentences/texts will have their quality assessed or post-editing measured? How many editors' output will be measured? Essentially these are questions of sampling, and statistical issues of sample adequacy, significance and confidence need to be taken into account here.

The third set of questions to be answering in designing an evaluation relates to choice of evaluation data. SJ&G characterise evaluation data in terms of its *sort* (e.g. test suite, typical input to setup), *status* (e.g. representativeness) and *nature* (presumably characterisation in terms of, e.g. domain, genre).

The final set of questions requires specification of the evaluation *procedure*, that is the sequence of actions to be taken in carrying out the evaluation.

2.5 The Process of Evaluation

The above gives a static picture of what constitutes an evaluation according to SJ&G. The process of carrying out an evaluation involves first unpacking the evaluation by trying to answer the questions implicit in specifying the remit and design of the evaluation as detailed above. Following this SJ&G recommend defining a grid of performance factors (environment variables and parameter settings) and then systematically filling in the grid through a series of runs. Of course, this cannot be done in a blind, mechanical manner. Overall the evaluation must be steered by reference to its motivation and an overarching requirement that the results be informative.

2.6 Assessment and Discussion

The SJ&G framework is an extremely rich one, both in breadth and depth. Few others have taken evaluation in language processing *in general* as an object of study in its own right, exceptions perhaps being the EAGLES work on evaluation (EAGLES Evaluation Workgroup, 1995) and the report of Crouch et al. (1995) which was commissioned by the European Commission as part of deliberations on whether to set up European programmes in language evaluation analogous to those run in the US. While there are many points in common between these frameworks and the SJ&G framework, neither is as extensively articulated or exemplified. Other work on evaluation (see for example the collection of papers in Gaizauskas (1998b)) tends to focus on specific evaluations of specific technologies or within specific task areas.

In a 1998 review of Sparck Jones and Galliers (1996), while generally supportive of the value of the framework, one of the present authors had two caveats (Gaizauskas, 1998a). The first was a concern with one possible consequence of the authors' final paraphrase of the content of the book, that "in evaluation it is always essential to look at environment factors. So the implication is that while NLP evaluation as such is fine, it is of limited value: what matters is the setup." The worry was that since genuinely novel technology can transform conventional setups, significant technological advances could be stifled by insistence on evaluating systems in setups which, since the transformational potential of the technology might not yet be well understood, were inappropriate. The second concern was with the combinatorics, and hence practicability, of the performance factor grid approach, if blindly pursued. Given a substantial number of environment variables and system parameters, each taking on a number of values/settings, the complexity of the grid rapidly becomes unmanageable. The result is that only some combinations will be tested – those corresponding to hunches about optimal or most informative settings. The review also noted that these issues were common to designing multi-factorial experiments in any area where a systems perspective is appropriate. For example, in cognitive psychology the object of study might be the effect of various teaching strategies on the learning of an individual operating within a social environment; in medical biology, the object of study could be the effects of drug treatments on the functioning of cells within an organ; in microeconomics the object of study could be the effects of the broader economy on individual firms. For each of these areas we must isolate and systematically investigate performance factors. In each of these areas the combinatorics of multi-factorial setups means that in practice inspired identification of relevant factors and selection of promising values/settings for variables/parameters is likely to be the way forward, not an exhaustive search of alternatives.

Gaizauskas (1998a) did not rate these as serious criticisms of the SJ&G approach and we still do not. The second concern is really no more than an observation that the grid approach needs to be applied selectively; we shall have no more to say about this here (though see 3.1 below), save that it highlights the necessity of creativity and insight in carrying out evaluations/experiments and that this is not well understood.

Concerning the first point, however, there is more to say – indeed the rest of this paper revolves around the role of the setup in NLP system evaluation. With time, we have come to agree with SJ&G on the central importance of the setup for evaluating NLP systems. In retrospect, the earlier concern with the stifling of new technologies appears to have been driven very much by a worry that technologies the first author of this paper was working on at the time (information extraction, as construed in the MUC enterprise) would be unfairly shut down because they were not quick enough to prove themselves in the market (ALPAC and Lighthill echoing down the years). We still believe this is a legitimate concern in general. In particular the choice of setup in which to evaluate novel technology must be made very carefully: is this a new technology that fits neatly into an existing setup, perhaps replacing an existing component with one which is functionally equivalent, but more reliable, efficient etc.? or does it require abstraction away from aspects of an existing setup, offering new ways to fulfil the setup's purpose and possibly transforming what and how things are done (e.g. consider the move from mail to telegraph as a setup for remote communication)?

However, ignoring the setup entirely can turn into a self-deluding defence for pursuing technological objectives that may not be achievable, at least not at the present time or given current understanding. Ill-considered or overly persistent commitment to intrinsic evaluation of systems designed to carry out a task outside of any genuine setup can have at least two unfortunate consequences. First, without a real setup it is impossible to know what levels of performance on the intrinsic evaluation are required for the embedded system to be deemed successful or useful (even assuming – and this may not be true– that there is at least some setup in which the task being assessed needs to be carried out, or in which the capability developed to tackle the task can be usefully deployed). Without this knowledge, efforts to optimise systems' performance against the task specification can divert attention from far more basic research which may be essential in order for acceptable performance to be achieved in the long run. Put crudely, if 95% performance, on some measure, is required for utility in a given setup and five years of research and evaluation of systems based on related approaches pushes performance from 50 to 70% with diminishing advances suggesting a ceiling being approached, then fundamental questions need to be asked. On the other hand if 75% performance is acceptable, then further effort in the same direction may be warranted.

Secondly, absence of a real setup may also divert attention from the exploration of novel ways in which imperfect technologies may still yield benefit if exploited appropriately in the appropriate setup, an activity which can in turn drive new developments in technologies and give rise to new understanding. A good example here is machine translation. Given current understanding, fully automatic translation yielding results which are comparable in quality to human translation is not possible. However, in certain setups, such as machine-assisted translation or browsing of web pages, existing MT technologies may offer significant benefits. Furthermore, such applications may also throw light on how humans carry out translation, yielding insights which can in turn help to develop our understanding of the underlying processes we are attempting to automate. An evaluation programme that focussed exclusively on intrinsic evaluation of the quality of fully automatic MT might lead to these benefits being missed.

Not only is paying attention to the setup within which an NLP system is to function important for these reasons, but arguably it is essential in order to identify what is distinctive about NLP evaluation as opposed to software system evaluation in general, a topic which the SJ&G framework does not address explicitly. All software systems are embedded in setups. In that respect a framework which calls for the identification of environment variables and system parameters and their systematic investigation, or which separates intrinsic evaluation in relation to system objectives from extrinsic evaluation in relation to system function within a setup, is appropriate for the proper evaluation of *any* software system. Indeed it could be argued that such a framework is appropriate for the evaluation of any *artifact*. In his essays on the "sciences of the artificial", Simon (1996) suggests just this. "An artifact can be thought of as a meeting point – an "interface" in today's terms – between an "inner" environment, the substance and organization of the artifact itself, and an "outer environment", the surroundings in which it operates. If the inner environment is appropriate to the outer environment, or vice versa, the artifact will serve its intended purpose." (p. 6) Later in discussing the science of design, and under the heading of evaluation of designs, he says

> The "inner environment" of the design problem is represented by a set of given
> alternatives of action ... commonly they are specified in terms of *command variables*
> that have defined domains. The "outer environment" is represented by a set of
> parameters ... The goals for adaptation of inner to outer environment are defined by a

utility function – a function ... of the command variable and environmental parameters – perhaps supplemented by a number of constraints' ... The optimization problem is to find an admissible set of values on the command variables, compatible with the constraints, that maximize the utility function for the given values of the environmental parameters. (p. 116)

For Simon the design problem can be seen as search for those inner environment settings (the "means") which, given the outer environmental constraints, optimize a utility function which characterises the intended purpose of the artifact (the "ends"). Note the dual parallels between (1) Simon's command variables characterising the inner environment and SJ&G's system parameter settings and (2) Simon's environment parameters and SJ&G's environment variables.

Thus, given that much of what SJ&G have to say about evaluation of NLP systems, can be seen as relevant for the evaluation of any artifact, what, if anything, is distinctive about NLP evaluation? One factor, at least at this point in the development of the field, surely is this: existing language processing systems do not work very well, at least not in comparison with humans given the same task. Certainly, for some limited tasks, such as named entity identification, systems have been shown to do almost as well as humans; and they can process colossal amounts of data which humans could not begin to tackle. But for many tasks, such as information extraction or summarisation or question answering, NLP systems are consistently and significantly outperformed by people. Note how different this is from embedded software systems in other areas of software engineering, e.g., database applications. In such setups, for example a banking database application, the system can be expected, with some verification, to meet its objective at or near the 100% level. Of course it may not deliver what users want, i.e. in SJ&G terms, while it meets its objective it may fail to fulfil its function in the setup. Hence the concern with validation as well as verification. Still this is very different from the NLP case where, crucially, *an imperfect language processing subsystem must be able to deliver useful functionality within the setup as a whole.* Thus no doubt one aspect of NLP evaluation must be to understand how well with respect to intrinsic criteria NLP systems perform and to attempt to drive understanding of why they perform as they do, with a view to improving them. However, another equally important task is to understand the delicate relation between system failure and utility in the context of a real setup. Can the user detect when the system has failed? How can they recover? What is the cost of failure? Do the benefits the system offers outweigh the costs of its mistakes?

2.7 Implications

Addressing these questions requires the design and execution of extrinsic evaluations, something which is rarely done. As we shall see in the next section the highest profile evaluations for question answering and summarisation technologies are intrinsic evaluations, carried out under the assumption, identified over ten years ago by Sparck Jones (1994), that "the nature of the evaluation data reflects real needs, and that the relative scores obtained correctly predict relative operational utility". At that time she drew attention to the fact the DARPA/NIST evaluations, while sound in their methodology and invaluable in enabling researchers to gain explanatory insight into system behaviour, were trading on this assumption of implied operational utility. And she called for more of the complementary concern with tests which are "properly situated, especially in relation to the ends the evaluation subject is intended to serve, and the properties of the context in which it does this".

The rest of this paper supports this view and develops some preliminary ideas about how to redress the situation in one particular context. Specifically we argue that the DARPA/NIST evaluations for question answering and summarisation (1) address tasks which it is presumed either need to be addressed or the addressing of which will lead to capability which carries over to tasks which do (2) have demonstrated that the level of performance achievable is far short of gold standard. Together these observations argue very heavily in favour of the need for a counterbalancing extrinsic evaluation of these technologies, to enable us to see whether there are real setups in which the capabilities and levels of performance developed through these evaluations are vindicated. We propose an extrinsic evaluation of systems designed to support journalists in writing background stories for breaking news events. Of course, failure to demonstrate the utility of existing QA or summarisation technology in this context would not mean they should be abandoned. There could be other setups in which they do prove themselves; or perhaps future small advances in their performance, as measured in intrinsic evaluations, might tip the balance in their favour in a comparative extrinsic evaluation; or perhaps the manner of their exploitation in a setup is not as effectual as it might be. Nonetheless, the onus is on any proponent of these technologies to show *some* real setup in which they can yield benefit. The attempt to do so will re-orient research effort towards addressing suboptimal performance in real settings. This should lead either to successful applications, or to the conclusion that more fundamental advances in NLP are necessary before applications can proceed. Seen in this light, evaluation properly construed is about research strategy, and not just about methodology.

3. RECENT DEVELOPMENTS IN EVALUATION FOR QUESTION ANSWERING, SUMMARIZATION, AND INTERACTIVE INFORMATION RETRIEVAL

In this section we review briefly recent NIST initiatives to evaluate open domain question answering (QA) in the TREC-QA track (started at TREC-8 in 1999) and summarisation in the Document Understanding Conferences (DUCs) and also interactive information retrieval. We review – that is explicate and then assess – these initiatives drawing on the SJ&G framework and ensuing discussion presented in the previous section. Sparck Jones has herself reviewed TRECs 1-6 in two papers (Sparck Jones, 1995, 2000), using, broadly, the SJ&G framework. We shall begin by summarizing her reviews, as it seems reasonable to take them as a benchmark of the sort of analysis of NIST-like evaluation programmes that one might expect within the SJ&G framework. We shall concentrate primarily on the tasks, data, and experimental setup and evaluation, and will only present results in a very summary form. We shall certainly not attempt to give an overview of the technological approaches participants have used or technological insights that have been gained. The emphasis is on evaluation design.

3.1 Reflections on Reflections on TRECs 1-6

In Sparck Jones (1995) and Sparck Jones (2000), Spark Jones presents a comprehensive assessment of the TREC programme, in the first case up to and including TREC-2 and in the second case up to and including TREC-6. In neither of these papers does she exhaustively characterise the evaluations by completing the sort of descriptive template we have outlined in Section 2 above. This may be because as laboratory experiments the TREC evaluations have a rather impoverished setting, i.e. no users. This has the consequence that some of the distinctions she has carefully elaborated, such as that between system objective and function, are less important than they would be in a real setting: effectively the function of an experimental system is to perform as well as possible against its design specification, which may be taken to be the TREC task specification (participants may have designed their systems to do more than the TREC task specification, but this is not of interest in the evaluation scenario). Nonetheless, she does bring some of the SJ&G framework to bear in these papers, especially the environment variable/parameter setting distinction.

The remit of TREC is discussed in both papers. TREC is co-sponsored by the US National Institute of Standards and Technology (NIST) and the US Department of Defense. Their motivation is to encourage research in information retrieval based on large test collections; to increase communication among industry, academia, and government by creating an open forum for the exchange of research ideas; to speed the transfer of technology from research labs into commercial products by demonstrating substantial improvements in retrieval methodologies on real-world problems; and to increase the availability of appropriate evaluation techniques for use by industry and academia, including development of new evaluation techniques more applicable to current systems.

For the most part (one exception is the interactive track – see below) the subject of TREC evaluations is a system which is presented with a task. In TREC-2 there were just two tasks, the so-called ad hoc retrieval task and a routing task. By the time of TREC-6 while these two tasks remained, a further eleven distinct tracks had been introduced, each of which specified at least one task. For each task, the TREC evaluation design includes:

1   a definition of the task (e.g. for the ad hoc retrieval task to retrieve documents relevant to a user information need);
2   the data which will be used for training and testing (e.g., a set of topics, i.e. user information requests, and a document collection)
3   human judgments of system outputs (e.g. relevance assessments in the case of the ad hoc task);

4   criteria which will be used in assessing the system (e.g. recall and precision at certain cutoffs averaged over the request set).

This experimental design fits well into the SJ&G analytical framework presented in the preceding section. The task specification is part of the definition of the subject of the evaluation. The data and human judgments can be seen as environment variables which are givens for the system, and are one component of the performance factors whose variation can be expected to affect system behaviour. Recall and precision are measures whose associated methods of application are specified as part of the TREC evaluation – e.g. averaging over system responses to the request set.

Moreover, it is clear that Sparck Jones views the TREC programme overall as conforming, albeit loosely, to her notion of the process of evaluation as the filling in of a performance grid in which environment variables and system parameter settings are systematically varied. Each year for each track a fixed set of values for environment variables – e.g. document and request set – is supplied. Thus subsequent years represent exploration of environment variable space. Furthermore, each participant's system represents a choice of parameter settings, a particular point in parameter space. Thus, TREC itself is slowly filling in a comprehensive performance grid as part of a grand IR experiment. In casting TREC as a single grid-style evaluation Sparck Jones (2000) notes that there are pressures pushing it away from this paradigm. Amongst these she notes "participants' natural instincts to pursue what works rather than why" as well as "the sheer effort of systematic comparative testing" (p. 84). In our view the former of these is a healthy, indeed inevitable, response to the combinatorics issue raised in Section 2.6 above.

3.2 The TREC-QA track

The TREC-QA track began in TREC-8 and has run every year since, making six evaluations since inception (at the time of writing participants have submitted system outputs for TREC 2004 – the 13th TREC – but assessment is still underway).

3.2.1 Evolution of the QA track

TREC-8 and TREC-9 In TREC-8 and TREC-9 the QA task required systems to process a file of natural language questions and to return, for each, up to five ranked answers, where each answer consisted of a document id and a text "snippet" drawn from the document of either 50 bytes, in one test condition, or 250 bytes in another (Voorhees and Tice, 2000, Voorhees, 2001). The answer snippets were to be drawn from a supplied text corpus of around 4GB of newswire text. The questions in the case of TREC-8 (around 200) were assembled from a variety of sources, including the NIST orgranizers and assessors and the track participants and were in many cases back formulations from the text corpus; in TREC-9, in a move towards increased realism, the questions (around 700) were obtained from search engine logs. For both evaluations each question was guaranteed to have an explicit answer in the collection. Like other TREC exercises system responses were judged by human assessors and in this way a pool of correct answers was established. The evaluation criterion was a single measure called *mean reciprocal recall (MRR)* where for each question the reciprocal of the lowest rank of the first correct submitted answer was taken as the score for the question and scores were averaged over all questions. In TREC-9 answers were additionally judged as either supported or unsupported, depending on whether the document containing the answer string provided a context which supported the string as an answer to the question. For each run two scores were then computed. The *strict* score counted only supported answers; the *lenient* score counted unsupported as well as supported answers.

TREC-2001 In TREC-2001 (the 10th TREC), several changes were made to the track (Voorhees, 2002). Three subtasks were distinguished. The first subtask was the same as the previous years, but now questions were no longer guaranteed to have an answer within the corpus and "nil" became a valid response. In the second subtask, called the *list* task, systems were required to assemble an answer from multiple documents and questions specified the number of instances to be retrieved – for example *What are nine novels written by John Updike?*. The target number of instances was guaranteed to exist in the corpus, and the evaluation measure was accuracy, defined for each list question as the ratio of number of correct distinct instances retrieved to number of target instances. In the third subtask, called the *context* subtask, systems were required to answer a series of related questions, where the meaning of a question in the series could depend upon the meaning of or answer to an earlier question. The intention here was to test system's ability to track discourse entities through multiple questions, for example by resolving referential links across questions – the sort of capability a user would expect in an extended interaction with a QA system. The evaluation measure was MRR for each component question in a series using lenient scoring.

TREC-2002 In TREC 2002 (Voorhees, 2003), a new corpus – the AQUAINT corpus – was introduced, consisting of just over a million documents (new stories) from three distinct newswire sources for the period 1996-2000. The main task, or as it became increasingly called, the *factoid* task remained, as did the list task. However, the context task was dropped as analysis of results from the preceding year's track showed no correlation between ability to answer earlier and later questions in a series, suggesting discourse entity tracking was still beyond system capabilities. Principal changes were that now one exact answer per question was required, not up to five text snippets, and that the evaluation measure was changed from MRR to a *confidence weighted score (CWS)*. Participants were required not only to submit one exact answer per question but to submit them in ranked order by confidence. The CWS was then computed by summing for each position in the ranking the proportion of correct answers up to that position and dividing this sum by the number of questions. Put differently CWS is the average proportion of correct answers to any ranking position. This measure favours systems that not only get correct answers, but are also able to assess their confidence in their own answers.

TREC-2003 In TREC 2003 (Voorhees, 2004), the factoid task remained as in TREC 2002. A passages task, using the same question set as the factoid task, was re-introduced in which systems were required return a text snippet of 250 bytes –

exactly one per question. The list task was modified slightly so that questions no longer specified a fixed target number of instances to return and instead all distinct, correct instances were to be returned (so, e.g., *What novels did John Updike write?*). However, the main development was the introduction of a definition task. Here the requirement was to return a set of "nuggets" of information describing the question target. For example, a question such as *Who is Aaron Copland?* or *What is Ph in biology?* would be expected to return multiple text strings each describing some aspect of the target (e.g. *American composer, born Brooklyn NY 1900*). Scoring changed significantly as well. For factoid questions, CWS was abandoned and simple accuracy (proportion correct) was adopted. For list questions an f-measure was used based on precision and recall of returned instances (there was no penalty for returning the same instance more than once). For definition questions an f-measure score was introduced based on the ideas of nugget precision and nugget recall. Nuggets were classified into two classes: vital and non-vital. For each definition target a set of vital nuggets was developed by the assessors, through system response pooling and exploration of the corpus. This set served as a basis for computing nugget recall – proportion of vital nuggets returned. Computing nugget precision is more difficult. The intuition is that it should be the proportion of nuggets returned by the system which are correct. However, in practice it proved impossible to ascertain of every system response precisely how many nuggets it contained. So, length of response was used as a surrogate for total nuggets returned in the following manner. An allowance of 100 bytes per correct (vital or non-vital) nugget returned was allocated and precision was set to 1 if the length of the response was less than its allowance and to 1 – (allowance / response-length) otherwise. In computing the overall f-measure recall was weighted as five times more important than precision, partly as a reflection of the importance placed on recall and partly as an acknowledgement of the crudeness of the precision measure.

TREC-2004 In TREC 2004, factoid, list and definition questions were folded into a single task[4]. A series of 65 *targets* was supplied and for each target there was an associated set of questions, each either a factoid, a list or an "other" question and flagged as such. The factoid and list questions were roughly as before; the *other* question was to be interpreted as a request for systems to return any information nuggets about the target not already returned in response to earlier questions. For example a target could be *Americorps* with associated factoid questions such as *When was AmeriCorps founded?*, *How many volunteers work for it?* and list questions such as *What activities are its volunteers involved in?*. Note the presence of pronouns in the questions which need resolving against the target or possibly other discourse entities introduced in the series (reminiscent of the context task in TREC 2001). Scoring measures were as before for each of the three question types, with the *other* question being scored as definition questions were in TREC 2003 except that the weighting of recall to precision was changed from 5 to 3. In scoring

---

[4] Details of TREC 2004 have not yet been published. The account here is taken from the QA track guidelines on the active participants web site: http://trec.nist.gov/act_part/tracks/qa/qa.04.guidelines.html. A series of 65 *targets*

other questions assessors were not to count as correct nuggets which had already been returned in response to earlier questions in the series, or which were included more that once.

3.2.2 Assessment

The QA track has proved very popular, attracting a large number of participants each year and spawning a set of workshops at community fora such as ACL and SIGIR conferences. Clearly this is a measure of its success; yet some questions need to be asked.

Context of Use As with the earlier TREC tracks the QA track follows the same paradigm of controlled laboratory experiment of systems designed to carry out a task which is presumed to have some real context of use. But just what are these contexts? We can all imagine situations in which an answer to a specific factoid or list question would be useful. However, how widespread are these situations and to what extent would QA functionality, assuming it worked perfectly, offer value above and beyond current search engine functionality? After all it is rare that we want information in the form of an exact answer extracted from documents – generally we will want textual context, either to confirm that system's proposed answer or to allow further exploration of the information need that prompted the question in the first place. Over the years the track has moved towards "more realism" by, e.g., introducing questions with no answers, focusing on exact answers, and most recently addressing definition questions, a question type found frequently in search engines logs. While the move away from satisfying very specific information needs towards satisfying less focused needs seems to be a move towards a more realistic setup, the assumptions made in order to make the task evaluable are problematic. Voorhees (2004) notes: "In evaluations such as TREC, questions are asked in isolation. This is not much of an issue for factoid questions, but becomes much more of an issue for definition questions. Without any idea of who the questioner is and why he or she is asking the question it is essentially impossible for a system to decide what level of detail in a response is appropriate – presumably an elementary-school-aged child and a nuclear physicist should receive different answers for at least some questions." To address this issue a scenario was assumed in which the questioner is an adult, native speaker of English and "average" reader of US newspapers, and so on. Given this scenario, human assessors are left to decide what information nuggets are relevant and furthermore to distinguish between vital and non-vital nuggets. While such a methodology is necessary to operationalise the evaluation, it would certainly be reassuring to look at evaluating this capability in a real setup.

Performance Levels In TREC2003 the best performing system achieved 70% accuracy in the main factoid task. Of the 25 sites participating only three scored above 50% and only 4 above 33%, the median site score being around 15%. The scores for the other tasks, while not directly comparable are, if anything, lower. There are several issues to consider here:

1. Is 70% acceptable for use in a real setup? If not what sort of accuracy is necessary for real use? Answering these questions requires a real context of use in which QA systems can be deployed and investigated *in situ*.
2. Will a user know when the system has failed and if so what options will he have? Presumably the textual context from which an answer has been drawn will be supplied along with the answer so that users can assess for themselves whether the system has answered correctly. If there has been an error, how will a user recover or proceed? Will they be offered alternative proposed answers? Or be induced to ask another question? Or to carry out a more conventional search?
3. Can remedial or supportive system behaviour in response to an incorrect answer reduce the accuracy requirement on the overall system? I.e. will users tolerate and productively use a system whose accuracy rate on its own is unacceptable if that system is supplied as part of a question answering assistant (as opposed to a fully automated question answering system)? If so what would such a system be like?
4. Why is the score distribution so skewed? Similar distributions, and roughly similar absolute scores, have been observed in the QA track for each of the four years preceeding TREC2003. The optimistic interpretation is that the task is getting harder each year, so that while general advances in QA are being made and becoming standard practice, overall improvements are not obvious. The pessimistic interpretation is that the leading systems are systems whose behaviour is not well-understood and hence not replicable by other participants, implying that as yet no general advance in understanding how to do QA has occurred.

These considerations, while in no way detracting from the substantial achievement of the evaluations, all point to the need for investigating QA in context.

3.3 The DUC Summarization Evaluations

3.3.1 The evolution of DUC

The objective of the Document Understanding Conferences is to further research in text summarisation. Like TREC they are organised by NIST and have as their central feature an open evaluation consisting of a set of tasks, training and test data, human assessments of correctness, and evaluation measures for assigning a score to participating systems. They have run annually since 2001.

DUC 2001 DUC 2001 was intended to be an exploration of the issues that might be involved in a large scale summarisation evaluation exercise (Over, 2001a, Duc01). Three tasks were specified: (1) to produce, automatically, a 100 word generic summary of a single newswire document; (2) to produce, automatically a set of four generic summaries of lengths 400, 200, 100 and 50 words for multiple newswire documents on a single subject; (3) exploratory summarization in which participants could explore alternative problems and approaches to summarization and evaluation. The data used for the evaluation was collected by NIST analysts each of whom put together sets of about 10 documents – newswire stories – which were meant to be about a single concept, where this could be a single event with causes and consequences, multiple events of the same type, or a single subject or person. Sixty such sets were collected, half to be used for training and half for testing. For each of the document sets the analysts were asked to write (1) a 100 word summary of each text in the set using the author's perspective and (2) a 400 word summary of the whole 10 document set written as a report for a contemporary adult newspaper reader. From the 400 word summary 200, 100 and 50 word summaries were then produced in succession, by cutting, pasting and reformulating the preceding summary so as to reduce it by one half.

Intrinsic evaluation was carried out by human assessors using a tool called SEE (Lin, 2001). Assessors were required to compare a model human-created summary, as described above, with a so-called peer summary created by a system, a baseline algorithm or another human. Their goal was to produce three sorts of judgements concerning: peer quality, coverage of content units in the model by the peer (i.e. analogue of recall), and other notable characteristics of material in the peer.

Peer quality assessments were carried out by rating the peer on a 5 point scale regarding *grammaticality* (answering the question "Do the sentences, clauses, phrases, etc. follow the basic rules of English?"), *cohesion* (answering the question "Do the sentences fit in as they should with the surrounding sentences?"), and *organization* (answering the question "Do the sentences fit in as they should with the surrounding sentences?").

Coverage assessments were made by the assessor using the SEE tool to move one-at-a-time through predefined content units – so-called *elementary discourse units (EDU's)*[5] in the model summary. For each such EDU all sentences in the peer summary which expressed any of the content of the EDU were marked and then a judgement was associated with this set of marked peer sentences that collectively they contained either all (4), most (3), some (2), hardly any (1), or none (0) of the content in the model summary EDU (Harmon and Over, 2004). An overall coverage score was assigned to the peer, defined as the mean of the judgement scores for each of the EDUs in the model. Additionally unmarked peer sentences were examined in the light of three categories: should be in the model in place of something already there; not good enough to be in the model, but relevant to the model's subject; unrelated to the model. For each peer abstract a judgement was made for each of these three categories as to whether all, most, some, hardly any or none of the unmarked peer units in the abstract belonged in that category.

For a subset of the DUC 2001 document sets two additional human summaries (50 and 200 words) were generated. These were gathered for use in analysing the effects of different models on the absolute and relative coverage scores. Unlike the main evaluation described above in which the assessor was the model summary creator, in this case the assessor was not the creator of either of the two additional models. Results reported in Harmon and Over (2004) show stability in absolute and relative coverage scores. That is, there is not a huge variation in coverage scores

---

[5] "Clauses or clause-like units that are unequivocally the nucleus or satellite of a rhetorical relation that holds between two adjacent spans of text'" [Soricut and Marcu, 2003].

between models, and for any system that is rated higher than another with respect to one model, this relative ordering tends to hold when other models are used instead.

DUC 2002 In DUC 2002 the experimental design was largely the same (Over and Liggett, 2002, DUC02). The tasks consisted of a single document summarisation task and two multiple document summarisation tasks. The first required the production of four generic *abstracts* of lengths 200, 100, 50 and 10 words (note 400 word abstract of DUC 2001 was dropped and a very short 10 word, or headline abstract, added) and, the second, new for DUC 2002, the production of two generic whole sentence *extracts* of lengths 400 and 200 words. DUC 2001 data served as training data and a further set of 60 document sets of about 10 documents each was created. As before each set had to contain documents about a single concept – a natural disaster event (e.g. Hurricane Gilbert) or other single event (e.g. outcome of the longest criminal trial in US history), where the documents fell within a seven day period, a set of events of the same type (e.g. grievances and strikes of miners around the world), or a person (e.g. Andrei Sakharov). Again as for DUC 2001 NIST assessors created 100 word single document abstracts for each single document. For each document set abstracts of approximately 200, 100, 50 and 10 word were created, as were 400 word and 200 word extracts (using source sentences in their entirety only).

Peer quality assessment was carried out this time by assessors responding to 12 separate quality related questions covering aspects such as capitalization, subject-verb agreement, pronoun-antecedent relations, dangling conjunctions, and so on. Questions were posed so as to elicit a numeric response (e.g. "About how many sentences have incorrect word order?") and the numeric responses were mapped to 4 values corresponding to the numerical ranges 0, 1-5, 6-10 and > 10.

Peer content assessment for abstracts was carried out, as in DUC 2001, using the SEE tool. The question that assessors were asked concerning the relation of marked peer units to a given model unit was changed slightly to ask explicitly what percentage of meaning the marked peer units expressed of the model unit (as opposed to the categories *all*, *most*, etc. specified in DUC 2001). The coverage metric was retained, and a variant of it called *length-adjusted coverage* was introduced as well. This is a weighted sum of coverage and brevity, brevity being defined as a measure whose value increased as the summary length shrank below the target length value.

DUC 2003 DUC 2003 identified 4 tasks (Over and Yen, 2003, DUC03). Overall the objective underlying the task design was to "incorporate focus of various sorts to reduce variability and better model real tasks". The first task was to generate a *very short summary* – approximately 10 words – given a single newswire document. These summaries were evaluated using coverage (as defined previously) and *usefulness*, a simulated extrinsic evaluation measure in which assessors were asked to read the text being summarized and the summary and then, assuming the text to be of interest, to judge on a five point scale the usefulness of the summary in getting its readers to select the full document as relevant. The second was to generate a short summary (around 100 words) focussed by *event*, given a cluster of around 10 documents and an event topic description. The summaries were evaluated intrinsically for quality, using 12 quality-related questions as in DUC 2002, and length-adjusted coverage, as in DUC 2002. The third was to generate a short summary (100 words) focussed by *viewpoint*, given a cluster of 10 documents and a point of view, specified as a single natural language sentence expressing the facets of a cluster to be captured. These facets were guaranteed to be present in at least all but one of the documents in the cluster. Again, the summaries were intrinsically evaluated using quality and length-adjusted coverage. The fourth task was to generate short summaries in response to a question. Systems were given a document cluster containing documents relevant to a particular question and the question itself. Additionally the sentences from each document that were deemed relevant to the question were identified, as were a subset of these sentences which were deemed the first to introduce the relevant information, given a relevance ordering over the set of documents in the cluster with respect to the topic of the question. These summaries we evaluated intrinsically, using the quality and length-adjusted coverage, as in the last two cases. They were also evaluated in a simulated extrinsic evaluation using a measure called *responsiveness*. To assess responsiveness human assessors were given the question, the sentences from the document cluster judged relevant to answering the question and the short summaries produced by the systems being assessed. They were instructed to read the question and all the short summaries, referencing the relevant sentences as needed, then assign to each summary a score of 0 (low) to 4 (high) based on how responsive to the question, in form and content, the summary was.

The data used for DUC 2003 differed by task, and re-used, in several cases, data and annotations created for other NIST assessment exercises. For task 2 (event focused summaries) the data used were 30 document clusters together with topic descriptions taken from the topic detection and tracking (TDT) evaluation exercises (see Wayne (2000) for an overview). In this exercise rich topic descriptions were generated for selected events and analysts were asked to read documents in a newswire corpus and for each topic to classify each story as on topic, not on topic or "brief" if the topic was mentioned but occupied less than 10% of the story. For each document cluster selected from the TDT data, DUC assessors created a short (100 word) summary of the cluster. For task 3 (viewpoint focussed summaries) the data used were 30 clusters of 10 documents each drawn from the TREC AQUAINT corpus (described in section 3.2.1 above) on topics of interest to the assessors, who also constructed the statements of viewpoint according to which systems were to focus their summaries. Again, for each cluster assessors created a short summary. These two sets of 30 document clusters, the TDT and TREC sets, also served as the source of data for task 1, the very short summary task. Assessors were required to create a very short (10 word) summary of each document in each cluster. For task 4 (short summaries in response to a question) the data used were 30 document clusters created for the TREC Novelty track (Harman, 2003). The DUC assessors were given these document clusters and the topic descriptions which contained a question and were asked to create short summaries using only information from the sentences marked relevant to the question by the Novelty track assessors, using the information about which of those sentences were novel if useful.

DUC 2004 DUC 2004 differed from DUC 2003 in a number of ways, most notably the introduction of two tasks involving the summarisation of noisy input produced by Arabic-English machine translation and several changes to evaluation procedures, described below (Over and Yen, 2004, DUC04). DUC 2004 included five tasks. The first two – very short summaries and event-focused summaries – were essentially the same as tasks 1 and 2 in DUC 2003. Task 3 and 4 involved production of very short cross-lingual single document summaries and short cross-lingual multi-document summaries focussed by events respectively (i.e. like tasks 1 and 2 only involving Arabic-English translations). For each of these two tasks there were two required and one optional run per participant. One required run was supplied automatic translations of the Arabic documents only; the other was supplied manual translations only; and the optional run was supplied the automatic translations, but allowed systems to use any other documents in English. Task 5 required systems to produce a short summary focused by a question, given a document cluster and a question of the form "Who is X", where X is a person or group of people. The data for tasks 1 and 2 were 50 English document clusters taken from TDT data; the data for tasks 3 and 4 were 25 Arabic document cluster also from TDT data. For task 5 50 document clusters of about 10 documents each were created from the AQUAINT corpus such that each cluster contained documents that each supplied part of the answer to a question which the assessor formed.

DUC 2004 differed significantly in respect of the evaluation measures used. For all tasks summaries were truncated to length limits before evaluation and no bonus was given for summaries under the length limit. Very short summaries were now required to be 75 bytes or less, and short summaries to be 665 bytes or less (these numbers were derived from examination of the manual summaries in DUC 2003). Tasks 1-4 were evaluated by means of an automated evaluation approach called ROUGE – Recall Oriented Understudy for Gisting Evaluation (Lin, 2004). ROUGE, which is actually a family of related measures, compares two summaries using n-gram (n = 1, 2, 3, or 4) co-occurrence statistics or longest common subsequences. Essentially these measures are a form of recall measure between a candidate summary and a benchmark summary produced by a human summariser. Clearly there are reasons to prefer an automated to a human evaluator – cheapness, speed, repeatability. DUC 2001-3 has provided sufficient data to be able to assess the correlation between manual assessments and ROUGE assessments. The correlation is high, especially for single document summaries; for multi-document summaries correlation is reasonable, but improvement still desirable. For tasks 2 and 5 the conventional DUC measures of quality and coverage were used (quality assessed by seven questions now rather than 12). For task 5 responsiveness, as used in the DUC 2003 task 4, was also used.

3.3.2 Assessment

Like the TREC QA track the Document Understanding Conferences have proved popular, though have attracted somewhat smaller numbers (~ 15-20 as opposed to ~ 25-35). As with the QA track we need to ask questions about the imagined context of use of the summarization capability which DUC is stimulating and also about performance levels and what their implications for use of the technology in real setups.

Context of Use DUC has investigated a wide range of summarization tasks: single vs. multiple document summaries, generic vs. topic- or viewpoint-focused summaries, abstracts vs. extracts, uni-lingual vs. cross-lingual summaries. It has also tried to assess both quality and content (in the form of "coverage"). Finally it has considered both intrinsic evaluation (for quality and content measures) and extrinsic evaluation with respect to simulated tasks. Again, as with the TREC QA evaluations, these are laboratory exercises that concentrate on assessing system output with respect to system objective, which in the case of most participants is just the task specification, since systems are built to carry out the specified task. While the evaluation of "usefulness" of very short summaries in DUC 2003 and of "responsiveness" of question-focused summaries in DUC 2003 and 2004 are a move towards extrinsic evaluation, these exercises are simulated – i.e. they are not the judgements of real users in a real setup. Thus we must ask whether the tasks being pursued and the measures used to assess them reflect concerns of real users. Certainly, there would seem to be a wide requirement for multi-document summarisation of, e.g., newswire stories concerning events that have run over an extended period. However, the failure of multi-document summarisation systems to do better than baselines which take the first n characters of the most recent text suggest that perhaps recapping is a feature of this genre (though human produced summaries are judged much better than the baseline). Thus the presumption of the need for and the usefulness of various forms of summarisation cannot be taken for granted and needs to be studied in the context of a real task.

Performance Levels As with QA systems, various questions need to be asked about the performance levels of summarisation technology and their implications for use of the technology. Risking travesty of the extensive performance results of DUC, here are what appear to us to be the main findings so far. First, regarding coverage, human summaries are significantly better than all machine produced summaries (e.g. on the single and multi-document summarisation task in DUC 2004 manual summaries' coverage was more than twice that of others (Over and Yen, 2004)). Secondly, baseline scores – typically the result of taking the first part of the most recent or most relevant text – are in general indistinguishable from systems' automated summaries. Thirdly, regarding quality, system summaries produce significantly more errors than do baselines, which in turn are judged poorer than manually produced summaries. Fourthly, unlike the QA track, variance across system scores is much less. Finally, in the extrinsic evaluations manual summaries are clearly separable from the rest – both for usefulness and responsiveness.

Thus machine generated summaries clearly fall well short of human levels of performance. A key question, though, is whether they are good enough for certain uses. Given that in many contexts human summaries are simply not going to be produced, because of time and effort, are machine generated summaries of use? Or are their errors of commission and omission such as to make them unusable – in any setting? or only in settings where their weaknesses are not compensated through alternatives? Once again it seems the only way to find out is through investigating the use of the technology in real setups.

3.4 The TREC Interactive Track

3.4.1 Evolution of the interactive track

The TREC Interactive track began officially with the introduction of specialised tracks at TREC-4 in 1995, though there was experimentation with the interactive construction of queries in TREC-3. The track ran annually following that until 2002. In 2003 it ran as an adjunct to the Web track and in 2004 it did not run. From the outset the primary goal of the track has been "the investigation of searching as an interactive task by examining the process as well as the outcome" (Over, 1996). A secondary goal has been the development of appropriate methodologies for interactive evaluation.

TREC-4 and TREC-5 In TREC-4 the interactive track consisted of two tasks (Harman, 1995). The first was to retrieve as many relevant documents as possible within a timeframe, given a topic from the ad hoc track and a document collection. The second was to construct the best query possible. Groups were asked to use the same topics and record the same information about how searches were done, but nonetheless there were significant difficulties in comparing results across groups. As a consequence the major push in TREC-5 was to develop further the methodology for interactive system evaluation to control for variables in the interactive environment. Due to late agreement on methodology that year, there were few participants and the methodology was carried over with minor modifications to TREC-6 the following year. For the sake of brevity we shall describe TREC-6 only here.

TREC-6 The key difference between the interactive track in TREC and the other tracks is that the interactive track inherently includes a human searcher as part of the setup. This has at least two profound implications for experimental design. First, since searcher time is limited, given the nature of unfunded participation in TREC, the number of topics that can be investigated in any single experiment is seriously limited. This is unlike the batch processing arrangements of most tracks in which humans are not involved and where the number of topics (or questions or documents to summarise) can therefore be increased so as to ensure with some convincingness the representativeness of the topic set and hence to minimise the likelihood of skewed results and unwarranted conclusions about system performance. Secondly, introducing searchers into the experimental setup means that possible interaction effects between searcher and system and searcher and topic need to be investigated.

The design arrived at for TREC-6 was as follows (Lagargren and Over, 1998). Participating sites minimally required four searchers and an experimental system. Six topics were selected from the TREC-6 ad hoc topic set and specially modified for the interactive track by adding a section called "Aspects" (see below). The document collection used was the Financial Times of London, 1991-1994 collection (~ 210K documents) which formed parted of the TREC-6 ad hoc collection. Each site was required to download and install a control system called ZPRISE, a public domain IR system developed at NIST. ZPRISE's role was to function as a cross-site control. The key measure for the track was the difference in performance between the experimental system at each site and the control, or $(E-C)$, for a given searcher. To factor out possible system-searcher and searcher-topic interactions a Latin square design was adopted in which each of the four searchers searched the six topics, three on the experimental system and three on the control. Each searcher used the same system for three searches and then the other system for the remaining three. Two searchers per site began with the control system and then switched to the experimental system; and two reversed this procedure. The order of topics presented to the searchers was the same across all sites and systems. Sites could optionally extend the experiment by introducing additional groups of four searchers or by introducing more that one experimental system which would be similarly tested against the control.

The task the searchers were required to complete was to read the topic and then to use to the system (experimental or control) to find and save relevant documents that covered as many different *aspects* of the topic as possible in 20 minutes. An aspect of a topic is "roughly one of many possible answers to a question which the topic in effect poses" (Lagergren and Over (1998), p. 166). For example for a topic about ferry sinkings, different ferry sinkings would count as different aspects; for a topic about a treatments for high blood pressure, different alternative treatments would count as different aspects. Each site submitted four sorts of results: sparse-format data (list of documents saved and elapsed clock time for each search); rich-format data (searcher input and significant events in the course of the interaction plus their timing); a full narrative description of one interactive session for one topic; any further guidance or refinement of the task specification given to the searchers. To evaluate these results NIST had human assessors create an aspect-document mapping for each topic. This was done by assembling from the participants' submitted lists of documents a pool of documents containing one or more relevant aspects and noting which documents contained which aspects. The chief quantitative evaluation measures used were *aspectual recall* – proportion of total aspects for a topic covered by the submitted documents – and *aspectual precision* – proportion of the submitted documents containing one or more aspects.

Following extensive statistical analysis of the participants' submissions by NIST there were several outcomes of interest from the perspective of assessing the experimental approach. First, at no site was it possible to assert that there was a significant difference between E and C. Secondly, for each site the effect of topic is the most significant, underscoring the importance of an experimental design where the topic effect is eliminated when assessing systems. Thirdly, for almost half of the systems there was no searcher effect; searcher-topic and searcher-system interactions were also negligible. Fourthly, while the results of an ANOVA comparing $E-C$ across sites showed that site was a statistically significant factor, no pair-wise difference between any two sites was significant. Additional experiments were conducted outside the TREC framework to examine the assumption that the use of a control system is effective in eliminating site-related effects. Interestingly, contrasting direct comparison of two sites versus indirect comparison via use of a control led to very different results, but results that were not statistically different. The organisers concluded that while the assumption of the effectiveness of a control system had not been refuted, the lack of positive evidence for its effectiveness combined with its large practical cost meant that it could not be recommended.

TREC-7 In TREC-6 not only was there lack of convincing evidence for the effectiveness of a common control system for cross-site comparison, use of a common control system also meant half of each group's experimental effort was expended on a system of no particular interest (Over, 2001b). TREC-7 dropped the idea of cross-site comparison altogether and instead invited participants to use a control system which suited their own research agenda. The task remained essentially the same as TREC-6, though searchers were now given 15 minutes per topic instead of 20 and were asked to return as many *instances* of the type of information requested in the topic in place of the aspects required in TREC-6. The text collection remained the same. Eight topics from the ad hoc task were used instead of six, with the topics modified for the track by specifying the nature of the instances sought. Assessor judgements were collected as in TREC-6 and the chief measures this time were instance recall and instance precision in place of aspectual recall and precision. The minimal experiment this time involved 8 searchers (instead of 4) and 8 topics (instead of 6) yielding an 8 x 8 matrix. As before a Latin square design was used to allow the effects of searcher and topic to be blocked and the main effect of system to be isolated. The same four types of results – sparse-format data, rich-format data, a narrative of one specified interaction and extra advice to searchers – were required from participants. In addition searcher questionnaires (searcher background, user satisfaction) and results of a psychometric test (verbal fluency) for each searcher were also required.

TREC-8 The TREC-8 experimental design remained more or less the same as TREC-7. The verbal fluency test for searchers was dropped. The task was the same but search times were returned to 20 minutes. The minimum number of searchers per site was increased to 12, but the number of topics reduced to 6. Instead of all searchers being presented with the topics in a single fixed order a pseudo-random topic order was used for each searcher.

TREC-9 In TREC-9 the task was altered slightly to move it closer to the QA track question answering task (Hersh and Over, 2000b). Searchers were given two types of questions, questions of the form "Find any n Xs", e.g. *Name four films in which Orson Welles appeared*, and questions which involved comparison of two specific Xs, e.g. *Is Denmark larger or smaller in population than Norway?* Eight questions, four of each type, were supplied. The text collection was the TREC text collection used for the TREC-9 QA track. The minimum configuration for each site was 16 searchers and two systems; and blocks of 8 searchers and additional systems could optionally be added. As before in TREC-7 and TREC-8 choice of control and experimental system was left to each site and so the experimental design did not support cross-site comparisons.

Searchers were given 5 minutes per question. Before searching began they were given some introductory information and a 15 minute tutorial on each system. Searchers were asked questions about the certainty of their answers before and after each question and were also asked to complete questionnaires before and after the experiment and after the use of each system. Sites were requested to submit the same results as for TREC-8. In this case the sparse-format data requested consisted of a list of zero or more answers to the question and a list of zero or more documents supporting these answers. NIST assessors evaluated only the sparse-format data, considering only whether the responses contained all, some, or none of the items requested by the question and whether the supplied documents supported all, some or none of the correct items in the response.

TREC-2001/2 A workshop was held at SIGIR 2000 to consider future directions for the track (Hersh and Over, 2000a). The chief recommendations to emerge from this forum were that the track should move onto a two-year cycle with observational studies in year one and metrics-based comparison of systems in the second; the track should start using live Web data rather than a test collection to more adequately reflect everyday searching conditions; search tasks should be in domains chosen from surveys of popular web usage, to allow searchers to easily identify with them; the experimental design should incorporate more questions, e.g. 25 rather than 6 or 8, so as to improve the scope of conclusions that could be drawn with respect to topic.

TREC 2001 adopted most of these recommendations. Since it was the first year in a two year cycle, the track ran in an observational mode. Participants were allowed to use data sources and search tools accessible via the Internet. Sites were obliged to recruit as many searchers as possible, 24 being suggested as a target. Each searcher worked in one or more of four domains which were common across all sites: finding consumer medical information on a given subject, buying a given item, planning to travel to a given place and collecting material for a project on a given subject. Each searcher carried out four searches, two from a list of fully specified tasks (e.g. *Tell me three categories of people who should or should not get a flu shot and why.*) and two from a set of partially specified tasks which the searcher/site completed (e.g. *Identify three interesting places to visit in X*). This approach broadened the set of topics/questions considered over previous years without completely unconstraining it. Sites were allowed to impose further restriction on searchers at their site in order to define an area of interest for observation, subject to the constraints that the restrictions had to hold for all searchers at the site and had to be reported before the observation began. So, for example some sites looked at the difference between expert and non-expert searchers within a domain, others with the effect of increased query length, others with choice of search engine. Beyond submitting a track report the only other output requirement was that sites propose a testable hypothesis for the succeeding year.

In 2002, the second year of the cycle, the track aimed at a more controlled laboratory-type experiment than the previous year. The collection used was an open version of the .GOV Web collection created for the TREC 2002 Web track – "open" in that some links pointed outside the collection and could be followed (this was not a design feature of the collection but the result of lack of time to prepare a closed version). Most participants used the collection as indexed and searched by the Panoptic search engine, experimenting with as they saw fit, e.g. by adding their own interfaces. There were eight searcher tasks similar to those used in TREC-2001 – looking for personal health information, seeking guidance on US government laws, regulations, etc., making travel plans, and gathering material for a report on a given subject. Search tasks had one of two forms: find any N short answers to a question with multiple answers of the same type and find any N websites that meet the need specified in the task statement. Each searcher had to carry out all eight searchers, four on one system and four on another system, permitting comparative judgements to made about the two systems or system variants. Search results after 10 minutes had to be reported; results after shorter or longer times were optional. Searches were evaluated for effectiveness, efficiency and user satisfaction as in previous interactive tracks (i.e. whether the task was completed successfully, elapsed time for each search, and searcher background and satisfaction questionnaires).

TREC-2003 In TREC-2003 the Interactive track was subsumed as a subtrack within the Web track. The task was a variant of the topic distillation task used within the non-interactive part of the Web track. The topic distillation task involves finding relevant homepages given a broad query, for example returning for the query "cotton industry" a set of .gov web sites which are home pages dealing with aspects of the cotton industry (Cotton Pathology Research Unit, Office of Textiles and Apparel, US Department of Agriculture Cotton Program, and so on) (Craswell et al., 2003). A home page was judged good if it meet three conditions: it is principally devoted to the topic, provides credible information on the topic, and is not part of a larger site principally devoted to the topic. Note how this task differs from the ad hoc task where the goal is to return all relevant pages, rather than an overview of relevant sites.

For the interactive track eight of the search topics from the non-interactive topic distillation task were adapted by adding a scenario to provide searchers with a context (not with additional content for searching). For example "You are to construct a resource list for high school students interested in the cotton industry ...". Participants were supplied with two versions of the Panoptic search engine, one optimised for the topic distillation task by balancing home pageness and relevance, the other using an Okapi-like relevance ranking. The collection to be searched was the closed .GOV collection distributed for the main Web track (18GB/1.25 million documents). Experimental protocol was left open to participants though a protocol similar to past tracks was suggested by the guidelines. This involved using comparing two systems by dividing the topics into two blocks, one half searched on each system, using a minimum of 16 searchers per site. Evaluation was based on four criteria for each of which assessors were asked to provide a rating on a 5-point Likert scale: relevance (of page for topic); depth (is the page too broad, just right, too narrow for the topic); coverage (does the set of saved entry points cover all aspects of the topic); repetition (how much repetition is there across the set of saved entry points).

3.4.2 Assessment

The TREC interactive track has consistently attracted fewer participants than the other tracks, and its future status is unclear. This lower level of participation is most likely a reflection of the difficulty of assembling a sufficient number of human searchers to take part in the task. Another factor may have been the difficulties in establishing an agreed and effective methodology. Finally, this track appeals to a different sort of researcher than do the other tracks, one with interests which reach beyond the narrow technical challenges of optimising system performance using a well-defined metric and embrace the less well-defined issues inherent in studying interaction.

The track's most substantial achievement has been in establishing a methodology for studying interactive searching. While the track has not been able to address cross-site comparative studies in the way that other tracks have, it has established a method for doing comparative analysis between systems. The Latin square technique for removing system-searcher and searcher-topic interactions is a major contribution. So is the track's acknowledgement that interactive searching is the dominant mode in which retrieval technology is used, and its emphasis on an extrinsic form of evaluation in which the setup consisting of user plus system are investigated, rather than simply the technology.

As with the other tracks we may ask whether the setup the track presumes is in fact a realistic one. Again, while it is not hard to think of contexts where the ability to assemble as many answers as possible to a specific question in a limited time is useful, this is not the same thing as studying information seeking in the context of a real task. For instance, are the topics an accurate reflection of information need in any real task setting? The task is conceived of very much as a *search* task – a clear question is posed (e.g. *tell me three categories of person who should or should not get a flu shot and why?*). But information seeking is recognised to be a rich activity with directed searching only one of many forms it may take (Wilson, 2000). Information needs evolve during interaction and in many contexts an information seeker is unlikely to pursue doggedly a single question for an extended period (e.g. finding all possible ferry sinkings), but will instead branch off to understand more about material already discovered, or turn to addressing other aspects of the task context which prompted the question in the first place (this type of information seeking behaviour has been observed in our investigations of journalists' practice discussed in the following section).

None of this is to fault the direction the track has taken. As with other TREC tasks in order for any kind of comparative, cross-site activity to be defined, an idealised task must be proposed and measures for assessing system performance on this task must be specified. However, as with other tracks, this means researchers must remain sensitive to whether the idealisation is helpful. This is especially true in a track that by including the user might be thought to have overcome all the problems of techno-centric laboratory experimentation.

4. A CASE STUDY FOR EVALUATION: THE CUB REPORTER SCENARIO

The Cub Reporter project aims to investigate ways language technology can assist news agency reporters in researching and writing background pieces to support breaking news stories, using a news archive as a resource. In current practice reporters typically use a basic search engine to attempt to find relevant information from the archive. Since, by definition, the breaking story has just happened, there will be nothing in the archive about it specifically. Thus one would expect no exact matches between a query formed from statement of the new event and the archive. Instead one is seeking information about role players in the new event, or about similar events in the past, or about events that may be causal antecedents of the current event. This would seem to be rich territory in which to deploy QA and summarization systems. Reporters may well want profiles of individuals; they may want to check individual facts or get answers to specific factoid-like questions; and since the archive has extensive coverage of major stories, reporters would appreciate multi-document summarization of earlier related stories to minimize redundant information. Finally, since their information needs will in general be imprecise and will evolve as their understanding of the background deepens, they will of necessity be engaged in interactive information seeking within a news archive, and will thus require a system that supports interactive searching effectively.

4.1 Information Seeking and the Production of News

The information seeking behaviour of newspaper journalists has been explicitly studied by Attfield and Dowell (2003). The chief outcome of their work, which involved interviews with 25 journalists from the *Times* including both news and features writers, was a model of journalistic information seeking in the context of the task of writing a story, or more broadly "constructing a new information artifact". This is a crucial point for them – information seeking must be viewed not as an isolated task, but in a particular context, where it is part of a combined process of information gathering and information use. Given a news topic assignment by a news editor and a set of product and resource constraints, the three stages in the Attwood and Dowell model are:

1. *Initiation*: A provisional "angle" is established and a deadline and word count constraints are determined. (This usually takes place during the initial assignment brief). The notion of an "angle" is central to their model. It is described by them elsewhere (Attfield et. al, 2003) as a "proposition, or central factual claim that is to be made by the report. Where the claim involves some speculation the angle takes the form of a working hypothesis or conjecture" and again as the "early focused perspective or guiding idea which determines both a solution's space and the writer's information requirements".

2. *Preparation*: The angle is tested and either confirmed or refuted. Potential content is gathered, personal understanding is developed and a plan for the report is evolved. During this stage an assignment-specific collection of materials, paper or electronic, is assembled for later use.

3. *Production*: The story is written, consulting the assignment collection, based on the understanding and plan developed so far. The writing process may provoke further information seeking and alteration of the plan.

These stages are carried out, perhaps iteratively with feedback, in the context of a set of dynamic constraints of two types: *product* constraints, i.e. constraints on the output of the process, and *resource* constraints, i.e. constraints on the materials and mechanisms employed in the production process. Product constraints include the deadline and word count, and also such requirements as originality, newsworthiness, and correspondence with the facts. Resource constraints are either constraints on external resources – archives, software, personal contacts, collected materials for the assignment, written plans, etc. – or constraints on internal resources – working memory of the journalist, accumulated subject knowledge, internal plans etc. Both product and resource constraints are dynamic: deadlines or word counts may change; new events may alter perceptions of newsworthiness or refute the hypothesis underlying the angle the journalist is pursuing; new sources of information may become available; internalised and externalised plans evolve with increase in understanding.

This is a compelling model for the task scenario, or setup, they have studied. However, the setup we have chosen to study initially is somewhat different from Attwood and Dowell's, so that while the general model of initiation, preparation, and production in the context of product and resource constraints is still valid, some of the constraints and some of the activities within the process are different. Furthermore, Attwood and Dowell stop short of pursuing in depth the process by which journalists iteratively gather potential content and refine their understanding of a topic. Insights into this process are important if we are to understand how language technology may be able to assist journalists.

Specifically the setup we have chosen to investigate differs from that studied by Attwood and Dowell in that we are concerned exclusively with the gathering of background information by a *news agency in the context of the production of a breaking news story*. This setting is different in at least three ways from that of a reporter working for a specific newspaper seeking information to fulfil an editorial assignment: (1) Speed really is of the essence. A news agency's role is to serve its subscribers (newspapers) with material as soon as possible after an event, so that the subscribing news organizations can incorporate it into their publications. (2) Copy length, on the other hand, is not so important since the agency can continue to publish stories in successive pages of electronic copy, so long as the editors judge the events to be worthy of coverage (thus permitting subscribers, who have their own constraints, to pick and chose what material they want).(3) More importantly, the nature of breaking news events is such that in the initial minutes of the story, when the decision to cover the story is made, very little is known about the event. Thus reporters and news editors have insufficient details to determine any "angle". Here, in contrast to what Attfield and Dowell have observed, our observational studies of journalists show that they begin the background information seeking task without a specific, articulated angle, but rather with expert knowledge of the typical ingredients that might be used to contextualise the new event, for example, accounts of similar events, role players in the event, or significant events leading up to the event (Barker, 2004). The precise quantities of these ingredients and the way in which they are brought together and presented in any report will only become clear once the reporter has explored the content of archive in the time available.

While in current practice, described in more detail in the next section, outputs from this background for breaking news setup are texts of various types, one can imagine scenarios of future use in which the information assembled in the current setup might be used in other ways. For example, were it available rapidly enough background information might be used to inform the decision to proceed with coverage of a story (a process known as "copy tasting"), something not currently done due to the limitations of existing systems. Thus, novel language technologies not only have the potential to improve the efficiency and effectiveness of the existing setup, but also have the potential to alter significantly current practices.

4.2 Current Practice: Writing a Backgrounder

The Press Association is the major UK domestic newswire service and provides copy to all major national daily newspapers. For breaking news stories (in contrast to say feature stories), the news cycle unfolds as follows (Barker and Foster, 2004): when breaking news is received a journalist writes one or two sentences summarising it and then passes this text, called a *snap* to a sub-editor for checking. When satisfied, the sub-editor "moves" the copy on the wire, marking the instalment of a new story. The story is then published as a series of instalments, where each instalment contains a new and updated account of the news. These instalments have names such as *substitute, lead, nightlead* which reflect their position and significance in the sequence of instalments and their intended function in the publishing cycle of the major daily papers (so, a nightlead is a major re-working prepared especially for use in evening news broadcasts and in the following morning's papers).

At least three types of written background material are produced for use in this cycle:

- *Background Snippets* These are brief bits of background information, for example descriptive appositives such as *former Chancellor of the Exchequer* or single sentences mentioning related events, that find their way into snapfuls (pages of copy that follow the opening snap) and subsequent instalments. They contextualize the breaking news story.

- *Fact Sheets* These are lists of facts deemed potentially relevant for newswire clients in the light of a new event. For example, following a train crash a fact sheet listing previous train crashes might be released.

- *Backgrounders* These are full narrative pieces in their own right, sometimes referred to as "sidebars", typically written when a news editor deems a particular story worthy of dedicated background material. They are usually not released till sometime after the first instalments as time is needed both to determine whether a story merits a backgrounder, but also for the research to be carried out to assemble the material. Their function is not to continue to report details of new events, but rather to provide text that supports and contextualises these events. Backgrounders are typically made up from the following four types of material: (1) accounts of similar events in the past (e.g. other train crashes, scandals of similar nature, etc.); (2) accounts of events which have led up to the current event (e.g. a chronology of company takeovers, store openings, price cuts and profit warnings in the months leading up to a supermarket's announcement of low annual profits); (3) profiles of persons or organisations or locations (usually role players in the new event) comprising some highly structured factual information about the role player, for example date and place of birth, career appointments; spouse etc; accounts of the role player in events leading up to the event and accounts of the role player in similar events to the current event; and (4) comment (quotes) on any of the preceding by notable individuals.

To make the discussion more concrete we will illustrate some of these concepts by reference to a particular story – the drowning of Chinese immigrant cockle pickers in Morecambe Bay in the UK in Feb, 2004. The story begins with a single sentence snap under the heading *SEA Rescue*: *Up to twenty-three people are trapped in rising tides at Morecambe Bay, the RAF said tonight.* (PA Snap, 05/02/04, 22:34 GMT). Subsequent snapfuls reveal that those trapped are Chinese cockle pickers. By 22:52 a three sentence snapful is released that mentions that in August of the previous year police had arrested 37 Chinese people in Morecambe in relation to concerns of the public over unregulated commercial cockle picking on a public beach. The first full backgrounder appears at 03:09 on 06/02/04. It consists of thirteen sentences. The first relates the backgrounder to the main event *The stretch of coastline where up to 26 people were reported stranded last night by a fast rising tide is renowned for its treacherous conditions.* The next three sentences give more detail on the location and the dangerous nature of the tides and quicksand. The remainder of the text discusses previous incidents in the bay: two separate relatively recent drownings (2002 and 1995); the appointment, over 600 years ago, of a Royal Guide to show travellers a safe route across the sands, with a reference to activities of the current Royal Guide; and a memorial in a local churchyard to over 140 people drowned on the sands.

4.3 How Current Language Technologies Might Help

Currently the PA access their archive via a conventional free text search system. After a story has broken and a news editor has deemed it of sufficient interest to merit a backgrounder, a journalist is assigned to produce the backgrounder. As noted above this may take the form of a profile of one or more of the role players (people, organisations, locations) in the event or of significant events which have led up to current event or are similar to the current event in some way. To complete this task the journalist will search the archive and possibly other sources, using his world knowledge in addition to the information given about the new event to guide his search.

The system the PA currently use allows boolean queries to be formed from single words or phrases. Searches may be restricted to story text, headlines or byline and they may be date range restricted as well. Results may be requested sorted by weighting (a relevance ranking of some sort) or date.

Let us now imagine how advances in language technology, in particular those being encouraged by the TREC and DUC programmes, might offer additional or improved functionality.

4.3.1 Question Answering

The TREC-QA programme is currently addressing three question types: factoid, list and definition questions, as described in Section 3.2.1 above. While fact checking is something that all journalists need to do from time to time, this is a secondary activity that follows on deciding what to include in a backgrounder. Hence factoid QA, as defined in TREC, is unlikely to be a journalist's primary mode of interaction with a text archive. List QA, suitably interpreted, could be useful for the preparation of fact sheets. For example, an answer to *List train crashes in the UK resulting in one or more fatalities* would be useful in building up a fact sheet about rail crashes. To date most of the list questions in TREC have been about entities (e.g. *novels written by John Updike*), rather than about events, however. Finding a set of events which share some property is probably harder to do than finding entities which share a property, and is probably a more central part of the activity of journalists writing backgrounders, who will very often be seeking information about related events in the past. It is also the case that events rarely get names, though particularly famous events may acquire them metonymously (*Lockerbie, 9/11*, etc.). This means that there are unlikely to be short, literal text strings from the document collection which serve unproblematically as answers, a condition of a question finding its way into the TREC QA track. Nonetheless, like fact checking, listing entities that share a characteristic is certainly a requirement from time to time in preparing background pieces (e.g. an answer to *Name British physicists who have won the Nobel prize* would be relevant in writing background should a new British winner be announced).

The third type of question currently addressed in the TREC-QA track, definition questions, is perhaps the most potentially relevant for the preparation of background stories, especially the "who is" subset of these questions. Journalists very frequently need to produce profiles on individuals, and this sort of question addresses this requirement. However, journalists certainly do not need to know every "nugget" (see Section 3.2.1 above) pertaining to an individual, especially for people who have been in the news scores or hundreds of times over decades. Rather a profile will include standard biographical data, such as date of birth, education, career progression and achievement. TREC has distinguished vital and non-vital nuggets, but it is not clear precisely what criteria underlie this distinction for "who is" definitional questions and to what extent these map onto what a journalist would take to be core profile material. Still, the capability required to answer correctly "who is" definitional questions would seem to be of significant relevance for the backgrounder task.

Overall then the TREC-QA track appears to be promoting capabilities which while not exactly satisfying the information gathering requirements for writing backgrounders, do match some of them. The question then is can these capabilities be usefully integrated into an information gathering system that will require additional searching capability as well (probably the traditional search capabilities)? Issues will be (1) will journalists understand the functional limitations of the QA component and know which information needs to address to it and which to a more traditional search engine? (2) how will QA performance affect acceptability and how will recovery be handled in cases where the system makes mistakes?

4.3.2 Summarization

The most relevant of the DUC tasks, from the perspective of writing a backgrounder, are the multi-document event and entity focused summarization tasks. One of the key aspects of writing a backgrounder is summarizing earlier, similar or related events. In their time these events may well have been reported over days or weeks and have yielded scores of instalments. Furthermore, any previous event may already have been cited in the background for some third, intervening event and hence may be found in the archive not only at the time of its original occurrence, but at other points between that time and the present. In the rush to put together a backgrounder for a current event the journalist must quickly find, assess for relevance and then summarize such related previous events. Thus, an automated summarizer that could take multiple documents referring to an earlier event and compress them into a much shorter text, removing the redundancy across the set, would be very useful, both for the task of assessing earlier events for relevance as background for the current event and, should they be relevant, for the task of generating a summary for inclusion in the backgrounder.

Generating profiles for individuals from multiple documents relating to that individual is also a task that journalists need to do. Again, in an archive this information will be distributed across many texts and parts of it will occur multiple times. Condensing the material and removing redundancy automatically would be of great assistance, both for assessing its relevance to current events and for generating a summary for the backgrounder.

Note that for the DUC multi-document summarization task systems are presented with a small set of documents (typically around 10) to summarize. Thus two aspects of the Cub Reporter backgrounder task have already been completed in the DUC scenario: (1) the *identification* of an event or person as something of relevance as background to the current event, and (2) the *selection* of a subset of documents from the archive which pertain to that identified event or person. Neither of these operations are part of the DUC task. They are more akin to tasks which form part of the Topic Detection and Tracking (TDT) evaluation mentioned in the discussion of DUC-2003 above in Section 3.3, but there are differences even with it. TDT starts with a rich topic description and then classifies stories as on topic or not.

In the backgrounder case the descriptions are not rich – they may be as little as one sentence snaps – and, more importantly, they do not define the topic to be found – the requirement is to find earlier related or similar events, not other texts about the same event, since by definition the event has just taken place.

Thus, DUC-like summarization capability should be highly useful for Cub Reporter. However, it presumes a context in which coherent sets of documents to summarize are made available, a context which itself is not easy to engineer and which will inevitably include some noise (interesting question: how do DUC event focused multi-document summarization systems perform when one or more off-topic documents are included in the set to be summarized? – documents which are likely to be textually related as they will probably have been assembled using existing IR technology).

4.3.3 Interaction

Some aspects of the background task are very much like the task posed in the TREC 6 – TREC 2001 interactive tracks, namely the assembly of as many aspects relating to a narrow topic or answers to a question as possible. In assembling fact sheets or lists of previous related events (e.g. previous drownings in Morecambe Bay), a journalist must at present interact with an archive using a search tool. Furthermore, speed is an important aspect of the task. However, as noted above in Section 3.5 in our assessment of the interactive track, while some of the information seeking that goes into assembling material for a backgrounder is of this nature (i.e. assembly of as many facts of the same sort as rapidly as possible), there are other less focused sorts of information seeking as well. For example, if a journalist wishes to explore the question of why just recently large numbers of Chinese cockle-pickers have started working the sands of Morecambe Bay he has a much less specified, more challenging search task. In such a task the nature of the interaction may be radically different from the "find as many instances of type X as possible" task characteristic of the interactive track.

4.3.4 Possible experimental systems

Since we aim to support the journalist not just in the task of information seeking, but also in the task of gathering together relevant material, and finally in the production of a new information artifact, i.e. the backgrounder, an interface that supports more than stateless seeking functionality is likely to be useful. For example, to assemble relevant materials a "keep list" or "shopping basket" approach which allows users to keep the results of selected searches is likely to be helpful. So is some representation of search history, since extended, complex search interactions are likely to take place and users may want to revisit documents they have seen before. Functionality, perhaps just cut and paste, to move materials into the new document which is being written is also required; it may be of benefit for such moved materials to retain provenance linkage, so that a journalist can follow them backwards into the archive, if necessary, as writing proceeds. These are just three examples of non-language technology functionality that are likely to add significant value to any system designed to offer combined searching/writing capability to journalists[6]. Thus, if extrinsic evaluation of different language technologies embedded in an information seeking/writing system is an objective then comparison across systems that embody different language technologies, different L-systems in SJ&G terminology, will only be meaningful if as much as possible of the non-language technology, the N-system, is held constant across comparisons.

With this in mind, let us consider how language technologies might be deployed in the backgrounder task setting. In each case we assume the input to the process is information about a breaking news event, perhaps just a snap or a snapful that contains at most a few sentences about a new event. Resource constraints on the process are the archive(s) to be used in discovering background information; product constraints are time limits.

For purposes of experimental control we will assume a baseline system (call it *Base*) which relies primarily on existing state-of-the-art IR technology. Since the current PA system is a black box to us, we intend to use an open source IR engine, such as Lucene[7]. Using *Base* we imagine a journalist would read the snap or snapful and then formulate queries as with any search engine in order to explore likely avenues for finding relevant background, using features of the N-system to assist in perhaps limiting the sources searched (which archives, title vs. full text search, date range constraints, etc.) and in saving results and navigating the search history.

At the other extreme from *Base* one can imagine a fully automatic cub reporter system, call it *Auto*, which analyses the input snap or snapful, gathers relevant background materials, summarizes them where necessary, and then edits the whole into a seamless narrative which is publishable as is, i.e. a system which completely replaces the journalist. Such a system is science fiction at this point, but it plays a useful role in marking the upper bound, in terms of the involvement of language technologies, in the possible system space we might explore. In between are a set of systems which make use of question answering, summarization and other language technologies to a greater or lesser extent and in various combinations. For example, the first stage could involve the automatic analysis of snap or snapful with a view to *question generation*, the generation of questions answers to which could form part of the information to be included in the backgrounder. Let us assume, simplistically for now, that events can be arranged hierarchically into types and that they involve role players (agents, patients), which are also typed, and take place at times and places. If a snap can analysed to extract and fill this sort of *event template* then one can generate questions by replacing one or more of the event type, role players, time, and place in the snap analysis by a variable, or by a more general type and asking for instantiations of this generalized pattern in the archive. For example, let us return to the drowning incident of the Chinese cockle pickers in Morecambe Bay (ignoring the fact that the initial snap mentions only that they are stranded – the drowning is reported slightly later) and suppose we are given a report of the form

---

[6] See Shneiderman et al. [1998] a discussion of a general issues underlying the construction of user-interfaces to support text searching.

[7] See http://jakarta.apache.org/lucene

Twenty-four Chinese cockle pickers were drowned by rising tides in Morecambe Bay last night. From this various questions could be generated in a mechanical fashion such as: *Have Chinese cockle pickers drowned in Morecambe Bay before? Where have Chinese cockle pickers drowned before? Who has drowned in Morecambe Bay before? What other events have Chinese cockle pickers been involved in Morecambe Bay? Who has drowned where before?* until most generally, and least helpfully, *What/who has been involved in what sort of events where?*

Clearly not all of these questions are useful in terms of seeking background, but some of them very much are. It should be feasible to control the generalisation in such a fashion that the likelihood of generating truly unhelpful questions could be made quite small. Other questions that are effectively just requests for profiles of role players in the events could also be generated, e.g. *Tell me about Chinese cockle pickers* or *Tell me about Morecambe Bay.* For stories involving specific individuals, e.g. the resignation of a cabinet minister, the utility of automatically identifying the named individual and generating a profile is obvious.

Following question generation a system could ask the journalist to select or deselect proposed questions before commencing to seek answers. Or it could simply proceed to answer the questions automatically and then make answers available under headings the journalist could chose to follow or ignore. The responses generated by the system would be hyper-linked back to their source in the archive. After an initial system response, various routes could be taken to support refinement of the initial query or follow-on questioning which arises from the response.

What language technologies would be involved in such a system? Question analysis would involve named entity recognition and some syntactic analysis. The resulting event template could be used to generate natural language factoid or list or definition questions of the sort appearing in the TREC QA track; or it could be used to define queries useful for building profiles of role players or detecting similar events without actually requiring transformation into a natural language question. Regardless, QA techniques are likely to prove useful. Multi-document summarisation techniques are also likely to prove useful. For every individual about whom information is sought and for every related event there is probably going to be more information in the archive than is useful. Coping with this glut requires two responses: first, redundancy must be eliminated; secondly, information must be prioritised. Summarisation technology addresses both of these issues.

The foregoing is a very rough sketch of sort of ways in which language technology could be integrated into an information access system designed to support journalists in the backgrounder task. A host of variations on this theme can be imagined. One could enhance *Base* to a system which automatically formulated a query from the snap and clustered the results (so that, for example, stories about cockle pickers and about Morecambe Bay fell into separate clusters). Or one could limit question analysis to identifying named entities and generate profiles of each of these, as an adjunct to a system like *Base*. One could do syntactic analysis of the question as well, but leave out any notion of type-based generalisation over events or role players, concentrating just on looking for identical event types involving different role players or looking for other events involving the same role players. All such systems are possible and could be built using technologies which now exist.

Given this possibility the pre-eminent question that then arises is: how are we to compare or evaluate these systems?

4.4 Envisaging a Cub Reporter Evaluation

Let us now attempt to specify an evaluation for the types of Cub Reporter system we have sketched above, adhering insofar as possible and useful to the SJ&G model. Recall that this involves specifying the remit and the design of the evaluation.

4.4.1 Remit

The goal of the evaluation is to learn whether current advances in language technology can be successfully deployed to assist journalists in preparing background articles for a wire service. Our perspective is a scientific one, our interest that of system developers; the consumers of the evaluation will be scientists/engineers. The evaluation will contain both intrinsic and extrinsic elements: we want to know both whether system components are doing their job and produce, with respect to their design objectives, high quality output, and also whether these outputs are figuring usefully in the setup. The form of yardstick will be comparative – we want to know whether new language technologies can be deployed to build a superior setup to the setup currently in use.

4.4.2 Design

Turning to design, we must first identify the subject of the evaluation.

Subject In our case this will be a system or systems – information gathering tools – embedded in a setup. First let us consider the setup. In describing above the current process by which backgrounders are produced, we have described most aspects of the newswire copy production setup. The purpose of the setup is to deliver timely and accurate coverage of newsworthy topics. Focusing on the provision of backgrounders only, we may narrow this prescription and say the purpose of the newswire service here is to provide timely and accurate coverage of background material relevant to another news story whose significance may be taken as given. The setup is composed of two key entities, a user, the journalist, and an information gathering system. Different setups result from varying the system, in particular by varying the boundary between how much the system attempts by way of "intelligent" interpretation of information-bearing textual data and how much this is left entirely to the user. As environment variables for the systems we will be primarily interested in the form of description of the news story for which a backgrounder is to be written (e.g. is the system given a snap, or a snapful or substitute produced later in the course of a story's evolution?) and the text archive that is to be used for discovering background information. The nature of any system parameters to be explored depends on the specifics of individual systems which it is not appropriate to discuss here.

Criteria This statement of the purpose of the setup, suggests two extrinsic criteria for the evaluation of any system figuring in the setup: (1) *efficiency* – does one system allow for backgrounders to be delivered more efficiently than another, in less time or with less effort? (2) *quality* – does one system result in higher quality backgrounders being written than another?

Operationalising efficiency in evaluation measure(s) is relatively easy. Given two systems for supporting background writing, a controlled experiment could be designed where journalists are asked to write backgrounders and their time taken to do so and number and type (e.g. productive/non-productive) of interactions with the system measured. The experimental design would need to control for topic and journalist, but this is relatively straightforward to do. One can envisage doing so using the sort of Latin square design introduced for the TREC interactive track (see Section 3.4 above).

However, proposing a measure to operationalise the criterion of quality is a much harder task. There are analogies with summarization here (indeed a backgrounder could in some sense be viewed as a sort of event-focused multi-document summary of a news archive). First, as with summaries, it seems unlikely that the notion of an ideal backgrounder (summary) for a given news story (document) can be made concrete. Backgrounders are read by different consumers with different requirements and states of prior knowledge and any attempt to define "background" precisely is doomed to failure. Nonetheless, while evaluation against an ideal backgrounder may not be possible, a comparative evaluation between backgrounders seems more promising. Suppose two journalists are asked to write a backgrounder for the same news story and are given the same resources and constraints (archive, search tools, time and length limits) and each duly produces a text. While it is an empirical question (which we aim to investigate) whether their backgrounders can be consistently ranked with respect to each other by independent evaluators, this should be possible for more extreme examples. Furthermore we might hope that for every proposition in a backgrounder, independent assessors could agree on (1) whether or not that proposition belonged in a backgrounder, or, using a slightly more fine-grained classification, whether it was essential for inclusion in a backgrounder, optional, or irrelevant (cf. the distinction between vital and non-vital nuggets introduced for answers to definitional question in the TREC QA track mentioned in Section 3.2.1 above) and (2) its relative importance in the backgrounder with respect to other propositions in the backgrounder. If (1) were true an annotation scheme could be defined in which propositions had associated with them a classification expressing their importance for inclusion in a backgrounder. If (2) were true an annotation scheme could be defined whereby each proposition is assigned a rank expressing its relative importance for inclusion. Finally, given a set of backgrounders for the same story written using the same closed set of resources, if each were annotated according to second of these schemes, it may be possible to get a set of assessors to agree a single merged ranking of propositions with respect to the their "background-worthiness". This is probably as close to an ideal backgrounder as it is reasonable to expect one might ever get.

Such consensual annotation of backgrounders, if possible, would provide the basis for a quantitative evaluation of the quality of backgrounders being generated in a given background-producing setup. Measures such as precision and recall (approximated through pooled judgements, as in ad hoc retrieval evaluation) could be used if categorical judgements of the sort suggested in scheme (1) above were available; more sophisticated measures could be used if ranked judgements of the sort suggested in scheme (2) were on hand.

The evaluation of the quality of backgrounders and the efficiency with which they are produced could form part of an intrinsic evaluation of the background writing setup. Of more relevance to our current concerns, however, they could also serve as the basis for an extrinsic evaluation of any system deployed to assist journalists in gathering materials from an archive for inclusion in a backgrounder. Given two setups which are identical save for the information gathering system being used to support the writing of backgrounders, which setup leads to the production of higher quality backgrounders? more rapidly? or with less effort?

4.4.3 Discussion

Note that while we have hinted at the similarities between evaluating backgrounders and summaries, there is an essential difference in the presumed setup here and that supposed in the evaluation of summaries or profiles being carried out in DUC or in TREC QA. In those evaluations what is being evaluated is the output of an automated *system*. Here we are proposing the evaluation of the output of a *setup* in which an information system plays a part. Only indirectly, through comparative evaluation in the setup, are systems being evaluated in relation to one another. This has two profound implications.

First, on the negative side, given the indirect nature of the system evaluation it will be difficult to assess the contribution of specific aspects of any embedded technologies since the human component of the setup (aka the journalist) will be able to compensate for system behaviour in various ways that will be hard to determine. However, depending on the nature of the embedded information gathering system, it may be more or less possible to derive an intrinsic evaluation of this system from the extrinsic one. For example, in the limiting case where the embedded system generates a full backgrounder entirely automatically and the journalist does nothing save submit what the system has generated, the setup effectively becomes the system alone, and extrinsic and intrinsic evaluations are collapsed together. In cases where the journalist plays a significant role in interpreting and selecting material which appears in the backgrounder it may still be possible to carry out some sort of intrinsic evaluation of the system. Suppose for example that one function of the system is to identify the names of any persons mentioned in a snap provided as input to the setup and then to assemble a profile each of these people. An evaluation of the profiles could be made on the basis of how much of the material in them makes its way into the final backgrounder and how much profile material in any profile of a person appearing in the backgrounder was not in the system-provided profile. Of course, the value of material read by a journalist but not included in a backgrounder is hard to assess: material may critically assist a journalist's understanding of a topic, while not being appropriate for inclusion in a backgrounder. Thus, derivatively using the extrinsic criteria for an intrinsic evaluation does raise problems. Nonetheless we are currently investigating how such criteria and possibly others can be used to evaluate a system in a complex interactive process.

Secondly, and much more positively, however, we believe this evaluation scenario provides a more realistic setting in which to explore the utility of question answering and summarisation technologies than the current TREC QA and DUC evaluations. In particular the effects of errors (e.g. a QA system providing mistaken answers) and of incomprehensibility (e.g. incoherent summaries or extracted information nuggets without context), issues we have highlighted in our assessments of existing evaluations of QA and summarisation technology above, should become apparent. Furthermore the issues of confidence and justification or support for automatically generated answers or summaries will also need to be addressed head-on in the design of any system using QA or summarisation for this task, since it is unlikely that journalists will want to use a system that does not allow them to track back to their original text sources any outputs from an automated system. This, in our view, will provide a salutary re-orientation of effort in QA and summarisation away from optimising scores on intrinsic evaluation measures and towards the construction of systems in which these technologies provide a genuine assistive role. After all if the existing measures are measuring anything "real" then this should be vindicated in an extrinsic evaluation which should show systems that score more highly on existing intrinsic metrics also score more highly on the extrinsic measures.

5. CONCLUSIONS

Let us now pull together some of the strands from the foregoing. First we would like to highlight the utility of SJ&G framework. The distinctions it makes, particularly the related distinctions of setup versus system, extrinsic versus intrinsic evaluation, system objectives versus setup function, and environment variables versus system parameters, are invaluable for any analysis of the evaluation of setups in which language technology plays a role. These distinctions, together with the emphasis placed throughout Sparck Jones's writings on the importance of the setup in evaluation, formed one key component of the analysis proposed in Section 3 of the current NIST/DARPA evaluation exercises being carried out for question answering and summarization systems.

The other key component, related but not raised by Sparck Jones, is the central role that sub-optimal performance needs to be given in discussions of the evaluation of language technology. Any framework that distinguishes extrinsic evaluation of a system in a setup from intrinsic evaluation of a system with respect to its design objectives inherently acknowledges the possibility of lack of fit between these two. In most systems engineering this comes about through the failure of the system, even if it has been built so that it achieves its objectives perfectly, to meet the requirements subsequently placed upon it in the setup. With language technology not only is this a problem, but since the technology cannot, in many cases, perform at desired levels, there is the additional problem of understanding what impact this underperformance will have in the setup.

This latter problem can be ignored if it looks like performance of an embedded component can shortly be raised to match design objectives. But if it cannot, or if looks like achieving it will require significant time and effort or perhaps even fundamental advances in the field, then the role of the setup and the investigation of the effect of sub-optimal performance in the setup becomes critical. For either: (1) a sub-optimally performing component will prove adequate in the setup (e.g. search technology while never achieving particularly high scores in evaluations – rarely have systems scored over .5 precision at rank 10 – has been a run away success in many setups) (2) or a new setup in which the sub-optimal component proves adequate needs to be found (e.g. machine-assisted translation), or (3) work needs to be done, be it incremental or fundamental, to shift the performance of the component upwards until it does become adequate.

Thus the setup is critical and this, in our view, is the key weakness (which is not to overlook the many strengths) of the current NIST/DARPA evaluation exercises. As an alternative we proposed an extrinsic evaluation of language technology based on the task of a journalist using a news archive in writing a background piece to support a breaking news story. A comparative extrinsic evaluation of language technologies in this setup should be possible, based only on the judgements of journalists as to the background-worthiness of items included in backgrounders written using one system or the other, together with non-quality criteria such as time and effort expended in the writing.

Such an evaluation should help to inform judgments as to the direction of research in language engineering. Should it be towards understanding how to use imperfect language components in useful systems? – i.e. should the emphasis be on studying information seeking behaviour and on interface design and support? Or will incremental advances in performance against the intrinsic measures studied in the DARPA/NIST exercises make all the difference? Or do we need to take a step backward and do more fundamental research into human language processing and understanding in order to make the sort of advances needed to feed into useful technology? Seen in this light, evaluation becomes not just a necessary though somewhat boring methodological adjunct to the "real" work of science, but a key issue of research strategy with which every researcher in language technology must engage.

In Sparck Jones and Galliers (1996) Sparck Jones characterised her recommendations on strategies for evaluation as "disappointingly mice from a mountain" but mice which she hoped might nonetheless be "healthy, vigorous, rapidly breeding and colonising". In informing all of the discussion above and, more generally, the discussion and practice of evaluation in language technology in so many ways and across so many years, this hope has more than been fulfilled.

Robert Gaizauskas is Professor of Computer Science at the University of Sheffield. His research interests lie in applied natural language processing, especially information extraction and retrieval, both from newswire text and from scientific writing, particularly medical and biological text. He also works on automatic question answering and summarisation, on the extraction of temporal information from texts and has an on-going interest in evaluation of language technology. He has published over 80 papers in peer-reviewed journals and conference proceedings.

Emma Barker is a research associate in the natural language processing (NLP) group in department of Computer Science at the University of Sheffield. Graduating with an MPhil in History and Computing from the University of Glasgow in 1996, she went on to complete a PhD (2001), at the University Sheffield, on creating a biographical database from historical texts, a case study of the Alumni Cantabrigienses *and its editor, the logician John Venn. She continued to pursue her interest in the problem of access to information in historical texts while working as a research assistant for what is now the Economic and Social Data Service (ESDS) Qualidata, led by the UK Data Archive at the University of Essex, (2001-2002). In 2003 she returned to Sheffield to work on the "Cub Reporter" project, a collaboration between the departments of Computer Science and Journalism, which is investigating the design and evaluation of human language technologies for assisting journalists in research and writing tasks using news archives. Her current interests are in human factors in NLP technologies, specifically interactive search and retrieval from text.*

ACKNOWLEDGEMENTS

We would like to thank Jonathan Foster and Horacio Saggion for their work on the Cub Reporter project which has contributed importantly to the argument above, and for their comments on drafts of this paper. We would also like to thank the UK Engineering and Physical Sciences Research Council for support under research grant R91465/01 which has made the work on Cub Reporter possible. Finally we would like to thank the Press Association for their collaboration with us on this project, both in making their archive available and granting us access to journalists.

REFERENCES

S. Attfield, A. Blandford and J. Dowell. Information seeking in the context of writing: a design psychology interpretation of the 'problematic situation'. *Journal of Documentation*, 59(4):430-453, 2003.

S. Attfield and J. Dowell. Information seeking and use by newspaper journalists. *Journal of Documentation,* 59(2):187-204, 2003.

E. J. Barker. Investigating the task of researching and writing background news. Technical Report CS-04-15, Department of Computer Science, University of Sheffield, 2004.

E. J. Barker and J. Foster. Current practice in gathering information and writing news at the Press Association. Technical Report CS-04-14, Department of Computer Science, University of Sheffield, 2004.

Boehm, B. Verifying and validating software requirements and design specifications. *IEEE Software*, Vol. 1(1), 1984.

J. Burger, C. Cardie, V. Chaudhri, R. Gaizauskas, S. Harabagiu, D. Israel, C. Jacquemin, C-Y. Lin, S. Maiorano, G. Miller, D. Moldovan, B. Ogden, J. Prager, E. Riloff, A. Singhal, R. Shrihari, T. Strzalkowski, E. Voorhees and R. Weischedel. Issues, tasks and program structures to roadmap research in question & answering (q&a). Technical report, 2002. URL www-nlpir.nist.gov/projects/duc/papers/qa.Roadmap-paper_v2.doc.

J. Carbonell, D. Harman, E. Hovy, S. Maiorano, J. Prange and K. Sparck Jones. Vision statement to guide research in question & answering (q&a) and text summarization. Technical Report Final version 1, 2000. URL http://www-nlpri.nist.gov/projects/duc/papers/Final-Vision-Paper-v1a.pdf

N. Craswell, D. Hawking, R. Wilkinson and M. Wu. Overview of the TREC 2003 web track. In *Proceedings of the twelfth Text Retrieval Conference (TREC-2003)*, 2003. URL http://trec.nist.gov/pubs/trec12/papers/WEB.OVERVIEW.pdf. NIST Special Publication 500-255.

R. Crouch, R.J. Gaizauskas and K. Netter. Interim report of the study group on assessment and evaluation. Technical report, EAGLES project, Language Engineering Programme, European Commission, 1995. URL http://lanl.arxiv.org/abs/cmp-lg/9601003.

DUC01. DUC 2001 guidelines, 2001. URL http://www-nlpir.nist.gov/projects/duc/guidelines/2001.html.

DUC02. DUC 2002 guidelines, 2002. URL http://www-nlpir.nist.gov/projects/duc/guidelines/2002.html.

DUC03. DUC 2003 guidelines, 2003. URL http://www-nlpir.nist.gov/projects/duc/guidelines/2003.html.

DUC04. DUC 2004 guidelines, 2004. URL http://www-nlpir.nist.gov/projects/duc/guidelines/2004.html.

EAGLES Evaluation Working Group. Evaluation of natural language processing systems. Technical Report EAG-EWG-PR.2, EAGLES: Expert Advisory Group on Language Engineering Standards, 1995. URL http//:issco-www.unige.ch/ewg95.

R.Gaizauskas. A Review of *Evaluating Natural Language Processing Systems: An Analysis and Review* by Karen Sparck Jones and Julia Galliers. *Journal of Natural Language Engineering*, 4(2), 1998a.

R. Gaizauskas, editor. *Journal of Computer Speech and Language, Special Issue on Evaluation*, volume 12(3). 1998b.

D. Harman. Overview of the TREC 2002 novelty track. In *Proceedings of the Eleventh Text Retrieval Conference (TREC 2002)*, 2003. URL http://trec.nist.gov/pubs/trec11/papers/NOVELTY.OVER.pdf. NIST Special Publication 500-251.

D. Harman. Overview of the fourth text retrieval conference (TREC-4). In *Proceedings of the Fourth Text Retrieval Conference (TREC-4)*, 1995. URL http://trec.nist.gov/pubs/trec4/overview.ps.gz. NIST Special Publication 500-236.

Donna Harman and Paul Over. The effects of human variation in DUC summarization evaluation. In Stan Szpakowicz Marie-Francine Moens, editor, *Text Summarization Branches Out: Proceedings of the ACL-04 Workshop*, pages 10-17, Barcelona, Spain, July 2004. Association for Computational Linguistics. URL http://acl.ldc.upenn.edu/acl2004/textsummarization/pdf/Harman.pdf.

W. Hersh and P. Over. SIGIR workshop on interactive retrieval at TREC and beyond. *SIGIR Forum*, 34(1), 2000a. URL http://www.sigir.org/forum/S2000/Interactive_report.pdf.

W. Hersh and P. Over. TREC-9 interactive track report. In *Proceedings of the Ninth Text Retrieval Conference (TREC-9)*, 2000b. URL http://trec.nist.gov/pubs/trec9/papers/t9irep.pdf. NIST Special Publication 500-249.

E. Lagergren and P. Over. Comparing interactive information retrieval systems across sites: The TREC-6 interactive track matrix experiment. In *Proceedings of the 21st Annual International ACM SIGIR Conference on Research and Development in Information Retrieval (SIGIR'98)*, pages 164-172, Melbourne, 1998.

C-Y. Lin. SEE – summary evaluation environment: Users guide, version 1.0. Technical report, Information Sciences Institute, University of Southern California, 2001. URL http://www.isi.edu/cyl/SEE/SEEManual.pdf.

C-Y. Lin. ROUGE: A package for automatic evaluation of summaries. In Stan Szpakowicz Marie-Francine Moens, editor, *Text Summarization Branches Out: Proceedings of the ACL-04 Workshop*, pages 74-81, Barcelona, Spain, July 2004. Association for Computational Linguistics. URL http://acl.ldc.upenn.edu/acl2004/textsummarization/pdf/lin.pdf.

P. Over. TREC-5 interactive track report. In *Proceedings of the Fifth Text Retrieval Conference (TREC-5)*, 1996. URL http://trec.nist.gov/pubs/trec5/papers/trackreport.ps.gz. NIST Special Publication 500-238.

P. Over. Introduction to DUC-2001: An intrinsic evaluation of generic news text summarization systems. In *Proceedings of the of the SIGIR 2001 Workshop on Text Summarization (DUC-2001)*, 2001a. URL http://www-nlpir.nist.gov/projects/duc/pubs/2001slides/pauls_slides/index.htm.

P. Over. The TREC interactive track: an annotated bibliography. *Information Processing and Management*, 37(3):369-381, 2001b.

P. Over and W. Liggett. Introduction to DUC-2002: An intrinsic evaluation of generic news text summarization systems. In *Proceedings of the ACL 2002 Workshop on Text Summarization (DUC-2002)*, 2002. URL http://www-nlpir.nist.gov/projects/duc/pubs/2002slides/overview.02.pdf.

P. Over and J. Yen. Introduction to DUC-2003: An intrinsic evaluation of generic news text summarization systems. In *Proceedings of the Human Language Technology 2003 Workshop on Text Summarization (DUC-2003)*, 2003. URL http://www-nlpir.nist.gov/projects/duc/pubs/2003slides/duc2003intro.pdf.

P. Over and J. Yen. . Introduction to DUC-2004: An intrinsic evaluation of generic news text summarization systems. In *Proceedings of the HLT/NAACL 2004 Document Understanding Workshop (DUC-2004)*, 2004. URL http://www-nlpir.nist.gov/projects/duc/pubs/2004slides/duc2004intro.pdf.

B. Shneiderman, D. Byrd and W.B. Croft. Sorting out searching: A user-interface framework for text searches. *Communications of the ACM*, 41(4):95-98, 1998.

H. Simon. *The Sciences of the Artificial*. MIT Press, third edition, 1996.

R. Soricut and D. Marcu. Sentence level discourse parsing using syntactic and lexical information. In *Proceedings of the Human Language Technology and North American Association for Computational Linguistics Conference (HLT/NAACL)*, 2003.

K. Sparck Jones. The Cranfield tests. In K. Sparck Jones, editor, *Information Retrieval Experiment*, pages 256-284. Butterworths, London, 1981a. URL http://www.nist.gov/itl/div894/984.02/projects/irlib.

K. Sparck Jones. Retrieval system tests: 1958-1978. In K. Sparck Jones, editor, *Information Retrieval Experiment*, pages 213-255. Butterworths, London, 1981b. URL http://www.nist.gov/itl/div894/984.02/projects/irlib.

K. Sparck Jones. Towards better NLP system evaluation. In *Proceedings of the Human Language Technology Workshop*, pages 102-107. Morgan Kaufmann, 1994.

K. Sparck Jones. Reflections on TREC. *Information Management & Processing*, 31(3):291-314, 1995.

K. Sparck Jones. Further reflections on TREC. *Information Management & Processing*, 36:37-85, 2000.

K. Sparck Jones. Factorial summary evaluation. In *Proceedings of the 1ˢᵗ Document Understanding Conference*, 2001. URL http://www-nlpir.nist.gov/projects/duc/pubs/2001papers/cambridge2.pdf.

K. Sparck Jones, J.R. Galliers. *Evaluating Natural Language Processing Systems*. Sprinter, Berlin, 1996.

E. Voorhees. Overview of the TREC-9 question answering track. In *Proceedings of the Ninth Text Retrieval Conference (TREC-9)*, 2001. URL http://trec.nist.gov/pubs/trec9/papers/qa_overview.pdf. NIST Special Publication 500-249.

E. Voorhees. Overview of the TREC 2001 question answering track. In *Proceedings of the Tenth Text Retrieval Conference (TREC 2001)*, 2002. URL http://trec.nist.gov/pubs/trec10/papers/qa10.pdf. NIST Special Publication 500-250.

E. Voorhees. Overview of the TREC 2002 question answering track. In *Proceedings of the Eleventh Text Retrieval Conference (TREC 2002)*, 2003. URL http://trec.nist.gov/pubs/trec11/papers/QA11.pdf. NIST Special Publication 500-251.

E. Voorhees. Overview of the TREC 2003 question answering track. In *Proceedings of the Twelfth Text Retrieval Conference (TREC 2003)*, 2004. URL http://trec.nist.gov/pubs/trec12/papers/QA.OVERVIEW.pdf. NIST Special Publication 500-255.

E. Voorhees and D. Tice. The TREC-8 question answering track evaluation. In *Proceedings of the Eighth Text Retrieval Conference (TREC-8)*, 2000. URL http://trec.nist.gov/pubs/trec8/papers/qa8.pdf. NIST Special Publication 500-246.

C. Wayne. Multilingual topic detection and tracking: Successful research enabled by corpora and evaluation. In *Proceedings of the Second International Conference and Evaluation (LREC2000)*, 2000. URL http://www.nist.gov/speech/tests/tdt/research_links/Wayne-LREC2000.ps.

T.D. Wilson. Human information behaviour. *Informing Science*, 3(2):49-55, 2000.

PETER WILLETT

THE EVALUATION OF RETRIEVAL EFFECTIVENESS IN CHEMICAL DATABASE SEARCHING

1. INTRODUCTION

The novel bioactive molecules that are the lifeblood of the pharmaceutical and agrochemical industries have massive research and development costs, and there has thus been much interest in ways to increase the cost-effectiveness of the discovery process for new drugs and agrochemicals. One such technology that has come very much to the fore over the last few years is *chemoinformatics*, the name given to the computational techniques that have been developed for the storage, retrieval and processing of the two-dimensional (2D) or three-dimensional (3D) structures of chemical compounds (Russo, 2002; Schofield *et al.*, 2001). There are many aspects to chemoinformatics, as detailed in two recent texts (Gasteiger & Engel, 2003; Leach & Gillet, 2003); here, we focus on the techniques that are used for database searching, i.e., the chemical equivalent of information retrieval (IR).

Chemoinformatics may appear to be rather far removed from Spärk Jones' work: however, the rigorous approach that she adopted for the measurement of retrieval effectiveness has provided a major input to the development of similarly rigorous ways of evaluating the performance of database systems in chemoinformatics. Specifically, the detailed and systematic approaches that she pioneered in the Seventies, most notably as detailed in Spark Jones & Bates (1979) and Sparck Jones & Webster (1980), provided my group with a model that, with appropriate modification, is now used very widely to support research in chemoinformatics. However, before discussing the concept of chemical retrieval effectiveness, it is necessary to put this into context by introducing the techniques that are used to represent and to search databases of chemical structures. In what follows, I consider only databases of 2D molecules, i.e., the conventional chemical structure diagram. However, many of the same basic techniques are also applicable to the inherently more complex task of processing databases of 3D molecules, where one has detailed information about the geometries of the molecules that are being searched (Martin & Willett, 1998).

John I. Tait (ed.), *Charting a New Course: Natural Language Processing and Information Retrieval. Essays in Honour of Karen Spärck Jones*. 239-254
© 2005 Springer.

2. SEARCHING CHEMICAL DATABASES

2.1 Representation and Substructure Searching

A 2D chemical structure diagram is normally represented in a chemical database system by a *connection table*, a data structure that contains a list of the atoms within a molecule, together with bond information that describes the exact manner in which the individual atoms are linked together. A connection table is an example of a labelled graph in which the nodes and edges of the graph represent the atoms and bonds, respectively, of a molecule. A chemical database can hence be regarded as a database of graphs that can be searched using algorithms derived from graph theory. Historically, the two types of retrieval facility available in a chemical information system were *structure searching* and *substructure searching*, these corresponding in the IR context to known-item searching and Boolean subject searching, respectively. Specifically, structure searching involves an exact-match search of a database to find the information pertaining to an individual query molecule, *e.g.*, how it could be synthesised or its infra-red spectrum. The search is effected using a graph isomorphism algorithm, in which the graph describing the query molecule is checked for isomorphism with the graphs of each of the database molecules. A variety of structural hashing procedures are used to ensure that the time-consuming graph isomorphism check needs to be carried out on only a very small fraction of the molecules in the database. Substructure searching involves a partial-match search of a database to find all those molecules that contain a user-defined query substructure, in just the same way as a Boolean text search finds all those documents that contain the user's set of query terms. For example, Figure 1 shows examples of molecules retrieved in a search for the diphenyl ether query at the top of the figure.

Substructure searching is effected by checking the graph describing the query substructure for inclusion in (subgraph isomorphism with) the graphs of each of the database molecules (Barnard, 1993). This retrieval mechanism is totally effective, in that searches will proceed with 100% recall and 100% precision (i.e., a search retrieves all of the molecules that contain the sought substructure, without any additional false-drops), but it is hopelessly inefficient because of the NP-complete nature of the subgraph isomorphism problem. Substructure searching is feasible only because of the availability of an initial *screening search*. A screen is a substructural feature, called a *fragment*, the presence of which is necessary, but not sufficient, for a molecule to contain the query substructure. These features are typically small, atom-, bond- or ring-centred fragment substructures that are algorithmically generated from a connection table when a molecule is added to the database that is to be searched. For example, a common type of screen is the *augmented atom*, which consists of an atom, and those atoms that are bonded directly to the chosen central atom.

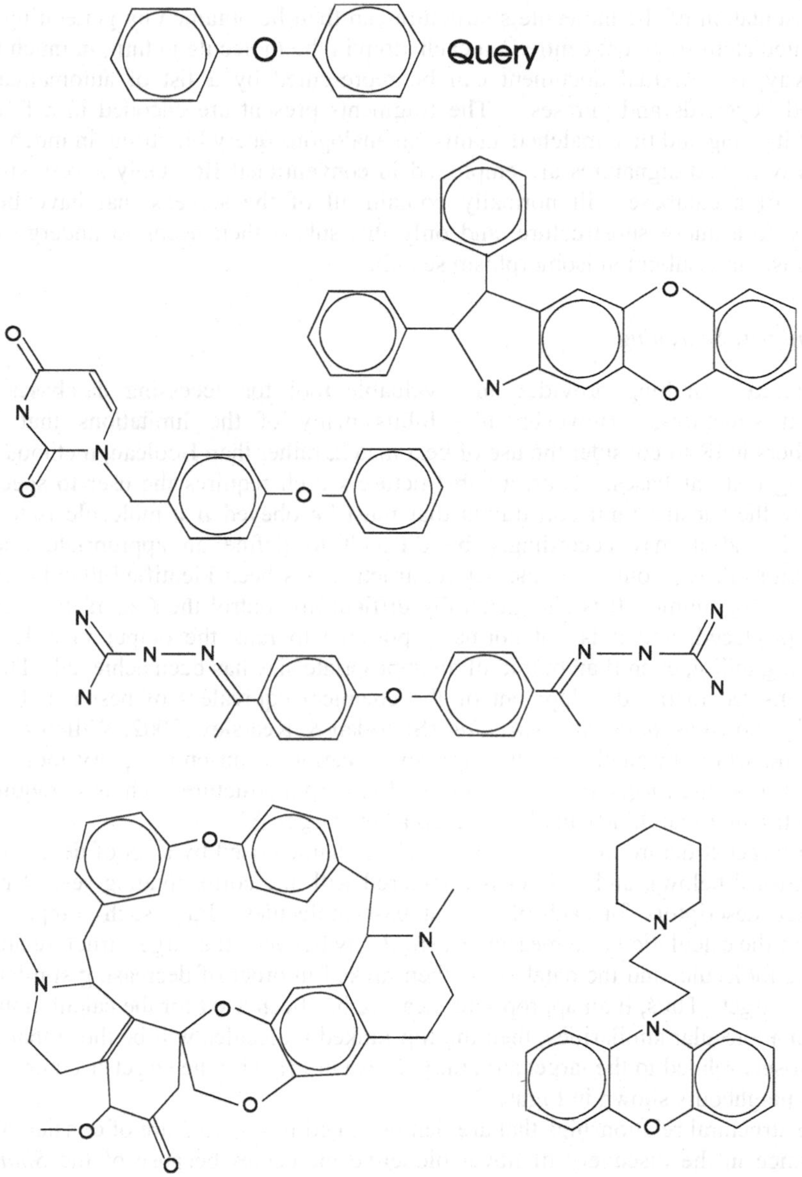

Figure 1. Example of a 2D substructure search. The search is for the diphenyl ether query substructure at the top of the figure, below which are shown five of the hits resulting from a search of the National Cancer Institute database of molecules that have been tested in the US government anti-cancer programme (see URL http://dtp.nci.nih.gov/)

A representation of the molecule's structure can then be obtained by generating an augmented atom fragment centred on each atom in the molecule in turn, in much the same way as a textual document can be represented by a list of automatically assigned keywords and phrases. The fragments present are encoded in a fixed-length bit-string and then matched against an analogous query bit-string, in much the same way as text-signatures are employed in conventional IR. Only a very small fraction of a database will normally contain all of the screens that have been assigned to a query substructure, and only this subset then needs to undergo the time-consuming subgraph isomorphism search.

2.2 Similarity Searching

Substructure searching provides an invaluable tool for accessing databases of chemical structures. However, it exhibits many of the limitations that led researchers in IR to consider the use of best match, rather than Boolean, methods for searching text databases. Thus, a substructure search requires the user to specify precisely the substructural constraints that must be obeyed if a molecule is to be retrieved, and it may accordingly be difficult to define an appropriate query substructure if, e.g., only a single active structure has been identified thus far in a synthetic programme. It is also generally difficult to control the size of the output that is produced, and it is not normally possible to rank the output in order of decreasing utility, even if an output of an appropriate size has been achieved. These limitations led to the development of the chemical equivalent of best match IR, which is known as similarity searching (Sheridan & Kearsley, 2002; Willett et al., 1998) and which normally involves the specification of an entire query molecule (referred to as the target structure), although a partial structure such as is required for substructure searching can also be used as the target.

The target structure in a similarity search is characterised by a set of descriptors (as discussed below), and this set is compared with the corresponding sets of pre-computed descriptors for each of the database molecules. Each such comparison results in the calculation of a measure of similarity between the target structure and a database molecule, and the database is then ranked in order of decreasing similarity with the target. Thus, if an appropriate measure has been used for the calculation of the inter-molecular similarities, then the top-ranked molecules will be those that are most closely related to the target structure, as exemplified by the target structure and nearest neighbours shown in Figure 2.

The structural relationships that are demonstrated in Figure 2 are of considerable importance in the discovery of novel bioactive molecules because of the Similar Property Principle (Johnson & Maggiora, 1990), which states that molecules that have similar structures will have similar properties (there is also the related neighbourhood behaviour approach of Patterson et al. (1996), which essentially states that property differences increase in line with structural dissimilarities). Hence, if the target structure has some interesting property, e.g., it lowers a person's cholesterol level or alleviates the symptoms of a migraine attack, then molecules that are structurally similar to it are more likely to exhibit that property than are molecules picked from a database at random (Martin *et al.*, 2002). This has led to similarity searching being widely used in systems for *virtual screening* (Bohm & Schneider, 2000). Biological testing in pharmaceutical and agrochemical research is resource intensive (in terms of both time and money), and the cost-effectiveness of such testing is hence maximised if it is possible to eliminate from consideration those molecules that have low *a priori* probabilities of exhibiting the biological activity of interest. Virtual screening is the name given to the use of computational methods to rank a dataset in decreasing order of such probabilities, so that attention can be focussed on the molecules at the top of the ranking. Similarity searching is just one type of virtual screening method: there are several others (Bohm & Schneider, 2000).

It will be clear that the Similar Property Principle can be regarded as the chemoinformatics equivalent of the Cluster Hypothesis in IR (Jardine & van Rijsbergen, 1971), which states that documents that are similar tend to be relevant to the same requests: replace "document" in the Cluster Hypothesis by "molecule" and "relevant to the same requests" by "exhibit the same biological properties" and one has the Similar Property Principle. In fact, there are many other analogies between chemoinformatics and IR, as I have discussed elsewhere (Willett, 2000, 2001), and it was this close relationship between the two subject domains that led me to commence a long-term programme of research at the end of the Seventies that sought to apply the concepts of best-match IR to the processing of chemical databases (Willett, 1987).

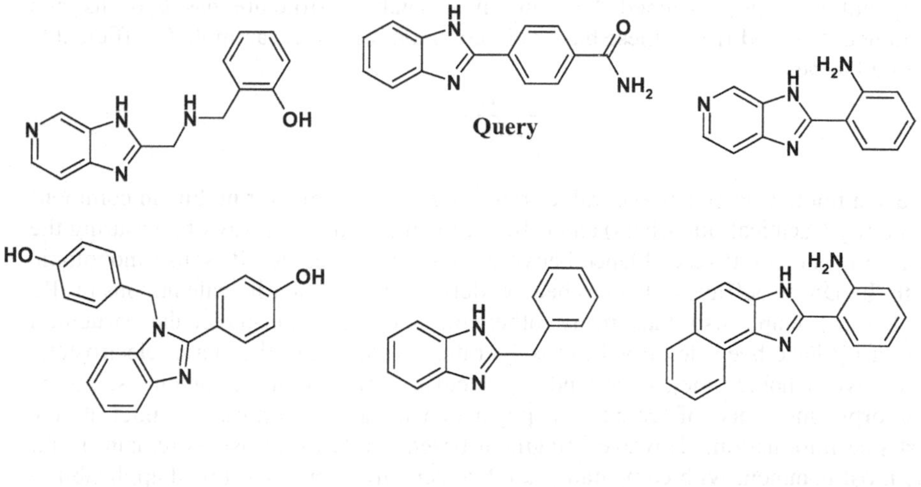

Figure 2. Example of a 2D similarity search, showing a query molecule and five of its nearest neighbours. The search is again of the National Cancer Institute database described in the caption to Figure 1, and the similarity measure for the search is based on fragment bit-strings and the Tanimoto coefficient.

2.3 Similarity Measures

At the heart of any similarity searching system is the measure that is used to quantify the degree of structural resemblance between pairs of molecules (Dean, 1994; Johnson & Maggiora, 1990; Sheridan & Kearsley, 2002; Willett *et al.*, 1998). My group took as its starting point a study by Adamson and Bush that considered inter-molecular similarities based on the fragment bit-strings that are normally used for 2D substructure searching (Adamson & Bush, 1973). Specifically, these authors suggested that two molecules should be regarded as being similar if they have a large number of bits, and hence substructural fragments, in common, in just the same way as a document and a query are judged to be similar if they have sufficient index terms in common; indeed, it is the close analogy between the document-index term and molecule-fragment substructure relationships that enables one to apply many IR techniques in chemoinformatics and *vice versa* (Willett, 2000, 2001). The study of Adamson and Bush (1973) focused on the similarities between the 20 naturally occurring amino acids and much of the subsequent work in Sheffield also considered such small datasets (Willett, 1987). However, the basic approach is applicable to the calculation of similarities in a database-searching context, and two near-contemporaneous papers in the mid-Eighties described experimental systems for large-scale similarity searching (Carhart *et al.*, 1985; Willett *et al.*, 1986). This is now an established component of chemoinformatics software systems (Gasteiger & Engel, 2003; Leach & Gillet, 2003), with the inter-molecular structural similarities in such systems being calculated using the Tanimoto Coefficient (Willett *et al.*, 1998). If the target structure in the similarity search has a of the bits in its fragment bit-string switched "on" and if a database structure has b of its bits switched "on" and if c of these bits are in common, then the Tanimoto Coefficient is defined to be

$$\frac{c}{a+b-c}.$$

The Tanimoto Coefficient has values ranging between zero (for no bits in common) and unity (identical bit-strings) and is by far the most common way of measuring the degree of structural resemblance between pairs of molecules. It is also monotonic with the Dice Coefficient that has been widely used for similarity calculations in IR.

I must emphasise that many other measures of inter-molecular structural similarity have been described in the literature, using, *e.g.*, the steric, electrostatic and hydrophobic fields around molecules, maximum common subgraph isomorphisms, sets of calculated physicochemical properties, or inter-atomic distance information. However, fragment-based similarity measures remain by far the most common, with comparative studies demonstrating their broad applicability (Brown & Martin, 1996; Willett, 1987), and their use for similarity-based virtual screening will be assumed in the remainder of this chapter.

		Active		
		Yes	No	
Retrieved	Yes	a	$n-a$	n
	No	$A-a$	$N-n-A+a$	
				$N-n$
		A	$N-A$	N

Figure 3. Contingency table describing the output of a similarity search in terms of active molecules and molecules retrieved. The dataset contains a total of N molecules, A of which are biologically active; the search retrieves n molecules, a of which are active.

3. EVALUATION OF RETRIEVAL EFFECTIVENESS

The criterion that one uses to evaluate the effectiveness of a similarity search depends on the use to which the results of that search are being put. In the context of a virtual screening system, the rationale for the search is to find additional molecules that exhibit the same biological activity as the user's target structure, where these activities are determined by carrying out some sort of *in vitro* or *in vivo* biological test. As noted above, we can view biological activity as being analogous to document relevance and it hence seems natural to adopt performance measures based on the numbers of biologically active molecules retrieved, in just the same way as IR performance measures are based on the numbers of relevant documents retrieved. If we accept this viewpoint then the results of a chemical database search can be summarised by the 2×2 contingency table shown in Figure 3.

In this figure, it is assumed that a search has been carried out resulting in the retrieval of the n nearest neighbours at the top of the ranked output. Assume that these n nearest neighbours include a of the A active molecules in the complete database, which contains a total of N molecules. Then, in the normal IR way, we can define the *recall*, R, as the fraction of the active molecules that are retrieved, *i.e.,*

$$R = \frac{a}{A},$$

and the *precision*, P, as the fraction of the retrieved molecules that are active, *i.e.,*

$$P = \frac{a}{n}.$$

3.1 Graphical Performance Measures

Precision-recall plots have always played a central role in the IR context, but their analogues have been little used in chemoinformatics. One reason for this may simply be a lack of awareness, in that few researchers in chemoinformatics have any IR experience; a rather better reason is a characteristic of chemical databases that differentiates them from document databases.

The normal synthetic approach in the pharmaceutical and agrochemical industries is to identify some compound, often called a *lead* compound, that exhibits the biological activity of interest and then to synthesise large numbers of close analogues, yielding what is commonly referred to as a *homologous series*. Historically, a company might well have synthesised some hundreds of analogues, but developments in robotic synthesis and combinatorial chemistry mean that it is now possible to synthesise thousands, or even tens of thousands, of analogues in parallel. Accordingly, a typical chemical database will contain very large numbers of closely related molecules. While there may well be some sets of documents in a text database that are closely related to each other (e.g., an initial conference report, a full journal article and a subsequent book chapter describing some piece of scientific research, or different wire services all reporting some fast-breaking news story), the overall incidence of such sets is on a far smaller scale than in the chemical context. Assume now that a similarity search is being carried out using a bioactive member of a homologous series as a target structure. The Similar Property Principle implies that the others in the series are also likely to be active, and the output of the search is hence likely to be very peaky, with large groups of closely related molecules all occurring at around the same position in a ranking.

Structural clustering resulting from analogue synthesis is exacerbated in some drug databases by the phenomenon of "me too" drugs. Once a pharmaceutical company has successfully brought a drug to market, other companies will (subject to the constraints of patent law) develop similar molecules with the same drug activity. This again increases the number of closely similar molecules that can be retrieved by a similarity search, as does the existence of "privileged substructures". A privileged substructure is a feature that occurs in molecules that exhibit several different types of biological activity (such as a benzodiazepine ring) and that will hence occur quite widely in databases of drug-like molecules; the existence of such common features again means that there may be some, or even many, molecules in a file that have a high degree of similarity with the target structure.

The resulting structural clustering was demonstrated in a detailed study of performance measures for chemical similarity searching (Edgar *et al.*, 2000). For example, in a search for blood substitutes - using 19102 molecules from the *World Drugs Index* database (World Drugs Index, no date) and using UNITY 2D fragment bit-strings (UNITY, no date) - there were two well-marked peaks at around rank positions 100-400. The corresponding molecules were all found to contain a phenyl trifluoromethyl moiety, with many of them also possessing a nitrogen atom immediately adjacent to the phenyl ring, as illustrated in Figure 4.

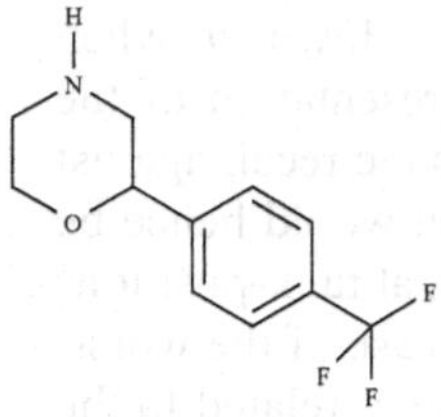
(119)

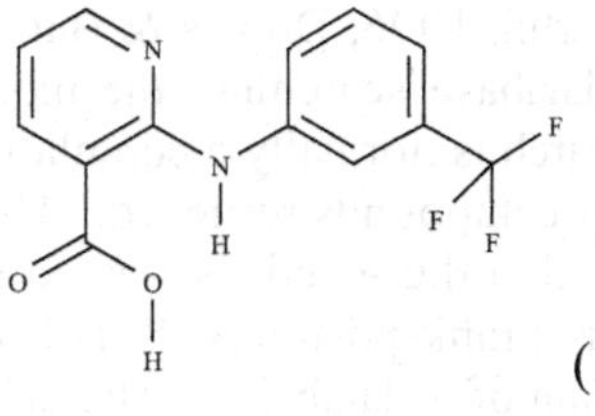
(151)

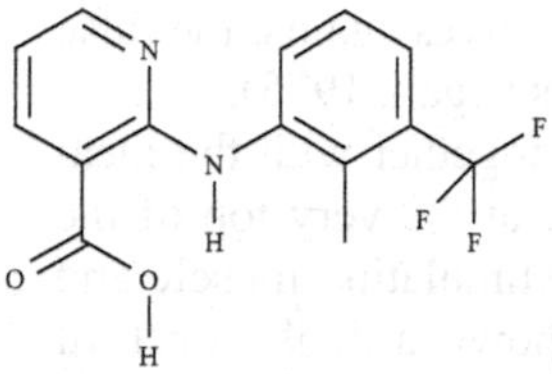
(211)

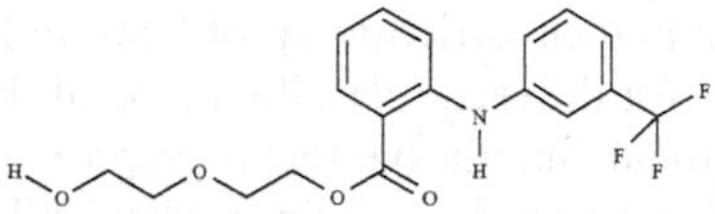
(219)

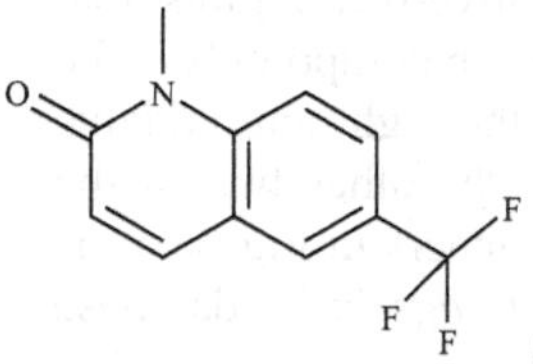
(245)

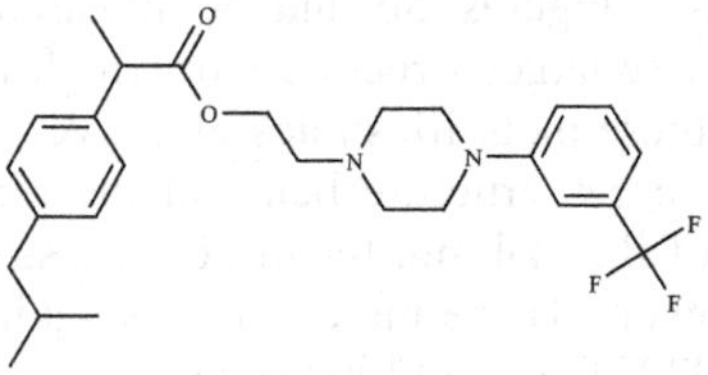
(271)

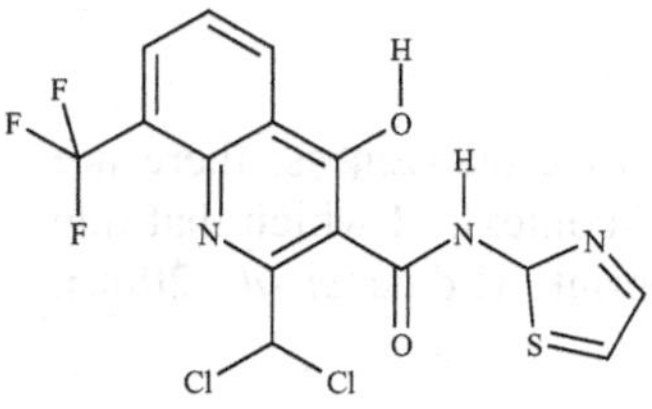
(291)

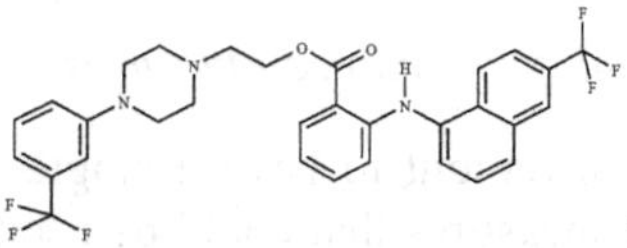
(308)

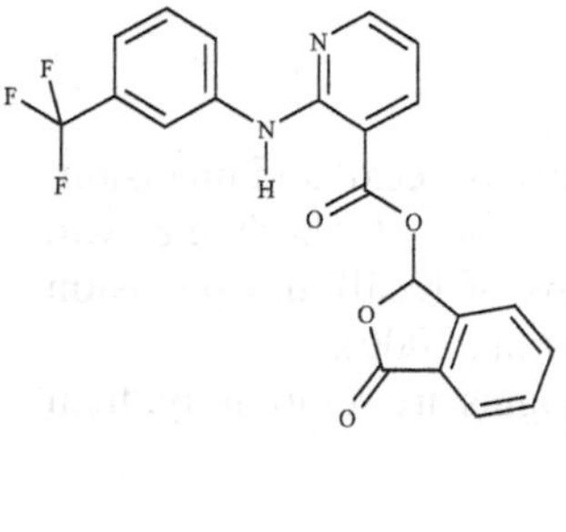
(389)

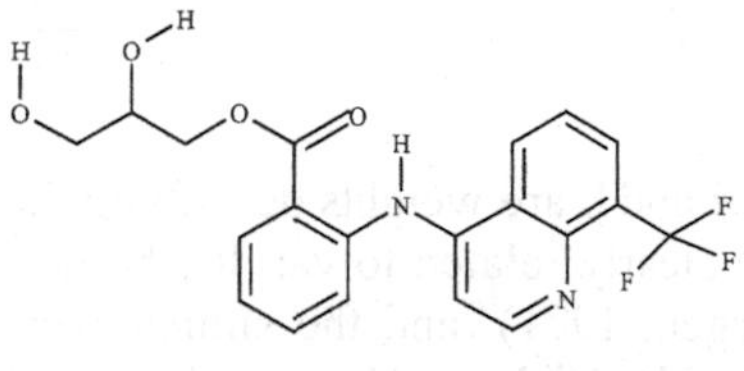
(399)

Figure 4. Retrieval position (in parentheses) of the active structures associated with the two peaks between n=100 and n=400 in the precision-recall plot for a blood-substitute target structure

The presence of such well-defined groupings goes some way to explaining the widespread and successful application of clustering methods to chemical databases (Brown & Martin, 1996; Downs & Barnard, 2002; Willett, 1987). However, when considering database searching, the most common graphical representation of the output of a search is normally a cumulative recall plot, which plots the recall against the number of compounds retrieved. The best possible such graph would hence be one in which all of the A actives were at the top of the ranking, *i.e.*, at rank-positions 1, 2, 3...A (or at rank-positions, N-A+1, N-A+2, N-A+3...N in the case of the worst-possible ranking of a database). The cumulative recall plot is closely related to the *receiver operating characteristic* (ROC) curves that are widely used in signal detection and classification problems and that plot the true positives against the false positives for different classifications of the same set of objects (Egan, 1975).

A typical cumulative recall graph is shown in Figure 5a, together with the ideal case (shown as a dashed line) where all of the actives occur at the very top of the ranking. The target structure used here shares its anabolic (stimulating muscle and bone growth) activity with 83 other compounds, and shows a high level of performance, with most of these actives being retrieved within the first 2000 positions. Figures 5b and 5c illustrate the stepped cumulative-recall plots that characterise target structures for which there are few other active compounds. The first of these plots illustrates effective searching, with six of the eight antioxidants for this target structure being at the top of the ranking, and the other two in the middle of the ranking; the effectiveness of the search for sweeteners in Figure 5c is much lower. These three searches again involved the *World Drugs Index* database and UNITY fragment bit-strings.

3.2 Numerical Performance Measures

It is often convenient to have a single-valued measure of effectiveness: there are several such measures that could be used in the chemical context, of which that due to Güner & Henry (2000) seems to be the most appropriate (Edgar *et al.*, 2000). Their *G-H* score is defined to be

$$\frac{\alpha P + \beta R}{2},$$

where α and β are weights describing the relative importance of recall and precision. This is clearly related to van Rijsbergen's effectiveness function, E (Jardine & van Rijsbergen, 1971), and the similar weighted combinations of recall and precision described by Vickery, Heine and Shaw, *inter alia* (Edgar *et al.*, 2000).

The lower bound for the G-H score is zero; if both weights are set to unity, then the score is simply the mean of recall and precision,

$$\frac{P + R}{2},$$

in which case it can be shown that the upperbound value is ½ (Edgar *et al.*, 2000). It is possible to obtain a graphical representation by plotting the G-H score at different values of *n*, the cut-off rank that is being used. The precise form of the plots obtained depends on the values of α and β, but the general shape is similar to cumulative recall plots, as would be expected from an analysis of their mathematical bases: this shows that when *n* molecules have been retrieved then the ratio of the cumulative recall at this point to the G-H score at this point (assuming $\alpha = \beta = 1$) tends to a limiting value of 2 (Edgar *et al.*, 2000).

Although the G-H score is being increasingly used as a way of combining the two parameters of recall and precision, there are other single-valued measures have been reported in the literature (Willett, 2004). For example, much of our early work in Sheffield quoted just the precision, i.e., *a/n*, without any consideration being given to the recall behaviour of the search. This may appear rather strange to workers in IR but is not unreasonable in that these studies were mostly comparative in nature, using several different mechanisms (e.g., types of similarity coefficients, of substructural fragment or of weighting schemes) with the same sets of active structures. Precision is also appropriate for evaluating virtual screening systems, given that their main purpose is rapidly to identify as many actives as possible so as to enable the subsequent formulation of a query for a more specific substructure search (either 2D or, preferably, 3D). In similar vein, the chemoinformatics group at Merck in the USA have used not only cumulative recall plots, but also *enrichment factors*, i.e., the number of actives retrieved relative to the number that would be retrieved if compounds were picked from the database at randomThus, using the notation of Figure 3, the enrichment factor at some point, *n*, in the ranking resulting from a similarity search is given by

$$\frac{a/n}{A/N}.$$

Since *A/N* is a constant, the enrichment is monotonic with precision. Finally, classification and machine learning methods in chemoinformatics often use a 'leave-one-out' approach. This assumes that the activity of one of the molecules in the database, *X*, is unknown and that a similarity search then identifies the top-*n* (where *n* is odd) nearest neighbours of *X*, by using it as a target structure. The activity or inactivity of *X* is then predicted on the basis of a majority vote (hence the requirement for an odd number) of the known activities of the selected nearest neighbours. This process is repeated for each of the *N* molecules in turn (or just the *A* active molecules in many comparative studies) and then the results summarised by

a measure such as Cohen's kappa statistic or the Rand statistic (Willett, 2004).

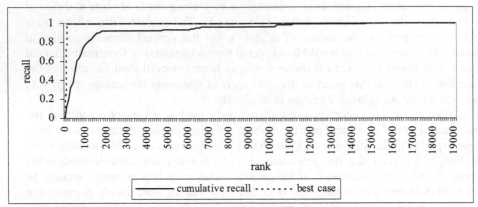

Figure 5a. Cumulative recall for an anabolic target structure

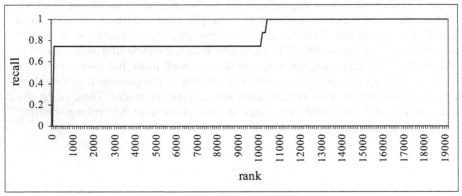

Figure 5b. Cumulative recall for an antioxidant target structure

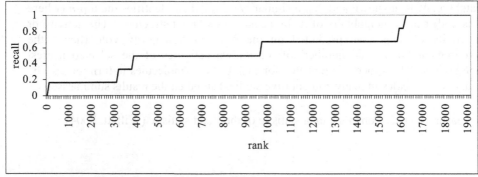

Figure 5c. Cumulative recall for a sweetener target structure

3.3 Quantitative Biological Data

Thus far, we have assumed a binary form of biological activity, in the sense that a molecule either is, or is not, active. This is, indeed, normally the case at an early stage in a drug discovery programme, where the aim is simply to identify at least some active lead compounds that can form the basis for a subsequent, more detailed optimisation programme. However, once the leads have been identified, far more precise experiments are carried out, resulting in molecules having quantitative, real-valued activity data associated with them; *e.g.*, the well-known LD50, which is the concentration of a molecule that is required to cause the death of 50% of the rats in a long-term carcinogenicity programme. A rather different approach to performance measurement is required when such quantitative data are available.

Assume that the value of some quantitative (*i.e.*, interval or ratio scale) property has been measured for each of the molecules in a dataset. The property value of the target structure, X, is assumed to be unknown, and a similarity search carried out to identify its n nearest neighbours. The predicted property value for X, $P(X)$, is then set equal to the arithmetic mean of the observed property values of its n nearest neighbours. This procedure results in the calculation of a $P(X)$ value for each of the N structures in the dataset (or some subset thereof): an overall figure of merit for the set of searches is then obtained by calculating the product moment correlation coefficient between the sets of N observed and N predicted values. A high value for the correlation coefficient is taken to mean that the similarity measure used in the making of the predictions provides an effective way of relating chemical structure with biological activity; alternatively, if the coefficient value is low, or even statistically insignificant, then there is no reason to believe that molecules judged as being structurally similar to the target structure are likely to exhibit similar properties.

There is no reason in principle why such quantitative approaches to performance evaluation could not also be used for IR: in practice, it is difficult enough to obtain relevance judgements on a binary scale, let alone on an interval or ratio scale, and there hence appears to be little scope for the adoption of such chemical approaches in the IR context.

4. CONCLUSIONS

In this chapter, I have illustrated some of the ways in which the rigorous approach to system evaluation that typifies both IR in general and much of Spärck Jones' work in particular, is also applicable to the evaluation of systems for virtual screening in chemical databases. This approach is now well established in chemoinformatics and provides a quantitative basis for the comparison of different types of chemical similarity measure. As noted previously, there are many links between information retrieval and chemoinformatics (Willett, 2000, 2001) and it would be remiss of me here not to mention the influence of other IR pioneers on the chemoinformatics research that has been carried out in Sheffield. Thus, the early work of van Rijsbergen and Salton on document clustering (Jardine & van Rijsbergen, 1971; Salton, 1971) inspired the development of tools for clustering databases of chemical structures (Willett, 1987), a technique that is now well established for the selection of compounds for biological screening (see, *e.g.*, Brown & Martin (1996) and Downs & Barnard (2002)). More recently, molecular diversity analysis (Dean & Lewis, 1999) has adopted tools from similarity searching and chemical clustering to maximise the cost-effectiveness of robotic synthesis procedures; the influence of IR research on this aspect of chemoinformatics is included in the historical review by Martin *et al.* (2001). As another example, Robertson's work with Spärck Jones on relevance feedback (Robertson & Sparck Jones, 1976; Spark Jones & Webster, 1980) provided the basis for some of our studies of substructural analysis (Cosgrove & Willett, 1996; Ormerod *et al.*, 1989); this is an alternative approach to virtual screening that assumes a training-set of known active and known inactive molecules (rather than the single known active required for similarity-based virtual screening).

To conclude on a personal note, Spärck Jones has played a pivotal role in the development of IR systems, in particular by her insistence on the need for extended and rigorous experimental comparisons if one is to be able to make unequivocal statements about the relative merits of different retrieval mechanisms. Such comparative studies were very rare in chemoinformatics when I started work in the late Seventies. I feel that I have been very lucky in being in a position to apply the methodologies of IR in a different area, with the result that detailed comparative studies are now a standard experimental methodology and a pre-requisite for the acceptance of new searching procedures (see, *e.g.*, the work of Brown & Martin (1996), Kearsley *et al.* (1996), Martin *et al.* (2002), Patterson *et al.* (1996), and Sheridan & Kearsley (2002)).

Peter Willett is the Head of the Department of Information Studies and a member of the Krebs Institute for Biomolecular Research at the University of Sheffield. He is a Fellow of the Chartered Institute of Library and Information Professionals, and was the recipient of the 1993 Skolnik Award of the American Chemical Society, of the 1997 Distinguished Lecturer Award of the New Jersey Chapter of the American Society for Information Science, of the 2001 Kent Award of the Institute of Information Scientists, and of the 2002 Lynch Award of the Chemical Structure Association Trust. He is included in Who's Who, is a member of the editorial boards of four international journals, and has been involved in the organisation of many national and international conferences in various aspects of chemical and textual information retrieval. Professor Willett heads a large research group studying novel computational techniques for the processing of chemical and biological information. His current interests include: database applications of cluster analysis, evolutionary computing and graph theory; molecular similarity and molecular diversity analysis; the comparison of chemical and biological 3D structures; and the use of citation data for the evaluation of academic research performance. He edited the book "Readings in Information Retrieval" with Karen Spärck Jones.

ACKNOWLEDGEMENTS

I thank the Royal Society, Tripos Inc. and the Wolfson Foundation for software and laboratory support, and the Biotechnology and Biological Sciences Research Council, the Engineering and Physical Sciences Research Council and my many industrial collaborators for their contributions to the work of the Sheffield chemoinformatics research group over the years. The Krebs Institute for Biomolecular Research is a designated biomolecular sciences centre of the Biotechnology and Biological Sciences Research Council.

REFERENCES

Adamson, G.W. & Bush, J.A. (1973). A method for the automatic classification of chemical structures. *Information Storage and Retrieval*, *9*, 561-568.

Barnard, J.M. (1993). Substructure searching methods: old and new. *Journal of Chemical Information and Computer Sciences*, *33*, 532-538.

Böhm, H.-J. & Schneider, G. (editors) (2000). *Virtual Screening for Bioactive Molecules*. Wiley-VCH.

Brown, R.D. & Martin, Y.C. (1996). Use of structure-activity data to compare structure-based clustering methods and descriptors for use in compound selection. *Journal of Chemical Information and Computer Sciences*, *36*, 572-584.

Carhart, R.E., Smith, D.H. & Venkataraghavan, R. (1985). Atom pairs as molecular features in structure-activity studies: definition and application. *Journal of Chemical Information and Computer Sciences*, *25*, 64-73.

Cosgrove, D.A. & Willett, P. (1998). SLASH: a program for analysing the functional groups in molecules. *Journal of Molecular Graphics and Modelling*, *16*, 19-32.

Dean, P.M. (editor) (1994). *Molecular Similarity in Drug Discovery*. Chapman and Hall.

Dean, P.M. & Lewis, R.A. (editors) (1999). *Molecular Diversity in Drug Design*. Kluwer.

Downs, G.M. & Barnard, J.M. (2002). Clustering methods and their uses in computational chemistry. *Reviews in Computational Chemistry*, *18*, 1-40.

Edgar, S.J., Holliday, J.D. & Willett, P. (2000). Effectiveness of retrieval in similarity searches of chemical databases: a review of performance measures. *Journal of Molecular Graphics and Modelling*, *18*, 343-357.

Egan, J.P. (1975). *Signal Detection Theory and ROC Analysis*. Academic Press.

Gasteiger, J. & Engel, T. (editors) (2003). *Chemoinformatics: from Data to Knowledge*. Wiley-VCH.

Güner, O.F. & Henry, D.R. (2000). Metric for analyzing hit lists and pharmacophores. In Güner, O (editor). *Pharmacophore Perception, Development and Use in Drug Design*. International University Line, pp. 193-212.

Jardine, N. & van Rijsbergen, C.J. (1971). The use of hierarchic clustering in information retrieval. *Information Storage and Retrieval*, *7*, 217-240.

Johnson, M.A. & Maggiora, G.M. (editors) (1990). *Concepts and Applications of Molecular Similarity*. Wiley.

Kearsley, S.K., Sallamack, S., Fluder, E.M., Andose, J.D., Mosley, R.T. & Sheridan, R.P. (1996). Chemical similarity using physicochemical property descriptors. *Journal of Chemical Information and Computer Sciences*, *36*, 118-127.

Learch, A.R. & Gillet, V.J. (2003). *An Introduction to Chemoinformatics*. Kluwer.

Martin, Y.C., Kofron, J.L. & Traphagen, L.M. (2002). Do structurally similar molecules have similar biological activities? *Journal of Medicinal Chemistry*, *45*, 4350-4358.

Martin. Y.C. & Willett, P. (editors) (1998). *Designing Bioactive Molecules: Three-Dimensional Techniques and Applications*. American Chemical Society.

Martin, Y.C., Willett, P., Lajiness, M., Johnson, M., Maggiora, G., Martin, E., Bures, M.G., Gasteiger, J., Cramer, R.D., Pearlman, R.S. & Mason, J.S. (2001). Diverse viewpoints on computational aspects of molecular diversity. *Journal of Combinatorial Chemistry*, *3*, 231-250.

Ormerod, A., Willett, P. & Bawden, D. (1989). Comparison of fragment weighting schemes for substructural analysis. *Quantitative Structure-Activity Relationships*, *8*, 115-129.

Patterson, D.E., Cramer, R.D., Ferguson, A.M., Clark, R.D.& Weinberger, L.E. (1996). Neighbourhood behaviour: a useful concept for validation of "molecular diversity" descriptors. *Journal of Medicinal Chemistry, 39,* 3049-3059.

Robertson, S.E & Spark Jones, K. (1976). Relevance weighting of search terms. *Journal of the American Society for Information Science, 27,* 129-146.

Russo, E. (2002). Chemistry plans a structural overhaul. *Nature, 419,* 4-7.

Salton, G. (editor) (1971). *The SMART Retrieval System.* Prentice-Hall.

Schofield, H., Wiggins, G. & Willett, P. (2003). Recent developments in chemoinformatics education. *Drug Discovery Today, 6,* 931-934.

Sheridan, R.P. & Kearsley, S.K. (2002). Why do we need so many chemical similarity search methods? *Drug Discovery Today, 7,* 903-911.

Sparck Jones, K. & Bates, R.G. (1979). *Research on Automatic Indexing 1974-1976.* British Library Research and Development Department.

Sparck Jones, K. & Webster, C.A. (1980). *Research on Relevance Weighting 1976-1979.* British Library Research and Development Department.

UNITY. The UNITY chemical information management software is available from Tripos Inc. at http://www.tripos.com/

Willett, P. (1987). *Similarity and Clustering in Chemical Information Systems.* Research Studies Press.

Willett, P. (2000). Textual and chemical information retrieval: different applications but similar algorithms. *Information Research,* at URL http://InformationR.net/ir/5-2/infres52.html

Willett, P. (2001). Applications of information retrieval methods in computer-aided drug discovery. *Jurnal Teknologi Maklumat, 1,* 17-31.

Willett, P. (2004). The evaluation of molecular similarity and molecular diversity methods using biological activity data. *Methods in Molecular Biology, 275,* 51-63.

Willett, P., Barnard, J.M. & Downs, G.M. (1998). Chemical similarity searching. *Journal of Chemical Information and Computer Sciences, 38,* 983-996.

Willett, P., Winterman, V. & Bawden, D. (1986). Implementation of nearest neighbour searching in an online chemical structure search system. *Journal of Chemical Information and Computer Sciences, 26,* 36-41.

World Drugs Index. The *World Drug Index* database is available from Derwent Information at http://www.derwent.co.uk/

YORICK A. WILKS

UNHAPPY BEDFELLOWS: THE RELATIONSHIP OF AI AND IR

1. AI AND NLP IN NEED OF IR?

1.1. Introduction

Speaking of Artificial Intelligence (AI) in the past, one sometimes refers to "classical" or "traditional" AI, and the intended contrast with the present refers to the series of shocks that paradigm suffered from connectionism and neural nets to adaptive behaviour theories. The shock was not of the new, of course, because those theories were mostly improved versions of cybernetics which had preceded classical AI and been almost entirely obliterated by it. The classical AI period was logic or symbol-based but not entirely devoid of numbers, of course, for AI theories of vision flourished in close proximity to pattern-recognition research. Although, representational theories in computer vision sometimes achieved prominence (e.g. with Marr, 1981), nonetheless it was always, at bottom, an engineering subdiscipline with all that that entailed. But when faced with any attempt to introduce quantitative methods into classical core AI in the 70s, John McCarthy would always respond "But where do all these numbers **come from**?"

Now we know better where they come from, and nowhere have numbers been more prominent than in the field of Information Retrieval (IR), one of similar antiquity to AI, but with which it has until now rarely tangled intellectually, although on any broad definition of AI as "modelling intelligent human capacities", one might imagine that IR, like machine translation (MT), would be covered; yet neither has traditionally been seen as part of AI. On second thoughts perhaps, IR does not fall there under that definition simply because, before computers, humans were not in practice able to carry out the kinds of large-scale searches and comparisons operations on which IR rests. And even though IR often cohabits with Library Science, which grew out of card indexing in libraries, there is perhaps no true continuity between those subfields, in that IR consists of operations of indexing and retrieval that humans could not carry out in normal lifetimes.

1.2. Sparck Jones' Case Against AI

If any reader is beginning to wonder why I have even raised the question of the relationship of AI to IR, it is because Karen Sparck Jones (KSJ from now on), in a

John I. Tait (ed.), *Charting a New Course: Natural Language Processing and Information Retrieval. Essays in Honour of Karen Spärck Jones.* 255-282
© 2005 Springer.

remarkable paper, has already done so (1999b) and argued that AI has much to learn from IR. In this paper my aim is to redress that balance a little and answer her general lines of argument. Her main target is AI researchers seen as what she calls "The Guardians of content". I shall set out her views and then contest them, arguing both in her own terms, and by analogy with the case of Machine Translation (MT) in particular, that the influence is perhaps in the other direction, and that is shown both by limitations on statistical methods that MT developments have shown in recent years, and by a curious reversal of terminology in IR that has taken place in the same period. However, the general purpose of this chapter will not be to redraw boundaries between these subfields, but will argue that subfields of NLP/AI are now increasingly hard to distinguish: not just MT, but Information Extraction (IE) and Question Answering (QA) are now beginning to form a general information processing functionality that is making many of these arguments moot. The important questions in Sparck Jones resolve to one crucial question: what is the primitive level of language data? Her position on this is shown by the initial quotation below, after which come a set of quotations from two sources (1990, 1999b) that capture the essence of her views on the central issues:

1. "One of these [simple, revolutionary IR] ideas is taking words as they stand" (2003)
2. "The argument that AI is required to support the integrated information management system of the future "Is the heady vision of the individual user at his workstation in a whole range of activities calling on, and also creating, information objects of different sorts." (1990)
3. "What might be called the intelligent library" (1990)
4. "What therefore is needed to give effect to the vision is the internal provision of (hypertext) objects and links, and specifically in the strong form of an AI-type knowledge base and inference system" (1990)
5. "The AI claim in its strongest form means that the knowledge base completely replaces the text base of the documents" (1990)
6. "It is natural, therefore, if the system cannot be guaranteed to be able to use the knowledge base to answer questions on the documents of the form 'Does X do Y?' as opposed to questions of the form 'Are there documents about X doing Y?' to ask why we need a knowledge base" (1990)
7. "The AI approach is fundamentally misconceived because it is based on the wrong general model, of IR as QA" (1990)
8. "What reason can one have for supposing that the different [multimodal, YW] objects involved could be systematically related via a common knowledge base, and characterised in a manner *independent of ordinary language*" [YW's italics] (1990)
9. "We should think therefore of having an access structure in the form of a network thrown over the underlying information objects" (1990)
10. "When the key properties of document retrieval are recognised .... and the technologies that have been developed in the last forty years of IR research have important lessons for AI" (1999b)

11. "A far more powerful AI system than any we can realistically foresee will not be able to ensure that answers it could give to questions extracted from the user's request would be appropriate" (1999b)
12. "Classical document retrieval thus falls in the class of AI tasks that assist the human user but cannot, by definition, replace them" (1999b)
13. This [IR] style of representation is the opposite of the classical AI type and has more in common with connectionist ones. (1999b)
14. "The paper's case is that important tasks that can be labelled 'information management' are fundamentally inexact". (1999b)
15. "Providing access to information could cover much more of AI than might be supposed". (1999b)

These quotations suffice to establish a complex position, and one should note in passing the prescience of quotations (2)(3)(4) and (10) in their vision of a system of information access something like the World Wide Web we now have. The quotations indicate three major claims in the papers from which they come, which I shall summarise as follows:

A. Words are self-representing and cannot be replaced by any more primitive representation; all we, as technicians with computers, can add are sophisticated associations between them (quotations (1), (10) and (14)).

B. Core AI-KR seeks to replace words, with their inevitable inexactness, with exact logical — or at least non-word based — representations. (quotations (5) (6) and (9))

C. Human information needs are vague: we want relevant information, not answers to questions. In any case, AI-KR cannot answer questions. (quotations (7)(8)(11) and (12))

D. The human reader/author relationship remains primary in the relationship, and is mediated by relevant documents. Anyway, systems based on association can do some kinds of (inexact) reasoning and could be used to retrieve relevant axioms in a KR system. (quotations (5)(13)(14) and (16)).

We should not see the issues here as simply ones of KSJ's critique (based on IR) of "core", traditional or symbolic AI, for her views connect directly to an internal interface within AI itself, one about which the subject has held an internal dialogue for many years, and in many of its subareas. The issue is that of the nature and necessity for structured symbolic representations, and their relationship to the data they claim to represent.

So, to take an example from NLP, Schank always held that Conceptual Dependency (CD) representations (1975) not only represented language strings but made the original dispensable, so that, for example, there need be no access to the source string in the process of machine translation after it had been represented by CD primitives; Charniak (1973) and I (1977) in our different ways, denied this and claimed that the surface string retained essential information not present in any representation. Schank's position here can be seen as exactly the type that KSJ is attacking, but it was not of course the only AI view.

But, more generally, the kind of AI view that KSJ had in her sights was the AI view that proclaimed the centrality and adequacy of knowledge representations, and their independence of whatever language would be used to describe what it is in the world they represent (that is the essence of her claims A and B). The key reference for the view she rejects would be McCarthy and Hayes (1969), and its extreme opposite, in machine vision at least, would be any view that has elements that could be termed Gibson (1968), one that insists on the primacy of data over any representation. The spirit of Chomsky, of course, hovers over the position, in language modelling at least, that asserts the primacy of a (correct) representation over any amount of data. Indeed, he produced a range of ingenious arguments as to why no amount of data could possibly produce the representations the brain has for language structure (1965), and those arguments continued to echo through the dispute, for example, between Fodor and Pollack (1990) as to whether or not nested representations could be derived by any form machine learning from language data: Pollack claimed his connectionist RAAM system could do exactly that, and Fodor denied it.

Again, and now somewhat further from core AI, one can see the issue in Schvaneveldt's Pathfinder networks (1990) which he showed, in psychological experiments, could represent the expertise of fighter pilots in associationist networks of terms, a form very close to the data from which it was derived. This work was a direct challenge to the contemporary expert-systems movement for representing such expertise by means of high-level rules.

1.3. Some Countervailing Considerations from AI

It should be clear from the last paragraphs that KSJ is not targeting all of AI, which might well be taken to include IR on a broad definition, but a core of AI, basically the strong representationalist tradition, one usually (but not always, as in the case of Schank above) associated with the use of first order predicate calculus. And when one writes of a broad definition, it could only be one that does not restrict AI to the modelling of basic human functionalities, the notion behind Papert's original observation that AI could not and should not model superhuman faculties, ones that no person could have. In some sense, of course, classic IR is superhuman: there was no pre-existing human skill, as there was with seeing, talking or even chess playing that corresponded to the search through millions of words of text on the basis of indices. But if one took the view, by contrast, that theologians, lawyers and, later, literary scholars were able, albeit slowly, to search vast libraries of sources for relevant material, then on that view IR is just the optimisation of a human skill and not a superhuman activity. If one takes that view, IR is a proper part of AI, as traditionally conceived.

However, that being said, it may be too much a claim (D above) in the opposite direction to suggest, as KSJ does in a remark at the end of one of the papers cited, that core AI may need IR to search among the axioms of a formalised theory (1999b) in order to locate relevant axioms to compose a proof. It is certain that resolution, or any related proof program, draws in potential axioms based on the appearance of identical predicates in them (i.e. to those in the theorem to be proved). But it would be absurd to see that as a technique borrowed from or in any way indebted to IR; it is simply the obvious and only way to select those axioms that might plausibly take part in proofs.

A key claim of KSJ's (in (A) and especially (B) above) is the issue one might call *primitives*, where one can take that to be either the predicates of a logical representation, as in McCarthy and Hayes and most AI reasoning work, or the more linguistic primitives, present in Schank's CD work and my own under the name *preference semantics* (Wilks and Fass, 1992, Wilks et al., 1996). Her argument is that words remain their own best interpretation, and cannot be replaced by some other artificial coding that adequately represents their meaning. KSJ's relationship to this tradition is complex: her own thesis (Sparck Jones, 1966 and see Tait and Wilks, this volume) although containing what now are seen as IR clustering algorithms applied to a thesaurus, was intended, in her own words, to be a search for semantic primitives for MT. Moreover, she contributed to the definition and development of Cambridge Language Research Unit's own semantic interlingua NUDE (for "naked ideas"). That tradition has been retained in AI and computational linguistics, both as a basis for coding lexical systems (e.g. the work of Pustejovsky, 1995) and as another form of information to be established on an empirical basis from corpora and can be seen in early work on the derivation of preferences from corpora by Resnik (1996), Grishman, (Grishman and Sterling, 1992), Lehnert (Riloff and Lehnert, 1993) and others. Work of this type certainly involves the exploitation of semantic redundancy, both qualitatively, in the early preference work cited above, and quantitatively, in the recent tradition of work on systematic Word Sense Disambiguation which makes use of statistical methods exploiting the redundancy already coded in thesauri and dictionaries. Unless KSJ really intends to claim that any method of language analysis exploiting statistics and redundancy (like those just cited) is really IR, then there is little basis to her claim that AI has a lot to learn from IR in this area, since it has its own traditions by now of statistical methodology and evaluation and, as I shall shown below, these came into AI/NLP from speech research pioneered by Jelinek, and indigenous work on machine learning, and not at all from IR.

Let us now turn to another of KSJ's major claims, (C above) that question-answering (QA) is not a real task meeting a real human need, but that the real task is the location of relevant documents, which is IR's classic function. First, one must be clear that there has never been any suggestion in mainstream AI that its techniques could perform the core IR task. To find relevant documents, as opposed to their content, one would have to invent IR, had it not existed; there simply is no choice. Information Extraction (IE), on the other hand, (Gaizauskas and Wilks, 1997) is a relatively recent content searching technique, usually with a representational non-statistical component, designed to access factual content directly, and that process usually assumes a prior application of IR to find relevant material to search. The application of an IR phase prior to IE in a sense confirms KSJ's "primacy of relevance", but also confirms the independence and viability of QA, which is nowadays seen as an extension of IE. IE, by seeking facts of specific forms, is always implicitly asking a question (i.e. What facts are there matching the following general form?).

However, recently Gaizauskas (2004) has questioned this conventional temporal primacy of IR in an IE application, and has done so by pointing out that the real answers to IE/QA questions are frequently to be found very far down the (relevance based) percentiles of returns from this prior IR phase. The reason for this is that if one asks, say, "What colour is the sky?" then, in the IR phase, the term "colour/color" is a very poor index term for relevant documents likely to contain the answer. In other words, "relevance" in the IR sense (and unboosted by augmentation with actual colour names in this case) is actually a poor guide to where answers to this question are to be found, and Gaizauskas uses this point to question the conventional relationship of IR and IE/QA.

One could, at this point, perhaps reverse KSJ's jibe at AI as the self-appointed "Guardians of Content" and suggest that IR may not be as much the "Guardian of relevance" as she assumes. But whatever is the case there, it seems pretty clear that wanting answers to questions is sometimes a real human need, even outside the world of TV quiz shows. The website Ask Jeeves seemed to meet some real need, even if it was not always successful, and QA has been seen as a traditional AI task, back to the classic book by Lehnert (1977). KSJ is, of course, correct that those traditional methods were not wholly successful and did not, as much early NLP did not, lead to regimes of evaluation and comparison. But that in no way reflects on the need for QA as a task.

In fact, of course, QA has now been revived as an evaluable technique (see below), as part of the general revival of empirical linguistics, and has been, as we noted already, a development of existing IE techniques, combined in some implementations with more traditional abductive reasoning (Moldovan, 2001). The fact of its being an evaluable technique should have made it very hard for KSJ to dismiss QA as a task in the way she does, since she has gone so far elsewhere in identifying real NLP with evaluable techniques (Galliers and Sparck Jones, 1996).

Over a twenty year period, CQA has moved from a wholly-knowledge based technique (as in Lehnert's work) to where it now is, as fusion of statistical and knowledge-based techniques. Most, if not all, parts of NLP have made the same transition over that period, starting with apparently straightforward tasks like part-of-speech tagging (e.g. Garside, 1987) and rising up to semantic and conceptual areas like word-sense disambiguation (e.g. Stevenson and Wilks, 1999) and dialogue management (Churcher et al., 1997) in addition to QA. In the next section we shall return to the origin of this empirical wave in NLP and re-examine its sources, then claim that new and interesting evidence can be found there for the current relationship of AI and IR. In her paper, KSJ acknowledges the recent empirical movement in NLP and its closeness in many ways to IR techniques, but she does not actually claim the movement as an influence from IR. I shall argue in the next section that, on the contrary, the influence on NLP that brought in the empirical revolution was principally from speech research, and in part from traditional statistical AI (i.e. machine learning) but in no way from IR. On the contrary, the influences detectable are all *on IR from outside*.

1.4. Jelinek's Revolution in Machine Translation and its Relevance

A piece of recent NLP history that may not be familiar to AI researchers is, I believe, highly relevant here. Jelinek, Brown and others at IBM New York began to implement around 1988 a plan of research to import the statistical techniques that had been successful in Automatic Speech Processing (ASR) into NLP and into machine translation (MT) in particular. DARPA supported Jelinek's system CANDIDE (Brown and Cocke, 1989, Brown et al., 1990) at the same time as rival symbolic systems (such as PANGLOSS (Nirenburg et al., 1994) using more traditional methods.

The originality of CANDIDE was to employ none of the normal translation resources within an MT system (e.g. grammars, lexicons etc.) but only statistical functions trained on a very large bilingual corpus: 200 million words of the French-English parallel text from Hansard, the Canadian parliamentary proceedings. CANDIDE made use of a battery of statistical techniques that had loose relations to those used in ASR: alignment of the parallel text sentences, then of words between aligned French and English sentences, and n-gram models (or language models as they would now be called) of the two language separately, one of which was used to smooth the output. Perhaps the most remarkable achievement was that given 12 French output words so found (output sentences could not be longer than that) the generation algorithm could determine the unique best order (out of billions) for an output translation with a high degree of success. The CANDIDE team did not describe their work this way, but rather as machine learning from a corpus that, given what they called an "equation of MT" produced the most likely source sentence for any putative output sentence.

The CANDIDE results were at roughly the 50% level, of sentences translated correctly or acceptably in a test set held back from training. Given that the team had no access to what one might call "knowledge of French", this was a remarkable achievement and far higher than most MT experts would have predicted, although CANDIDE never actually beat SYSTRAN, the standard and traditional symbolic MT system that is the world's most used system. At this point (about 1990) there was a very lively debate between what was then called the rationalist and empiricist approaches to MT, and Jelinek began a new program of trying to remedy what he saw as the main fault of his system by what would now be called a "hybrid" approach, one that was never fully developed because the IBM team dispersed.

The problem Jelinek saw is best called "data sparseness": his system's methods could not improve even applied to larger corpora of any reasonable size because language events are no rare. Word trigrams tend to be 85% novel in corpora of any conceivable size, an extraordinary figure. Jelinek therefore began a hybrid program to overcome this, which was to try to develop from scratch the standard NLP resources used in MT, such as grammars and lexicons, in the hope of using them to generalise across word or structure classes, so as to combat data sparseness. So, if the system knew elephants and dogs were in a class, then it could predict a trigram [X Y ELEPHANT] from having seen the trigram [X Y DOG] or vice versa.

It was this second, unfulfilled, program of Jelinek that, more than anything else, began the empiricist wave in NLP that still continues, even though the statistical work on learning part-of-speech tags actually began earlier at Lancaster under Leech (Garside, 1987). IBM bought the rights to this work and Jelinek then moved forward from alignment algorithms to grammar learning, and the rest is the historical movement we are still part of.

But it is vital to note consequences of this: first, that the influences brought to bear to create modern empirical, data-driven, NLP came from the ASR experience and machine learning algorithms, a traditional part of AI by then. They certainly did not come from IR, as KSJ might have expected given what she wrote. Moreover, and this has only recently been noticed, the research metaphors have now reversed, and techniques derived from Jelinek's work are now being introduced into IR under names like "MT approaches to IR" (Berger and Laferty, 2001, and see below) which is precisely a reversal of the direction of influence that KSJ argued for.

We shall mention some of this work in the next section, but we must draw a second moral here from Jelinek's experience with CANDIDE and one that bears directly on KSJ's claim that words are their own best representations (Claim A above). The empiricist program of recreating lexicons and grammars from corpora, begun by Jelinek and the topic of much NLP in the last 15 years, was started precisely because working with self-representations of words (e.g. n-grams) was inadequate because of their rarity in any possible data: 80% of word trigrams are novel, as we noted earlier under the term "data sparseness". Higher-level representations are designed to ameliorate this effect, and that remains the case whether those representations are a priori (like Wordnet, LDOCE or Roget's Thesaurus) or themselves derived from corpora.

KSJ could reply here that she did not intend to target such work in her critique of AI, but only core AI (logic or semantics based) that eliminates words as part of a representation, rather than adds higher level representation to the words. There can be no doubt that even very low-level representations, however obtained, when added to words can produce results that would be hard to imagine without them. A striking case is the use of part-of-speech tags (like PROPERNOUN) where, given a word sense resource structured in the way Longmans LDOCE is, (Stevenson and Wilks, 1999) were able to show that those part of speech tags alone can resolve large-scale word sense ambiguity (called homographs in LDOCE) at the 92% level. Given such a simple tagging, almost all word sense ambiguity is trivially resolved against that particular structured resource, a result that could not conceivably be obtained without those low-level additional representations, which are not merely the words themselves, as KSJ expects.

1.5. Recent Developments in IR

In this section, we draw attention to some recent developments in IR that suggest that KSJs characterisation of the relationship of IR to AI may not be altogether correct and may in some ways be the reverse of what is the case.

That reverse claim may also seem somewhat hyperbolic, in response to KSJ's original paper, and in truth there may be some more general movement at work in this whole area, one more general than either the influence of AI on IR or its opposite, namely that traditional functionalities in information processing are now harder to distinguish. This degree of interpenetration of techniques is such that it may be just as plausible (as claiming directional influence, as above) to say that MT, QA, IE, IR as well as summarisation and, perhaps a range of technologies associated with ontologies, lexicons, inference, the Semantic Web and aspects of Knowledge Management, are all becoming conflated in a science of information access. Without going into much detail, where might one look for immediate anecdotal evidence for that view?

Salton (1972) initiated CLIR (Cross-language Information Retrieval) using a thesaurus and a bilingual dictionary between languages, and more recent forms of the technique have used Machine-Readable Bilingual Dictionaries to bridge the language gap (Ballasteros and Croft, 1998), and Eurowordnet, a major NLP tool (Vossen, 1998), was designed explicitly for CLIR. CLIR is a task rather like MT but recall is more important and it is still useful at low rates of precision, which MT is not because people tend not to accept translations with alternatives on a large scale like "They decided to have {PITCH, TAR, FISH, FISHFOOD} for dinner".

(Gaizauskas and Wilks, 1997) describe a system of multilingual IE based on treating the templates themselves as a form of interlingua between the languages, and this is clearly a limited form of MT. (Gollins and Sanderson, 2001) have described a form of CLIR that brings back the old MT notion of a "pivot language" to bridge between one language and another, and where pivots can be chained in a parallel or sequential manner. Latvian-English and Latvian-Russian CLIR could probably reach any EU language from Latvian via multiple CLIR pivot retrievals (of sequential CLIR based on Russian-X or English-X). This IR usage differs from MT use, where a pivot was an interlingua, not a language and was used once, never iteratively. (Oh et al., 2000) report using a Japanese-Korean MT system to determine terminology in unknown language. (Gachot et al., 1998) report using an established, possibly the most established, MT system SYSTRAN as a basis for CLIR. (Wilks et al., 1996) report using Machine Readable Bilingual Dictionaries to construct ontological hierarchies (for IR or IE) in one language from an existing hierarchy in another language, using redundancy to cancel noise between the languages in a manner rather like Gollins and Sanderson.

All these developments indicate some forms of influence and interaction between traditionally separate techniques, but are more suggestive of a loss of borderlines between traditional functionalities. More recently, however, usage has grown in IR of referring to any technique related to Jelinek's IBM work as being a use of an "MT algorithm": this usage extends from the use of n-gram models under the name of "language models" (Ponte and Croft, 1998, Croft and Laferty, 2000), a usage that comes from speech research, to any use in IR of a technique like sentence alignment that was pioneered by the IBM MT work. An extended metaphor is at work here, one where IR is described as MT since it involves the retrieval of one string by means of another (Berger and Laferty, 1999). IR classically meant the retrieval of documents by queries, but the string-to-string version notion has now been extended by IR-researchers who have moved on to QA work where they describe an answer as a "translation" of its question (Berger, 2000). On this view questions and answers are like two "languages". In practice, this approach meant taking FAQ questions and their corresponding answers as training pairs.

The theoretical underpinning of all these researches is the matching of language models i.e. what is the most likely query given this answer, a question posed by analogy with Jelinek's "basic function of MT" that yielded the most probable source text given the translation. This sometimes sounds improbable, but is actually the same way up as theoretical science, namely that of proving the data from the theory, even though actually inferring the theory from the data, by abduction.

1.6. Preliminary Conclusion

What point have we reached so far in our discussion? We have not detected influence of IR on AI/NLP, as KSJ predicted, but rather an intermingling of methodologies and the dissolution of borderlines between long-treasured application areas, like MT, IR, IE, QA etc. One can also discern a reverse move of MT/AI metaphors into IR itself, which the opposite direction of influence to that advocated by KSJ in her paper. Moreover, the statistical methodology of Jelinek's CANDIDE did revolutionise NLP, but that was an influence on NLP from speech research and its undoubted successes, not IR. The pure statistical methodology of CANDIDE was not in the end successful in its own terms, because it always failed to beat symbolic systems like SYSTRAN in open competition. What CANDIDE did, though, was to suggest a methodology by which data sparseness might be reduced by the recapitulation of symbolic entities (e.g. grammars, lexicons, semantic annotations etc.) in statistical, or rather machine learning, terms, a story not yet at an end. But that methodology did not come from IR, which had always tended to reject the need for such symbolic structures, however obtained e.g. in the on going, but basically negative, debate on whether or not Wordnet or any similar thesaurus, can improve IR.

In the second part of this paper, we shall return to, and focus on, this key hard issue, that of whether NLP, taken broadly to include both resources and techniques, can improve the performance of IR systems, again broadly construed. KSJ has taken a number of positions on this issue, from the agnostic to the mildly sceptical. This is a complex issue and one quite independent of her theme examined in this first part of the paper, namely that IR methods should play a larger role than they do in NLP and AI.

One interesting question to ask at the end of this initial discussion is: if GOFAI (good old fashioned AI) and its logic did not produce the results in NLP that had been hoped for, and I agree with KSJ that it did not in its original form, then where did GOFAI go off to? The answer to which is that part of it has returned, replete with new claims about the nature of natural language, in the form of the Semantic Web (SW) movement (Berners-Lee et al., 2001). This is not the place for any full description of that development and its aims, but it incorporates aspects of the formal ontologies movement, which now can be taken to mean virtually all the content of classical AI Knowledge Representation, rather than any system of merely hierarchical relations, which is what the word "ontology" used to convey. More particularly, the Semantic Web movement envisages the (automatic) annotation of the texts of the World Wide Web with a hierarchy of annotations up to the semantic and logical, which is a claim virtually indistinguishable from the old GOFAI assumption that the true structure of language was its underlying logical form. Fortunately, SW comes in more than one form, some of which envisage statistical techniques, of the sort already discussed, as he basis of the assignment of semantic and logical annotations, but the underlying similarity to GOFAI is clear. One could also say that semantic annotation, so conceived, is the inverse of Information Extraction, done not at analysis time but, ultimately, at generation time without the writer being aware of this (since one cannot write and annotate at the same time). SW is as, it were, producer, rather than consumer, IE.

Two other aspects of the SW link it back directly to the goals of GOFAI: one is the rediscovery of a formal semantics to "justify" the SW. This is now taken to be expressed in terms of URIs (basic objects on the web), which are usually illustrated by means entities like lists of zip codes, with much indication of how such a notion will generalize to produce objects into which all web expressions can "bottom out". This concern, for non-linguistic objects as the ultimate reality, is of course classic GOFAI. Secondly, one can see this in KSJs terms with which we began this paper, namely her emphasis on the "primacy of words" and words standing for themselves, as it were: this aspect of the SW is exactly what KSJ meant by her "AI doesn't work in a world without semantic objects" (1990). In the SW, with its notion of universal annotation of web texts into both semantic primitives of undefined status and the ultimate URIs, one can see the new form of opposition to that view. The WWW was basically words—if we ignore pictures, tables and diagrams for the moment—but the vision of the SW is that of the words backed up by, or even replaced by, their underlying meanings expressed in some other way, including annotations and URIs. Indeed, the current SW formalism for underlying content, usually called RDF triples, is one very familiar indeed to those with memories of the history of AI: namely, John-LOVES-Mary, a form reminiscent at once of semantic nets (of arcs and nodes Woods et al., 1974), semantic templates (Wilks, 1964), or, after a movement of LOVES to the left, standard first order predicate logic. Only the last of these was full GOFAI, but all sought to escape the notion of words standing simply for themselves.

KSJs position here, an opposition to any kind of symbolic primitives standing behind words, has been a long held one, although at earlier periods (e.g. that of her thesis, see Tait and Wilks, this volume) she found such notions more congenial. One can also see the SW revival as again taking head on David Lewis' classic critique of what he called "markerese" (1972), an attack he aimed at the semantic markers of Fodor and Katz but which can be transferred to any project like the SW that makes use of "special languages", separate from natural languages, but not clearly grounded in any formal semantics, which was what Lewis considered the only plausible grounding, though KSJ differs on this, of course.

It is not obvious, that the SW needs any of the systematic justifications on offer, from formal logic to URIs, to annotations to URIs: it may all urn out to be a practical matter of this huge structure providing a range of practical benefits to people wanting information. Critics like Ted Nelson (1997) still claim that the

WWW is ill-founded and cannot benefit users, but all the practical evidence shows the reverse. Semantic annotation efforts are widespread, even outside the SW, and one might even cite recent work by Jelinek (Chelba and Jelinek, 1998), who is investigating systematic annotation to reduce the data sparseness that limited the effectiveness of his original statistical efforts at MT.

KSJ's position under discussion in this first part of the paper has been that words are just themselves, and we should not become confused (in seeking contentful information with the aid of computers) by notions like semantic objects, no matter what form they come in, formal, capitalized primitives or whatever. However, this does draw a firm line where there is not one: I have argued in many places—most recently against Sergei Nirenburg in (Nirenburg and Wilks, 2001)----that the symbols used in knowledge representations, ontologies etc., throughout the history of AI, have always appeared to be English words, often capitalized, and indeed are, in spite of the protests of their users, no more or less than English words. If anything else, they are slightly privileged English words, in that they are not drawn randomly from the whole vocabulary of the language. Knowledge representations, annotations etc. work as well as they do—and they do, and the history of machine translation using such notions as interlinguas is the clearest proof of that (1990)------because it is possible to treat some words as more primitive than others and to obtain some benefits of data compression thereby, but these privileged entities do not thereby cease to be words, and are thus at risk, like all words of ambiguity and extension of sense. In (Nirenburg and Wilks, 2001) that was my key point of disagreement with my co-author Nirenburg who holds the same position as Carnap who began this line of constructivism in 1936 with Der Logische Aufbau der Welt, namely that words can have their meanings in formal systems controlled by fiat. I believe this is profoundly untrue and one of the major fissures below the structure of formal AI.

This observation bears on KSJs view of words in the following way: her position could be characterised as a democracy of words, all words are words from the point of view of their information status, however else they may differ. To this I would oppose the view above, that there is a natural aristocracy of words, those that are natural candidates for primitives in virtually all annotation systems e.g. ANIMATE, HUMAN, EXIST and CAUSE. The position of this chapter is not as far from KSJ's as appeared at the outset and we both remain opposed to those in AI who believe that things-like-words-in-formal-codings are no longer words.

KSJs position in the sources quoted remains basically pessimistic about any fully automated information process; this is seen most clearly in her belief that humans cannot be removed from the information process. There is a striking similarity between that and her former colleague Martin Kay's famous paper on human-aided machine translation and its inevitability, given the poor prospects for pure MT. I believe his pessimism was premature and that history has shown that simple MT has a clear and useful role if users adapt their expectations to what is available, and I hope the same will prove true in the topics covered so far in this paper.

2 . IR IN NEED OF AI AND NLP?

In this section we turn the hard question, ignored in part 1 though long debated, as to whether or not the representational techniques, familiar in AI and NLP as both resources and the objects of algorithms, can improve the performance of classical statistical IR. The aim is go beyond the minimal satisfaction given by Croft's immortal phrase about IR "For any technique there is a collection where it will help".

Artificial Intelligence (AI), or at least non-Connectionist non-statistical AI, remains wedded to representations, their computational tractability and their explanatory power; and that normally means the representation of propositions in some more or less logical form. Classical Information Retrieval (IR), on the other hand, often characterised as a "bag of words" approach to text, consists of methods for locating document content independent of any particular explicit structure in the data. Mainstream IR is, if not dogmatically anti-representational (as are some statistical and neural net-related areas of AI and language processing), is at least not committed to any notion of representation beyond what is given by a set of index terms, or strings of index terms along with numbers themselves computed from text that may specify clusters, vectors or other derived structures.

This intellectual divide over representations and their function goes back at least to the Chomsky versus Skinner debate, which was always presented by Chomsky in terms of representationalists versus barbarians, but was in fact about simple and numerically-based structures versus slightly more complex ones.

Bizarre changes of allegiance took place during later struggles over the same issue, as when IBM created the machine translation (MT) system (CANDIDE, see Brown and Cocke, 1989), discussed earlier, based purely on text statistics and without any linguistic representations, which caused those on the representational side of the divide to cheer for the old-fashioned symbolic MT system SYSTRAN in its DARPA sponsored contests with CANDIDE, although those same researchers had spent whole careers dismissing the primitive representations that SYSTRAN contained. Nonetheless it was symbolic and representational and therefore on their side in this more fundamental debate! In those contests SYSTRAN always prevailed over CANDIDE for texts over which neither system had been trained, which may or may not have indirect implications for the issues under discussion here.

Winograd (1971) is often credited in AI with the first natural language processing system (NLP) firmly grounded in representations of world knowledge yet, after his thesis, he effectively abandoned that assumption and embraced a form of Maturana's autopoesis doctrine (see Winograd and Flores, 1986), a biologically-based anti-representationalist position that holds, roughly, that evolved creatures like us are unlikely to contain or manipulate representations. On such a view the Genetic Code is misnamed, which is a position with links back to the philosophy of Heidegger (whose philosophy Winograd began to teach at that period at Stanford in his NLP classes) as well as Wittgenstein's view that messages, representations and codes necessarily require intentionality, which is to say a sender, and the Genetic Code cannot have a sender. This insight spawned the speech act movement in linguistics and NLP, and also remains the basis of Searle's position that there cannot therefore be AI at all, as computers cannot have intentionality. The same insight is behind Dennett's more recent view that evolution necessarily undermines AI, as it does so much else.

The debate within AI itself over representations, as within its philosophical and linguistic outstations, is complex and unresolved. The Connectionist/neural net movement of the 1980's brought some clarification of the issue into AI, partly because it came in both representationalist (localist) and non-representationalist (distributed) forms, which divided on precisely this issue. Matters were sometimes settled not by argument or experiment but by declarations of faith, as when Charniak said that whatever the successes of Connectionism, he didn't like it because it didn't give him any perspicuous representations with which to understand the phenomena of which AI treats.

Within psychology, or rather computational psychology, there have been a number of recent assaults on the symbolic reasoning paradigm of AI-influenced Cognitive Science, including areas such as rule-driven expertise which was an area where AI, in the form of Expert Systems, was thought to have had some practical success. In an interesting revival of classic associationist methods, Schvaneveldt developed an associative network methodology for the representation of expertise (1990), producing a network whose content is extracted directly from subjects' responses, and whose predictive power in classic expert systems environments is therefore a direct challenge to propositional-AI notions of human expertise and reasoning.

Within the main AI symbolic tradition, as I am defining it, it was simply inconceivable that a complex cognitive task, like controlling a fighter plane in real time, on the basis of input from a range of discrete sources of information from instruments, could be other than a matter for constraints and rules over coded expertise. There was no place there for a purely associative component based on numerical strengths of association or (importantly for Pathfinder networks) on an overall statistical measure of clustering that establishes the Pathfinder network from the subject-derived data in the first place.

The Pathfinder example is highly relevant here, not only for its direct challenge to a core area of classic AI, where it felt safe, as it were, but because the clustering behind Pathfinder networks was in fact very close, formally, to the clump theory behind the early IR work such as Sparck Jones (1966/1986) and others. Schvaneveldt and his associates later applied Pathfinder networks to commercial IR after applying them to lexical resources like LDOCE. There is thus a direct algorithmic link here between the associative methodology in IR and its application in an area that challenged AI directly in a core area. It is Schvaneveldt's results on knowledge elicitation by associative methods from groups like pilots, and the practical difference such structures make in training, that constitute their threat to propositionality here.

This is no unique example, of course: even in more classical AI one thinks of Pearl's long-held advocacy (1985) of weighted networks to model beliefs, which captured (as did fuzzy logic and assorted forms of Connectionism since) the universal intuition that beliefs have strengths, and that these seem continuous in nature and not merely one of a set of discrete strengths, and that it is very difficult indeed to combine any system expressing that intuition with central AI notions of logic-based machine reasoning.

2.1. Information Extraction (IE) as a Task and the Adaptivity Problem.

In this chapter, I am taking IE as a paradigm of an information processing technology separate from IR; formally separate, at least, in that one returns documents or document parts, and the other linguistic or data-base structures. IE is a technique which, although still dependent on superficial linguistic methods of text analysis, is beginning to incorporate more of the inventory of AI techniques, particularly knowledge representation and reasoning, as well as, at the same time, finding that its rule-driven successes can be matched by machine learning techniques using only statistical methods (see below on named entities).

IE is an automatic method for locating facts for users in electronic documents (e.g. newspaper articles, news feeds, web pages, transcripts of broadcasts, etc.) and storing them in a data base for processing with techniques like data mining, or with off-the-shelf products like spreadsheets, summarisers and report generators. The historic application scenario for Information Extraction is a company that wants, say, the extraction of all ship sinkings, from public news wires in any language world-wide, and put into a single data base showing ship name, tonnage, date and place of loss etc. Lloyds of London had performed this particular task with human readers of the world's newspapers for a hundred years.

The key notion in IE is that of a "template": a linguistic pattern, usually a set of attribute-value pairs, with the values being text strings. The templates are normally created manually by experts to capture the structure of the facts sought in a given domain, which IE systems then apply to text corpora with the aid of extraction rules that seek fillers in the corpus, given a set of syntactic, semantic and pragmatic constraints.

IE has already reached the level of success at which Information Retrieval and Machine Translation (on differing measures, of course) have proved commercially viable. By general agreement, the main barrier to wider use and commercialisation of IE is the relative inflexibility of its basic template concept: classic IE relies on the user having an already developed set of templates, as was the case with intelligence analysts in US Defense agencies from whose support the technology was largely developed. The intellectual and practical issue now is how to develop templates, their filler subparts (such as named entities or NEs), the rules for filling them, and associated knowledge structures, as rapidly as possible for new domains and genres.

IE as a modern language processing technology was developed largely in the US, but with strong development centres elsewhere (Cowie et al., 1993), (Grishman, 1997), (Hobbs, 1993), (Gaizauskas and Wilks, 1997). Over 25 systems, world wide, have participated in the DARPA-sponsored MUC and TIPSTER IE competitions, most of which have the same generic structure (as shown by Hobbs, 1993). Previously unreliable tasks of identifying template fillers such as names, dates, organizations, countries, and currencies automatically — often referred to as TE, or Template Element, tasks — have become extremely accurate (over 95% accuracy for the best systems). These core TE tasks were initially carried out with very large numbers of hand-crafted linguistic rules.

Adaptivity in the MUC development context has meant beating the one-month period in which competing centres adapted their system to new training data sets provided by DARPA; this period therefore provides a benchmark for human-only adaptivity of IE systems. Automating this phase for new domains and genres now constitutes the central problem for the extension and acceptability of IE in the commercial world beyond the needs of the military sponsors who created it.

The problem is of interest in the context of this paper, to do with the relationship of AI and IR techniques, because attempts to reduce the problem have almost all taken the form of introducing another area of AI techniques into IE, namely that of machine learning, and which is statistical in nature, like IR but unlike core AI.

2.2. Previous Work on ML and Adaptive Methods for IE

The application of Machine Learning methods to aid the IE task goes back to work on the learning of verb preferences in the Eighties by Grishman and Sterling (1992) and Lehnert (et al., 1992), as well as early work at MITRE on learning to find named expressions (NEs) (Bikel et al., 1997). Many of the developments since then have been a series of extensions to the work of Lehnert and Riloff on Autoslog (Riloff and Lehnert, 1993), the automatic induction of a lexicon for IE.

This tradition of work goes back to an AI notion that might be described as lexical tuning, that of adapting a lexicon automatically to new senses in texts, a notion discussed in (Wilks and Catizone, 1999) and going back to work like Wilks (1979) and Granger (1977) on detecting new preferences of words in texts and interpreting novel lexical items from context and stored knowledge. These notions are important, not only for IE in general but, in particular, as it adapts to traditional AI tasks like QA.

The Autoslog lexicon development work is also described as a method of learning extraction rules from <document, filled template> pairs, that is to say the rules (and associated type constraints) that assign the fillers to template slots from text. These rules are then sufficient to fill further templates from new documents. No conventional learning algorithm was used by Riloff and Lehnert but, since then, Soderland has extended this work by using a form of Muggleton's ILP (Inductive Logic Programming) system for the task, and Cardie (1997) has sought to extend it to areas like learning the determination of coreference links.

Grishman at NYU (Agichtein et al., 1998) and Morgan (Morgan et al., 1995) at Durham have done pioneering work using user interaction and definition to define usable templates, and Riloff (Riloff and Shoen, 1995) has attempted to use some version of user-feedback methods of Information Retrieval, including user-judgements of negative and positive <document, filled template> pairings.

2.3. Supervised Template Learning

Brill-style transformation-based learning methods are one of the few ML methods in NLP to have been applied above and beyond the part-of-speech tagging origins of virtually all ML in NLP. Brill's original application triggered only on POS tags; later (Brill, 1994) he added the possibility of lexical triggers. Since then the method has been extended successfully to e.g. speech act determination (Carberry, Samuel and Vijay-Shanker, 1998) and a Brill-style template learning application was designed by Vilain (1993).

A fast implementation based on the compilation of Brill-style rules to deterministic automata was developed at Mitsubishi labs (Roche and Schabes, 1995, Cunningham, 1999). The quality of the transformation rules learned depends on factors such as:

1. The accuracy and quantity of the training data;
2. The types of pattern available in the transformation rules;
3. The feature set available used in the pattern side of the transformation rules.

The accepted wisdom of the ML community is that it is very hard to predict which learning algorithm will produce optimal performance, so it is advisable to experiment with a range of algorithms running on real data. There have as yet been no systematic comparisons between these initial efforts and other conventional machine learning algorithms applied to learning extraction rules for IE data structures (e.g. example-based systems such as TiMBL (Daelemans et al., 1998) and ILP (Muggleton, 1994). A quite separate approach has been that of Ciravegna (Ciravgna and Wilks, 1993) which has concentrated on the development of interfaces (ARMADILLO and MELITA) at which a user can indicate what taggings and fact structures he wishes to learn, and then have the underlying (but unseen) system itself take over the tagging and structuring from the user, who only withdraws from the interface when the success rate has reached an acceptable level.

2.4. Unsupervised Template Learning

We should also remember the possibility of unsupervised notion of template learning: in a Sheffield PhD thesis Collier (Collier, 1998) developed such a notion, one that can be thought of as yet another application of the early technique of Luhn (1957) to locate statistically significant words in a corpus and then use those to locate the sentences in which they occur as key sentences. This has been the basis of a range of summarisation algorithms and Collier proposed a form of it as a basis for unsupervised template induction, namely that those sentences, with corpus-significant verbs, would also contain sentences corresponding to templates, whether or not yet known as such to the user. Collier cannot be considered to have proved that such learning is effective, only that some prototype results can be obtained. This method is related, again via Luhn's original idea, to recent methods of text summarisation (e.g. the British Telecom web summariser entered in DARPA summarisation competitions) which are based on locating and linking text sentences containing the most significant words in a text, a very different notion of summarisation from that discussed below, which is derived from a template rather than giving rise to it.

2.5. *Linguistic Considerations in IR*

Let us now quickly review the standard questions, some unsettled after 30 years, in the debate about the relevance of symbolic or linguistic (or AI taken broadly) considerations in the task of information retrieval.

Note too that, even in the form in which we shall discuss it, the issue is not one between high-level AI and linguistic techniques on the one hand, and IR statistical methods on the other. As the last section showed, the linguistic techniques normally used in areas like IE have in general been low-level, surface orientated, pattern-matching techniques, as opposed to more traditional concerns of AI and linguistics with logical and semantic representations. So much has this been the case that linguists have in general taken no notice at all of IE, deeming it a set of heuristics almost beneath notice, and contrary to all long held principles about the necessity for general rules of wide coverage. Most IE has been a minute study of special cases and rules for particular words of a language, such as those involved in template elements (countries, dates, company names etc.).

Again, since IE has also made extensive use of statistical methods, directly and as applications of ML techniques, one cannot simply contrast statistical (in IR) with linguistic methods used in IE as Sparck Jones (1999a) does when discussing IR. That said, one should note that some IE systems that have performed well in MUC/TIPSTER — Sheffield's old LaSIE system would be an example (Gaizauskas and Wilks, 1997) — did also make use of complex domain ontologies, and general rule-based parsers. Yet, in the data-driven computational linguistics movement in vogue at the moment, one much wider than IE proper, there is a goal of seeing how far complex and "intensional" phenomena of semantics and pragmatics (e.g. dialogue pragmatics as initiated in (Carberry et al., 1998)) can be treated by statistical methods.

A key high-level module within IE has been co-reference, a topic that linguists might doubt could ever fully succumb to purely data-driven methods since the data is so sparse and the need for inference methods seems so clear. One can cite classic examples like:

{A Spanish priest} was charged here today with attempting to murder the Pope. {Juan Fernandez Krohn}, aged 32, was arrested after {a man armed with a bayonet} approached the Pope while he was saying prayers at Fatima on Wednesday night. According to the police, {Fernandez} told the investigators today that he trained for the past six months for the assault. He was alleged to have claimed the Pope "looked furious" on hearing {the priest's} criticism of his handling of the church's affairs. If found guilty, {the Spaniard} faces a prison sentence of 15-20 years. (The London Times 15 May 1982, example due to Sergei Nirenburg)

This passage contains six different phrases {enclosed in curly brackets} referring to the same person, as any reader can see, but whose identity seems a priori to require much knowledge and inference about the ways in which individuals can be described.

There are three standard techniques in terms of which this infusion (of possible NLP techniques into IR) have been discussed, and I will mention them and then add a fourth.

i. *Prior WSD (automatic word sense disambiguation) of documents by NLP techniques i.e. so that text words, or some designated subset of them, are tagged to particular senses.*

ii. *The use of thesauri in IR and NLP, the major intellectual and historical link between them.*

iii. *The prior analysis of queries and document indices so that their standard forms for retrieval reflect syntactic dependencies that could resolve classic ambiguities not of type (i) above.*

Topic (i) is now mostly regarded as a diversion as regards our main focus of attention in this chapter; even though large- scale WSD is now an established technology at the 95% accuracy level (Stevenson and Wilks, 1999), there is no reason to believe it bears on this issue, largely because the methods for document relevance used by classic IR are in fact very close to some of the algorithms used for WSD as a separate task (in e.g. Yarowsky, 1992, 1995). IR may well not need a WSD cycle because it constitutes one as part of the retrieval process itself, certainly when using long queries as in TREC, although short web queries are a different matter, as we discuss below.

This issue has been clouded by the "one sense per discourse" claim of Yarowsky (1992, 1995), a claim that has been contested by Krovetz (1998) who has had had no difficulty showing that Yarowsky's figures (that a very high percentage of words occur in only one sense in any document) are wrong and that, outside Yarowsky's chosen world of encyclopaedia articles, is not at all uncommon for words to appear in the same document bearing more than one sense on different occasions of use.

This dispute is not one about symbolic versus statistical methods for tasks, let alone AI versus IR. It is about a prior question as to whether there is any serious issue of sense ambiguity in texts to be solved at all, and by any method. In what follows I shall assume Krovetz has the best of this argument and that the WSD problem, when it is present, cannot be solved, as Yarowsky claimed in the one-sense-per-discourse paper, by assuming that only one act of sense resolution was necessary per text. Yarowsky's claim, if true, would make it far more plausible that IR's distributional methods were adequate for resolving the sense of component words in the act of retrieving documents, because sense ambiguity resolution would then be only at the document level, as Yarowsky's claim makes clear.

If Krovetz is right, then sense ambiguity resolution is still a local matter within a document and one cannot have confidence that any word is univocal within a document, nor that a document-span process will resolve such ambiguity. Hence one will have less confidence that standard IR processes resolve such terms if they are crucial to the retrieval of a document. One will expect, a priori, that this will be one cause of lower precision in retrieval, and the performance of web engines confirms this anecdotally in the absence of any experiments going beyond Krovetz's own.

Let us now turn to (ii), the issue of thesauri: there is less in this link in modern times, although early work in both NLP and IR made use of a priori hand-crafted thesauri like Roget. Though there is still distinguished work in IR using thesauri in specialised domains, beyond their established use as user-browsing tools (e.g. Chiaramella and Nie, 1990), IR moved long ago towards augmenting retrieval with specialist, domain-dependent and empirically constructed thesauri, while Salton early on (1972) claimed that results with and without thesauri were much the same.

NLP has rediscovered thesauri at intervals, most recently with the empirical work on word-sense disambiguation referred to above, but has remained wedded to either Roget or more recent hand-crafted objects like WordNet (Miller, 1990). The objects that go under the term thesaurus in IR and AI/NLP are now rather different kinds of thing, although in work like Grefenstette and Hearst (1992) an established thesaurus like WordNet has been used to expand a massive lexicon for IR, again using techniques not very different from the NLP work in expanding IE lexicons referred to earlier.

Turning now to (iii), the use of syntactic dependencies in documents, their indices and queries, we enter a large and vexed area, in which a great deal of work has been done within IR (e.g. back to Smeaton and van Rijsbergen, 1988). There is no doubt that some web search engines routinely make use of such dependencies: take a case like

> measurements of models

as opposed to

> models of measurement

which might be expected to access different literatures, although the purely lexical content, or retrieval based only on single terms, might be expected to be the same. In fact they get 363 and 326 hits respectively in Netscape but the first 20 items have no common members. One might say that this case is of type (i), i.e. WSD, since the difference between them could be captured by, say, sense tagging "models" by the methods of (i), whereas in the difference between

> the influence of X on Y

and (for given X and Y)

> the influence of Y on X

one could not expect WSD to capture the difference, if any, if X and Y were 'climate' and 'evolution' respectively, even though these would then be quite different requests.

These are standard types of example and have been a focus of attention, both for those who believe in the role of NLP techniques in the service of IR (e.g. Strzalkowski and Vauthey, 1991), as well as those like Sparck Jones (1999a) who do not accept that such syntactically motivated indexing has given any concrete benefits not available by other, non-linguistic, means. Sparck Jones' paper is a contrast between what she call LMI (Linguistically Motivated Information Retrieval) and NLI (Non-Linguistically etc.), where the former covers the sorts of efforts described in this paper and the latter more 'standard' IR approaches. In effect, this difference always comes down to one of dependencies within, for example, a noun phrase so marked, either explicitly by syntax or by word distance windows. So, for example, to use her own principal example:

URBAN CENTRE REDEVELOPMENTS

could be structured (LMI-wise) as

REDEVELOPMENTS of [CENTRE of the sort URBAN]

or as a search for a window in full text as (NLI-wise)

[URBAN =0 CENTRE]<4 REDEVELOPMENTS

where the numbers refer to words that can intrude in a successful match.

The LMI structure would presumably be imposed on a query by a parser, and therefore only implicitly by a user, while the NLI window constraints would again presumably be imposed explicitly by the user, making the search. It is clear that current web engines use both these methods, with some of those using LMI methods derived them directly from DARPA-funded IE/IR work (e.g. NetOWL and TextWise). The job advertisements on the Google site show clearly that the basic division of methods at the basis of this chapter have little meaning for the company, which sees itself as a major consumer of LMI/NLP methods in improving its search capacities.

Sparck Jones' conclusion is one of measured agnosticism about the core question of the need for NLP in IR: she cites cases where modest improvements have been found, and others where LMI systems' results are the same over similar terrain as NLI ones. She gives two grounds for hope to the LMIers: first, that most such results are over queries matched to abstracts, and one might argue that NLP/LMI would come into play more with access to full texts, where context effects might be on a greater scale. Secondly, she argues that some of the more negative results may have been because of the long queries supplied in TREC competitions, and that shorter more realistic and user-derived, web queries (which over 2.5 terms) might show a greater need for NLP. The development of Google, although proprietary, allows one to guess that this has in fact been the case in Internet searches.

On the other hand, she offers a general remark (and I paraphrase substantially here) that IR is after all a fairly coarse task and it may be not in principle optimisable by any techniques beyond certain limits, perhaps those we have already. Here the suggestion is that other, possibly more sophisticated, techniques should seek other information access tasks and leave IR as it is. This demarcation has distant analogies to one made within the word-sense discrimination research mentioned earlier, namely that it may not be possible to push figures much above where they now are, and therefore not possible to discriminate down to the word sense level, as oppose to the cruder homograph level, where current techniques work best, on the ground that anything "finer" is a quite different kind of job, and not a purely linguistic or statistical one, but rather one for future AI.

iv.   The use of proposition-like objects as part of document indexing.
This is an additional notion, which, if sense can be given to it, would be a major revival of NLP techniques in aid of IR. It is an extension of the notion of (iii) above, which could be seen as an attempt to index documents by template relations, e.g. if one extracts and fills binary relation templates (X manufactures Y; X employs Y; X is located in Y) so that documents could be indexed by these facts in the hope that much more interesting searches could in principle be conducted (e.g. find all documents which talk about any company which manufactures drug X, where this would be a much more restricted set than all those which mention drug X).

One might then go on to ask whether documents could profitably be indexed by whole scenario templates in some interlingual predicate form (for matching against parsed queries) or even by some chain of such templates, of the kind extracted as a document summary by co-reference techniques (e.g. by Azzam et al., 1999).

Few notions are new, and the idea of applying semantic analysis to IR in some manner, so as to provide a complex structured (even propositional) index, go back to the earliest days of IR. In the 1960s researchers like Gardin (1965), Gross (1964) and Hutchins (1970) developed complex structures derived from MT, from logic or "text grammar" to aid the process of providing complex contentful indices for documents, entities of the order of magnitude of modern IE templates. Of course, there was no hardware or software to perform searches based on them, though the notion of what we would now call a full text search by such patterns so as to retrieve them go back at least to (Wilks, 1964, 1965) even though no real experiments could be carried out at that time. Gardin's ideas were not implemented in any form until (Bely et al., 1970), which was also inconclusive.

Mauldin (1991), within IR, implemented document search based on case-frame structures applied to queries (ones which cannot be formally distinguished from IE templates), and the indexing of texts by full, or scenario, templates appear in Pietrosanti and Graziadio (1997). The notion is surely a tempting one, and a natural extension of seeing templates as possible content summaries of the key idea in a text (Azzam et al., 1999). If a scenario template, or a chain of them, can be considered as a summary it could equally well, one might think, be a candidate as a document index.

The problem will be, of course, as in work on text summarisation by such methods: what would cause one to believe that an a priori template could capture they key item of information in a document, at least without some separate and very convincing elicitation process that ensured that the template corresponded to some class of user needs, but this is an empirical question and one being separately evaluated by summarisation competitions.

Although this indexing-by-template idea is in some ways an old one, it has not been aired lately, and like so much in this area, has not been conclusively confirmed or refuted as an aid to retrieval. It may be time to revive it again with the aid of new hardware, architectures and techniques. After all, connectionism/neural nets was only an old idea revived with a new technical twist, and it had a ten year or more run in its latest revival. What seems clear at the moment is that, in the web and Metadata world, there is an urge to revive something along the lines of "get me what I mean, not what I say" (see Jeffrey, 1999). Long-serving IR practitioners will wince at this, but to many it must seem worth a try, since IE does have some measurable and exploitable successes to its name (especially Named Entity finding) and, so the bad syllogism might go, Metadata is data and IE produces data about texts, so IE can produce Metadata.

2.6. Question Answering within TREC

No matter what the limitation on crucial experiments so far, another place to look for evidence of the current of NLP/AI influence on IR might be the QA track within TREC since1999, already touched on above in connection with IRs influence on AI/NLP, or vice versa.

QA is one of the oldest and most traditional AI/NLP tasks (e.g. Green et al., 1961, Lehnert, 1977) but can hardly be considered solved by those structural methods. The conflation of the rival methodologies distinguished in this paper, can be clearly seen in the admitted possibility, in the TREC QA competition, of providing ranked answers, which fits precisely with the continuous notion of relevance coming from IR, but is quite counterintuitive to anyone taking a common sense view of questions and answers, on which that is impossible. It is a question master who provides a range of differently ranked answers on the classic QA TV shows, and the contestant who must make a unique choice (as opposed to re-presenting the proffered set!). That is what answering a question means; it does not mean "the height of St Pauls is one of [12, 300, 365, 508]feet"! A typical TREC question was "Who composed Eugene Onegin?" and the expected answer was Tchiakowsky – which is not a ranking matter, and listing Gorbachev, Glazunov etc. is no help.

There were examples in the competition that brought out the methodological difference between AI/NLP one the one hand, and IR on the other, with crystal clarity: answers could be up to 250 bytes long, so if your text-derived answer was A, but wanting to submit 250 bytes of answer meant that you, inadvertently, could lengthen that answer rightwards in the text to include the form (A AND B), then your answer would become wrong in the very act of conforming to format. The anecdote is real, but nothing could better capture the absolute difference in the basic methodology of the approaches: one could say that AI, Linguistics and IR were respectively seeking propositions, sentences and byte-strings and there is no clear commensurability between the criteria for determining the three kinds of entities. More recently, Tait and colleagues (Stokoe & Tait, 2003, Stokoe, Oakes & Tait, 2003) have shown that if the queries are short (a crucial condition that separates off modern democratic and Google-based IR from the classic queries of specialists) then WSD techniques do improve performance.

3. CONCLUSION

One can make quite definite conclusions but no predictions, other than those based on hope. Of course, after 40 years, IR ought to have improved more than it has---its overall Precision/Recall figures are not very different from decades ago. Yet, as Sparck Jones has shown, there is no clear evidence that NLP has given more than marginal improvements to IR, which may be a permanent condition, or it maybe one that will change with full text search, and a different kind of user-derived query, and Google may be one place to watch for this technology to improve strongly. It may also be worth someone in the IE/LMI tradition trying out indexing-by-scenario templates for IR, since it is, in one form or another, an idea that goes back to the earliest days of IR and NLP, but remains untested.

It is important to remember as well that there is a deep cultural division in that AI remains, in part at least, agenda driven: in that certain methods are to be shown effective. IR, like all statistical methods in NLP as well, remains more result-driven, and the clearest proof of this is that (with the honourable exception of machine translation) all evaluation regimes have been introduced in connection with statistical methods, often over strong AI/linguistics resistance.

In IE proper, one can be moderately optimistic that fuller AI techniques using ontologies, knowledge representations and inference, will come to play a stronger role as the basic pattern matching and template element finding is subject to efficient machine learning. One may be moderately optimistic, too, that IE may be the technology vehicle with which old AI goals of adaptive, tuned, lexicons and knowledge bases can be pursued. IE may also be the only technique that will ever provide a substantial and consistent knowledge base from texts, as CYC (Lenat et al., 1986) has failed to do over twenty years. The traditional AI/QA task, now brought within TREC, may yield to a combination of IR and IE methods and it will be a fascinating struggle. The curious tale above, of the use of "translation" with IR and QA work, suggests that terms are very flexible at the moment and it may not be possible to continue to draw the traditional demarcations between IR and these close and merging NLP applications such as IE, MT and QA.

Yorick Wilks is Professor of Computer Science at the University of Sheffield and Director of ILASH, the Institute of Language, Speech and Hearing, since 1993. During the period 1985-93 he was the first Director of the Computing Research Laboratory at New Mexico State University, which became a major US centre for research in artificial intelligence and its applications to natural language processing.

He was a researcher at Stanford AI Laboratory, a SERC Senior Fellow at Edinburgh University, and then Professor of Computer Science and Linguistics at the University of Essex. He has published numerous articles and six books in that area of artificial intelligence, of which the most recent are Artificial Believers (1991 with Afzal Ballim) from Lawrence Erlbaum Associates and Electric Words: dictionaries, computers and meanings (1996 with Brian Slator and Louise Guthrie) from MIT Press. He has also produced recent edited collections Machine

Conversations (2000, Kluwer) and Readings in Machine Translation (2003 with Sergei Nirenburg and Harold Somers). He is also a Fellow of the American and European Associations for Artificial Intelligence, a member of the EPSRC College of Computing, a member of the UK Computing Research Council and on the boards of some fifteen AI-related journals. He designed CONVERSE, the dialogue system that won the Loebner prize in New York in 1998.

ACKNOWLEDGMENTS

The paper has benefited from discussions with Mark Sanderson, Rob Gaizauskas, Ted Dunning and others, but the errors are all mine of course

REFERENCES

Agichtein, E., Grishman, R., Borthwick, A. and Sterling, J. (1998) Description of the named entity system as used in MUC-7. In Proc. of the MUC-7 Conference, NYU.

Azzam, S., Humphries, K., Gaizauskas, R. and Wilks, Y. (1997) Using a language-independent domain model for multilingual Information Extraction. *Journal of Applied* AI. 13.

Azzam, S., Humphreys, K. and Gaizauskas, R. (1999) Using coreference chains for text summarization. In Proc. ACL'99 Workshop on Coreference and its Applications, Maryland.

Ballasteros, L., and Croft, B. (1998) Statistical Methods for Cross Language Information Retieval. In Grefenstette (ed.) Cross Language Information Retrieval. Kluwer: Dordrecht.

Bely, N., Borillo, A., Virbel, J. and Siot-Decauville, N. (1970) Procedures d'analyse semantique appliquees a la documentation scientifique. Gauthier-Villars: Paris.

Berger, A. et al. (2000) Bridging the lexical chasm: statistical approaches to question answering. SIGIR'00.

Berger, A. and Lafferty, J. (1999) Information retrieval as statistical translation. SIGIR'99.

Berners-Lee, T., Hendler, J. and Lassila, O. (2001) The Semantic Web. Scientific American.

Bikel, D., Miller S., Schwartz, R. and Weischedel, R. (1997) Nymble: a High-Performance Learning Name-finder. In Proc. of the 5th conference on Applied Natural Language Processing (ANLP'97).

Brill, E. (1994) Some Advances in Transformation-Based Part of Speech Tagging. In Proc. of 12th National Conference on AI (AAAI'94), Seattle, Washington.

Brown, P.F. and Cocke, J. (1989) A Statistical Approach to Machine Translation, IBM Research Division, T.J. Watson Research Center, RC 14773.

Brown, P.F., Cocke, J., Della Pietra, S., Della Pietra, V., Jelinek, F., Lafferty, J., Mercer, R.L. and Roossin, P. (1990) A Statistical Approach to Machine Translation. *Computational Linguistics*, 16:2: 79-85

Bruce, R., and Guthrie, G. (1992) Genus disambiguation: a study in weighted preference. In Proc. COLING92, Nantes.

Carberry, S., Samuel, K. and Vijay-Shanker, K. (1998) Dialogue act tagging with transformation-based learning. In Proc. of COLING-ACL'98 Conference, vol. 2, pp. 1150-1156, Montreal, Canada.

Cardie, C. (1997) Empirical methods in information extraction. AI Magazine, 18(4), Special Issue on Empirical Natural Language Processing.

Cardie, C. and Lehnert, W. (1991) Preference Semantics and message Understanding. In Proc. DARPA Workshop on Spoeech and Language.

Charniak, E. (1973) Jack and Janet in search of a theory of knowledge. In Proc. IJCAI-73.

Charniak, E. (2001) Immediate-Head Parsing for Language Models. In Proc. of the 39th Annual Meeting of the Association for Computational Linguistics (ACL'01).

Chiaramella, Y. and Nie, J. (1990) A retrieval model based on an extended modal logic and its application to the RIME experimental approach. In Proc. of the 13th ACM International Conference on Research and Development in Information Retrieval (SIGIR'90), pp. 25-43.

Chomsky, N. (1965) Aspects of the Theory of Syntax. Cambridge, MA: MIT Press.

Churcher, G., Atwell, E. and Souter, C. (1997) Dialogue Management Systems—a survey. Research Report, University of Leeds, Department of Computer Science.

Chelba, C. and Jelinek, F. (1998) Exploiting Syntactic Structures for Language and Modelling. In Proc. of ACL'98, Montreal, Canada.

Ciravegna, F. and Wilks, Y. (2003) Designing Adaptive Information Extraction for the Semantic Web in Amilcare, In S. Handschuh and S. Staab (eds). Annotation for the Semantic Web in the Series Frontiers in Artificial Intelligence and Applications by IOS Press, Amsterdam.

Colby, K.M. (1973) Simulation of Belief Systems, in Schank and Colby (eds.) Computer Models of Thought and Language, San Francisco, CA: W. H. Freeman.

Collier, R. (1998) Automatic Template Creation for Information Extraction. PhD thesis, University of Sheffield, Computer Science Dept., UK.

Cowie, J., Guthrie, L., Jin, W., Odgen, W., Pustejowsky, J., Wanf, R., Wakao, T., Waterman, S. and Wilks, Y. (1993) CRL/Brandeis: The Diderot System. In Proc. of Tipster Text Program (Phase I), Morgan Kaufmann.

Croft, W. and Lafferty, J. (eds.) (2000) Language Modelling for Information Retrieval. Kluwer: Dordrecht.

Cunningham, H. (1999) JAPE – a Java Annotation Patterns Engine. Technical Report, Department of Computer Science, University of Sheffield.

Daelemans, W., Zavrel, J., van der Sloot, K. and van den Bosch, A. (1998) TiMBL: Tilburg memory based learner version 1.0. Technical report, ILK Technical Report 98-03.

Gachot, D., Lage, E., and Yang, J. (1998) The SYSTRAN NLP Browser: an application of MT technique in multilingual IR. In Greffenstette (ed.) Cross Language Information Retrieval, Kluwer: Dordrecht.

Gaizauskas, R. and Wilks, Y. (1997) Information Extraction: beyond document retrieval. *Journal of Documentation*.

Galliers, J. and Sparck Jones, K. (1996) Evaluating Natural Language Processing Systems. Lecture Notes in AI. Springer Verlag: berlin.

Gardin, J. (1965) Syntol. New Brunswick, NJ: Rutgers Graduate School of Library Science.

Garside, R. (1987) The CLAWS word-tagging system. In Garside, Leech and Sampson (eds.), The Computational Analysis of English. London and New York: Longman.

Gibson, J.J. (1968) The senses considered as a perceptual system. Allen and Unwin: London.

Gollins, T. and Sanderson, M. (2001) Improving Cross Language Information Retrieval with triangulated translation. SIGIR'01.

Granger, R. (1977) FOULUP: a program that figures out meanings of words from context. In Proc. 5th International Joint Conference on Artificial Intelligence (IJCAI'77).

Green, B., Wolf. A., Chomsky, C. and Laughery, K. (1961) BASEBALL, an automatic question answerer. In Proc. Western Joint Computer Conference 19, pp. 219-224

Grefenstette, G. and Hearst, M.A (1992) Method for Refining Automatically-Discovered Lexical Relations: Combining Weak Techniques for Stronger Results. In Weir (ed.) Statistically-based natural language programming techniques. In Proc. AAAI Workshop, AAAI Press, Menlo Park, CA.

Grishman, R. (1997) Information extraction: Techniques and challenges. In M-T. Pazienza (ed.) In Proc. of the Summer School on Information Extraction (SCIE'97), LNCS/LNAI. Springer-Verlag.

Grishman, R. and Sterling, J. (1992) Generalizing automatically generated patterns. In Proc. of COLING'92.

Gross, M. (1964) On the equivalence of models of language used in the fields of mechanical translation and information retrieval. *Information Storage and Retrieval*. 2(1).

Hobbs, J.R. (1993) The generic information extraction system. In Proc. of 5th Message Understanding Conference (MUC-5), pp. 87-91. Morgan Kaufman.

Hutchins, W.J. (1970) Linguistic processes in the indexing and retrieval of documents. *Linguistics*, 61.

Jeffrey, K. (1999) What's next in databases? ERCIM News (www.ercim.org) 39.

Krovetz, R. (1998) More than one sense per discourse. NEC Princeton NJ Labs., Research Memorandum.

Lehnert, W. (1977) A Conceptual Theory of Question Answering. In Proc. of 5th IJCAI, Cambridge, MA. Los Altos: Kaufmann, pp. 158-164.

Lehnert, W., Cardie, C., Fisher, D., McCarthy, J. and Riloff, E. (1992) University of Massachusetts: Description of the CIRCUS system as used for MUC-4. In Proc. of the 4th Message Understanding Conference MUC-4, pp. 282-288. Morgan Kaufmann.

Lenat, D., Prakash, M. and Shepherd, M. (1986) CYC: Using common sense knowledge to overcome brittleness and knowledge acquisition bottlenecks, *The AI Magazine*, 6(4).

Lewis, D. (1972) General Semantics. In Davidson and Harman (eds.) Semantics of natural language. Reidel: Dordrecht.

Luhn, H.P. (1957) A statistical approach to mechanized encoding and searching of literary information. *IBM Journal of Research and Development*, 1:309-317.

Marr, D. (1981) Artificial Intelligence: a personal view. In Haugeland, J. Mind Design. Cambridge, MA: MIT Press.

Mauldin, M. (1991) Retrieval performance in FERRET: a conceptual information retrieval system. SIGIR'91.

McCarthy, J. and Hayes, P. (1969) Some Philosophical Problems from the Standpoint of Artificial Intelligence, In Machine Intelligence 4. Edinburgh Univ. Press, Edinburgh.

Miller, G.A. (ed.) (1990) WordNet: An on-line Lexical Database, In *International Journal of Lexicography*, 3(4).

Moldovan, D. (2001) Question Answering Systems in Knowledge Management. In *Proc. IEEE Intelligent Systems*. 16.

Morgan, R., Garigliano, R., Callaghan, P., Poria, S., Smith, M., Urbanowicz, A., Collingham, R., Costantino, M. and Cooper, C. (1995) Description of the LOLITA System as used for MUC-6. In Proc. of the 6th Message Understanding Conference (MUC-6), pp. 71-86, San Francisco, Morgan Kaufmann.

Muggleton, S. (1994) Recent advances in inductive logic programming. In Proc. 7th Annual ACM Workshop on Computer Learning Theory, pp. 3-11. ACM Press, New York, NY.

Nelson, T. (1997) The future of information. ASCII Press: Tokyo.

Nirenburg, S., Frederking, R., Farwell, D., and Wilks, Y. (1994) Two types of adaptive MT environments. In Proc. COLING94, Kyoto.

Nirenburg, S. and Wilks, Y. (2001) What's in a symbol: ontology, representation and language. *Journal of Experimental and Theoretical Artificial Intelligence (JETAI)*.

Oh, J., Chae, Y. and Choi, K. (2000) Japanese term extraction using a dictionary hierarchy and an MT system. Terminology 6.

Pearl, J. (1985) Bayesian Networks: A Model of Self-Activated Memory for Evidential Reasoning, In Proc. of Cognitive Science Society (CSS-7).

Pollack, J. (1990) Reursive Distributed Representations. *Artificial Intelligence*. 46.

Ponte, J. and Croft, B. (1998) A language modelling approach to Information Retrieval. In Proc. 21st ACM SIGIR, Melbourne.

Pustejovsky, J. (1995) The Generative Lexicon. Cambridge, MA: MIT Press.

Resnik, P. (1996) Selectional Constraints: information theoretic model. *Cognition*. 61.

Riloff, E. and Lehnert, W. (1993) Automated dictionary construction for information extraction from text. In Proc. of 9th IEEE Conference on Artificial Intelligence for Applications, pp. 93-99.

Riloff, E. and Shoen, J. (1995) Automatically acquiring conceptual patterns without an annotated corpus. In Proc. of 3rd Workshop on Very Large Corpora.

Roche, E. and Schabes, Y. (1995) Deterministic Part-of-Speech Tagging with Finite-State Transducers. *Computational Linguistics*, 21(2):227-254.

Salton, G. (1972) A new comparison between conventional indexing (MEDLARS) and automatic text processing (SMART). *Journal of the American Society of Information Science*, 23(2).

Schank, R. (1975) Conceptual Information Processing, North Holland, Amsterdam.

Schvaneveldt, R. (ed.) (1990) Pathfinder Networks: Theory and Applications. Ablex, Norwood, NJ.

Smeaton, A. and van Rijsbergen, C. (1988) Experiments in incorporating syntactic processing of user queries into a document retrieval strategy. In Proc. 11th ACM SIGIR.

Sparck Jones, K. (1966/1986) Synonymy and Semantic Classification. Edinburgh University Press, Edinburgh.

Sparck Jones, K. (1990) Retrieving Information or Answering Questions? British library Annual research Lecture, London: British Library.

Sparck Jones, K. (1999a) What is the role of NLP in text retrieval. In Strzalkowski (ed.) Natural language Information Retrieval. Kluwer: New York.

Sparck Jones, K. (1999b) Information Retrieval and Artificial Intelligence. *Artificial Intelligence Journal*, vol. 114.

Sparck Jones, K. (2003) Document Retrieval: shallow data, deep theories, historical reflections and future directions. In Proc. 25th European IR Conference (ECIR03). Lecture Notes in Computer Science. Berlin: Springer. Pp.1-11.

Stevenson, M. and Wilks, Y. (1999) Combining Weak Knowledge Sources for Sense Disambiguation. In Proc. of the International Joint Conference for Artifical Intelligence (IJCAI'99)

Stevenson, M. and Gaizauskas, R. (2004) Recognition using annotated corpora. In Proc. European Conference on Information Retrieval (ECIR04), Sunderland.

Stokoe, C & Tait, J; Towards a Sense Based Document Representation for Internet Information Retrieval. The Twelth Text Retrieval Conference (TREC 2003) Notebook, National Institute of Standards and Technology, Gaithersburg, MD, USA pp732- 736. November 2003.

Stokoe, Chistopher, Michael Oakes and John Tait Word Sense Disambiguation in Information Retrieval Revisited. Proceedings of the 26th ACM SIGIR Conference on Research and Development in Information Retrieval (SIGIR 2003), Toronto, July 2003. pp 159-166. ISBN 1-58113-646-3

Strzalkowski, T. and Vauthey, B. (1991) Natural Language Processing in Automated Information Retrieval, PROTEUS Project Memorandum. Department of Computer Science, New York University.

Vilain, M. (1993) Validation of terminological inference in an information extraction task. In Proc. of ARPA'93 Human Language Workshop.

Vossen, P. (ed.) (1998) Eurowordnet . Kluwer: Dordrecht.

Wilks, Y. (1964) Text Searching with Templates. Cambridge Language Research Unit Memo, ML 156.

Wilks, Y. (1965) The application of CLRU's method of semantic analysis to information retrieval. Cambridge Language Research Unit Memo, ML.173.

Wilks, Y. (1977) Good and Bad Arguments About Semantic Primitives. In Communication and Cognition, Vol. 10, No 3/4.

Wilks, Y. (1979) Frames, semantics and novelty. In Metzing (ed.) Frame Conceptions and Text Understanding. Berlin: de Gruyter.

Wilks, Y. (1990) "INterlinguas in Japanese Machine Translation" In Report of the National Science Foundation JTEC Panel, to assess Japanese Natural Language Processing (eds. Carbonell and Rich), National Science Foundation, Washington DC.

Wilks, Y. and Fass, D. (1992) Preference Semantics: a family history. In Computing and Mathematics with Applications, Vol. 23, No. 2.

Wilks, Y., Slator, B. and Guthrie, L. (1996) Electric Words: dictionaries, computers and meanings. Cambridge, MA: MIT Press.

Wilks, Y. and Catizone, R. (1999) Making information extraction more adaptive. In M-T. Pazienza (ed.) In Proc. of Information Extraction Workshop, Frascati.

Winograd, T. (1971) Understanding Natural Language, MIT Press, Cambridge, MA.

Winograd, T. and Flores, A. (1986) Understanding Computers and Cognition: A New Foundation for Design, Ablex: Norwood, NJ.

Woods, W., Kaplan, R. and Nash-Webber, B. (1974) The Lunar Sciences Natural Language Information System, Final Report 2378, Bolt, Beranek and Newman, Inc., Cambridge, MA.

Yarowsky, D. (1992) Word-sense disambiguation using statistical models of Roget's categories trained on large corpora. In Proc. COLING'92, Nantes, France.

Yarowsky, D. (1995) Unsupervised word-sense disambiguation rivalling supervised methods. In Proc. of ACL'95.

Yngve, V.H. (1960) A model and an hypothesis for language structure. In Proc. of American Philosophical Society, Vol. 104, No. 5, pp. 444-466.